INDIVIDUAL DIFFERENCES AND PERSONALITY

INDIVIDUAL DIFFERENCES AND PERSONALITY

THIRD EDITION

MICHAEL C. ASHTON

ACADEMIC PRESS
An imprint of Elsevier

Academic Press is an imprint of Elsevier
125 London Wall, London EC2Y 5AS, United Kingdom
525 B Street, Suite 1800, San Diego, CA 92101-4495, United States
50 Hampshire Street, 5th Floor, Cambridge, MA 02139, United States
The Boulevard, Langford Lane, Kidlington, Oxford OX5 1GB, United Kingdom

Notices
Knowledge and best practice in this field are constantly changing. As new research and experience broaden
our understanding, changes in research methods, professional practices, or medical treatment may become
necessary.

Practitioners and researchers must always rely on their own experience and knowledge in evaluating
and using any information, methods, compounds, or experiments described herein. In using such
information or methods they should be mindful of their own safety and the safety of others, including parties
for whom they have a professional responsibility.

To the fullest extent of the law, neither the Publisher nor the authors, contributors, or editors, assume
any liability for any injury and/or damage to persons or property as a matter of products liability, negligence
or otherwise, or from any use or operation of any methods, products, instructions, or ideas contained in the
material herein.

Library of Congress Cataloging-in-Publication Data
A catalog record for this book is available from the Library of Congress

British Library Cataloguing-in-Publication Data
A catalogue record for this book is available from the British Library

ISBN: 978-0-12-809845-5

For information on all Academic Press publications visit our website at
https://www.elsevier.com/books-and-journals

Working together
to grow libraries in
developing countries

www.elsevier.com • www.bookaid.org

Publisher: Nikki Levy
Acquisition Editor: Nikki Levy
Editorial Project Manager: Barbara Makinster
Production Project Manager: Caroline Johnson
Designer: Matthew Limbert

Typeset by TNQ Books and Journals

CONTENTS

PREFACE

The central aim of personality psychology is to understand differences between people. With this in mind, my purpose in writing this textbook was to describe the main questions about the nature of personality variation, and to explain the answers that have been learned so far.

The organization of this textbook largely follows from this aim, and differs from that of most other textbooks in this discipline. In the past, most authors structured their textbooks around the theorists who had written about personality psychology, with each chapter being devoted to the work of a different theorist. More recently, some authors have organized their textbooks in terms of several distinct "domains" or "approaches" within the discipline of personality psychology. The structure of this textbook is closer to the latter than to the former, in the sense of being organized around issues rather than around theorists. But the present textbook emphasizes the unity of the discipline, by treating the diverse areas of research in personality psychology as efforts to answer a series of related questions about the same basic phenomenon—human personality variation.

This book begins with some basic orientation to the discipline, by explaining the nomothetic approach to personality and by introducing the basic principles of personality measurement. The idea of a personality trait is then described, along with the evidence for the existence (and the measurability) of those traits. At this point, the stage is set for an examination of the big questions of personality psychology.

The first issue to be examined is that of personality structure—of finding the basic dimensions that summarize personality traits. The next topic is that of the development of personality, in terms of stability and change in personality trait levels across the life span. Then follows an examination of the origins of personality variation, in the sense of its proximal biological causes (i.e., in brain structures and substances) and its more distal sources (i.e., in genes and environmental features). This leads to the question of the function of personality variation throughout human evolution, and of the consequences of personality variation in modern society, with attention to personality disorders and also to diverse life outcomes—involving relationships, work, health, and so on—that are influenced by personality.

All of those chapters deal with personality variation as defined in a somewhat narrow sense, and thereby leave aside some important areas of psychological variation: mental abilities, vocational interests, religion and politics, and sexuality. These individual differences are often omitted altogether from personality textbooks, but I have included them here in recognition of their importance to personality in a broader sense of the term. Each of the remaining chapters of the textbook examines a different one of these domains, discussing its relations with the major personality dimensions and also addressing the same questions as those considered for personality traits throughout the earlier chapters of the book. Finally, a concluding chapter summarizes and integrates the previous sections of the book, drawing attention to the major findings of personality research as well as the important questions that remain to be answered.

ACKNOWLEDGMENTS

I would like to thank many people for their help in making the third edition of this textbook.

At Elsevier/Academic Press, my publisher, Nikki Levy, was highly supportive of the plans for a third edition. My developmental editor, Barbara Makinster, helpfully allowed me a great deal of flexibility in the timing and format of the new manuscript. My production manager Caroline Johnson was efficient and very accommodating in organizing the preparation and correction of page proofs. Harsha Vardhanan of TNQ Books and Journals did the big job of typesetting the manuscript and incorporating my late edits.

Several individuals generously allowed me to include their test items or not-yet-published data in this book. Ted Jackson of Sigma Assessment Systems kindly permitted me to reproduce example items from the Nonverbal Personality Questionnaire and the Multidimensional Aptitude Battery. Lew Goldberg shared the data from his Eugene-Springfield Community Sample. David Schmitt provided further analyses of his data on personality and sexuality. Ingo Zettler gave preliminary findings about the HEXACO Elementary School Inventory.

I want to thank the professors who supervised me—and taught me so much—during my years as a student: Jerry Hogan, the late Doug Jackson, and the late Sam Paunonen.

I also thank several course instructors and colleagues who have provided valuable suggestions for improvement to the previous editions of this textbook: Gordon Hodson, Reinout de Vries, Ulrich Schimmack, Edward Cokely, John Antonakis, Tanya Martini, Sid Segalowitz, Robert Hogan, Benjamin Hilbig, and Paul Tremblay. An undergraduate student, Mohammed Aldawsari, helpfully brought my attention to an error in a figure of the previous edition.

A special thanks goes to Vassilis Saroglou, who provided several helpful corrections and suggestions and who also organized the French translation of the second edition of this textbook.

A special thanks also goes to Kibeom Lee, whose detailed comments on previous editions and whose feedback on drafts of several chapters were particularly helpful. Kibeom also created the figures for Chapter 1.

Finally, and most of all, I thank my family members for all of their encouragement and support: my parents, my sister and her family, all my in-laws, and especially my wife, Narnia. This edition is dedicated to Nathan and Darren and to their cousins Ewan and Torin and John, Michael, Caroline, and Alexander.

INTRODUCTION

THE STUDY OF PERSONALITY

Welcome to the fascinating world of personality psychology!

One of the most intriguing aspects of life is the variety that we notice in the people around us. People differ, of course, in their outward physical characteristics. But the variety among human beings is not just "skin deep": People also differ in their typical ways of behaving, thinking, and feeling. And it is these differences in psychological characteristics—these differences in *personality*—that seem so important to us for defining who a person is. All around the world, people notice the personalities of the people around them, and all around the world, people find it useful to describe each other's personalities: Is this person outgoing or shy? Sensitive or tough? Creative or conventional? Quick-tempered or patient? Sincere or deceitful? Disorganized or self-disciplined?

You have probably observed these differences in personality all throughout your life. Even when you were a young child playing in the playground, you probably realized very early that the other kids had different styles of playing: Some shared their toys more than others did, some would "tattle-tale" more than others would, some liked to compete more than others did, and so on. (You probably also realized that the adults who supervised that playground were not all the same either: Some punished more readily than others did, some watched the playground more closely than others did, and so on.) And ever since that time, you have no doubt noticed the different personalities of the people around you—relatives, friends, classmates, coworkers, or anyone else you have encountered.

But have you ever *wondered* about personality? Have you ever been struck by the sheer variety of people's personalities—by the many ways that one person can be similar to and different from another person? Have you ever speculated about *why* people have such varied personalities—about what causes the differences between one person and the next? Have you ever wondered whether personality really matters in life—whether someone's personality will influence their relationships, their career, their health? If so, then you have come to the right place: These are exactly the kinds of questions that we will try to answer in this book.

Of course, these questions are not new: People have speculated and debated about them for centuries. More than 2000 years ago, the ancient Greeks were fascinated by the variety of personalities that people exhibit. One philosopher, Theophrastus, even wrote a book describing the many characteristics he observed in others. Greek doctors, such as Hippocrates and Galen, wrote that different bodily fluids were responsible for the major personality characteristics. But the first attempts to examine personality in a systematic, scientific way were not undertaken until much more recently: There were some promising beginnings in the late 19th century, then some scattered (but sometimes substantial) progress leading up to the late 20th century, and then an explosion of discoveries that continues into the 21st century. And this is what makes the field of personality research so exciting: It examines fundamental, age-old questions about the human condition—questions whose answers are only now finally being revealed.

THE UNIVERSAL, THE UNIQUE, AND THE IN-BETWEEN

Before going any further, we should examine what kinds of questions this book will consider, and what kinds of questions it will not. A good way to do so is to consider three categories of topics that psychologists can study in regard to human behavior.

At one extreme, some psychologists study the *universal* aspects of human nature—the ways in which everyone tends to be similar in their behavior. That is, some researchers investigate the circumstances in which people in general are likely to behave in a certain way. For example, one could try to find the conditions that cause all (or almost all) people to show a particular reaction, such as conforming to group norms, retaliating against an attacker, feeling closely attached to one's parents, helping a person in distress, rebelling against authority, changing opinions on a topic, boasting about achievements, feeling sexually attracted to someone, and so on.

At the other extreme, some psychologists examine the *unique* combinations of very specific features that make a given person different from everyone else. For example, perhaps one of your friends is concerned about achieving academically, wants more independence from family members, and has always loved playing music, and perhaps another of your friends is concerned about having an attractive appearance, wants to avoid conflict with family members, and has always loved being outdoors. Some psychologists are interested in exploring these details in a given person's life story and personality.

In between these two extremes, some psychologists explore the ways in which any given person can be similar to some people yet different from other people. That is, some researchers investigate the important characteristics (or traits) along which people vary, with the aim of measuring those characteristics—and of learning about their causes and their consequences. For example, how can we measure different people's overall levels of honesty or of creativity? What are the reasons why people differ from one another in their usual levels of fearfulness or of impulsiveness? What are the consequences—for relationships or for work or for health—of differences among people in their typical levels of cheerfulness or of stubbornness?

The focus of this book will be on this third, intermediate category of topics. The first category—that of the universal features of human nature—is studied in great detail by researchers in many areas of psychology, particularly social psychology. The topics of that category are obviously very interesting, and they are certainly relevant to an understanding of personality. But because those topics have been so thoroughly investigated by researchers in other areas of psychology, we will not consider them here.

The second category—that of the unique aspects of each individual—is examined in a subjective way by many insightful observers of the human condition, including novelists, playwrights, poets, philosophers, biographers, and historians. In addition, the topics of that category are also studied in a more systematic way by some personality psychologists. However, many personality psychologists believe that we can learn much more about personality by studying the third category of topics. To understand the reason for this opinion, consider two different ways in which we could approach the study of personality: The *idiographic* approach and the *nomothetic* approach (e.g., Allport, 1937).

IDIOGRAPHIC VERSUS NOMOTHETIC APPROACHES

As just noted, one way of studying personality is to examine individual persons in detail, with the aim of identifying the unique features of each individual's personality. You have already encountered this approach used many times, whenever you have read or watched a biography or a "case study" of a person's life.

Let us consider an example of how this approach might work. Suppose that we wanted to write a detailed description of the personality of our classmate, Alice. To do so, we would study Alice's personality in depth. For example, we might conduct interviews with her, with her family members, and with her friends, and we might observe her behavior directly, across many situations and over a long period of time. (We will assume that Alice would agree to some invasions of her privacy.)

After all of this careful investigation, we might conclude that the most striking features of Alice's personality are her fear of the disapproval of others and her strong sense of responsibility in her dealings with others. So, when writing our biography of Alice, we would draw attention to these aspects of her personality, and we would illustrate them with various episodes from her life. But in writing this biography, we might also want to try to *explain* why these are the outstanding features of her personality. In looking for clues, we might notice that Alice's parents had a very strict style of raising their children, and expressed strong disapproval whenever Alice behaved "badly" as a child. From these observations, we might decide that it was Alice's strict upbringing that caused her fear of disapproval of others, and that this fear of disapproval in turn caused her to be a very responsible person. It might be difficult to prove this conclusively, but we could certainly make a persuasive argument that this was how these prominent aspects of Alice's personality had developed.

This strategy of studying the many unique details of an individual's personality is called the idiographic approach, and it has some obvious strengths. By its very nature, it can give us some interesting insights into the really distinctive features of an individual's personality, and it can even give us some clues as to the origins of those features. These strengths might help to explain why most of us find the biographies of famous people and the stories of fictional characters to be so captivating.

On the other hand, the idiographic approach also has some weaknesses. One obvious shortcoming is inefficiency: It would simply be too expensive and too time-consuming to study a large number of people in so much detail, and as a result our knowledge of personality would be based on a very small number of cases. This inefficiency is also seen in the relatively small segment of "personality" that really stands out in any one person. Remember that Alice did not strike us as being, say, especially ambitious, or especially artistic. So, if we had been hoping to learn more about those particular aspects of personality, we would need to keep looking for other individuals to study.

But perhaps an even more serious shortcoming of the idiographic approach is that it does not allow us to figure out any *general laws* about personality. Recall that when we studied Alice, we decided that her very responsible and dependable nature was caused by her need for approval of others, which was in turn the result of the strict upbringing given to her by her parents. But, do we really know for sure that people who are responsible also tend to be fearful of the disapproval of others? And do we really know that people whose upbringing was strict also tend to be responsible, or to be afraid of disapproval? Perhaps if we looked at a large number of people, we would find that, on average, responsible people are no more afraid of others' disapproval than irresponsible people are. And maybe we would find that people raised by strict parents are no more fearful of disapproval than are people raised by very permissive parents. So, although the idiographic approach can give us some interesting ideas about personality, it does not allow us to test whether or not those ideas are actually correct.

Because of these drawbacks associated with the idiographic approach, most personality researchers now prefer the other strategy, which is called the nomothetic approach. In the nomothetic approach, the researcher studies certain features of the personalities of many different people, and then compares those people in an effort to figure out some general rules about personality. The nomothetic approach usually involves measuring some interesting variables in a large group of people, and then finding out how those variables are related. For example, our study of Alice might suggest to us that traits such as responsibility and fear of disapproval might be worth measuring in a large sample of people, to find out whether or not those traits usually go together. Using the nomothetic approach, we could also study the hypothesized causes of one's personality, such as parental child-rearing style or the levels of a certain hormone or neurotransmitter chemical; likewise, we could also study the hypothesized consequences of one's personality, such as job performance, marital satisfaction, or criminal record.

The great strength of the nomothetic approach is that it *does* allow us to find general laws of personality. Because the aim of any scientific research is to discover the laws that govern nature, the nomothetic approach is clearly the best choice for researchers who wish to understand the laws of personality. For example, we can use the nomothetic approach to find out whether two personality characteristics are related to each other, or to find out whether some presumed "causes" or "consequences" of a personality characteristic are really related to that trait. By using the nomothetic approach, we can gradually learn more and more about the personality characteristics that differentiate people, and about the origins and the effects of those personality differences. But, in addition, the nomothetic strategy can also teach us a great deal about the personalities of individual persons. For example, if we can assess an individual's personality in terms of several important characteristics, then the overall pattern produced by this combination of variables is likely to be very informative, and to give a description that is virtually unique.

Thus, for these reasons we will study personality using the nomothetic approach rather than the idiographic approach. By focusing on the ways in which people differ from (and are similar to) each other, we can learn some general laws about personality. Moreover, we can also learn a great deal about any individual person, perhaps more than we could learn by trying to study individuals one at a time.

Of course, all of this is not to say that idiographic approaches are not valuable, or that a study of the unique features of an individual is uninteresting. On the contrary, a creative personality psychologist will probably derive some insights from observations in everyday life, from works of fiction, or from biographies of famous persons.

OUTLINE OF THIS BOOK

Now that we have established the general approach that we will adopt in our study of personality, let us have a brief overview of the major questions to be addressed in this book.

First, we will start with some basic concepts in psychological measurement, and with some basic issues about the existence of personality: How do we know that personality traits really exist? How can we measure those characteristics? What are the main traits that make up our personalities?

Then we will look at the nature of personality: How does personality change throughout the life span? In what ways do the workings of our brains and bodies influence our personalities? Are personality differences shaped more by genes or by environments? How did personality differences evolve in our early ancestors?

Next we will consider the practical importance of personality: Are there "disorders" of personality? What is the role of personality in aspects of life such as relationships, work, health, the law, and satisfaction with life?

Finally, we will look at personality in relation to some other important psychological characteristics—characteristics that we will also examine in their own right. How does personality relate to mental abilities? To occupational interests? To religious beliefs and political attitudes? To sexuality?

Personality psychology is an exciting field of knowledge—get ready to enjoy studying it for the first time!

CHAPTER 1

Basic Concepts in Psychological Measurement

Contents

Before we can really begin to understand personality, we need to figure out how to measure it. And before we can measure personality, it would be useful to have some common terms for describing our measurements.

In this chapter, we will introduce some basic concepts that allow us to describe psychological measurements. By using these concepts, we will have some quick and simple ways of understanding the results of personality research. For example, if a researcher reports that women average higher than men on some personality characteristic, we would want to know *how much* higher. Or, if a researcher reports that a given personality characteristic is related to enjoyment of a particular kind of music, we would want to know *how much* they are related.

Also in this chapter, we will consider the basic ways of evaluating the accuracy of our measurements. Whenever we try to measure a psychological characteristic, we need to make sure (1) that we really have measured some meaningful characteristic, and (2)

Individual Differences and Personality
ISBN 978-0-12-809845-5, http://dx.doi.org/10.1016/B978-0-12-809845-5.00001-9

that this characteristic is really the same one that we are trying to measure. It is important to have some ways of expressing *how well* our measurements meet these requirements.

And finally, we will also explore in this chapter some of the methods that psychologists use when measuring personality and related characteristics.

1.1 SOME SIMPLE STATISTICAL IDEAS

1.1.1 Levels of Measurement

One challenge in psychological measurement, as opposed to measurements of many physical characteristics, is that it is difficult or even impossible to measure someone's absolute amount of a psychological characteristic. With physical measurements, such as height or weight, it is meaningful to say that someone is 50% taller than someone else, or twice as heavy as someone else, because measurements of height and weight begin from zero. But with psychological measurements, there might not be a meaningful zero at all. For example, a person might get a score of zero on an intelligence test, but it does not seem meaningful to say that the person has zero intelligence—presumably, he or she would get a score higher than zero if the test were easier. Likewise, if someone has a score of zero on a questionnaire scale measuring "unconventionality," we cannot be sure that this person really has no unconventionality at all. (And likewise, if someone had a score of 100% on this unconventionality scale, this would not necessarily mean that he or she truly had the highest possible level of unconventionality.) Because psychological measurements do not usually have a true zero level, the *ratios* between measurements are not meaningful—we cannot really say that one person is "twice as intelligent" or "50% more unconventional" than another person is.

But there are still ways by which we can meaningfully compare people's levels of psychological characteristics. One way is simply to rank people according to their scores: We could measure people's levels of a characteristic by whatever method, and then record their positions relative to each other, such as 1st, 2nd, 3rd,..., 654th,... . Ranking people by their scores is a sensible approach, but it has some shortcomings. One difficulty is that the *differences (or intervals)* between the ranks are not always meaningful. For example, the person with the highest level of a trait in a given sample might be just slightly higher than the person with the 2nd highest level, but the person who is 2nd highest might be far, far ahead of the person in 3rd. This fact means that ranks are less than ideal for calculating statistics based on our measurements. For example, when we want to compute the average level of a trait, our computation is meaningful only if the differences between the numbers always mean the same thing. So, the numbers provided by ranks are not as useful as we might like them to be.

In measuring people's characteristics, therefore, psychologists would like to obtain scores that have meaningful *differences* between them (even though the *ratios* need not be meaningful). For example, if we are trying to measure the trait of assertiveness, we would like to be confident that a score of 60 really does mean a level of assertiveness that is halfway between the levels indicated by a 50 and a 70. Note that assertiveness is not really being measured in any particular "units," and that it does not matter if the average score is 60, or 360, or −60, or whatever. The important thing—for comparing people and for calculating averages—is simply that equal differences, or intervals, between scores represent roughly equal differences in the level of the trait. For example, when psychologists measure intelligence using an "IQ" test, they would hope that the difference between an IQ of 110 and an IQ of 120 really does have the same meaning as the difference between an IQ of 130 and an IQ of 140. (Note again, by the way, that an IQ of 0 does not indicate zero intelligence.)

How do psychologists know if their measurements meet the requirement of having meaningful differences? The methods for testing this are beyond the scope of this textbook, but we can say here that most well-designed psychological measurements are close enough to this ideal to be useful for statistical analysis.

1.1.2 Standard Scores

It was mentioned earlier that psychological characteristics are not measured in any particular units and that it does not matter how high or low the scores on a characteristic tend to be, as long as the differences between scores are meaningful. But differences in the numbers used for measuring variables might cause difficulties when we want to compare someone's scores across two or more traits. For example, suppose that Bob has an IQ of 90 (where the average person's IQ is 100) and that Bob also has a score of 60 on a "sociability" scale (which, let us say, has an average score of 50). At first glance, it seems that Bob's IQ score (90) is higher than his sociability score (60), but in fact Bob is below the average on IQ and above the average on sociability. Therefore, we need some way to relate scores on one scale to scores on another scale, so that we can compare levels of one characteristic with levels of another, or to compare levels of the *same* characteristic as measured by different scales.

Psychologists are able to make meaningful comparisons across different measurement scales by converting the original or "raw" scores into *standard scores*. The first step in calculating a standard score is to take an individual's original ("raw") score on a given scale, and then subtract the mean score (i.e., the average score) for the persons who have been measured. This difference between the individual's score and the mean score tells us whether the person is above the average (if the difference is positive) or below the average (if the difference is negative).

But this is not the only step. If we merely subtract the mean score from the individual's score, we still might not have a meaningful idea of *how far* above or below the average that person is. This is because scales measuring psychological characteristics differ in terms of how "spread out" people's scores are. For example, on a typical IQ test, about two-thirds of people are within 15 points of the average (i.e., between 85 and 115), and about 95% of people are within 30 points of the average (i.e., between 70 and 130). So, a person who has an IQ of 110 is above average, but not very far above average. But now imagine that we have a different IQ test, again with an average score of 100, but on which people's scores are much more tightly bunched (say, two-thirds of people between 95 and 105, and 95% of people between 90 and 110). On this scale, a score of 110 would be very high. So, we need some way to compare scales that have different amounts of *variability* in people's scores, as well as different average scores.

To do this, psychologists use a second step, after having first subtracted the average score on a scale from the individual's score on that scale. They then divide this difference by the standard deviation, a number that indicates how much variability there is among people on a variable.[1] For many psychological characteristics, about two-thirds of people are within one standard deviation above or below the mean, and about 95% of people are within two standard deviations above or below the mean. (For example, in the situation mentioned previously for the typical IQ test, the standard deviation is 15.)

The result of the preceding two steps—finding the difference between the individual's score and the average score, and then dividing this difference by the variability (standard deviation) of the scores—is to give a universal or standard way of expressing people's scores on a given characteristic, regardless of the original distribution of scores on that characteristic. These scores, known as standard scores (or *z-scores*), have two special properties: First, the average score on a standard score scale is exactly zero, and second, the standard deviation of a standard-score scale is exactly one. So, after we have calculated standard scores for our variables, we can meaningfully compare a person's scores across different variables. This applies not only to different scales measuring the same variable (e.g., two different IQ test scales), but also to scales measuring different variables (e.g., an IQ test scale and a sociability scale, or an "orderliness" scale and an "originality" scale).[2]

---

[1] In any sample of persons, the standard deviation of scores is calculated by, first, finding the difference between each person's score and the average score across all of those persons, then squaring each of these differences, then adding up all of the squared differences, then dividing this sum by the number of people who were measured (minus one), and then finding the square root of this result. For example, suppose that there is a sample of n individuals, and each of the individuals, i, has a score of X_i on variable X, with a mean score of $\overline{X}$ for those individuals. The formula for the standard deviation, s, will then be as follows:

$$s = \sqrt{\frac{\sum_{i=1}^{n} (X_i - \overline{X})^2}{n-1}}$$

If we do not take the square root, then we have the *square* of the standard deviation of scores, which is called the *variance* of scores, s^2.

[2] Sometimes, standard scores are converted from their basic z-score form, in which the mean is 0 and the standard deviation is 1, into some other form. As mentioned earlier, IQ scores are nowadays calculated as standard scores, but with the mean set to 100 and the standard deviation set to 15. Many other tests use a form of standard scores called T-scores, whereby the mean is set to 50 and the standard deviation to 10. Scores on the well-known SAT examination, used in admissions to higher education in the United States, were originally standard scores for which the mean was set to 500 and the standard deviation to 100.

Box 1.1 The Normal Distribution

The examples in the text are based on what is called a *normal distribution* of scores; when drawn as a graph, this produces the well-known bell-shaped curve (see Fig. 1.1). For many physical and psychological characteristics, the distribution of scores is roughly normal: Most people have scores close to the average value, with relatively few people being far above or far below that average. Notice that a person whose score is equal to the mean (i.e., a z-score of 0) will have a score that is higher than that of 50% of people. If a person's score is 1 standard deviation above the mean ($z = 1$), then his or her score is higher than that of about 84% of people; if it is 2 standard deviations above ($z = 2$), then it is higher than that of about 98% of people. Conversely, a score that is 1 standard deviation below the mean ($z = -1$) is higher than that of about 16% of people, and a score that is 2 standard deviations below ($z = -2$) is higher than that of about 2% of people. (Note that, for any distribution, the percentage of scores below a given score is often called a *percentile*.)

1.1.3 Correlation Coefficients

Psychologists often want to know how much people's scores on one variable "go together" with their scores on another variable. For example, they might want to know how people's scores on one personality characteristic are related to their scores on another personality characteristic. Or, they might want to know how people's scores on one personality characteristic are related to their levels of some other kind of variable, such as their job performance or their blood pressure.

The correlation coefficient, known by the symbol r, tells us how strongly two variables covary, or "go together," in a given sample of persons. The values of the correlation coefficient can range from a maximum of $+1$ (indicating a perfect positive correlation between two variables) to a minimum of -1 (indicating a perfect negative correlation between two variables). A correlation of 0 means that the two variables are unrelated to each other.

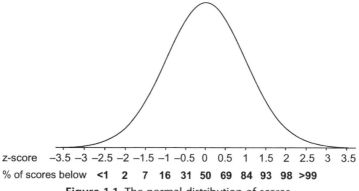

z-score	−3.5	−3	−2.5	−2	−1.5	−1	−0.5	0	0.5	1	1.5	2	2.5	3	3.5
% of scores below	<1		2	7	16	31	50	69	84	93	98	>99			

Figure 1.1 The normal distribution of scores.

The correlation coefficient tells us an important fact about how people's standard scores (i.e., z scores) on the two variables are related: A difference of 1 standard deviation unit on one variable is associated with a difference of r standard deviation units on the other variable. Let us consider some examples that show what this means.

Suppose that variables X and Y have a perfect positive correlation with each other (i.e., $r = 1$): the higher variable X is, the higher variable Y must be, and vice versa. In this case, we know that a person's level of variable X (expressed in z-score units) will be equal to his or her level of variable Y (expressed in z-score units). For example, a person who is 1 standard deviation above the mean on variable X must also be 1 standard deviation above the mean on variable Y. Likewise, a person who is 2 standard deviations below the mean on variable Y must also be 2 standard deviations below the mean on variable X.

Fig. 1.2 (panel A) shows a graph that depicts what a correlation of +1 looks like; notice that the dots (each of which represents a person's score on the two variables) make a straight line from the lower left of the graph (indicating low levels of both variable

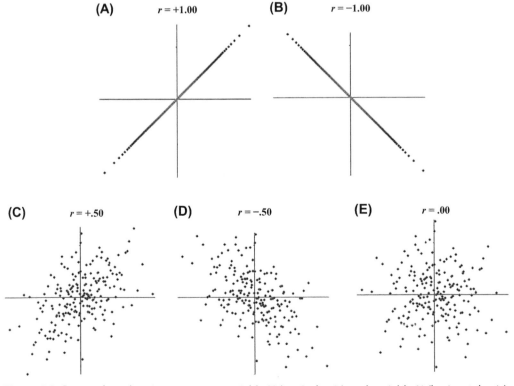

Figure 1.2 Scatterplots showing scores on variable Y (vertical axis) and variable X (horizontal axis) having correlations of (A) $r = +1.00$, (B) $r = -1.00$, (C) $r = +.50$, (D) $r = -.50$, and (E) $r = .00$.

X and variable Y) to the upper right of the graph (indicating high levels of both variable X and variable Y).

Now suppose instead that variables X and Y have a perfect negative correlation with each other (i.e., $r = -1$): the higher variable X is, the lower variable Y must be, and vice versa. In this case, we know that a person's level of variable X (expressed in z-score units) will be equal in size *but opposite in sign* to his or her level of variable Y (expressed in z-score units). A person who is 1.5 standard deviations above the mean on variable X must be 1.5 standard deviations *below* the mean on variable Y. Likewise, a person who is 0.5 standard deviations above the mean on variable Y must be 0.5 standard deviations *below* the mean on variable X.

Fig. 1.2 (panel B) shows a graph that depicts what a correlation of -1 looks like; notice that the dots (each of which represents a person's score on the two variables) make a straight line from the upper left of the graph (indicating high levels of Y and low levels of X) to the lower right of the graph (indicating low levels of Y and high levels of X).

It is unusual for two variables to correlate perfectly with each other, either positively or negatively. In fact, even when we measure the same characteristic in two different ways, we usually find a correlation smaller than $+1$, due to various sources of error in measurement (as we will discuss in Section 1.2.1). When the correlation between two variables is not $+1$ or -1, then we do not know exactly what a person's level of one variable will be, simply by knowing his or her level of the other variable. However, for a large group of people who have a given level of one variable, the correlation does let us know roughly what the *average* level of the other variable will be for those particular people.

For example, if the correlation between variable X and variable Y is .50, and if we have some people who are all 2 standard deviations above the mean on variable X, then their average level on variable Y will be about 1 standard deviation above the mean (because $2 \times .50 = 1$). Likewise, if the correlation between variable X and variable Y is $-.50$, and if we have some people who are all 2 standard deviations above the mean on variable X, then we know that their average level on variable Y will be about 1 standard deviation *below* the mean (because $2 \times -.50 = -1$).

To get a sense of what a correlation of a given size "means," consider the remaining panels of Fig. 1.2. Notice that in these panels, the association between X and Y is not perfect, but you can still notice a *tendency* for X and Y to go together positively (panel C) or negatively (panel D).

Fig. 1.2 (panel C) shows a correlation of about $+.50$, which is a moderately large positive correlation. As an example, this might be close to the correlation that you would find, for a group of adults, between body weight and weight-lifting ability. (On average, heavier people can lift more weight than lighter people can, but there are still some light people who can lift a lot and some heavy people who cannot lift very much.)

Fig. 1.2 (panel D) shows a correlation of about $-.50$, which is a moderately large negative correlation. This might be close to the correlation that you would find, for a group of adults, between body weight and distance-running ability. (On average, heavier people cannot sustain as fast a running pace as lighter people can, but there are still some heavy people who can run at a faster pace and some light people who cannot.)

Fig. 1.2 (panel E) shows a correlation of .00, which means that the two variables are completely unrelated to each other. In this case, people's levels of variable X do not go along in either direction with their levels of variable Y. No matter what is the level of variable X shown by a given person, your best guess for that person's level of variable Y is simply the average level for the entire sample of persons (i.e., 0 standard deviations from the mean). In this kind of situation, we say that the two variables are perfectly uncorrelated. A similar result might happen if we were to examine, in a group of healthy adults, the correlation between height and IQ. On average, there is probably not much tendency for taller people to be any more or any less intelligent than shorter people are.

There is no strict rule as to what value of a correlation makes it a "small" (or "low," "weak") as opposed to a "large" (or "high," "strong") correlation. But as a rough guideline, correlations between −.20 and +.20 are often considered small; correlations between −.20 and −.40 and between .20 and .40 are considered moderate in size; and correlations beyond −.40 or beyond +.40 are considered large. (A correlation of, say, +.80 is very large and usually in personality research would be found only when the same characteristic is being measured by two similar methods.)

Sometimes people downplay the importance of correlations that are not very large. But even a rather modest correlation can provide useful information about large groups of people, even though it tells us little about any one person. For example, suppose that a personality characteristic correlates .25 with some outcome variable (such as job performance or marital satisfaction). This correlation means that people with very high levels of this personality characteristic (say, 2 standard deviation units above the mean) would, on average, be about 0.5 standard deviation units above the mean on the outcome variable (because $2 \times .25 = .50$). Likewise, people with very low levels of this personality characteristic (say, 2 standard deviation units below the mean) would, on average, be about 0.5 standard deviation units below the mean on the outcome variable (because $-2 \times .25 = -.50$). Therefore, there would be about a 1 standard deviation unit difference in the outcome variable between people who are very high and people who are very low in the personality characteristic (because $.50 - (-.50) = 1.0$). A difference of 1 standard deviation unit is fairly large, so the information provided by this rather modest correlation coefficient is important.

Here is the formula for calculating the correlation, r, between two variables, x and y, in a sample of n persons, where Zx_i and Zy_i are standard scores on those variables for each of those n persons, i:

$$r_{xy} = \frac{\sum_{i=1}^{n} Zx_i Zy_i}{n - 1}$$

The idea is that for each of the n individuals in our sample, we find the product of his or her standard scores on the two variables. Then we add together the products obtained from each individual, and we divide this total by $n - 1$ (i.e., the number of persons in our sample, minus one). Notice that, if most people have positive z scores on both variables or negative z scores on both variables—rather than a positive z score on one variable and a negative z score on the other—then most of the products will be positive, and their sum will be a positive number, thereby producing a positive correlation. If instead most people have a positive z score on one variable and a negative z score on the other, then most of the products will be negative, and their sum will be a negative number, thereby producing a negative correlation.[3]

1.1.4 Sample Representativeness and Sample Size

Whenever researchers measure psychological characteristics in a given sample of people, it is usually because they want to learn something about people *in general*—not just about the particular sample of people who are measured. For example, a researcher might want to know the average level of some variable—such as religiousness or reading comprehension or responsibility—and will measure that variable in a sample of people in order to estimate the average level for the whole population. Or, a researcher might want to know how much two variables are correlated with each other—such as anxiety and blood pressure, or sociability and attractiveness—and will measure the two variables in a sample of people in order to estimate the correlation in the whole population. To gain accurate estimates of averages or of correlations, researchers must measure variables in groups of people—that is, in *samples* of people—that meet two important requirements.

The first requirement is that the sample of people should be reasonably representative of the population that the researcher wants to learn about. For example, if a researcher wants to learn about the typical political attitudes among adults in a given country, then he or she should try to assess those attitudes in a sample that resembles the population in all the ways that might be related to political attitudes—sex ratio, age distribution, geographical background, education level, income level, ethnic origin, and so on. If instead he or she simply assessed political attitudes in a sample of students at his or

---

[3] Sometimes researchers investigate the differences between the means of two groups on a variable, rather than the correlation between two variables. For a given variable, differences between two groups' averages can be expressed in terms of standard deviation units. For example, if the standard deviation of height for men or for women is 8 cm, and if the average man is 12 cm taller than the average woman, then we can say that the difference in height between men and women equals 1.5 standard deviation units (because $12/8 = 1.5$). This method of expressing the differences between groups is related to the correlation coefficient. If, for example, men and women differ by 1.5 standard deviation units on a variable, then this is equivalent to a correlation of .60 between that variable and a person's sex; likewise, a difference of 0.5 standard deviation units is equivalent to a correlation of about .25, and a difference of 1.0 standard deviation units is equivalent to a correlation of about .45. (The formula for this conversion is beyond the scope of this textbook.)

her university, he or she would likely get an inaccurate estimate of the typical attitudes in the population he or she wants to learn about.[4]

The second requirement is that the sample of people should be reasonably large. Even if samples are representative of the general population, they will not all give the same results, simply because of chance differences between them. If a sample is small, then it is more likely to give unusual results just by chance. Suppose, for example, that you wanted to estimate the average height of all the men students at your school. If you picked a sample of 10 men at random, you might end up—just by chance—with a sample of men who are mostly taller than average (or, instead, with a sample of men who are mostly shorter than average). This would in turn lead you to overestimate (or to underestimate) the average height of all the men at your school. But if you picked a sample of 100 men at random, you would probably get an average height that is pretty close to the true average for the whole population of men students at your school. This is because it is very unlikely that this larger sample would just happen to have mostly quite tall men or mostly quite short men—any "flukes" would tend to cancel each other out in a larger sample. For this reason, it is better to measure characteristics in large samples of persons.

When calculating means (i.e., averages) or correlations, the amount of chance fluctuation across samples gets smaller when the samples have more people in them.[5] There is no single "magic number" that represents the minimum sample size for estimating means or correlations. However, some results from computer simulations suggest that correlations computed from samples of 250 people usually are reasonably close to the population correlations (Schönbrodt & Perugini, 2013), and these results correspond well with researchers' experience. But samples that are even larger will give more accurate estimates, and samples that are somewhat smaller can still give some rough indications about the values in the population at large.

1.2 ASSESSING QUALITY OF MEASUREMENT: RELIABILITY AND VALIDITY

The preceding sections have described some of the basic statistical concepts that are used by psychologists who measure people's levels of various characteristics. But now we need to consider the question of how to assess the *quality* of psychological measurements: When we try to measure a characteristic in a sample of people, how do we know whether

---

[4] Sometimes this requirement is less crucial for examining correlations between variables, because for many variables the correlations are roughly similar even in samples that are much different from each other. However, the ideal case is still to have a sample that closely resembles the population that we want to learn about.

[5] Specifically, when the samples get larger by a given ratio, the chance fluctuations get smaller by the square root of that ratio. For example, if one sample is four times bigger than another, the fluctuations are only one-half as big; if one sample is nine times bigger than another, the fluctuations are only one-third as big.

or not we have been successful? In other words, how can we know *how accurately* we have measured that characteristic? There are several aspects of measurement quality to be considered, but these are generally classified into two broad properties known as reliability and validity.

1.2.1 Reliability

The *reliability* of a measurement is the extent to which it is consistent with similar measurements of the same characteristic. When there is good agreement between measurements, this tells us that they are in large part assessing some real characteristic, rather than just being meaningless random numbers.

It is important to evaluate reliability because even quite similar measurements of a characteristic are unlikely to agree perfectly with each other. For example, suppose that we measure people's political conservatism by giving them a set of several questions about various political issues. If we were to use instead another set of questions, we would probably not get exactly the same results. Or suppose that we measure people's public-speaking ability by asking a set of several observers to rate each person's ability. If we were to use instead another set of observers, we would probably not get exactly the same results. Or now suppose that we make either of these measurements on a given day. If we were to make that measurement on a different occasion—maybe a week or a month later—we would probably not get exactly the same results.

The reason for the imperfect agreement between measurements of a characteristic is that each measurement is only partly capturing the intended characteristic. It is also capturing something else—something specific to that measurement. This specific part—which is due to the particular set of items, or the particular set of observers, or the particular occasion—is called "error" variance by psychologists. Note that "error" as used here does not usually mean that anyone is making a mistake; it just means that the measurement contains some random element other than the intended characteristic. When we evaluate the reliability of our measurements, we are evaluating how much (or really, how little) of the variance in the measurements is error variance. In the following sections we consider the different kinds of reliability that can be examined, where each kind of reliability is concerned with a different kind of error.

1.2.1.1 Internal-Consistency Reliability

When evaluating the quality of a psychological measurement, we can consider the error that results from differences among the "items" or parts of the measurement, such as the various questions on a test or a scale. Whenever we try to measure a characteristic by giving people a test or scale, we ask them to respond to some set of questions or statements, which we call "items." These items are combined to produce an overall score for the test or scale. You are already familiar with this idea in other aspects of life: For example, a golfer adds up his or her scores for each of the 18 holes to get his or her overall score for the round of golf.

The process of averaging across the items is usually very important for obtaining a reliable measurement. Any particular item is not a pure measure of the characteristic that we are trying to assess. Instead, each item will assess that characteristic only partially, and will also assess some other characteristic that is specific to that item—what we call the "error" variance. But if we can average a person's score across many items, then the error associated with any single item will tend to be canceled out. The overall, average score will therefore have less error—it will be a more reliable indication of whatever the items have in common.

To appreciate this point, consider the golf analogy again. A golfer's score on any given hole will depend partly on how good a golfer he or she is, but it will also depend on random chance, and on specific features of that hole. Regardless of a person's golf ability, he or she might be very lucky or very unlucky on any particular hole. And even if two golfers were equal in overall golf ability, one of them might find a particular hole to be easy, and the other might find that hole to be difficult. Therefore, we would not want to assess someone's golf ability based on his or her score on a single hole of golf. But if we were to find each golfer's overall score for an entire round of golf, then each golfer's good luck or bad luck on any particular hole—and each golfer's strengths and weaknesses for any particular hole—would tend to be canceled out. The overall score would give us a much better idea of how good a golfer he or she really is. In other words, we get a more reliable indication of a golfer's ability by averaging out (or adding up) across the holes of a golf course.

But even when we average a person's score across items, the resulting overall score will not be perfectly reliable—it will still have some error. The reliability of that score mainly depends on two things: the number of items, and the correlations between the items. If you think about this for a moment, you will understand why these things matter.

First, if we are averaging out people's responses to items that have something in common, that common element will become stronger and stronger when we add more and more items. The more items are averaged, the less important the "error" of any single item will be. To return to the golf example, if we have people play one hole of golf, there will be a lot of error in their scores, so we would not have a reliable indicator of how good the people are at golf. We would get a better idea by having them play (say) three holes—but nine holes would be even better, and 18 holes would be better still. So, by averaging out across a larger number of items, we get a more reliable overall score—in other words, we get a better measurement of whatever characteristic the items are measuring in common.

Second, if we are averaging out people's responses to items that have something in common, then that common element will be stronger to the extent to which the items are correlated with each other. This is because the correlations tell us how much each individual item is measuring the common characteristic: the higher the correlations, the more each item measures the common characteristic. In the golf example, suppose that people's scores on any one hole tend to be correlated rather strongly with their scores on any other hole. This would suggest that each hole is mainly measuring the same thing (presumably, golf ability). In this case, the score for a whole round of golf will be very reliable. But if instead people's scores on any one hole were correlated weakly with their scores on any other hole, then this would suggest that each hole is in large part measuring something different—maybe luck, or maybe the particular aspect of golf ability demanded by that hole. In this case, the score for a whole round of golf will be less reliable.

To maximize reliability—in other words, to obtain a very strong measure of the common characteristic measured by a set of items—it is better to have both a large number of items and high correlations between the items. But to some extent, a large number of items can compensate for low correlations between items, and high correlations between items can compensate for a small number of items.

Table 1.1 shows the level of reliability for tests or scales that have different numbers of items and different average correlations between the items. Notice that the reliability values are all between zero and one. This index of reliability has a special property, in that it represents the proportion of variance in the measurement that is due to the common element. Conversely, if we subtract the reliability value from one, then we obtain the proportion of variance in the measurement that is due to "error," or to the unique aspects of the various items individually. To the extent that the reliability value is high, it tells us that our scale does measure a common characteristic, not just a collection of unrelated characteristics.

The kind of reliability just described is called *internal-consistency reliability*, because it depends in part on the extent to which the items in a test are correlated with each other, or "internally consistent." As noted earlier, internal-consistency reliability represents the proportion of variance in a test that is common to the various items of the test. This is the kind of reliability that is most commonly reported in research on personality characteristics and related individual differences.

Table 1.1 Internal-consistency reliability of a measurement, as a function of the number of items (k) and the mean correlation between items ($\bar{r}$)

Mean correlation between items ($\bar{r}$)	Number of items (k)				
	2	5	10	20	50
.05	.10	.21	.34	.51	.72
.10	.18	.36	.53	.69	.85
.20	.33	.56	.71	.83	.93
.50	.67	.83	.91	.95	.98

Note that commonly used formulas for internal-consistency reliability—such as the "alpha" coefficient of Box 1.2—have an important drawback: Even if a scale shows a high alpha coefficient, this does not necessarily mean that its items are measuring only one common characteristic. For example, a scale could show a high alpha even if it

Box 1.2 Calculating Internal-Consistency Reliability

There are various formulas for estimating the internal-consistency reliability of a test by using the number of items and the average correlation between the items. The following is one of the simpler formulas, known as the *Spearman—Brown formula*; it is less precise than some of the others, but it is good enough for many purposes. In this formula, r_{xx} is internal-consistency reliability, k is the number of items, and $\bar{r}$ is the average correlation between the items.

$$r_{xx} = \frac{k\bar{r}}{1 + (k-1)\bar{r}}$$

Another formula for calculating internal-consistency reliability is called *Cronbach's alpha*, or *coefficient alpha*. Unlike the Spearman—Brown formula, the formula for Cronbach's alpha (α) takes into account the differences in correlations between items and the differences in the items' standard deviations. The alpha formula is the most widely used method of calculating internal-consistency reliability. The formula is as follows, where α is internal-consistency reliability, k is the number of items in the test, s_i^2 is the variance of each item i, and s_x^2 is the variance of the entire test:

$$\alpha = \frac{k}{k-1}\left[1 - \frac{\sum_{i=1}^{k} s_i^2}{s_x^2}\right]$$

Here the variances are given as s^2 (as for a sample of persons drawn from a population) but you will often see this formula written with the variances given as σ^2 (as for an entire population of persons).

A simpler method for calculating internal-consistency reliability is simply to split the items of a test into two halves and to calculate each individual's score on each half of the test, so that one can then find the correlation between the two halves. In this *split-half* method of calculating the reliability of a test, the Spearman—Brown formula is then applied to this correlation, using 2 as the value of k. This method is easy to use, but it is less accurate than the previous methods in which scores on each item are considered separately.

An even simpler method of calculating internal-consistency reliability is to take two different but comparable versions of a test—that is, two "parallel forms" of a test—and to calculate the correlation between them. The idea of this *parallel forms* method is that the reliability of a test is given by the correlation of the whole test with another version of the test meant to measure the same characteristic but using a different set of items. This is a useful way to estimate reliability, as it indicates directly the correlation between similar measures of the same characteristic. However, it can only be applied in the somewhat unusual case when one actually has two parallel forms of a test.

consisted of two unrelated sets of items, where the items within each set are closely related to each other. In such a case, the high alpha for the entire scale would conceal the fact that the scale essentially contains two separate subscales, each measuring its own characteristic. Therefore, when researchers compute a scale's internal-consistency reliability, they should make sure that the scale does not actually consist of two or more unrelated (or weakly related) sets of items.

If a scale has a very low level of internal-consistency reliability, then it will probably not be very useful in psychological research, because such a scale cannot have a very high level of validity (an important property that we will discuss later in this chapter). Some researchers have suggested guidelines about the levels of internal-consistency reliability that should be considered "acceptable," with .70 often being suggested as a minimally acceptable level. However, a scale that has only a modest level of internal-consistency reliability, say in the .50s or .60s, might still have a reasonably high level of validity (McCrae, Kurtz, Yamagata, & Terracciano, 2011) and therefore be quite useful in psychological research.

1.2.1.2 Interrater (Interobserver) Reliability

Another kind of reliability is analogous to internal-consistency reliability, but instead of being based on the items of a test, it is based on the observers or raters of a characteristic. To understand this other kind of reliability, known as interrater reliability (or interobserver reliability), consider the following example.

A team of psychologists (three of them, let us say) is trying to assess the personality characteristics of many people. The psychologists conduct an interview with each of the persons being studied. Then, for each of those persons, each psychologist independently observes the interview, and each psychologist independently estimates that person's levels of various personality characteristics. Now, for any given characteristic, we would expect to see at least some tendency for the psychologists to agree with each other's ratings. If we assume that the interviews provide some indication of people's personality differences, and if we assume that each of our psychologists can observe that evidence accurately, then they should end up with estimates that are at least somewhat similar. For example, if one psychologist rates person A as being much more confident than person B is, then we would expect the other psychologists also to rate person A as being more confident than person B is. That is, we would likely find some positive correlations between the psychologists' ratings.

However, we would not expect the correlations to be extremely high. For example, even if the psychologists' ratings are broadly in agreement that person C and person D are both about average in confidence, these estimates might not be identical. Perhaps one of the psychologists would rate person C as being slightly more confident than person D, whereas another would rate person D as being slightly more confident than person C. For any given person and any given trait, any of our psychologists will likely overestimate or underestimate that person's level of that characteristic to at least some extent. In other words, there is some error in the ratings of the persons' levels.

By averaging out the ratings across our three psychologists, we should get a more reliable idea of each person's level of a given characteristic. This is because the average rating will depend more heavily on the common element of those ratings. In contrast, the specific aspect of each rating—that is, the "error" associated with any particular psychologist's subjective estimate—should become relatively weak.

Notice that, much like the situation when we calculate internal-consistency reliability, we will have higher reliability if we have more raters. (In the case of interrater reliability, these raters take the place of the items that are used in computing internal-consistency reliability.) If we added three more psychologists who could observe the same interviews, and if we based our overall estimates on the average response from all six, then the common element of the ratings would be even more strongly represented.

Also, and again much like the situation when we calculate internal-consistency reliability, we will have higher reliability if our raters' ratings are more highly correlated with each other. (This is similar to the situation in which items are highly correlated with each other.) For example, if we had selected three psychologists who were all very skilled observers of interviews, then each psychologist's ratings would contain little subjective error. The correlations between the ratings would be rather high, and hence interrater reliability would also be high. But if we had selected three psychologists who were less-skilled observers (perhaps if this were their first time observing interviews), then each psychologist's ratings would contain much subjective error. The correlations between the ratings would be rather low, and hence interrater reliability would not be very high.

Thus, whenever we obtain some ratings of individuals' levels of characteristic as made by different observers, we can calculate the interrater (or interobserver) reliability of those ratings. This interobserver reliability represents the proportion of variance in the overall ratings that is common to the different observers' ratings; the remaining proportion of variance is the error that is specific to each of the different observers.[6]

1.2.1.3 Test–Retest Reliability

Another kind of error in our measurements is due to random fluctuations across short periods of time. If we measure some characteristic of people at a given time, and then we measure that same characteristic again a few days or weeks later, we will probably find that people's scores, relative to each other, will not be exactly the same: Some people

---

[6] The calculation of interrater reliability, and the interpretation of the resulting values, is the same as in the case of internal-consistency reliability, except that we have raters instead of items. For example, in the Spearman–Brown formula described earlier, k now represents the number of raters, and $\bar{r}$ represents the average correlation between the raters.

will have standard scores a bit higher, and some will have standard scores a bit lower, than they were when the variable was measured the first time.

The fluctuations in people's scores on many psychological characteristics across short periods of time are usually not very large, but psychologists like to have some indication of the extent to which those scores fluctuate—that is, of the extent to which there is error across occasions of measurement. To obtain this information, psychologists measure the characteristic in the same group of individuals on two different occasions, usually separated by a few days or weeks. The correlation between the two measurements is called the *test—retest reliability* of the measurements. If individuals' relative levels of the characteristic tend to be consistent across different occasions of measurement, then the correlation will be high; this indicates that there is little error due to the occasion of measurement, and that there is a high level of test—retest reliability.

Note that when evaluating test—retest reliability, the measurements are taken at relatively short time intervals. If, instead, these time intervals were much longer, then changes in individuals' relative scores might not be due to random fluctuations. Instead, the shifting positions of individuals might be due to real differences among them in their long-term development of the characteristic. As an example, consider the trait of height in children. If we measured children's heights on one occasion, and then measured the same children's heights again a week later, then the correlation between the two sets of measurements would tell us about the test—retest reliability of our measurement. However, if the time interval separating the measurements was much longer, say several years, then the correlation between the two measurements would not necessarily tell us about the reliability of our measurement. Instead, it would probably tell us more about the long-term stability of differences between children in the characteristic of height. That is, a low correlation would tell us that different children were growing at different rates during the years between the two measurements, which would cause changes in the children's standard scores for height. (In Chapter 4, we will discuss the extent to which personality characteristics are stable across long periods of time.)

As noted earlier, most measurements of psychological characteristics tend to show relatively little fluctuation across short periods of time, so test—retest reliability tends to be quite high. However, test—retest reliability can be low under some circumstances. For example, suppose that we are interested in measuring an individual's level of some emotion, such as anxiety, anger, fatigue, joy, sadness, or sentimentality. If the items used to measure these variables are phrased in such a way as to ask about the individual's current, temporary state, then there might be quite low correlations between scores obtained one week apart (or one day apart, or even one hour apart). These low correlations would reflect the tendency for most people's moods to fluctuate at least somewhat over short periods of time. So, if we were interested in measuring an individual's typical level of these emotions, we would need to make sure that the items ask how much the individual *generally* experiences these emotions, over the long run. In this way, test—retest reliability will likely be high, because an individual's perceptions of his or her *typical* level of the emotions will not be influenced so much by his or her temporary mood.

Before ending our discussion of reliability, we should note that the reliability of a measurement can also be computed in such a way as to take into account more than one kind of error variance. For example, a psychologist can examine error due to the occasion of measurement along with error due to the particular set of items used in a scale, by administering two different versions of a scale to the same group of persons on two different occasions. The correlation between the two versions of the scale administered on two occasions would give a reliability estimate that takes into account both sources of error.

1.2.2 Validity

The *validity* of a measurement is the extent to which it assesses the *same* characteristic that it is supposed to assess. Notice that this definition is different from, and more restrictive than, the definition of reliability. When we evaluate reliability, we are concerned only with the extent to which our measurements represent *some* meaningful characteristic, whatever that might be, rather than error. By contrast, when we evaluate validity, we are concerned with precisely *which* characteristic is being assessed. (In the last section, we were more or less assuming that the measurements were assessing the intended characteristic, but it is important to verify that this is really the case.)

You might wonder why we consider reliability at all, given that validity would seem to be more important. But there is a good reason for considering reliability. By knowing the reliability of a measurement, we get an idea of its maximum possible validity: If a measurement has poor reliability—that is, if it is not measuring any characteristic very well—then we know that it cannot have a very high level of validity—that is, it cannot be a good measurement of the characteristic we had in mind. This is important to know, because we might sometimes realize that a measurement having moderate validity could potentially have much higher validity, if its reliability could be improved (e.g., by adding more items or raters or by choosing some different items or raters). This contrasts with the situation in which a measurement with high reliability has low validity, in which case we know that the scale is measuring something, but something different from what we had in mind. In the latter case, we need to make some radical changes to the measurement or even to abandon it entirely.

There are different ways of evaluating the validity of a measurement of a characteristic. One way involves examining the *content* of the scale, and other ways involve examining the relations of scores on the scale with other variables. Let us consider these aspects of validity.

1.2.2.1 Content Validity

For measurements such as tests or scales, an important aspect of their validity is the extent to which their items are relevant to the characteristic that is supposed to be measured. For a measurement to have *content validity*, its items should assess all of the features of the intended characteristic and should not assess the features of other, irrelevant characteristics.

As an example, suppose that we wanted to construct a scale to measure people's enjoyment of the arts. In making this scale, we would try to include items describing the full variety of art forms, rather than only one or two. For example, we would include some items about different kinds of music, different kinds of visual art, different kinds of dramatic arts, different kinds of literature, and so on; we would not want our scale to consist only of items describing one of these categories of art. In addition, we would also avoid including items describing activities that clearly are not forms of art (e.g., tennis, accounting, welding, poker, etc.). By ensuring that our "enjoyment of the arts" scale contains items about all categories of art, and does not contain items about activities outside the arts, our scale would have good content validity.

In thinking about these examples, it might seem to you that achieving good content validity is fairly easy and that simple common sense can prevent us from constructing a scale that has poor content validity. But sometimes there are some subtle and difficult issues involved in making sure that content validity is strong. One difficulty is that it can often be tricky to decide exactly what kinds of content ought to be included, and what ought not to be included, in our definition of a characteristic. For example, in the case of "enjoyment of the arts," would we include popular culture, such as television comedies or pop music? Would we include sports that have an artistic component, such as figure skating or gymnastics? Sometimes it is difficult to decide exactly which content should be considered as part of the characteristic to be measured, and which content should be considered as something separate.

Difficulties with content validity can sometimes arise when we try to achieve a high level of internal-consistency reliability. Recall from the earlier section about reliability that the items of a scale should be substantially correlated with each other, so that the scale will have a high level of internal-consistency reliability. But it is possible to go too far in selecting items that show high correlations with each other, because we could end up with a set of very similar items that would only represent a small part of the range of content that our characteristic is supposed to include. For example, in the case of our "enjoyment of the arts" scale, perhaps we would find that our scale would have very high internal-consistency reliability if it included only items about visual arts, such as drawing, painting, and sculpture. However, an "enjoyment of the arts" scale consisting only of those items would have poor content validity.

1.2.2.2 Construct Validity: Convergent and Discriminant

Another aspect of validity is called *construct validity* (Cronbach & Meehl, 1955). The word "construct" (pronounced here as CON-struct) indicates that the property being measured is imagined or "constructed," not something concrete or tangible. Therefore, characteristics such as intelligence or sociability or impulsivity are constructs. (In the same way, many variables assessed in the physical sciences—such as temperature, mass, and length—are also constructs.) When we say that a measurement has construct validity, we are saying that this measurement really does assess the same construct that we are trying to assess.

Researchers evaluate the construct validity of a measurement by examining its correlations with other variables. If our scale is really measuring the characteristic that it is intended to measure, then it should correlate in certain specified ways with other variables. The sizes of these correlations should correspond closely to the degree of similarity between the characteristic to be measured by our scale and the characteristics believed to be measured by the other variables.

One aspect of construct validity is called *convergent validity*. When we examine the convergent validity of a scale, we investigate how strongly it correlates with variables that measure characteristics very similar (or *opposite*) to the one that our scale is intended to measure. If a variable is believed to measure something roughly the same as what our scale is supposed to measure, then we would expect our scale to show strong positive correlations with that variable. Similarly, if a variable is believed to measure something rather *opposite* to what our scale is supposed to measure, then we would expect our scale to show strong negative correlations with that variable. (This is still considered an aspect of convergent validity, because the relation is still supposed to be strong, but just in the negative direction.) If instead our scale has only weak correlations with variables assessing characteristics very similar (or opposite) to that which our scale is supposed to measure, then this would be evidence that our scale is not really measuring its intended characteristic. Ideally, these other variables would be measured using methods different from that of the measurement we are examining (see Box 1.3 and Box 1.4).

For example, suppose that we wanted to evaluate the convergent validity of students' self-ratings of their mathematical ability. If these self-ratings of math ability are valid, then they should correlate positively with the students' actual scores on a math aptitude test. They should also correlate negatively with teachers' ratings of the students' difficulties in learning math.

Another aspect of construct validity is called *discriminant validity*. When we examine the discriminant validity of a scale, we investigate how strongly it correlates with variables that measure characteristics *unrelated* to the one that our scale is intended to measure. If a variable is believed to measure something neither similar nor opposite to what our scale is supposed to measure, then we would expect our scale to show a weak correlation with that variable; in other words, the observed correlation, whether positive or negative, should be quite close to zero. If instead our scale showed a strong correlation (positive or negative) with that other variable, then this would be evidence against the discriminant validity of our scale; it would suggest that perhaps our scale was measuring some characteristic other than the one intended.

For example, consider once again the variable of self ratings of math ability. If these ratings are valid, then we would expect them not to correlate much with the students' levels of self-esteem. (If instead the self-ratings of math ability were strongly correlated with self-esteem, this might suggest that self-esteem was influencing the self-ratings of math ability.)

1.2.2.3 Criterion Validity

Another form of validity involves the relations of a measurement with an outcome or "criterion" variable that has some practical significance. In many cases, psychological

Box 1.3 Evaluating Construct Validity by Measuring Different Traits with Different Methods

One useful way to examine the construct validity of measurements is to consider two or more *different methods* of measuring each of two or more *different traits* (Campbell & Fiske, 1959). Suppose, for example, that we decide to measure the traits (i.e., characteristics) of sweet-toothedness (liking of sweet foods) and "spicy-toothedness" (yes, liking of spicy foods). Suppose also we measure both traits by using a person's own self-reports and by using observer reports about that person from someone who knows him or her very well (perhaps his or her spouse). ("Self-reports" and "observer reports" are defined in detail in Sections 1.3.1 and 1.3.2.) Let us assume that sweet-toothedness and spicy-toothedness are quite different traits, almost unrelated to each other.

If our self-report measure of sweet-toothedness is valid, then we would expect it to show a fairly high positive correlation with our observer report measure of sweet-toothedness. This would be evidence of convergent validity, because the *same* trait is being measured by the two different methods.

And if our self-report measure of sweet-toothedness really is valid, then we would also expect it to show only a weak correlation (whether positive or negative) with our observer report measure of spicy-toothedness. This would be evidence of discriminant validity, because two distinctly *different* traits are being measured by the two different methods.

Finally, if our self-report measure of sweet-toothedness really is valid, we would also expect it to show only a weak correlation (whether positive or negative) with our self-report measure of spicy-toothedness. This would also be evidence of discriminant validity, because two *different* traits are being measured by the same method. Sometimes when different traits are measured by the same method, the correlations between them are rather high, indicating a lack of discriminant validity. This can happen when there is something about the *method* of measurement that tends to influence people's scores on measurements of different traits. (For example, as we discuss in Chapter 2, self-reports on quite different characteristics might be positively correlated if some people tend to give more socially desirable responses in general than other people do.) Psychologists try to make their measurements so that people's scores depend as much as possible on their levels of the trait and as little as possible on the method of measuring the trait.

measurements are used to predict some important future outcomes, such as performance in a job or at school, response to a treatment program, or committing a crime. (In these cases of predicting future outcomes, criterion validity is also called *predictive* validity.) For example, if we developed a scale to measure sweet-toothedness (i.e., liking of sweet foods), we might use it to predict a person's future level of sugar consumption or their risk of developing tooth cavities or type 2 diabetes. In this case, the correlations between scores on the sweet–toothedness scale and these various criteria would be evidence of the criterion validity of the scale, at least for these particular criteria. (A scale that is valid for predicting one criterion might not be valid for predicting another.)

Note that in the case of criterion validity, the outcome (criterion) variables might depend only to a modest extent on the construct that our scale is trying to measure.

> **Box 1.4 Agreement between Raters: Interrater Reliability or Convergent Validity?**
>
> You might have noticed that both interrater reliability and convergent validity can be examined by finding the correlations between ratings or reports from different people. This might make you wonder about what is the difference between interrater reliability and convergent validity.
>
> Interrater reliability involves the case in which the persons who provide the information are more or less interchangeable—when they are all observing the same people at the same time, and when they are likely to have similar perspectives about the people they observe. Recall the example of the psychologists who were all observing the same interviews of the same people: Each of these psychologists is the same kind of observer.
>
> In contrast, convergent validity involves the case in which the persons who provide the information are not so interchangeable—when their information might be based on different observations, or when they would likely have different perspectives on the people they observe. For example, consider the differences in reports of someone's level of a personality trait from that person himself or herself, from that person's spouse, and from that person's friend. Each of these people observes the person in somewhat different circumstances, and each of them is likely to interpret those observations differently; in other words, each of these people is a different kind of observer.

For example, we might use our sweet-toothedness scale to predict sugar consumption, tooth cavities, or type 2 diabetes, even though those criterion variables depend on many causes other than sweet-toothedness. For this reason, we would not necessarily expect to find very high correlations between our measure and the criterion outcome. But the main question to be considered is whether the correlations would be high enough for the test to be useful in predicting the outcomes. For example, even if scores on a standardized test of academic aptitude showed only modest correlations with grade-point average in college, the test might still have practical value for improving accuracy in predicting which students will perform well in college.

1.3 METHODS OF MEASUREMENT: SELF- AND OBSERVER REPORTS, DIRECT OBSERVATIONS, BIODATA

Next we will discuss *how* psychological measurements are actually made. When we want to know about someone's personality characteristics—his or her patterns of behavior, thought, and emotion—we have several strategies for making our measurements.

1.3.1 Self-Reports

One approach is simply to ask the person a series of questions about his or her actions, thoughts, and feelings in various situations. An important feature of this approach is that the measurements are "structured" or "objective," in the sense that (1) every person is asked the same set of questions, and also (2) there is a fixed set of response alternatives for every question (e.g., yes/no, or a number from 1 to 7). In this way, we can make meaningful comparisons of the responses that different persons provide. If we ask a series of questions that involve related behaviors (e.g., talking on the phone, visiting friends, inviting guests, and attending parties), then we can make some inference about the person's level of some underlying characteristic (e.g., sociability).

This method is known as *self-report*, and it is the most widely used method of measuring personality. Perhaps the main reason for the popularity of self-report is the belief that it usually provides a fairly accurate measurement and does so cheaply and efficiently. The accuracy of self-report depends on a couple of important assumptions: first, that people generally know their behaviors, thoughts, and feelings fairly well, and second, that people are willing (at least under some circumstances) to report those behaviors, thoughts, and feelings. Of course, these assumptions are probably not entirely true: Most people are unlikely to be able to report all aspects of their personality with near-perfect accuracy, and some people may be quite poor at judging their own personality. And in some circumstances, some people are likely to distort their responses intentionally, to a greater or lesser extent, to present a good impression (or even, in some cases, to present a bad impression).

As described earlier, the self-report method of assessing personality involves asking an individual about his or her behaviors, thoughts, and feelings, and then inferring that individual's personality on the basis of the responses. But sometimes, the self-reports can simply involve an overall rating of the individual's level of a personality trait. For example, an individual might be asked to rate his or her own level of impulsivity, perhaps with a number from 0 to 10. These self-ratings might have an advantage relative to other self-reports, insofar as the rating is a more direct indication of the trait. To the extent that people agree about what is actually meant by a given trait name, this method could be quite accurate. But, on the other hand, people might differ in their understandings of which behaviors, thoughts, and feelings would indicate an individual's level of a given trait. (For example, one person might interpret impulsivity as a spontaneous, fun-loving tendency whereas another person might interpret impulsivity as an inability to control one's urges.) To the extent that these understandings may differ, the accuracy of self-ratings would be limited, relative to self-reports of the kind described earlier. For many purposes, however, the distinction between "reports" and "ratings" is not so clear; many personality questionnaires, for example, contain a mixture of items that represent reports of behaviors, thoughts, and feelings, and items that represent direct ratings of traits.

1.3.2 Observer Reports

Another method of assessing an individual's personality is analogous to self-report, but instead of asking the individual about his or her own behaviors, thoughts, and feelings, it involves asking someone else for that information. Ideally, this other person should be someone who knows the individual well, for example a spouse, a close relative, or a close friend, but for some purposes and some traits a coworker or classmate might be a suitable rater. Compared with self-report, this *observer report* method (also called *other report* or *informant report* or *peer report*) has the advantage that an individual's personality might in some cases be judged more objectively by someone who actually *observes* that individual from the outside. But then again, the people who know someone very well might be strongly inclined to present a good impression for that individual—for example, your parents might overestimate your level of desirable traits and underestimate your level of undesirable ones. Also, it is likely that even the other people who know the individual very well still do not know that person quite as well as the individual himself or herself does; there are some aspects of his or her thoughts and feelings, and even behaviors, that others might never really observe. This is particularly true when the other people are only acquainted with the individual in a limited range of contexts, such as in the workplace or at school. (Note that, just as we distinguished between self-reports and self-ratings in the previous section, we can also distinguish between observer reports and observer ratings in the same way.)

1.3.3 Direct Observations

Another method of measuring personality, quite different from self- and observer reports or ratings, is to observe a person's behavior directly. If the behaviors that indicate a given personality trait can be observed directly, then it is possible to measure that trait by observing the frequency or intensity with which the individual performs those behaviors. These observations might be made by watching the individual in his or her own natural habitat. For example, a researcher could try to assess your level of a trait such as sociability by actually watching how frequently you talk on the phone, visit friends, invite guests, and attend parties. Alternatively, the individual could be observed in an artificial setting: For example, a researcher could try to assess your sociability level by observing your behavior in a social situation created in a laboratory, in which you would have the opportunity to interact and converse (or to *avoid* interacting and conversing) with other research participants or with research assistants. By observing various features of your behavior, such as how much talking you did, how many questions you asked, how many people you spoke with, and how closely you stood to the other people, the researcher might be able to estimate your level of sociability.[7]

---

[7] Notice how direct observations differ from observer reports: With direct observations, a researcher deliberately observes a person's behavior in a specific situation or period of time. With observer reports, the person's typical behavior tendencies are described by someone who knows that person.

The method of direct observation has sometimes been used in personnel selection. One example of this occurred in the United States during World War II, when the Office of Strategic Services (OSS)—the former name of today's Central Intelligence Agency—used direct observations to assess personality when selecting secret agents for overseas assignments (e.g., MacKinnon, 1967). In one of the OSS selection tests, the (male) applicant was observed in a role-playing scenario. In this scenario, he was told to imagine that he had just been caught looking through secret documents at a government building, and that he was not authorized to do so. The applicant was then given 10 minutes to come up with a detailed explanation that would justify what he had been caught doing and would preserve his "cover" as an agent. Subsequently, the applicant was interrogated by several officers who would try to confuse and intimidate him, to catch him in contradictions, to make him feel stressed, and to trick him into breaking his cover. The OSS officials who made this selection test observed the extent to which the applicant could maintain his composure and poise during the interrogation, and how well he was able to maintain a plausible cover story. Some applicants did these things well; others plainly did not. (In a few cases, the OSS officials were impressed by some applicants who had fooled the interrogators by pretending to break down emotionally, giving a fake but irrelevant "confession" that actually maintained their cover.)

The method of direct observation is potentially very informative, as by definition it involves observation of people's behavior. But it has the disadvantage that it requires a lot of time and effort to use and is therefore very expensive. To observe an individual's behavior, either in natural or artificial settings, can be a very large undertaking, particularly if one hopes to measure many different individuals or to measure many different traits. Even for any single trait, it might be necessary to observe each individual over a wide variety of situations and on many occasions, to ensure that one is obtaining a reliable measurement of the trait. These considerations make direct observation very difficult, or almost impossible, to use on a large scale.[8]

1.3.4 Biodata (Life Outcome Data)

Yet another method for assessing personality is to obtain "biodata"—that is, to obtain some records of the person's life that seem likely to be relevant to an individual's personality. For example, I might use your cell phone talking time as an indication of your

---

[8] Tests of ability or achievement can also be considered as examples of direct observations within artificial settings—but these are observations that can be made very efficiently. For example, consider tests of mental abilities: Here, individuals are placed into an artificial setting (specifically, the situation of taking the test), and their behavior is observed simply by recording their answers to the test questions. In other words, the researcher is able to measure each individual's level of ability by directly observing that individual's performance on the test. Notice that this is quite different from the self-report or observer report methods, which in this case would involve *asking about* the individual's level of ability.

sociability, your grade point average (GPA) as an indication of your industriousness, or your speeding tickets as an indication of your recklessness. These records have the advantage that they often represent important outcomes in a person's life, and that they are objective indicators of behavior rather than merely reports. But, on the other hand, it is not always clear that a particular piece of information about an individual's life is really an accurate indication of his or her level of the personality trait that we hope to assess. Instead, a particular outcome might be influenced by other traits or by a variety of circumstances that are unrelated to one's personality. For example, a sociable person who prefers to talk in person might have relatively little cell phone talking time; an industrious person who has no interest or aptitude for schoolwork might have a low GPA; and a reckless person who rarely drives a car might have no speeding tickets. Nevertheless, it seems likely that many kinds of life outcome data will give at least some indirect information about an individual's personality.

1.3.5 Comparing the Methods of Measurement

How do we know that any of the previous methods actually provide valid indicators of individuals' levels of various personality traits? The main source of evidence on this question has been the convergent validity correlations between measures of the same or similar traits, as assessed by different methods. As we will discuss in more detail in Chapter 2, there are generally rather strong correlations between self-report and observer report measurements of personality characteristics, and strong correlations also between observer report measurements of personality characteristics as provided by two different observers.[9] In addition, self-report and observer report measurements of personality generally show good convergent validity with regard to direct observations of behavior and biodata; we will discuss the relations of personality reports with various life outcomes in Chapter 9.

Some researchers have criticized the heavy reliance on personality reports (especially self-reports) by other researchers. However, it is easy to see why self- and observer reports are so widely used: They provide extremely quick, cheap, and efficient methods of measuring a wide array of traits, with generally good levels of reliability and validity. Although some researchers view direct observation as the ideal method—as a kind of "gold standard" for personality measurement—it is likely that self- and observer reports will provide better measures of personality overall. This is because of the extreme difficulty of obtaining enough observations of individuals, across a wide enough variety of situations, and involving a wide enough variety of relevant behaviors, for each of the traits that researchers would like to measure.

---

[9] Self-ratings of abilities, or of desirable characteristics such as attractiveness, tend to be less valid than self-reports of personality, however.

1.4 SUMMARY AND CONCLUSIONS

In this chapter, we have introduced some basic statistical concepts, some ways of assessing the quality of measurement, and some methods for measuring psychological characteristics. We can summarize these topics as follows.

First, most psychological measurements are reported using numbers that show which people have higher or lower levels of a characteristic, and also show how large is the difference (or interval) between any two people. However, those numbers do not show an absolute "zero" level of a characteristic, nor do they allow us to talk about ratios between people's levels—for example, it would not make sense to say that one person is twice as organized as another. Also, measurements of psychological characteristics are often reported in terms of standard scores, where the mean level is given as 0 (or some other round number) and the standard deviation as 1 (or some other round number). In addition, the relations between measurements of psychological characteristics are reported in terms of correlation coefficients, whose possible values range from -1 (perfect negative relation) through 0 (no relation) to $+1$ (perfect positive relation). By knowing the correlation coefficient, we gain a clear idea of the extent to which higher levels of one characteristic tend to go along with higher (or lower) levels of another characteristic.

Next, let us review the concepts that are used in evaluating the quality of psychological measurements. The reliability of a measurement is its consistency with similar measurements of the same characteristic; it therefore indicates the extent to which the measurement is assessing some meaningful characteristic. The reliability of a test or a questionnaire scale can be examined by finding the correlation between different parts (or different versions) of the test or questionnaire scale. When the measurement consists of ratings made by judges (observers), reliability can be examined by finding the correlation between the observers. Another way of evaluating reliability is to determine whether people's scores are stable across time, by finding out how much people's scores on different occasions are correlated.

The validity of a measurement is the extent to which it really does measure the intended characteristic. One way to evaluate the validity of a measurement is by examining the extent to which the content of the measurement (e.g., items on a personality questionnaire scale) corresponds to the concept of the characteristic that is supposed to be measured. Another way of evaluating validity is to find out the extent to which scores on this measurement are (1) strongly correlated with other variables that are believed to be good indicators of the same characteristic, and (2) weakly correlated with other variables that are believed to be unrelated to this characteristic. Validity is also evaluated by examining how well scores on a measurement can predict outcome variables (criteria) of practical importance.

Finally, we considered some of the basic methods used in evaluating personality. Self-report methods ask the individual to describe his or her own behaviors, thoughts, and feelings, and from this the researcher can figure out the individual's levels of various characteristics. Observer report methods ask some other person to describe the behaviors, thoughts, and feelings of the person to be measured. (Sometimes, the person who provides personality descriptions is asked to make self- or observer *ratings*, whereby he or she makes a direct estimate of the level of a given characteristic, rather than a report of some behavior that is relevant to the characteristic.) With direct observation methods, the researcher watches and records the behavior of the person whose personality is to be assessed and thus infers that person's level of a characteristic from his or her behaviors. (Direct observations can be made both in "natural" settings, such as the person's home or workplace, and in "artificial" situations, such as the psychologist's laboratory.) Biodata (or life outcome data) methods involve the use of records about various aspects of a person's life to make inferences about his or her personality characteristics. Each of the preceding methods has its advantages and disadvantages, but self- and observer report methods are used most frequently because of their great efficiency in providing accurate measurements.

CHAPTER 2

Personality Traits and the Inventories That Measure Them

Contents

2.1 THE IDEA OF A PERSONALITY TRAIT

In the previous chapter, we used terms such as "personality characteristic" or "personality trait" simply in the way that you would use those terms in everyday conversation. This familiar meaning is pretty close to what psychologists have in mind when they discuss personality traits. However, it would be useful to have at least a rough definition. Briefly, a personality trait refers to differences among individuals in a typical tendency to behave, think, or feel in some conceptually related ways, across a variety of relevant situations and across some fairly long period of time. But this definition has several parts, some of which could be stated more precisely. Let us discuss this definition a bit further.

2.1.1 Differences Among Individuals

First, the idea of "differences among individuals" is important, because the description of an individual's personality is meaningful only to the extent that it gives us, directly or

Individual Differences and Personality
ISBN 978-0-12-809845-5, http://dx.doi.org/10.1016/B978-0-12-809845-5.00002-0

indirectly, a comparison with others. For example, if we are told that Bob tends to show or feel fatigue after concentrating intensely for a long time, this does not really tell us very much, because the same is true of everyone. What is more informative is to know the degree to which Bob shows or feels fatigue after having concentrated for a long time, relative to that shown or felt by other people. This would give us some indication of how "fatigable" Bob is.

2.1.2 In a Typical Tendency to Behave, Think, or Feel

Next, "in a tendency to behave, think, or feel" refers to a *likelihood* of showing some behaviors or of having some thoughts or feelings. When we say that a person has a high level of a trait, we do not suggest that a person always exhibits certain behaviors, thoughts, or feelings; instead, we suggest that they have a relatively strong inclination or predisposition to exhibit those behaviors, thoughts, or feelings. For example, when we say that Bob is very optimistic, we do not mean that he is always optimistic about everything; instead, we just mean that he is frequently optimistic or is optimistic about many things. Note also that "a tendency to behave, think, or feel" includes not only the external or behavioral aspects of a trait, as shown by the person's actions or words, but also the internal aspects, as shown by the person's ideas and emotions. Some traits might be expressed in all of these ways; for example, the trait of optimism might be shown by what a person does (e.g., taking on difficult challenges) and what a person says (e.g., telling others that things will turn out well), but also what a person thinks (e.g., estimating the likelihood of success to be high) and what a person feels (e.g., experiencing excitement rather than anxiety when confronted by difficulties).

2.1.3 In Some Conceptually Related Ways

In the next phrase, "in some conceptually related ways," the idea is that a trait is expressed by various behaviors, thoughts, and feelings that appear to have some common psychological element. Sometimes, those expressions of the trait might share some obvious similarities to each other: For example, a person with a high level of the trait of "thrill seeking" might enjoy activities such as skydiving, bungee jumping, motorcycle racing, and jet-skiing. But sometimes, a trait can be expressed in ways that superficially appear to be quite different: For example, consider behaviors such as wearing flashy clothes, complimenting others loudly, stating extreme opinions, or giving large tips at a restaurant. These behaviors all look rather different from each other, but they might all reflect the same underlying trait of "showing off." (Related to this point, note that a given behavior might be related to two or more different traits: For example, some people who give large tips at a restaurant may be show-offs, but others may be very generous people, and still others may be careless with money.)

2.1.4 Across a Variety of Relevant Situations

The phrase "across a variety of relevant situations" is important, because a personality trait is not simply a habit that is confined to one specific situation; instead, it is shown across a variety of settings in which people differ in trait-relevant behavior. Suppose that we describe Bob as inquisitive: We mean that he is curious across a wide range of situations in which a person might feel this curiosity. But if Bob reads books *only* about mathematics, or asks questions *only* about sports, or watches documentaries *only* about gardening, then we probably would not describe him as inquisitive.

2.1.5 Over Some Fairly Long Period of Time

Finally, the phrase "over some fairly long period of time" means that there is some pattern that can be observed over the long run, rather than simply on a temporary basis. For example, a person who is generally very cheerful might be quite subdued for a few weeks after a very depressing event, such as the loss of a loved one. But this would not necessarily mean that the person's level of the *trait* of cheerfulness had actually changed; instead, it would probably mean that this temporary condition was interfering with the normal expression of that trait. The idea of a trait is that there is some reasonably stable, long-lasting tendency to show the relevant pattern of behaviors. It is difficult to specify exactly what a "fairly long period of time" should be, but it can probably be considered as a period of at least a few years. Note, though, that the idea of a trait does not require that the person show the same tendency across the entire life span: Instead, it is possible that even the rather stable, long-run tendencies of an individual might change considerably during the course of a lifetime. For example, we could at least imagine that a person might have a stable tendency to be lazy throughout his or her adolescence, but then a stable tendency to be hardworking throughout his or her early adulthood, and then a stable tendency to be "in between" these levels during middle age. During each of these three stages, it would have been meaningful to describe this individual in terms of the personality trait of being lazy versus hardworking, even though her level of that trait did change across this long period. The question of whether personality traits tend to be stable across the life span is an interesting one, and in Chapter 4 we will look at the results of studies that have compared people's personalities across very long periods of time.

2.2 PERSONALITY TRAITS AND OTHER PSYCHOLOGICAL CHARACTERISTICS

Using the preceding definition of a personality trait, we can also consider the issue of which kinds of individual differences should be considered as personality traits, and which kinds should be considered separately from personality traits, as distinct categories of psychological characteristics. For the purpose of this textbook, we will treat several important individual differences as belonging to categories different from the category of personality traits. For example, mental abilities—such as verbal or mathematical skills— differ from personality traits by representing one's maximum level of performance in some tasks, rather than one's typical way or style of behaving, thinking, or feeling. As another example, beliefs and attitudes differ from personality traits by being focused on some particular "object"—such as a specific set of religious or political issues—rather than standing alone as a general style of behaving, thinking, or feeling. A similar point can also be made about individual differences in sexuality. This is not to say that these "other" kinds of individual differences—mental abilities, beliefs and attitudes, and sexuality—are not important parts of one's personality; on the contrary, we will consider these individual differences in some depth in later chapters of this textbook. However, we will examine those individual differences separately from the more general personality traits that will be the focus of the next few chapters of this book.

In those following chapters, we will explore several interesting questions about personality traits: How are those traits related to each other? What are the causes of individual differences in personality traits? What are the "real-world" consequences of those differences? But first, we need to discuss another question—one that occupied much of the attention of personality psychologists between the late 1960s and the early 1980s: Do personality traits really exist?

2.3 DO PERSONALITY TRAITS EXIST?

By the 1960s, psychologists were conducting many research studies aimed at understanding and measuring a variety of personality traits. But some psychologists—most notably a researcher named Walter Mischel—argued that the results of those studies indicated that personality traits were of limited value for predicting behavior (e.g., Mischel, 1968). One important reason why some researchers reached this conclusion was that, in several studies, results showed that behaviors supposedly related to the same underlying trait were only weakly correlated across situations.[1] Mischel and others argued that these results contradicted the idea that personality traits would be useful for predicting or explaining people's behaviors.

2.3.1 Research Studies Testing the Existence of Traits

Let us consider an example of the findings that led some psychologists to doubt the value of personality traits. An early research study by Hartshorne and May (1928) examined the

---

[1] Notice that the issue here is about behavior in *different situations*, and not just about behavior in the same situation on different occasions. Even though any given person may vary from one occasion to the next in his or her response to the same situation, his or her typical response to the same situation becomes clear over the long run (see discussion by Fleeson, 2004). Mischel and others understood this, and their concern was instead about behavior in different situations.

behaviors of 11,000 elementary- and high-school students, who were observed in a variety of situations in which individual differences in traits of "moral character" would emerge. For example, Hartshorne and May watched to see whether each child would perform various behaviors related to altruism (e.g., voting to spend class money on a charity rather than on oneself, donating to charity various items from a pencil-case given to the child), self-control (e.g., resisting temptation to eat candy, persisting in a puzzle-solving task), and honesty (e.g., not stealing coins from a puzzle-box, not cheating in various contests). The children were observed several times in each situation, so that for each child, a reliable score could be calculated to indicate his or her tendencies to be altruistic, self-controlled, or honest. (The researchers designed each situation so that the observations would be subtle, to prevent the children from realizing that their moral character was being assessed.) What Hartshorne and May found was that the correlations between altruistic behaviors in any two situations were rather weak, generally not much above .20. That is, there was only a weak tendency for the children who were highly altruistic in one situation (compared with their peers) to be highly altruistic in another situation. Instead, many children who were relatively altruistic in one situation were not particularly altruistic in another. Similar results were obtained for self-controlled behaviors and for honest behaviors.

On the basis of this and similar findings, Mischel (1968) and others concluded that personality traits were much less important than had previously been thought. Instead, those researchers argued, individual differences in a given kind of behavior depend overwhelmingly on the specific situation involved. But soon after Mischel's points were published, other psychologists disputed his conclusions. Although the facts cited by Mischel were true, other researchers disagreed with the interpretation of what those facts meant. The chief problem, they suggested, was that a high level of cross-situational consistency can be shown when observations of behavior are *aggregated*, or averaged, across many situations (e.g., Epstein, 1979). For example, even though altruistic behavior (or self-controlled behavior, or honest behavior, etc.) may depend heavily on the situation involved, it is still possible that individuals will differ consistently from each other when we consider their *overall* level of altruism (or self-control, or honesty), as based on their average behavior across many situations. (Recall the importance of averaging as discussed in Section 1.2.1.)

To illustrate this point, Rushton, Brainerd, and Pressley (1983) noted that Hartshorne and May had also calculated each child's *average* level of altruism within each of two sets of *several* situations. They found that the children's overall scores for altruism on one set correlated about .50 or .60 with their overall scores for altruism on the other set. This is obviously a much higher value than the .20 correlation observed for any two *single* situations.

The meaning of these aggregated results is that, even though an individual's level of altruism (or self-control, or honesty) in one kind of situation is not a particularly accurate indicator of his or her level of altruism (or self-control, or honesty) in another kind of situation, people still differ consistently in their overall level as observed across many situations. The important point is that, even though behavior in any one situation does depend a great deal on the nature of that specific situation, the importance of traits becomes clear when we consider people's overall patterns of behavior, as shown by their typical tendencies, averaged across many situations. (For example, a child who is usually honest but who is worried about failing a course in school might be tempted to cheat on a test; or, a child who is usually dishonest but does not especially like sweet foods might not feel much urge to steal a particular kind of candy. But when we consider the "big picture" of how honestly those children usually behave, we could see the consistent differences between the two of them.) The effect of aggregating is important, because even though we may have a difficult time in predicting people's behavior in any one specific situation, we can still be rather successful in predicting people's overall patterns of behavior, which is usually our primary aim.

In addition to citing the results of previous research, such as the Hartshorne and May study, Mischel and his colleagues also conducted some investigations of their own to address the question of whether or not personality traits existed. Mischel and Peake (1982) made detailed observations of the behaviors of a sample of college students, with attention to behaviors that might be considered as indicators of a trait of conscientiousness. Mischel and Peake observed each student on repeated occasions to measure many conscientiousness-related variables, such as class attendance, appointment attendance, assignment neatness, class-note neatness, desk neatness, bed neatness, assignment punctuality, class reading punctuality, lecture punctuality, class reading completion, note thoroughness, and others. What Mischel and Peake found was that each of these indicators of conscientiousness tended to be only weakly correlated with the others, with an average correlation of only .13. They interpreted this finding as evidence that there was no important trait of conscientiousness, but that instead a student's "conscientiousness" depended very strongly on the situation.

Other researchers reached different conclusions, however. Jackson and Paunonen (1985) showed, using the data from the Mischel and Peake study, that the trait of conscientiousness emerges more clearly when one aggregates across the various behaviors assessed by Mischel and Peake. For example, if the 19 variables are randomly divided into two roughly equal sets, the correlations between overall conscientiousness levels on the two sets would typically be in the .50s. This again shows that, even though situations have an important influence on behavior, we can still see the very strong influence of traits when we consider people's typical behavior, as averaged across many different situations.

We can summarize this section as follows. First, differences among people in their tendencies to behave in ways related to a given trait will depend a great deal on the situation. As a result, we often cannot guess very accurately how individuals will behave in one situation just by knowing how they behave in another situation. However, if we know how individuals typically behave across several situations, then we can likely guess rather accurately how they typically behave across several other situations. In other words, even though the situation is important, we can still see very consistent differences among people when we consider their overall behavior as observed across many different situations: Traits clearly do exist.[2]

BOX 2.1 Situations, Persons, and Person-by-Situation Interactions

The question of whether or not traits exist can be considered in terms of "analysis of variance," the statistical technique that you have likely learned about in your statistics class. As an example, suppose that we observe each of many people as they experience various situations that might cause them to feel and express some anger toward another person. In doing so, we are likely to find that the level of anger is not the same for every person in every situation; that is, there will be some variance in angry behavior. Some of this variance is likely due to the situation alone, because different situations can provoke more or less anger: For example, pretty much everyone will feel more anger in response to being intentionally insulted than in response to being accidentally (and gently) bumped into. The idea that some variance is due to situations is considered obvious by all personality psychologists, regardless of whether or not they believe that personality traits are important (Fleeson & Noftle, 2009; Hogan, 2009). In fact, they tend to ignore this source of variance as a rather uninteresting one, focusing instead on the other two possible sources of variance.

Another potential source of variance involves the interaction between persons and situations. To see this, let us continue with our example of anger-related behaviors. Some people might tend to become angry when a driver "cuts them off" in traffic but not when a retail salesperson is very slow, whereas other people might show the opposite pattern. As was the case for variance due to situations, all personality psychologists agree that person-by-situation interactions can be important. (When we say that specific situations have an important influence on behavior, we are referring not only to the effects of situations alone, but also to person-by-situation interactions.) But psychologists have disagreed about the question of whether or not the person-by-situation interactions can account for pretty much all of the variance that is not already accounted for by situations alone. Researchers who consider personality traits to be unimportant believe that person-by-situation interactions can account for nearly all of that variance. In contrast, researchers who consider personality traits to be important believe that there is a considerable amount of variance that is attributable to another source, namely, that of persons alone.

Consider our example of anger-related behaviors. Some researchers believe that, when we take an average across various situations of each person's amount of anger-related behavior, we will find that some people have been much more angry than others overall. In other words, researchers who believe that there is a trait of anger would expect to find

(Continued)

---

[2] For further reading on the controversy about the existence of traits, and the issue of consistency across situations, see Lucas and Donnellan (2009), Fleeson and Noftle (2009), and Hodson (2009).

BOX 2.1 Situations, Persons, and Person-by-Situation Interactions—cont'd

that some people tend to get angry much more easily than others do. In contrast, researchers who do not believe that there is a trait of anger would expect to find very little difference among people in the overall tendency to become angry. Thus, the debate about the existence of personality traits is a debate about the question of whether or not there is any considerable amount of variance in behavior due to persons. As noted in this chapter, that debate has been resolved: it is clear that much of the variance in behavior is indeed variance between persons.

When examining the effects of persons (i.e., traits) and situations on behavior, researchers treat the situations as being independent of persons—that is, as if the situations one encounters did not depend on one's personality. But researchers who study personality traits have also realized that people's personalities do influence the situations they experience, in at least two ways (Buss, 1979; Funder, 2008).

One influence of persons on situations is that to some extent people can select the situations that they experience. For example, consider two kinds of parties that a person might attend. At one party, everyone gets involved in some wild and uninhibited behavior; at the other party, no one does so. Maybe the situation represented by the first party encouraged people to behave wildly, whereas the situation represented by the second party discouraged them from doing so. (And perhaps if you had attended the first party, your behavior would have been less inhibited than if you had attended the second party.) But it is also likely that people choose which kind of party to attend, such that people tend to go to the party where the expected behavior matches their own preferences.

A second influence of persons on situations is that to some extent people can evoke or influence the situations that they experience. For example, consider two new employees at a workplace. After a few weeks on the job, one employee is treated with coldness and hostility by her coworkers, and she becomes less motivated to work hard; meanwhile, the other employee is treated with warmth and friendliness by her coworkers, and she becomes more motivated to work hard. Perhaps these situations would have elicited the same reactions from almost any employee. But it is also possible that the behavior of the first employee toward her coworkers had provoked their hostility, whereas the behavior of the second employee had encouraged their friendliness.

Thus, the situations that people experience are not always independent of people's personalities; instead, people tend to select or evoke different situations, as a function of their own personalities. This is not to say that all, or even most, situations are influenced by people's personalities; on the contrary, many situations will be just about equally likely to happen to anyone, and some situations will happen in spite of a person's own personality. (To continue with the examples, sometimes an inhibited person will find himself at a wild party, and sometimes a well-intentioned employee will find herself treated coldly by her coworkers.) But the point is that some of the situations that influence behavior are themselves influenced by people's personalities.

2.4 MEASURING TRAITS BY SELF- OR OBSERVER REPORT: STRUCTURED PERSONALITY INVENTORIES

Self- and observer reports are the methods most frequently used by psychologists to assess people's levels of personality traits. Given this wide use, it is worth considering the workings of the questionnaires that are used for obtaining self- and observer reports of personality. These questionnaires are generally known as "structured personality inventories." They are structured in the sense that the individuals being measured are given a predetermined set of options for responding to the various "items" (i.e., the statements or questions): For example, they might answer questions on a yes/no basis, or they might indicate their levels of agreement with statements using a one-to-five scale, and so on. (In contrast, an inventory would be *unstructured* if it allowed individuals to respond freely rather than requiring them to choose one of several specified options. Later in this chapter, we will consider some methods of personality assessment that are unstructured.)

Most personality inventories assess several different personality traits. Each trait is assessed by its own "scale," which contains several different "items."[3] An individual's responses to the items of a given scale are averaged out (or added up) to produce an overall score, which can then be compared with the scores of other individuals on that scale. The reason why each trait is measured by a scale containing several different items is that this allows for good reliability and good content validity. When a scale has several related items, the scores on that scale will largely represent whatever is common to those items; if the items really do assess the trait that is supposed to be measured, then this common element will correspond to that trait. Also, a scale containing several items can assess the various features of the trait, because each item can capture a different aspect of the trait. Consider as an example a scale that measures the trait of intellectual curiosity: Such a scale might contain items describing interests in history, in geography, in literature, in the arts, in life sciences, and in physical sciences. This scale would probably show good reliability, because the average response to these items would likely be a good indicator of the element that is common to those items (presumably, intellectual curiosity). This scale would also have good content validity, because the items describe a wide array of interests, all of which are intellectual interests.

Most scales contain some items for which responses indicating greater agreement will contribute to higher scores on the trait. For example, a sociability scale might contain items about greatly enjoying parties or about frequently going out with friends, and

---

[3] Note that the word "scale" is used in different ways. "Scale" sometimes refers to a group of several items that are averaged out or added up to give an overall score for a given trait. However, "scale" sometimes refers to the set of options that an individual can use in responding to a given item; for example, an item might have a *response scale* with options ranging from 1 (very inaccurate) to 5 (very accurate).

individuals who agree with those statements will tend to get high scores on that sociability scale. But one interesting feature of personality inventory scales is that many of the
scales contain some items that suggest the *opposite* of the trait in question. That is,
most scales also contain some items for which responses indicating greater *disagreement*
will contribute to higher scores on a trait. To use the example of the sociability scale
again, such a scale might contain some items about preferring to be alone or about rarely
engaging in small talk, and individuals who *disagree* with those statements will tend to get
high scores on the sociability scale. Such items are generally known as "negatively-keyed" or
"reverse-coded" items, among other names.[4]

Why do psychologists bother to include reverse-coded items in their scales? The
main reason is that there are differences among individuals in their general tendency
to agree with statements (or to say "yes" to questions) independently of the content
of those statements (or questions). For example, when individuals respond to the items
of a personality inventory, there will frequently be some items for which they are not
absolutely sure of their precise responses. When faced with such items, some people
tend to respond in the direction of greater agreement; other people, however, tend
to respond in the direction of greater disagreement. This difference between people
is sometimes called "acquiescence," because it is as if some people "acquiesce" (agree)
with statements more than others do. As a result of this variance in "acquiescence,"
some people will tend to have substantially higher scores than other people when we
average responses across many such items. Therefore, it is difficult to interpret scores
on a scale that consists of items for which greater agreement always contributes to a
higher score. If a person has a high score, does this indicate a high level of the trait,
or does that score reflect (at least in part) a tendency to agree with items in general?
Similarly, does a low score necessarily indicate a low level of the trait, or does that score
reflect in part a tendency to disagree with items in general? To avoid this uncertainty,
psychologists try to make roughly half of the items of a scale reverse-coded or
negatively-keyed items. In this way, agreeing with items sometimes contributes to a
high score (in the case of regular items), but sometimes contributes to a low score (in
the case of reverse-coded items). By having roughly equal numbers of regular and
reverse-coded items, the tendency to agree or disagree with statements in general is
balanced out, with the result that higher scores on the scale really do indicate higher
levels of the trait, and lower scale scores really do indicate lower trait levels.

---

[4] Doing the math of reverse-coded items is very easy. Suppose that we have a trait scale from an inventory
whose items use a one-to-five response scale. For reverse-coded items, an individual's responses must first be
"reversed," so that a one is converted to a five, a two to a four, a three to a three, a four to a two, and a five to a one.
After the reversal of these negatively-keyed items, scores on all items can then be averaged (or added) to give the
overall scale score.

2.5 STRATEGIES OF PERSONALITY INVENTORY CONSTRUCTION

Now that you understand how personality inventories work, you might wonder how they are constructed in the first place. That is, how exactly do psychologists decide what items will be used when assessing a given personality trait? Is there one universal approach, or are there many different ways of constructing a personality inventory?

In some sense, the number of different ways of developing a personality questionnaire is very large, because every psychologist who constructs such questionnaires will do so a bit differently from every other psychologist. But we can say that there are three basic strategies or approaches to developing personality inventories, and that every psychologist uses one (or more) of these strategies. These three approaches are each known by various names, but here we will refer to them as the *empirical* approach, the *factor-analytic* approach, and the *rational* approach. The approaches differ in the ways that the items are generated and selected for inclusion in the inventory.

2.5.1 The Empirical Strategy

In the empirical strategy of constructing personality inventories, the psychologist begins by writing many items that together describe a very wide variety of actions, thoughts, and feelings, as well as (in many cases) items that ask for ratings on various characteristics. The psychologist then obtains self-reports (or observer reports) on this large pool of items from a large sample of persons. But in addition, the psychologist also obtains some other information from these individuals, and it is this extra information that is used in deciding which items should be kept to assess the traits that are of interest to the psychologist. In fact, the idea of the empirical approach is that items should be selected "empirically"— that is, on the basis of observed evidence of the relations of those items with some other information that is believed to indicate the individual's level of a given trait. Let us consider how this might be done.

Suppose, for example, that the psychologist would like to measure the trait of "femininity versus masculinity." For the purpose of measuring this trait, the psychologist who uses an empirical approach would want to choose items that are empirically related to some variable that should be a good indicator of femininity versus masculinity. You can probably think of several variables that should be strongly associated with femininity versus masculinity, and would therefore be a good basis for deciding which items were the better measures of this trait. For now, let us consider one such variable: The individual's own gender. We would expect that items that are empirically related to an individual's gender—that is, items that show a difference in responses between the average woman and the average man—would tend to be good indicators of an individual's level of femininity versus masculinity. Therefore, the psychologist who was using the empirical strategy could select the items that show the largest differences between the responses of women and the responses of men.

As another example, suppose that another trait of interest to the psychologist is "achievement orientation." If the sample of individuals being measured by the psychologist was from a college or high school, the psychologist might obtain information about the individuals' grade point averages, on the assumption that grade point average is a good indicator of achievement orientation. That is, the items measuring achievement orientation most effectively should be those that are empirically associated with grade point average. The psychologist would therefore select the items for which individuals' responses show the strongest correlations with grade point average.

These examples give some idea of how the empirical method works. Note that, in using this approach, psychologists are not concerned about the "content" of an item—in other words, they are not really interested in what kind of action, thought, or feeling is described by the item. For example, if responses to the item, "I like to eat apples," show a large difference between women and men (or a strong correlation with grade point average) then the psychologist will choose that item, even though it does not appear to have anything to do with femininity versus masculinity (or with achievement orientation). In other words, the empirical strategy is based solely on the observed, empirical links between the items and some variable that is assumed to be a good indicator of the trait.

To some extent, the fact that the empirical strategy may select items having no obvious relevance to a trait could be considered a strength of that approach. The potential advantage is that, if items are not obviously related to the trait they are intended to measure, it will be difficult for individuals to know how to adjust their responses in such a way as to give a desired impression—that is, it will be hard to "fake" responses. However, psychologists have raised some serious concerns about the use of the empirical strategy.

One criticism of the empirical method involves the samples of individuals from whom data are obtained: Specifically, an item selected on the basis of its observed associations with a given variable within a certain sample of individuals might not show such strong associations within every sample of individuals. Consider the example of selecting items to measure achievement orientation on the basis of their correlations with grade point average. Perhaps the items that show the strongest associations with grade point average in a sample of big-city high school students will not show the largest differences within a sample of small-town high school students. Or, the items that are most strongly correlated with grade point average in a sample of high school students might not be so strongly correlated with grade point average in a sample of college students. In addition to these concerns, it is also important that the sample whose data are used for selecting items be very large (generally, at least several hundred persons and ideally several thousand); otherwise, if the sample is small, then the selected items might have been related to the trait simply by chance, having had a "fluke" association with the trait. Thus, one criticism of the empirical approach is that very different sets of items might be selected, depending on the sample of individuals that is used as the source of the empirical data.

Another criticism of this approach involves the variables that are used as the basis for selecting items. For example, in the previous case involving achievement orientation, we used grade point average as an indicator of that trait, and used items' relations with grade point average as a basis for selecting the best items for measuring achievement orientation. But, even if we agree that grade point average tends to be a good indicator of achievement orientation, there are presumably several other variables that we could have used instead, and each of these might have been an equally good indicator. To take a couple of examples, we could have measured how many hours the individuals worked at paid jobs, or how many hours they spent practicing at sports or music, or how highly their friends rated their achievement orientation levels. Presumably, the items that were selected on the basis of relations with grade point average would not all be the same as those selected on the basis of relations with these other variables. In such a case, it would be difficult to know which set of items would represent the "best" measures of achievement orientation. Thus, another concern about the empirical strategy is that very different sets of items can be selected, depending on the variable that is used as the indicator of the trait.

The preceding criticisms are potentially important ones, but there are ways that their impact can be reduced. First, if the items can be selected on the basis of empirical relations that are observed within several different samples of individuals, then it is more likely that the selected items really will produce a scale that is a valid measure of the trait. Also, if the items can be selected on the basis of their empirical relations with several different variables that are all good indicators of the trait, then it is also more likely that the selected items will make a valid scale. However, the use of these procedures may not be very practical, as it may be very difficult to obtain several different, large samples of individuals who can all be measured on several variables that are all good indicators of a given trait.

2.5.2 The Factor-Analytic Strategy

In the factor-analytic strategy of constructing personality inventories, the psychologist begins with a large and diverse pool of items, much as is done with the empirical strategy. Also as is done in the empirical approach, the factor-analytic approach involves administering these items to a large sample of individuals. But in the factor-analytic approach, the basis for selecting items is different: Rather than examining the items' relations with some outside variable that serves as an indicator of a given trait, as is done in the empirical approach, the psychologist who uses the factor-analytic method instead finds groups of related items, such that each group measures a different trait.

In Chapter 3, we will describe the technique of factor analysis in some detail. For now, it is enough to say that factor analysis provides a way of sorting correlated items together into the same category (i.e., the same *factor*), while putting uncorrelated items into different categories (i.e., different factors). Because the items belonging to the same factor are correlated with each other, they tend to measure the same broad personality trait. When psychologists apply factor analysis to the construction of a personality inventory, they use the results to find out (1) what personality trait is being measured by each of the resulting factors, and (2) which items clearly belong to each factor, so that these items can be selected to make up the scales of the personality inventory. For example, imagine a very simple case in which the factor analysis shows only two factors, one of which contains items describing "risk-taking" behaviors, and the other of which contains items describing "energy level" behaviors. In the factor-analytic approach, the psychologist would select the items that clearly belong to the risk-taking factor and the items that clearly belong to the energy level factor, and would use those two sets of items to measure those two traits.

Notice that the factor-analytic strategy also differs from the empirical strategy in several other ways. In the empirical strategy, the psychologist starts out with a clear idea in mind as to which trait or traits are to be measured. In the factor-analytic strategy, however, the researcher does not necessarily have any specific plan as to which traits should be measured: Instead, the identity of these traits is revealed by the results of the factor analysis. This might be considered an advantage of this approach, insofar as the use of factor analysis will allow the psychologist to measure whatever are the major traits that are assessed by the items of the pool that has been administered to the individuals. But on the other hand, if the item pool does not contain a wide variety of items, then the product of the factor-analytic strategy will be an inventory that measures a rather limited set of traits.

2.5.3 The Rational Strategy

In the rational strategy of constructing personality inventories, the first step is usually different from that of empirical and factor-analytic approaches. Instead of beginning with a large existing pool of items, the psychologist writes items specifically for the purpose of assessing each trait that is to be measured. This process of writing the items to measure each trait is conducted "rationally," in the sense that the psychologist tries to produce items that are clearly relevant to the trait in question. In other words, the items are intended to describe actions, thoughts, or feelings that reveal a high level of the trait (or, for reverse-coded items, a low level of the trait), and to represent all the various aspects of the trait. The next step in the rational strategy is to figure out which of the items are the "best" ones, which ought to be kept in a final version of the scale measuring the trait. Sometimes, the psychologist might make these decisions by asking several experts—for example, graduate students or professors of personality psychology—to rate each item in terms of how well it appears to measure the trait, and then by keeping the items with the highest ratings on average. But usually, the psychologist will administer the items to a large sample of persons, and then select the items that show the strongest correlations with the entire set of items overall—that is, the items that will produce the most reliable scale. (At first, this might sound very much like the empirical strategy, but note the crucial difference: The rational strategy involves choosing the items that are most strongly related to *each other*, whereas the empirical strategy involves choosing the items that are most strongly related to *some outside variable* that is supposed to be a good indicator of the trait.)

In addition to examining the items' correlations with each other, the psychologist will also consider breadth of content when selecting items. In some cases, the psychologist might decide to keep an item that shows a somewhat modest correlation with the other items, instead of an item that shows a higher correlation, if the former item captures some important aspect of the trait that is not well represented by the other items. But on the other hand, if items representing a certain aspect of the trait are found to have very low correlations with the remaining items, then this might suggest to the psychologist that these items are actually measuring a different trait entirely. In such a case, the items would be discarded, but the psychologist might then construct a new scale to measure this separate trait.

One potential limitation of the rational approach is that the resulting scales can only be as good as the sets of items that the psychologist had written to measure the traits: If some important aspects of a trait have been neglected, and other aspects overemphasized, then these will probably be shortcomings of the final scale also. Another potential drawback is that the items of rationally constructed scales might be so clearly relevant to their intended traits that it would be easy for individuals to figure out what is being measured by the inventory, and to adjust (or "fake") their responses in such a way as to give a good impression. (We will discuss the issue of faking on personality inventories in Chapter 9, when we discuss the use of personality measures in personnel selection.)

One final note about the rational approach: Although, as described before, this strategy usually involves writing items "from scratch," it can also be applied to an existing pool of items. In the latter case, the psychologist would consider all of the items in such a pool, and select those that seemed theoretically most relevant to the trait.

2.5.4 Comparisons of the Three Strategies

By now you are probably wondering which of these methods is most successful in producing good personality inventories. Beginning in the 1960s, psychologists conducted many studies that were intended to compare the three strategies, in terms of the validity and the reliability of the scales that those strategies produced. In some of these comparison studies, the rational strategy outperformed one or both of the other two strategies. For example, Jackson (1975) found that rationally constructed self-report scales—even those made by psychology students as a classroom exercise—showed higher correlations with observer reports on the same traits than did empirically constructed scales of published inventories. An earlier study by Ashton and Goldberg (1973) found similar results. Another comparison study by Knudson and Golding (1974) found that rationally constructed self-report scales showed higher validity than did factor-analytically constructed self-report scales, as judged in terms of correlations with observer reports on the same traits.

Several other investigations generally reported similar levels of reliability and validity for scales produced by all three strategies, and one review of this research (Burisch, 1984) suggested that there was little difference among the three approaches in their usefulness for constructing personality inventories. However, Burisch noted that the rational approach is generally much simpler and easier to implement than the other two approaches, because the rational approach does not require a large existing item pool; instead, the psychologist can simply write the items as needed for a given trait. Nowadays, most personality inventories are constructed mainly according to the rational strategy, but often in combination with some aspects of the other two strategies as well. For example, a psychologist might use the rational approach to generate the items for a given scale and to guide the selection of items for the final scale; however, she might also use factor analysis to make sure that the items intended to measure different traits really do belong to different factors, and she might use some empirical data, such as correlations with observer ratings on a trait, as one of the bases for selecting items.

2.6 SELF- AND OBSERVER REPORTS ON PERSONALITY INVENTORY SCALES

Many of the personality inventories commonly used in research (see Box 2.2) were developed in self-report format only, but several of them have also been adapted for measurement using observer reports. The use of observer reports is important, because it provides a way of verifying results obtained by self-report; moreover, the use of self- and observer reports in combination may produce measurements that are more accurate than can be obtained from either kind of report on its own.

2.6.1 Agreement Between Self- and Observer Reports

One way in which the construct validity of personality inventory scales is often judged is by examining the correlations between self-reports and observer reports for each trait. That is, for each scale, researchers obtain self-reports from a large sample of persons on that scale and also obtain reports about those same persons on that same scale from others who are well acquainted with them. (Of course, these reports must be made independently, so that the persons giving the self- and observer reports do not influence each other's responses.) The researchers can then calculate the extent to which people who have higher self-report scores for a given trait also tend to have higher observer report scores for that trait. In other words, the researchers try to determine how much agreement there is between people's self-reports and the reports by others who know them well.

The results of these investigations generally show fairly high levels of agreement between self-reports and observer reports, and therefore support the convergent validity of the personality inventory scales. For example, one recent study examined self- and observer reports on the scales of the NEO Five-Factor Inventory (NEO-FFI) and the short version of the HEXACO-PI-R, as obtained from over 600 college students who participated in pairs, where the two persons of each pair were well acquainted with each other. Correlations between self-reports and observer reports on the same scale ranged from the low .40s to the low .60s, averaging above .50 for the HEXACO scales and above .45 for the NEO-FFI scales (Lee & Ashton, 2013). In other research, in which the full-length versions of these instruments were used and in which the members of each pair were spouses or close relatives, the self/observer correlations have been even higher, reaching about .60 (for spouses; Costa & McCrae, 1992b) or above (for spouses and close relatives; De Vries, Lee, & Ashton, 2008). (Note that, because these correlations involve the same scale, they support the *convergent* validity of each scale. When, instead, correlations are calculated between self-reports on one scale and observer reports on a different scale, the obtained values tend to be small, thus supporting the *discriminant* validity of the scales.) These levels of convergent validity can be considered to be fairly high. In fact, we probably would not expect the correlations to be much higher than this, given that the two individuals who make the reports have such different perspectives—people are unlikely to see themselves in exactly the same way that others see them.

BOX 2.2 Some Widely Used Personality Inventories

When reading about personality research, you will often come across the names of several inventories that are widely used by psychologists. This box will give you some familiarity with these inventories and might be a useful reference, but there is no need to memorize its details. Although all of these instruments are structured personality inventories assessing normal personality variation, they differ in the response formats of their items (some are true/false, others use a five-point response scale, etc.) and in their length (from a few dozen to a few hundred items). (As a rule of thumb, it might take the average college student up to 10 min to respond carefully to 100 typical personality inventory items.)

The California Psychological Inventory

The California Psychological Inventory (CPI) was developed by Gough (1996) as a measure of various psychological characteristics that he found to be useful in predicting important outcome variables. This inventory contains over 400 items, which are grouped into 20 "basic" scales as well as various other scales that have been constructed more recently. The CPI was developed according to an empirical approach, and as noted before, this strategy has sometimes been found to produce scales less valid than those produced by the rational strategy. However, the CPI scales have frequently been used in predicting important criterion variables (delinquent behavior, academic performance, etc.).

Incidentally, the construction of the CPI was guided in part by that of another inventory, called the Minnesota Multiphasic Personality Inventory (MMPI). The MMPI was also developed

(Continued)

BOX 2.2 Some Widely Used Personality Inventories—cont'd

according to an empirical approach, but unlike the CPI, the MMPI was intended to measure characteristics associated with mental illness, rather than characteristics of normal variation.

The Hogan Personality Inventory

The development of the Hogan Personality Inventory (HPI) (Hogan & Hogan, 1995) was inspired in large part by the CPI, but Hogan's inventory is aimed more directly at the prediction of variables associated with job performance. The HPI contains slightly more than 200 items, which are grouped into many short scales that measure specific characteristics, and also into several longer scales that measure broader characteristics. This inventory has been widely used in predicting various aspects of job performance.

The 16 Personality Factors Questionnaire

The 16 Personality Factors Questionnaire (16PF) (Conn & Rieke, 1994) was originally constructed in 1949 by Cattell, whose factor-analytic research suggested to him that a set of 16 traits would summarize personality characteristics. (As such, the 16PF is perhaps the only major inventory to have been developed using the factor-analytic approach. Although other psychologists have decided what traits to measure on the basis of factor analyses, they have usually used the rational approach when actually constructing the scales of their inventories.) Earlier versions of the 16PF were often criticized for the low internal-consistency reliabilities of their scales, but the scales have been improved in the most recent version of the 16PF (Conn & Rieke, 1994), which contains nearly 200 items. The 16 scales of this inventory can be combined into five broader factors that assess more general personality characteristics. (Note, however, that one of the 16PF scales is actually not a self-report personality scale at all, but rather an intelligence test.) The 16PF has been used in personality research and in contexts such as school and the workplace.

The Eysenck Personality Questionnaire and Eysenck Personality Profiler

A series of questionnaires of varying length was developed by Eysenck (Eysenck & Eysenck, 1975; Eysenck & Wilson, 1991) to measure the three personality characteristics that he believed were the basic dimensions of personality, each governed by its own structures in the brain and nervous system (see Chapter 5). Eysenck's scales have been widely used in studies of the biological basis of personality.

The Myers—Briggs Type Indicator

The Myers—Briggs Type Indicator (MBTI) (Myers & McCaulley, 1985) is loosely based on a theory of psychological "types" developed by the Swiss psychologist Carl Jung. The MBTI consists of nearly 100 self-report items that each contain two statements; the respondent chooses which item best describes him or her. The MBTI assesses four characteristics. Unlike most other inventories, people do not obtain numerical scores for each characteristic, but instead are assigned to one pole or another of each characteristic. For example, instead of obtaining a certain score on the extraversion scale, an individual is declared as an "extravert" (E) if he or she answers most questions in the extraverted direction, or alternatively is declared as an "introvert" (I) if he or she answers most questions in the introverted direction. (Sometimes, a difference in response to one question could make the difference between being declared, say, an extravert as opposed to an introvert.) On the basis of this method of scoring, each person is assigned one of 16 possible "types" based on the combination of his or her results for the four scales.

BOX 2.2 Some Widely Used Personality Inventories—cont'd

The MBTI has not been widely used in psychological research but it has been used very widely in business settings, for example, in seminars aimed at improving employees' self-understanding and understanding of each other. Moreover, some studies have shown some support for the construct validity of the MBTI (McCrae & Costa, 1989). However, one shortcoming of the MBTI is that it loses a great deal of precision by describing people in terms of only two levels of each characteristic rather than in terms of a more specific score on each characteristic. For example, consider a person who is slightly on the "extraverted" side of the boundary between extraverts and introverts: This person would actually be more similar to a slightly "introverted" person than to an extremely "extraverted" person. (In the same way, suppose that we had to describe everyone's height as being either "tall" or "short." A "tall" 5-foot-10 person would actually be much closer in height to a "short" 5-foot-6 person than to a "tall" 6-foot-6 person.)

The Temperament and Character Inventory

The Temperament and Character Inventory (TCI) was developed by Cloninger, Przybeck, Svrakic, and Wetzel (1994) to measure the basic dimensions of his biological model of temperament (described in Chapter 5), as well as additional dimensions of "character," whose biological bases are thought to be less direct. Several versions of the TCI have been used widely in research, particularly in studies of the biological basis of personality; the more recent versions generally contain between 200 and 300 items, and measure roughly 30 narrower personality traits that are grouped into seven scales representing the broader temperament and character variables. The TCI scales have been widely used in studies of the biological basis of personality.

The Multidimensional Personality Questionnaire

The Multidimensional Personality Questionnaire (MPQ) was constructed by Tellegen (2016) to assess a variety of traits of normal personality variation. This questionnaire contains nearly 300 items and measures 11 traits, which are classified into three groups intended to represent basic dimensions of personality. The MPQ scales have been widely used in studies of emotions, impulsivity, and imagination.

The Zuckerman—Kuhlman Personality Questionnaire

The Zuckerman—Kuhlman Personality Questionnaire (ZKPQ; e.g., Zuckerman, 2002) was developed as a self-report measure of the biologically based "alternative five" factors proposed as basic personality dimensions (see Chapter 5). The ZKPQ contains 99 items, but a 50-item version is also available, and recently an expanded 200-item version has been constructed (Aluja, Kuhlman, & Zuckerman, 2010). The ZKPQ has been widely used in studies of the biological basis of personality.

The Jackson Personality Inventory and Personality Research Form

These two instruments (Jackson, 1984b, 1994) were originally developed during the 1960s by Jackson, who employed a rational strategy carried out using very large numbers of items and very large participant samples. Each of the resulting inventories contains 300 or more items, which are grouped into 15 scales (Jackson personality inventory, JPI) and 22 scales (personality research form, PRF) measuring a wide variety of traits. Although the JPI and PRF scales are not usually grouped into broader scales representing broad personality factors, those scales span a very wide variety of personality characteristics, and some research suggests that the PRF and JPI in combination can assess all of the major dimensions of personality (e.g., Ashton, Jackson, Helmes, & Paunonen, 1998).

(Continued)

BOX 2.2 Some Widely Used Personality Inventories—cont'd

The Nonverbal Personality Questionnaire

The Nonverbal Personality Questionnaire (NPQ) (Paunonen, Jackson, & Keinonen, 1990) differs from all of the other inventories considered here in that its items are cartoon sketches rather than written statements. Each item shows a stick figure drawing of a person performing some behavior, and the individual who responds to the inventory is asked to indicate how likely he or she would be to perform the kind of behavior shown in the drawing. The NPQ scales were developed to measure the same traits as those of the PRF, and have shown levels of reliability and validity approaching those of the original scales. Fig. 2.1 shows two example items from the NPQ, which contains 136 items.

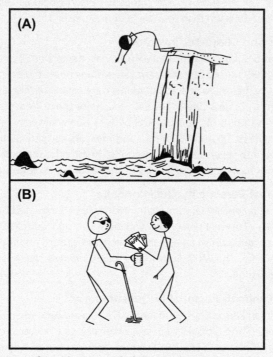

Figure 2.1 *Example items from the Nonverbal Personality Questionnaire.* The item in panel A assesses the trait of thrill seeking; the item in panel B assesses the trait of nurturance (i.e., help-fulness). For each item, self-reports (or observer reports) are made using a scale from 1 (extremely unlikely to perform this kind of behavior) to 7 (extremely likely to perform this kind of behavior). *(Reproduced by permission of SIGMA Assessment Systems, Inc. P.O. Box 610984, Port Huron, MI 48061-0984. See also Paunonen, S.V., Jackson, D.N., & Keinonen, M. (1990). The structured nonverbal assessment of personality.* Journal of Personality, 58, 481—502.)

The Big Five Inventory

The Big Five Inventory (BFI) (John, Donahue, & Kentle, 1991) was developed as a short measure of five broad personality characteristics known as the "Big Five" (see Chapter 3; see also the following description of the "NEO" inventories). The original BFI consisted of 44 items, but a recent revision has increased its length to 60 items (Soto & John, 2016). The BFI has been very widely used in personality research.

BOX 2.2 Some Widely Used Personality Inventories—cont'd

The NEO Personality Inventory Revised and NEO Five-Factor Inventory

The NEO Personality Inventory Revised (NEO-PI-R) (with its earlier version, the NEO-PI) and the NEO Five-Factor Inventory (NEO-FFI) were developed to measure five major dimensions of personality (Costa & McCrae, 1985, 1992b). The NEO-PI-R is the longer inventory, with 240 items that are grouped into 30 scales measuring narrower personality traits, with those scales in turn grouped into the five scales measuring broader characteristics: Neuroticism (N), Extraversion (E), Openness to Experience (O), Agreeableness (A), and Conscientiousness (C). (See Chapter 3 for descriptions of the 30 scales.) The NEO-FFI is a shorter, 60-item inventory that measures the five broad dimensions only. The scales of both questionnaires have been very widely used in personality research.

The HEXACO Personality Inventory—Revised

The HEXACO Personality Inventory was constructed recently (Ashton & Lee, 2009a; Lee & Ashton, 2004, 2006, 2013) to measure the six dimensions of personality that were found in personality research conducted in various cultures. The revised inventory, the HEXACO Personality Inventory—Revised (HEXACO-PI-R), has forms of three lengths: 200 items, 100 items, and 60 items. The items of each form are grouped into scales measuring narrower personality traits. These scales are in turn grouped into broader scales measuring the six dimensions called Honesty—Humility (H), Emotionality (E), Extraversion (X), Agreeableness (A), Conscientiousness (C), and Openness to Experience (O). (See Chapter 3 for descriptions of the scales.) The HEXACO-PI-R scales have increasingly been widely used in personality research.

The International Personality Item Pool

The International Personality Item Pool (IPIP) (Goldberg, 1999) is actually not a personality inventory, but rather a list of personality questionnaire items that has been developed on an ongoing basis since the early 1990s (The IPIP website is found at http://ipip.ori.org.). The IPIP contains over 2000 different items, and these items are grouped together into short scales (generally about 10 items each) to measure a variety of personality characteristics. In particular, Goldberg has provided lists of items that he has selected to measure each of the traits assessed by most of the published inventories listed earlier. Each scale can be administered separately or in combination with other scales, as desired by the researcher. Table 2.1 shows some example IPIP items. (Note that these items, unlike those of most personality questionnaires, generally omit the pronoun "I" at the beginning of each self-report statement.)

Table 2.1 Example items from the International Personality Item Pool

Pay attention to details
Get upset easily
Feel other people's joy
Do crazy things
Keep in the background
Am not interested in abstract ideas
Am usually active and full of energy
Try to impress others
Like to take it easy

These items can be used for self-reports or observer reports. The person who provides the reports is asked to indicate the accuracy of each statement on a scale from 1 (very inaccurate) to 5 (very accurate).
http://ipip.ori.org/; see also Goldberg, L. R. (1999). A broad-bandwidth, public-domain, personality inventory measuring the lowerlevel facets of several five-factor models. In I. Mervielde, I. Deary, F. De Fruyt, & F. Ostendorf (Eds.), Personality psychology in Europe (Vol. 7, pp. 7–28). The Netherlands: Tilburg University Press.

2.6.2 Why Do Self- and Observer Reports Tend to Agree?

In the preceding paragraphs, the high correlations between self-reports and observer reports on a given personality inventory scale are described as evidence of convergent validity—that is, as evidence that the scale is really providing an accurate measurement of some personality trait. But let us consider some alternative possibilities. One alternative explanation is that the agreement between self- and observer reports might happen simply because people who know each other have developed a shared opinion about each other's personality, but an opinion that is not necessarily accurate. (For example, perhaps you and your friend have somehow decided that you are a wild, uninhibited person, even if your actual behavior is not really so wild and uninhibited. Or, perhaps you and your friend have somehow decided that your friend is a stubborn, obstinate person, even if your friend's actual behavior is not really so stubborn or obstinate.)

This explanation may not sound very likely, but it is a possible explanation, and personality researchers have taken it seriously. One way in which this explanation can be tested is by examining how much agreement there is between two different observer reports of an individual's personality, where the observer reports are taken from two people who do not know each other, even though they both are well acquainted with the individual whose personality they describe. The logic of this approach is that, if these two people do not know each other, then any agreement between them in their assessment of the personality of their mutual acquaintance cannot be due to any discussion between them about that individual's personality. Also, if those two observer reports show fairly high agreement, then it is unlikely that this could be due to any discussion between each observer and the person being described. Let us consider a research study that used this strategy.

Funder, Kolar, and Blackman (1995) compared reports of college students' personalities as provided (1) by their friends from their hometowns, and (2) by their friends from college (which was in a different town). In some cases, the hometown friend and the college friend had never met, thus satisfying the requirement described previously, but in other cases, those friends had met. This allowed Funder et al. to examine whether the observer reports obtained from two friends who had met each other were any more similar than the observer reports obtained from two friends who had never met. (Again, keep in mind that in every case, both of these friends were well acquainted with the mutual friend whose personality they were describing.)

The results of this study showed that there was a moderate degree of agreement between the observer reports obtained from "hometown friends" and from "college friends." The correlations between these two observer reports, as averaged across five broad personality characteristics, were about .30. On average, the results were the same regardless of whether or not the hometown friend and the college friend had ever met each other. Therefore, the agreement between those persons in their assessment of their mutual friend's personality could not be the result of any discussions about that individual's personality. Instead, these results suggest that the hometown friend and the college friend have simply observed similar tendencies on the part of their mutual friend.

Funder et al. (1995) also examined the links between self-reports and observer reports of personality. Interestingly, the correlations between the two observer reports were almost as high as the correlations between self-reports and observer reports: When averaged across the five broad characteristics, self-reports correlated about .35 with observer reports from the hometown friend, and about .45 with observer reports from the college friend. The fact that the correlations between the two observer reports were almost as high as the correlations of self-reports with observer reports is also important: It indicates that the agreement between the hometown friend and the college friend (i.e., about .30, as mentioned before) cannot be due to each friend having discussed the mutual friend's personality with that mutual friend.[5] Instead, again, the results indicate that the hometown friend and the college friend have both observed similar tendencies on the part of their mutual friend.

2.6.3 The Validity of Self- and Observer Reports in Predicting Behavior

The substantial correlations between self-reports and observer reports on personality inventory scales provide some important evidence for the validity of those scales. However, it would also be useful to examine the validity of personality inventory scales in predicting actual behaviors or outcomes. For example, if we have a personality inventory scale that is intended to measure the trait of talkativeness, we would expect not only that self- and observer reports of talkativeness would be correlated, but also that those reports would correlate with direct observations of how much people talk. Or, if a scale is intended to measure the trait of orderliness, we would expect not only that self- and observer reports of orderliness would be correlated, but also that those reports would correlate with direct observations of the orderliness of people's rooms, desks, and so on.

When considering this issue of the validity of self- and observer reports on personality inventory scales in predicting trait-relevant behaviors and outcomes, another interesting question also comes to mind: Which kind of report is more accurate in predicting those criteria? That is, are self-reports more accurate indications of an individual's personality, or are observer reports (from close acquaintances) more accurate? Some investigations of self-reports and observer reports of personality as predictors of behaviors have allowed comparisons of the validity of the two kinds of reports.

In one study (Kolar, Funder, & Colvin, 1996), 140 college students each participated in a series of videotaped interactions with others (e.g., meeting another person,

---

[5] If the correlation between observer reports were simply due to the mutual friend having discussed his or her personality with both the hometown friend and the college friend, then that correlation would be no higher than the product of the correlations between self-reports and the two observer reports. But the average correlation between the two observer reports (.30) was considerably higher than the product of the average correlations between self-reports and observer reports (.35 × .45 ≈ .16).

participating in a debate) in the researchers' laboratory. In addition, the students' personality characteristics were assessed by self-report and also by observer reports given independently by two close acquaintances. The researchers compared the validity of self- and observer reports of personality in predicting four different kinds of behaviors, as rated by several research assistants who watched the videotapes (without knowing the self- and observer report personality scores). The results showed that the personality self-reports had some validity for predicting behavior, with an average correlation of slightly under .30 across the four kinds of behavior. However, each of the observer reports was slightly better in predicting behavior; even the less-accurate acquaintance averaged about .35, and in combination, the average of the two observer reports correlated over .40 with behavior. Thus, the results of the Kolar et al. study suggest that personality might be assessed somewhat more accurately by observer reports than by self-reports, at least when the observer reports are provided by rather close acquaintances.

Another interesting implication of the Kolar et al. (1996) study is that an individual's personality is likely to be assessed even more accurately by *averaging* his or her self-report with the observer reports provided by two or more persons who know him or her well. Taken individually, the self-report and each of the observer reports are fairly accurate, but by combining them into an overall average, we can obtain an even more accurate indication of the individual's personality. This is because each of the reports provides some accurate information that might not be provided by some of the remaining reports; consequently, the averaged reports will give a better indication than any one report alone will give.

In a similar study (Borkenau, Riemann, Angleitner, & Spinath, 2001), 600 adults were videotaped as they participated in a variety of situations in the researchers' laboratory (telling a joke, introducing someone, singing a song, solving a complex problem, etc.). The personalities of the participants were assessed in terms of five personality characteristics, both by self-reports and by observer reports from two close acquaintances. The researchers' assistants (who did not know about the self- and observer report personality scores) then watched the videotapes and provided their own ratings of the participants' personalities, again in terms of the same five characteristics. The results showed that self-reports were modestly correlated with the video-based judgments, averaging slightly above .20 for the five characteristics. The observer reports (as averaged across the two acquaintances) showed somewhat higher correlations, averaging above .30. These results are therefore consistent with those of Kolar et al. (1996), suggesting that observer reports (specifically, observer reports from two or more close acquaintances) are likely to be more accurate indicators of personality than are self-reports.

A more recent comparison has suggested that the relative validity of self- and observer reports depends on *which* personality traits are considered. Vazire (2010) studied 165 people, comparing those persons' self-reports with observer reports from their friends and from strangers. She hypothesized that some personality traits, such as talkativeness and dominance, would be very easily observed by friends and even by strangers, and that for these traits, observer reports from those persons would be just as valid as self-reports. She also hypothesized that some other traits, such as anxiety and low self-esteem, would not be so easily observed by strangers or even by friends, and that for these traits, observer reports (even those of friends) would be less valid than self-reports. Finally, she also hypothesized that some traits, such as creativity and intelligence, would be subject to a great deal of bias in self-reports, which would make those self-reports less valid than observer reports, at least when observer reports are provided by friends.

To evaluate the validity of the self- and observer reports, Vazire (2010) obtained some direct observations of behavior. In one of the behavior tasks, participants had to participate in a group discussion; participants' behavior in this situation was the criterion for participants' talkativeness and dominance. In another task, participants had to make a speech on a somewhat embarrassing topic; participants' behavior in this situation was the criterion for participants' anxiety and self-esteem. Finally, in another task, participants completed standardized tests of creativity and intelligence.

The results of the validity comparisons were generally consistent with Vazire's predictions. Behavioral indications of talkativeness and dominance were about equally well predicted by self-reports, by observer reports from friends, and by observer reports from strangers. Behavioral indications of anxiety and low self-esteem were better predicted by self-reports than by observer reports from friends; observer reports from strangers showed almost no validity. Behavioral indications of creativity and intelligence (i.e., test scores) were better predicted by observer reports from friends than by self-reports; observer reports from strangers, however, showed almost no validity. Thus, the study by Vazire (2010) suggests that the relative validity of self- and observer reports might differ according to which personality traits are considered.

In considering the results of the various studies just described, keep in mind that the participants' behaviors in these situations are unlikely to provide a completely accurate indication of their personalities in general. Presumably, personality would be more precisely revealed through observations of participants' behaviors in a wide variety of natural settings (i.e., outside the personality research laboratory) over a long period of time. If behaviors were observed in this way, thereby providing a more accurate criterion for judging the validity of self- and observer reports of personality, it is likely that both the self- and observer reports would show much higher levels of validity. Moreover, it is possible that this increase in correlations would be particularly large for self-reports, because an individual might be a better judge of his or her own behavior across a wide range of situations than would his or her acquaintances, who do not observe him or her in all situations.

2.6.4 Biases in Self- and Observer Reports

In the previous section, we saw that self-reports and observer reports of personality tend to agree with each other. We also saw that self-reports and observer reports also tend to agree with other indicators of personality. These results suggest that we can use self-reports or observer reports to measure people's personality characteristics rather accurately. But this is not to say that self-reports or observer reports are perfectly accurate. One limitation of these methods involves the biases that people may have when describing their own personality or the personality of someone they know. Some of these biases might be specific to a particular personality trait, but we will focus on a kind of bias that applies across many personality traits.

Suppose that you are responding to a self-report personality inventory. Even if you are trying to respond objectively and accurately, your responses might still be a bit biased. On the one hand, maybe you tend to describe yourself in a more positive or socially desirable way than is really accurate. Or on the other hand, maybe you tend to describe yourself in a more negative or socially undesirable way than is really accurate. Again, you might have these biases even if you are trying to be objective in describing yourself.

Likewise, the same kind of biases could apply to observer reports of personality. Suppose that some person who knows you well is responding to an observer report personality inventory. Even if that person is trying to describe you objectively and accurately, his or her responses might still be a bit biased, whether in the positive or socially desirable direction or in the negative or socially undesirable direction.

Researchers have tried to find out how much influence these biases have on self-reports and observer reports of personality. By using both self-reports and observer reports to measure people's personalities, they have been able to examine the biases that exist in both sources of data. For example, by comparing self-reports with observer reports, they have found that some people's self-reports are unrealistically favorable, whereas other people's self-reports are unrealistically unfavorable (e.g., Anusic, Schimmack, Pinkus, & Lockwood, 2009; Ashton & Lee, 2010; Paulhus & John, 1998; Paulhus & Trapnell, 2008). Likewise, by comparing observer reports with self-reports, they have found that some people's observer reports are unrealistically favorable, whereas other people's observer reports are unrealistically unfavorable.

These biases tend to distort self-reports and observer reports of personality, but under normal circumstances the amount of distortion is fairly small for most personality traits, as long as the personality inventory has been constructed properly (e.g., Ashton & Lee, 2010). Note that, even though self-reports and observer reports can both be biased, they are not necessarily biased in the same direction. For example, if your self-reports are biased in the socially undesirable direction, your friend's observer report of your personality might well be biased in the socially desirable direction (if biased at all). What this means is that the bias in any one source of data (either self-reports or observer reports) usually becomes weaker if we take those two sources of data together. That is, we can usually get a more accurate indication of someone's personality if we use information from both self-reports and observer reports.

BOX 2.3 Social Desirability Scales

Some researchers have developed scales to measure a person's tendency to give socially desirable responses—or socially *undesirable* responses—to self-report items. These desirability scales contain items that describe a wide variety of socially desirable or undesirable tendencies, which represent many different traits. Because the scales have many diverse items, each being a very desirable or undesirable statement, a person's score will tend to reflect his or her overall tendency to give desirable or undesirable responses in general, and not his or her level of *any one particular* personality trait.

In a typical desirability scale, half of the items are very desirable statements (such that agreeing is the more desirable response) and half of the items are very undesirable statements (such that disagreeing is the more desirable response); in other words, half of the items are reverse coded (recall Section 2.4). A person who generally agrees with the desirable statements and disagrees with the undesirable statements therefore gets a high score on the desirability scale; conversely, a person who generally agrees with the undesirable statements and disagrees with the desirable statements therefore gets a low score.

Desirability scales have been useful for researchers who want to make sure that other personality scales—each of them meant to measure a different personality trait—are not simply measuring the tendency to respond desirably or undesirably. If scales meant to measure various personality traits were all very highly correlated with a social desirability scale, then this would suggest that those scales are actually measuring (at least in considerable part) the tendency to respond desirably or undesirably. This result would therefore mean a lack of discriminant validity for the scales.

During the 1950s and 1960s, personality researchers were shocked by findings indicating that many widely used personality scales were very heavily influenced by socially desirable responding (e.g., Jackson & Messick, 1961). As a consequence, some researchers began to develop ways to construct personality trait scales that would be less-strongly "contaminated" by social desirability (Jackson, 1970, 1971). Those improved scales usually contained items that mostly describe more objective behavioral tendencies and do not simply give evaluations of oneself as having good or bad characteristics. (Consider a couple of artificial examples: the item "I rarely tidy things up" is less extreme in undesirability than the item "I am a real slob"; likewise, the item "I often think a lot about what is the right thing to do" is less extreme in desirability than the item "I always do what is right.") For many traits, it is not feasible to make a scale completely neutral in desirability, but it is feasible to make a scale only modestly desirable or undesirable.

Another use for desirability scales is to identify persons who are responding in a way that is very desirable or very undesirable. For such persons, the researcher may be concerned that their scores on various other scales—the scales intended to measure personality traits—will

(Continued)

BOX 2.3 Social Desirability Scales—cont'd

be inaccurate, being "pushed" in the desirable or undesirable direction by those persons' general style of responding to self-report personality items. However, it is not easy to interpret a given person's score on a desirability scale: a high score might reflect a tendency to give desirable responses, but it might reflect truly high levels of several quite different personality traits that all happen to be desirable.

For some desirability scales, a high score is interpreted as indicating that a person is "faking," or trying to appear more virtuous than he or she really is. In one way, this interpretation makes sense, because when people are actually instructed to fake on those scales, they generally do get higher scores than they do under normal instructions. But in another way, this interpretation is not very accurate: Under normal instructions, the people who get high scores on such scales actually are perceived by people who know them as truly having desirable characteristics (De Vries, Zettler, & Hilbig, 2014; Lee, Gizzarone, & Ashton, 2003), and actually do tend to show more honest or unselfish behavior than most people do (e.g., Cunningham, Wong, & Barbee, 1994; Zettler, Hilbig, Moshagen, & de Vries, 2015). Therefore, it seems that desirability scales are not usually able to distinguish people who are trying to "look good" from people who really do have desirable characteristics. But some desirability scales can still be useful in constructing personality trait scales that are not too heavily contaminated by socially desirable (or undesirable) responding (e.g., Jackson, 1970, 1971).

BOX 2.4 Projective Tests

Although there are some differences among the *structured* personality inventories described in this chapter, those instruments are all similar in the sense of providing a structured set of alternative responses to each item or stimulus (true/false, one-to-five scale, etc.). In sharp contrast to these inventories are instruments that use *unstructured* responses, which allow the individual to respond in his or her unique fashion—and often at great length—to each of the items or stimuli that are presented. These unstructured measures of personality are generally known as *projective* tests. A projective test provides the individual with some ambiguous stimulus—for example, a strangely shaped inkblot, a drawing of two or more people interacting in some uncertain way, or a paragraph that tells the beginning of a story. The individual is then asked to respond to this stimulus—for example, by describing what he or she sees in the inkblot, by explaining the situation depicted in the drawing, or by completing the story that begins with the paragraph. Usually, a series of such stimuli is presented to the individual, and when the entire test is completed, the psychologist can then attempt to assess the individual's personality by considering his or her responses to the stimuli.

One well-known projective test is the Rorschach inkblot test (Rorschach, 1921). The Rorschach contains a series of inkblot patterns. For each inkblot, the individual is asked to give an interpretation, by explaining what he or she sees in the pattern. The scoring of the Rorschach tends to differ from one psychologist to another—thereby limiting the reliability and validity of the test—but some efforts have been made to produce standard rules for

BOX 2.4 Projective Tests—cont'd

scoring the test (Exner, 1974). The interpretation of Rorschach responses sometimes involves the content of those responses: For example, responses that describe violence or weapons are thought—not surprisingly—to indicate a hostile personality (Gleitman, 1986). However, many interpretations of Rorschach responses focus on what aspects of the pattern are interpreted, rather than on the specific content of the interpretation: For example, responses that discuss the colors of the inkblots are taken to suggest emotionality and impulsivity; responses that describe movement are thought to indicate imagination; responses that refer to the white space around the inkblot are seen as signs of rebelliousness and negativity (Gleitman, 1986).

Although the Rorschach inkblot test is still widely used by some clinical psychologists, the test has some serious shortcomings (Wood, Lilienfeld, Garb, & Nezworski, 2000). Many psychologically normal people appear to be pathological when compared with the normative data (i.e., the results obtained on samples of people from the general population), a problem that suggests some inaccuracy with those norms. The scoring of the Rorschach test is complex and painstaking, and levels of test–retest reliability and interrater reliability are frequently rather low. Although a few Rorschach scoring scales have shown moderate validity in predicting thought disorders (e.g., schizophrenia), most have not provided much additional validity in predicting clinical psychologists' diagnoses, beyond what is provided by the much simpler self-report measures. These limitations of the Rorschach inkblot test, and the impracticality of administering and scoring the test, have led most personality researchers to choose other methods of assessment instead.

Another well-known projective test is the Thematic Apperception Test (TAT; Murray, 1943). The stimuli used in the TAT are less abstract than those of the Rorschach, as the TAT stimuli typically involve either a picture of some people interacting or a paragraph that describes the beginning of a story. The individual who takes the TAT is asked to tell a story about the picture or to complete the story started by the paragraph. Based on various features of the individual's responses, the psychologist can attempt to assess the individual's levels of various characteristics. To take a few examples, responses describing goal-setting suggest "need for achievement," responses describing conflict suggest "need for power," and responses describing friendship suggest "need for affiliation."

Some investigations do suggest at least modest correlations between TAT scores for these various "needs" and relevant criterion variables. Spangler (1992) reviewed over 100 previous investigations, and found average correlations of about .20 between TAT need for achievement scores and outcomes such as occupational success or school performance. However, there has been a lack of studies in which the TAT has been administered along with self- and observer reports of personality, and thus it is difficult to know the extent to which the TAT would add to the predictive validity of those other methods of assessing personality. In general, the TAT is not widely used in personality research, in large part because use of this test does not readily allow the researcher to assess large numbers of people on a wide variety of characteristics; testing time is long, and scoring of the test is labor intensive.

Thus, although there is some evidence to suggest that at least some projective tests may have adequate levels of validity, these instruments are not widely used in personality research.

(Continued)

BOX 2.4 Projective Tests—cont'd

In contrast, structured methods of assessment—particularly self- and observer reports—can be used much more efficiently, in the sense that structured inventories allow many individuals to be assessed quickly on many traits, with good reliability and validity, and without any difficult judgments to make about the scoring of any given item.

2.7 SUMMARY AND CONCLUSIONS

Let us summarize briefly the main points of this chapter. First, the idea of a personality trait refers to differences among individuals in a tendency to behave, think, or feel in some conceptually related ways, across a variety of relevant situations and across some fairly long period of time. During the 1970 and 1980, many researchers doubted the importance of personality traits, arguing that there was little consistency across situations in the differences among people's behaviors. However, when people's behaviors are considered across a wide variety of situations, by taking an overall average of each person's tendencies, the differences among people are found to be very important. This supports the idea of personality traits.

Researchers often measure people's levels of personality traits using self-report or observer report questionnaires called structured personality inventories. Such inventories typically contain several scales, each measuring a different trait, with each scale consisting of several items. A participant's responses to the items of a given scale are aggregated to produce his or her score for that scale. To construct a personality inventory, researchers generally use one or more of the three approaches known as the empirical, factor-analytic, and rational strategies.

Many research studies have examined the validity of personality inventory scales by investigating the extent to which self-reports and observer reports agree for a given trait. These studies generally show fairly high levels of agreement between self-reports and reports from other persons (observers) who are well acquainted with the person being described. Both self-reports and observer reports can predict behavior with moderate levels of validity, and recent findings suggest that the relative validity of self-reports and observer reports depends on the trait being measured. Self-reports and observer reports on personality inventory scales can be influenced by the tendency to give socially desirable (or undesirable) responses. However, those scales can be constructed in such a way as to limit the impact of these biases.

CHAPTER 3

Personality Structure: Classifying Traits

Contents

People differ in hundreds of personality traits, but each trait is correlated with many others. An important task for personality researchers has been to classify personality traits into a few large groups, where each group consists of many correlated traits. By finding these groups of traits, researchers can measure personality more efficiently and thoroughly, and they might even gain some ideas about why personality differences exist. In this chapter, we review the research that has been aimed at finding these basic groups of personality traits—the major dimensions or "factors" of personality.

3.1 WHICH TRAITS TO MEASURE? COMPLETENESS WITHOUT REDUNDANCY

Imagine that you are planning to do some research about personality. Perhaps you are interested in assessing the extent to which personality can predict job performance, or marital satisfaction, or political attitudes. Or perhaps you are interested in finding out how a certain brain chemical, or a certain kind of experience in childhood, can influence one's personality. Whatever research question you might have, you will need to decide which personality traits to measure. In some cases, you might have a specific interest in a particular personality trait, and so your decision is already made. But in other cases, you might be interested in personality *in general*, in which case your task is quite difficult: How can you choose a set of personality traits that will represent the whole domain of personality as broadly as possible?

Individual Differences and Personality
ISBN 978-0-12-809845-5, http://dx.doi.org/10.1016/B978-0-12-809845-5.00003-2

In the absence of any real knowledge about which traits to select, you might simply choose a few traits that, in your opinion, seem to be interesting, important, and diverse. In fact, this is exactly what many researchers have done in the past when investigating research questions or when constructing personality inventories. But this approach has some serious problems. First, it is subjective, because the set of traits that strike you as interesting, important, and diverse might be quite a bit different from the set of traits that another researcher would select. If each researcher uses a different set of traits, it will be difficult for researchers to communicate with each other about their findings or to compare and combine the results of different studies.

But suppose that this first problem could be overcome—suppose that you could somehow convince other researchers that your set of favorite traits was the best set to measure. How would *you* know that your set of traits was really complete or comprehensive? It seems likely that at least some important traits would be left out of your original set. To solve this second problem, you might try adding more traits to your set, to fill in any gaps that you noticed. But even if you added many more traits, you still might not be certain of having captured every important trait. Moreover, by adding these other traits, you would now have so many traits that measuring them reliably would take a very long time. And, with such a large set of traits, it seems likely that some traits in your set would be very similar to each other, and thus somewhat redundant. Therefore, in an attempt to measure personality comprehensively—an attempt whose success would be uncertain—you would likely make the measurement of personality very inefficient. Much time would now be needed to measure a large set of traits, at least some of which would be redundant with each other.

Thus, when a researcher simply chooses his or her own favorite set of traits, the measurement of personality is incomplete and inefficient, and communication among researchers is difficult. These problems have led many psychologists to believe that a systematic approach is needed for deciding which personality traits to measure. Although these psychologists have often disagreed about the details of this approach, they have generally agreed that it will need to use the statistical technique known as *factor analysis*. This technique, which is described in the following section, allows researchers to reduce many variables into a few unrelated groups of related variables. Personality researchers can use factor analysis to classify a vast array of personality traits into a few basic groups of traits. By doing this, researchers can then measure a few traits from each group, so that all of the major aspects of personality are represented, but without redundancy.[1,2]

---

[1] The results of factor analysis might also teach us some interesting insights about personality characteristics. For example, if we find that certain traits tend to go together on the same factor, then this might help us to understand what those traits have in common and might give us some clues about what causes those traits or why those traits are important. We will address these kinds of questions in the following chapters of this book.

[2] For the purpose of this chapter, we will use the term "factor analysis" broadly to include principal components analysis as well as common factor analysis. These two techniques have important conceptual differences, but those differences do not affect the findings reported in this chapter.

3.2 A GENTLE INTRODUCTION TO FACTOR ANALYSIS

When a researcher has measured many variables that show some substantial correlations with each other, it may be useful to reduce the number of variables by categorizing them into groups according to the correlations. However, when the number of variables is large and the pattern of correlations among them is complex, it is not easy to see which variables ought to be combined into a group. This is where the statistical technique of factor analysis is used. Factor analysis allows the researcher to reduce many specific traits into a few more general "factors" or groups of traits, each of which includes several of the specific traits.

Factor analysis can be used with many kinds of variables, not just personality characteristics. Consider the following example of a factor analysis. Suppose that I have persuaded a few hundred of my fit, healthy, young personality students to change into their gym clothes and to do a battery of physical tests. Here are the variables on which my student participants are to be measured:

1. vertical jump (height of jump from a crouching position),
2. 40-yard dash (time to sprint 40 yards or 36.5 m),
3. standing triple jump (distance of hop, step, jump from standing start),
4. 12-min run (distance run in 12 min),
5. 2-km row (time to row 2 km, or 1.25 miles, on rowing machine),
6. 20-min cycle (distance cycled in 20 min on standard exercise bike),
7. percent fast-twitch muscle fiber (from tissue sample taken from thigh), and
8. percent body fat (measured by skin-fold calipers).

Now, suppose that I have measured my students on these variables. The correlations among the variables are shown in Table 3.1. (Note that all of these data are artificial.

Table 3.1 Correlations among physical fitness and physiological measurements

Variables	VJ	Dash	TJ	Run	Row	Cycle	Type	Fat
Vertical jump height (VJ)	1.00							
40-Yard (36-m) dash time (dash)	−.52	1.00						
Standing triple jump distance (TJ)	.56	−.60	1.00					
12-min run distance (run)	.00	.01	.00	1.00				
2-km (1.25-mile) rowing time (row)	−.01	.00	.01	−.54	1.00			
20-min cycle distance (cycle)	.00	−.01	.00	.58	−.50	1.00		
Fast-twitch muscle fiber type percentage (type)	.30	−.26	.22	−.29	.25	−.21	1.00	
Body fat percentage (fat)	−.20	.28	−.24	−.21	.25	−.29	.00	1.00

These are hypothetical (imaginary) data.

I have not really measured anyone for these variables, so these correlations are just invented for the purpose of this example. But the correlations are probably not too far from what would be found in real life.)

The correlation matrix in Table 3.1 shows how each variable is correlated with each other variable. By looking for the name of one variable across the top and for the other variable down the side, and then finding the cell where the column of one variable and the row of the other variable meet, you can see the correlation between those two variables. (If the cell is blank, just switch the two variables around; I have only filled in one half of the matrix, because the correlation of A with B is the same as the correlation of B with A. I have put 1.00s in the diagonals because the correlation of each variable with itself is 1.00.)

Notice in Table 3.1 that there are fairly strong correlations among the first three variables. The vertical jump and standing triple jump show a strong positive correlation with each other, and the 40-yard dash time correlates negatively with both variables. Apparently, the ability to jump up and the ability to jump forward are related to each other, and both are related to the ability to sprint quickly. Note that the correlations of the jumps with the 40-yard dash are negative, because people who *took a long time* to sprint 40 yards did not jump very high or very far.

Notice also that there are fairly strong correlations among the second three variables. The 12-min run distance and the 20-min cycle distance are positively correlated with each other, and negatively correlated with 2-km rowing time. Apparently, the ability to run a long distance and to cycle a long distance are related to each other, and both are related to the ability to row a long distance. Note that the correlations of the run and cycle distances with rowing times are negative, because people who *took a long time* to row 2 km did not run or cycle very far.

With regard to these two groups of three variables, notice that the correlations across the two groups tend to be quite weak. The correlations of the vertical jump, the 40-yard sprint time, and the standing triple jump with the 12-min run, the 2-km row, and the 20-min cycle are all about zero. This indicates that a person's performance on the first three tests does not give us any indication as to how that person will perform on the second three tests, and vice versa.

Now let us consider the last two variables. First, the fast-twitch muscle fiber percentage shows some modest correlations with the first three variables (positive with vertical jump, negative with 40-yard sprint time, and positive with standing triple jump), and also with the second three variables (negative with 12-min run distance, positive with 2-km row time, and negative with 20-min cycle distance). These results indicate that people with a higher percentage of fast-twitch muscle tended to do relatively well in the first three events, but relatively poorly in the last three events.

Finally, the body fat percentage shows some modest correlations with all six variables (negative with vertical jump, positive with 40-yard sprint time, negative with standing

Table 3.2 Loadings of physical fitness and physiological measurements on two factors

Variables	Factors	
	I	II
Vertical jump height	.71	−.01
40-yard (36-m) dash time	−.76	−.01
Standing triple jump distance	.77	.01
12-min run distance	−.02	.77
2-km (1.25-mile) rowing time	.01	−.70
20-min cycle distance	.01	.74
Fast-twitch muscle fiber type percentage	.35	−.34
Body fat percentage	−.32	−.34

These are hypothetical (imaginary) data.

triple jump, negative with 12-min run distance, positive with 2-km row time, and negative with 20-min cycle distance). These results indicate the people with a higher percentage of body fat tended to do relatively poorly in all six events.

Now, let us see what happens when we factor analyze these correlations. According to the factor analysis, the correlations among the eight variables measured here indicate that those variables can be sorted into two groups or factors.[3] Table 3.2 shows these two factors by indicating how strongly each variable belongs to each group—or, to use more technical terms, how much each variable "loads on" each "factor."

Look first at the column of numbers on the left for factor I. These numbers are called *factor loadings*, and they can range in size between −1 and +1, just like correlation coefficients. Notice that, for this column, the numbers beside vertical jump, 40-yard sprint time, and standing triple jump are quite large: Vertical jump has a "loading" of .71, 40-yard sprint time has a loading of −.76, and standing triple jump has a loading of .77. These large loadings indicate that these variables very clearly are part of the first factor. This factor apparently represents a general jumping and sprinting ability, because the three jumping and sprinting variables have high loadings (the highest of any of the variables) on this factor. Notice that, unlike the loadings of the two jumping variables, the loading for 40-yard sprint time is negative; however, this makes sense, because a person who takes a long time to sprint 40 yards is slow, and would be unlikely to jump very high or very far.

Now look at the column of numbers on the right for factor II. Notice that, for this column, the numbers beside 12-min run, 2-km row time, and 20-min cycle are quite large: 12-min run has a loading of .77, 2-km row time has a loading of −.70,

---

[3] The mathematical calculations involved in factor analysis are fairly complex and are beyond the scope of this book. You can learn how to do factor analysis in a course on measurement, but when you actually do factor analysis, you will use a computer, which is much faster. Doing factor analysis by hand is nowadays done only on small, simple variable sets, for the purpose of understanding how it is done.

and 20-min cycle has a loading of .74. These large loadings indicate that these variables very clearly are part of the second factor. This factor apparently represents a general long-distance racing ability, because the three long-distance variables—running, rowing, and cycling—have high loadings (the highest of any of the variables) on this factor. Notice that, unlike the loadings of running and cycling, the loading for 2-km rowing time is negative; however, this makes sense, because a person who takes a long time to row 2 km is unable to maintain a fast rowing pace and would be unlikely to run or cycle a very long distance.

So, the factor analysis has revealed one factor that includes variables associated with sprinting and jumping ability, and another factor that includes variables associated with endurance or long-distance performance. It is important to understand that these are two separate, independent factors; they are not two opposite poles of the same factor. If the sprinting/jumping variables and the long-distance variables had been opposite to each other—if they had been strongly negatively correlated—then they would have belonged to the *same* factor, but would have shown *opposite* loadings on it. Instead, each of these groups of variables defined its own factor. Notice that the sprinting and jumping variables all had loadings close to zero on the second factor, and that the long-distance variables all had loadings close to zero on the first factor. This indicates that each set of variables is unrelated to the factor that is defined by the other set of variables; that is, each set is neither positively nor negatively related to the other set.

There are two other variables that we have not yet considered. First, look at the loadings for percent fast-twitch muscle fiber. As you can see, this variable showed a modest-sized positive loading on the first factor (.35) and a modest-sized negative loading on the second factor (−.34). These results indicate that this variable does not fit neatly within either factor but is instead partly within both factors. The positive loading on the first factor indicates that having a high percentage of fast-twitch muscle fibers is associated with good sprinting and jumping performances. However, the negative loading on the second factor indicates that having a high percentage of fast-twitch muscle fibers is associated with poor long-distance, endurance performances. (This makes sense given the function of fast-twitch muscle fiber: If you have taken a kinesiology class, you might be aware that these muscle fibers contract quickly and allow rapid, explosive movement, but become tired easily and do not enable sustained steady effort.)

Next, look at the loadings for percent body fat. As you can see, this variable showed a modest-sized negative loading on both the first factor (−.32) and also the second factor (−.34). As was the case for the muscle fiber variable mentioned in the previous paragraph, these results indicate that percent body fat does not fit neatly within either factor but is instead partly within both factors. But notice that the pattern is different, because percent body fat loads negatively on both the first and the second factors. These loadings indicate that high body fat percentage is associated both with poor sprinting and jumping performance and with poor long-distance, endurance performance. This makes sense, because having a lot of body fat means a lot of extra "dead" weight that will make it harder to sprint and jump explosively and harder to cover a long distance at a sustained speed.

As shown by these results, we can see that factor analysis allows us to summarize the relations among a large number of variables in terms of only a small number of groups, or factors. Whereas we began with eight variables in the previous case, we were able to show that these represented two major groups of variables, and we were able to understand the nature of each group by considering the identity of the variables within it. From now on, if I want to measure these kinds of physical abilities of my students, I could probably save some time by using just one sprinting or jumping test, and just one long-distance test, instead of the full battery of eight variables. For example, perhaps I could just measure the standing triple jump (which represents the "sprinting and jumping ability" factor) and the 12-min run (which represents the "long-distance" factor). (Of course, if I were interested in every variable for its own sake, I would continue to use all eight.)

In the example just shown, the number of variables was fairly small, and the pattern of correlations among those variables was relatively simple. By looking at the matrix of correlations among the variables, you could probably see that the variables would fall into two main factors. But in most cases when psychologists use factor analysis, the results are not nearly so obvious: There are often many variables, and the pattern of correlations among them is very complex, with many medium-sized correlations and fewer correlations that are very large or very small. When this is the case, factor analysis can be of much help to the researcher, by taking an extremely complicated pattern of correlations among a large number of variables and reducing those variables to a small number of factors.

Exactly how many factors are there in a given set of variables is not always easy to figure out. There are various rules that a researcher can use to decide how many factors there really are, but these rules do not always give the same result. One important way to figure out the true number of factors is to see which sets of factors can be found in many different studies, using different research participants or even different sets of variables measuring the same general kinds of characteristics. For example, you might find that the same set of three factors can be recovered consistently in many different studies, but that no single set of four factors is consistently found. If this were true, then you would probably decide that there were three, but not four, factors that underlie this domain of characteristics.

One important note about factor analysis: The groups of variables identified by this technique should be thought of as *dimensions* along which people differ, and not as "types" of people. In the example just given, people have different levels of the factor (or dimension) of sprinting and jumping ability, with a few people being very good at these abilities and a few others being very poor, but with most people somewhere in between. Similarly, for the other factor (or dimension) of long-distance racing ability, there are also a few people with very high levels, a few others with very low levels, and most others somewhere in between. That is, for *each* of these two dimensions, we can describe an individual in terms of some number (such as a standard score) that represents his or her *level* of that dimension.

3.3 FACTOR ANALYSIS OF PERSONALITY TRAITS: HOW TO FIND A REPRESENTATIVE SET OF TRAITS?

The use of factor analysis might seem like an ideal way to find a set of personality trait categories that would together account for all of the important personality traits. If we measure many people on a wide variety of personality traits, a factor analysis of those traits should reveal the major groups of traits. But we still face the problem of deciding which traits should be factor analyzed. This decision is a crucial step, because if there are some important aspects of personality that are not well represented in our list of traits, then factor analysis will probably fail to reveal any groups defined by those traits. Therefore, we need to select a set of traits in such a way that all of the important aspects of personality are well represented.

This brings us back to the problem that was discussed in the previous sections. Just as a researcher's list of a few favorite traits might miss some important aspects of personality, so too might a researcher's list of all of the important traits. If a researcher simply tries to assemble a list of traits that represents the personality domain as a whole, it is difficult for anyone to judge whether or not this list really does cover all of the important aspects of personality. Another researcher might well generate a very different list of traits, and in fact it seems likely that every researcher would provide a somewhat different collection.

At this point, you might wonder whether these disagreements could be resolved by holding a big meeting of all personality researchers, who would collectively try to decide on the complete list of important traits. (For example, perhaps they could put together the scales measured by the personality questionnaires that have been developed by various researchers.) This would probably produce a more complete list than any lone researcher could produce, but there is no guarantee that the collective choices of these researchers would represent all aspects of personality. Instead, it is still possible that some important personality traits would be underrepresented in their list, if those researchers tended to neglect some aspects of personality in favor of other aspects. For example, researchers might be particularly interested in characteristics that are associated with good (or poor) mental health or with good (or poor) job performance. Consequently, they might tend to include many of those traits at the expense of other traits that are also interesting parts of personality but that are less strongly related to those criterion variables. Therefore, we might not feel much confidence in the results of a factor analysis of a list of traits that was generated according to the interests of personality researchers.

3.3.1 The Idea of the Lexical Approach

Given the difficulties described in the preceding section, you might wonder how it would ever be possible to obtain a list of important personality traits, in which all aspects of personality are represented fairly. The solution that most researchers have adopted is one that takes much of the decision making out of their own hands and instead uses an already existing list of traits. This existing list is simply the set of personality-descriptive adjectives that can be found in the dictionaries of any language.

The idea behind the use of the dictionary as a source of personality characteristics is based on the *lexical hypothesis*. The lexical hypothesis states that people will want to talk about the personality traits that they view as important. As a result, people will inevitably invent some words to describe people who have high or low levels of these important traits. Over long periods of time, words that describe important traits should become established in every language. Therefore, by considering the full list of personality-descriptive adjectives in a given language—in other words, a language's personality "lexicon"—we should be able to get a reasonably complete list of important personality traits. If we then do a factor analysis of the adjectives in this list, we should be able to find the major groups of personality traits. (Or, to be more precise, we should be able to find the major groups of the personality traits that people have found important enough to talk about.)

In the next section, we will discuss the results obtained using the lexical approach to finding the basic categories of personality traits. But first, let us consider how researchers typically implement this approach. First, the researchers search systematically throughout the dictionary of the language to be studied, to obtain a list of adjectives that can each describe people in terms of a personality trait. When going through the dictionary, the researchers try to identify every word that is mainly used for the purpose of describing normal personality variation. (Yes, this is a boring job.) After obtaining such a list, the researchers exclude terms that are very rarely used (and hence not widely understood). The resulting list—usually several hundred adjectives in length—is then administered to a large sample of people who are willing to serve as the participants in the research study. Those people are asked to provide self-ratings on these adjectives, indicating the extent to which each adjective describes their own personalities. (Or, sometimes, the participants are asked to provide observer ratings on the adjectives for some other persons whom they know well.) For example, the participant might be asked to rate how accurately a given adjective describes himself or herself, using a scale from, say, 1 (very inaccurate) to 5 (very accurate). When ratings have been obtained from several hundred participants, the researcher can then calculate the correlations among the adjectives, and conduct a factor analysis to find the major categories of personality traits.[4]

---

[4] See Ashton and Lee (2005a) for a detailed discussion of many criticisms of the use of the lexical hypothesis in personality research.

3.3.2 The Early Use of the Lexical Approach

As early as the nineteenth century, some psychologists understood the basic idea of the lexical approach: Galton (1884) noted that the various personality-descriptive words listed in the dictionary would overlap and blend into each other, with each word partly sharing its meaning with other words, and partly having some unique meaning of its own. But the first systematic attempts to list the personality lexicon of a given language were only made in the 1930s. Baumgarten (1933) undertook an inventory of German personality-related words, and Allport and Odbert (1936) did the same in the English language, using Webster's dictionary. The result of Allport and Odbert's work was a list of nearly 18,000 English words that described people, of which about 4500 actually described people's personality traits.

The first researcher to factor analyze ratings on the adjectives assembled by Allport and Odbert was Raymond Cattell (e.g., Cattell, 1947). Cattell did not analyze all 4500 terms, however. This full list would be too long for research participants to complete, but even more importantly, it was far too large a variable set to be factor analyzed during the 1940s. (In the days before computers, factor analysis had to be performed by hand, and the calculations are very complex and time-consuming.) To allow a study whose computations would be manageable, Cattell sorted through the adjectives, putting synonyms and antonyms together, and produced a set of 35 variables. He then asked research participants to provide observer ratings of their peers on those variables and factor analyzed the responses.

Cattell (1947) reported that his data revealed 12 factors, which is a rather large number. However, when other researchers later reanalyzed Cattell's data, or when they collected new data from other research participants using the same variables, they were unable to recover those same 12 factors. This is probably because Cattell's method of using factor analysis—a technique that was still being refined at the time of his research—tended to produce more factors than really existed among the variables being analyzed. But although it was not possible to replicate Cattell's finding of 12 personality factors, some researchers did notice a striking similarity in the results of several studies in which Cattell's 35 adjective-based variables had been factor analyzed. These results showed a consistent set of only five personality factors (Tupes & Christal, 1961; later republished as Tupes & Christal, 1992).

3.4 LEXICAL STUDIES IN THE ENGLISH LANGUAGE: THE BIG FIVE PERSONALITY FACTORS

3.4.1 The Big Five

The summary of studies using Cattell's list of personality variables was conducted by two researchers—Ernest Tupes and Raymond Christal—who analyzed many different personality data sets. The consistent result from these data sets was that the 35 variables of Cattell's list could be classified in terms of a set of five factors. Soon after Tupes and Christal's research, these five groups of traits were also recovered in several new studies. This finding was an important one, because it suggested that the wide variety of personality characteristics—and hence the personalities of individuals—could be summarized reasonably well by a set of only five basic dimensions.

At this point, you are probably wondering about the content of these five personality factors: Just what are they, exactly? Let us consider each of these "Big Five" dimensions in turn. These factors and longer lists of their defining traits are also given in Table 3.3.

Extraversion. This factor includes traits such as talkativeness, liveliness, and outgoingness versus shyness, quietness, and passivity.

Agreeableness. This factor includes traits such as kindness and gentleness versus rudeness and harshness.

Conscientiousness. This factor includes traits such as organization, discipline, and thoroughness versus sloppiness, laziness, and unreliability.

Emotional Stability (vs. Neuroticism). This factor includes traits such as relaxedness versus moodiness, anxiety, and touchiness. You will often see this factor described in terms of its opposite pole and referred to as Neuroticism. In other words, the opposite end of Emotional Stability is Neuroticism, which roughly means the same thing as emotional instability.

Intellect or Imagination. The fifth factor includes traits such as philosophicalness, complexity, and creativity versus shallowness and conventionality. The choice of name for this fifth

Table 3.3 Examples of adjectives that have high loadings on the Big Five personality factors as obtained in lexical studies of personality structure in the English language

Factor	Adjectives
Extraversion	Talkative, extraverted, sociable, assertive, enthusiastic, verbal versus withdrawn, silent, introverted, shy, reserved, inhibited
Agreeableness	Sympathetic, kind, warm, cooperative, sincere, compassionate versus cold, harsh, rude, rough, antagonistic, callous
Conscientiousness	Organized, systematic, efficient, precise, thorough, practical versus careless, sloppy, absent-minded, haphazard, disorderly, unreliable
Emotional stability (vs. Neuroticism)	Relaxed, unemotional, easy-going, unexcitable versus moody, jealous, possessive, anxious, touchy, high-strung
Intellect/Imagination[a]	Intellectual, complex, philosophical, innovative, unconventional versus simple, conventional, uninquisitive, unintelligent, shallow

[a]Intellect/Imagination is also known as Openness to Experience.
Based on Hofstee, W. K. B., De Raad, B., & Goldberg, L. R. (1992). Integration of the Big Five and circumplex approaches to trait structure. *Journal of Personality and Social Psychology, 63*, 146–163; Saucier, G., & Goldberg, L. R. (1996). Evidence for the Big Five in analyses of familiar English personality adjectives. *European Journal of Personality, 10*, 61–77.

factor was a difficult one for researchers; it was originally called Culture by Tupes and Christal, and many researchers now refer to this factor as Openness to Experience.

Keep in mind that the various traits belonging to the same Big Five factor are correlated with each other, with the traits at the same pole being positively correlated and the traits at opposite poles being negatively correlated. Traits belonging to different Big Five factors would generally be roughly uncorrelated with each other. This means that in principle you could summarize people's personalities by measuring a few traits within each of the Big Five factors.

Now we return to the history of the Big Five factors. By the 1960s, these five personality dimensions had been found in several different studies, but nearly all of this research had been based on Cattell's 35 variables. (Recall that Cattell had obtained this list of 35 by taking the list of 4500 personality-descriptive words from Allport and Odbert's list, and then forming groups of roughly synonymous words.) Because Cattell's method had been quite subjective, some researchers wondered whether other personality factors, additional to the "Big Five," might be found if a larger, more complete list of personality-descriptive adjectives were administered to research participants.

The researcher who undertook such a project was Warren Norman, a psychologist who had earlier used Cattell's variables in his own research. Norman and his assistants used the original list that Allport and Odbert had compiled during the 1930s and added some new words from a more recent edition of the dictionary. Norman (1967) took the resulting list and reduced it to approximately 2800 terms that he considered to be descriptive of personality. Norman himself never conducted a factor analysis of these terms, but a colleague of his, Lewis Goldberg, did. Goldberg used about 1700 of these terms, excluding the ones whose meanings were unfamiliar to the university students who participated in his research.

When Goldberg performed his factor analyses during the 1970s and 1980s, computers were not yet powerful enough to analyze all 1700 adjectives separately. So, before conducting the factor analysis, he combined similar adjectives into 75 clusters that Norman had recommended. Goldberg (1990) factor analyzed the 75 clusters of adjectives, using responses from college students who provided self-ratings and observer ratings on the adjectives. The results were clear: Again, the Big Five factors—and only the Big Five factors—were found. Moreover, even when Goldberg rearranged the adjectives into other clusters, based on his own judgment, he again recovered the Big Five factors, and nothing else. These results were strong evidence in favor of the Big Five factors, because they showed that the emergence of these categories of personality traits did not depend on the variables that Cattell had used. Instead, the Big Five categories emerged even when different researchers assembled adjectives in different ways (see also Saucier & Goldberg, 1996).

3.4.2 Personality Inventories and the Five-Factor Model

By the 1980s, many researchers had begun to accept the Big Five factors as the major categories of personality traits. Among the psychologists who adopted the Big Five factors were Paul Costa and Robert McCrae. Costa and McCrae were interested in studying personality in relation to the aging process, but they wanted to develop a complete and efficient system for measuring personality. They conducted some analyses of questionnaire scales that Cattell had developed on the basis of his earlier lexical research, and then combined the results of those analyses with results from recent lexically based findings. Taken together, these results convinced Costa and McCrae that the Big Five framework was the best way to organize personality traits. To measure the factors of this "Five-Factor Model," Costa and McCrae (1985) constructed a questionnaire called the NEO Personality Inventory, and this instrument was soon being widely used in personality research. Its later versions, the NEO Personality Inventory—Revised and the shorter NEO Five-Factor Inventory (Costa & McCrae, 1992b; see Box 2.2), became so popular that many psychologists were familiar with the Big Five factors chiefly through the high profile of those instruments and were not even aware of the lexically based research that led to the discovery of those factors. These NEO questionnaires were used in a series of studies by Costa and McCrae during the 1980s and 1990s, in which they showed that nearly all of the scales of other personality inventories were related to one or more of the five factors (e.g., Costa & McCrae, 1988a), and that the NEO scales themselves produced five factors even when administered (in translation) in other countries (e.g., McCrae & Costa, 1997; McCrae, Zonderman, Costa, Bond, & Paunonen, 1996).

For most purposes, the Five-Factor Model as assessed using the NEO inventories can be considered to be the same as the Big Five structure. As seen in Table 3.4, the characteristics that are measured within the five broad factors of the NEO Personality Inventory—Revised are generally very similar to those that defined the Big Five factors in lexical studies (see Table 3.3). But one difference involves the name of the Big Five Intellect or Imagination factor, which in the Five-Factor Model is instead labeled Openness to Experience. This alternative name emphasizes the characteristics that Costa and McCrae view as the central elements of this factor, such as a willingness to examine new ideas, to explore one's imagination, and to try new things. It also downplays the role of intellectual ability, which Costa and McCrae (and many other researchers) consider to be something different from a personality characteristic. Another minor difference involves the Agreeableness factor, within which Costa and McCrae have included some traits—such as straightforwardness and modesty—that were only weakly related to the Big Five Agreeableness factor as found in early English lexical studies of personality structure.

Table 3.4 Broad personality factors and narrower personality traits assessed by the NEO Personality Inventory (NEO-PI-R)

Neuroticism	**Agreeableness**
Anxiety	Trust
Angry hostility	Straightforwardness
Depression	Altruism
Self-consciousness	Compliance
Impulsiveness	Modesty
Vulnerability	Tender-mindedness
Extraversion	**Conscientiousness**
Warmth	Competence
Gregariousness	Order
Assertiveness	Dutifulness
Activity	Achievement striving
Excitement-seeking	Self-discipline
Positive emotions	Deliberation
Openness to experience	
Openness to fantasy	
Openness to aesthetics	
Openness to feelings	
Openness to actions	
Openness to ideas	
Openness to values	

The five headings refer to the five broad factors (i.e., dimensions, domains) assessed by the NEO-PI-R; the six names under each heading refer to the six narrower traits (i.e., facets) that form each of the broad factors.
Based on Costa, P.T., Jr., & McCrae, R.R. (1992b). *NEO personality inventory—revised (NEO-PI-R) and NEO five-factor inventory (NEO-FFI) professional manual.* Odessa, FL: Psychological Assessment Resources.

3.5 LEXICAL STUDIES IN MANY LANGUAGES: THE HEXACO PERSONALITY FACTORS

3.5.1 Different Languages, Same Six Factors

Now let us return to our discussion of the results of lexical studies of personality structure. As we have seen, the repeated emergence of the Big Five factors in English-language research led many psychologists to conclude that these five dimensions represented the major groups of human personality characteristics. But personality researchers wanted to find out whether or not these results would also occur when other languages were studied. By conducting lexical studies of personality structure in a variety of languages, psychologists could hope to learn whether or not there existed a universal set of basic groups of personality traits. One possibility was that the Big Five factors would be found in each language, in much the same form as in English. Another possibility was that one or more of the factors would fail to emerge in most other languages; if so, this would suggest that those missing factors were not really among the main groups of personality traits.

Still another possibility was that most other languages would contain one or more factors that were missing in the English-language results; if so, this would suggest that the English lexical studies had missed some major aspects of personality variation.

Beginning in the late 1980s, lexical studies of personality structure were conducted in several languages, using methods similar to those of the English-language studies described in the previous section. However, unlike those English investigations, the studies conducted in other languages generally each used several hundred adjectives that could all be factor analyzed individually, rather than in clusters of synonyms as had been done in English. The reason for this change was that, at about this time, advances in computing power had made it feasible to factor analyze very large numbers of variables. By the early 2000s, lexical studies of personality structure had been conducted in many languages, including Croatian, Dutch, Filipino, French, German, Greek, Hungarian, Italian, Korean, Polish, and Turkish. Interestingly, the results of these studies showed some striking similarities among these languages, but also some surprising differences from the earlier English-language studies (see Ashton, Lee, Perugini et al., 2004; Lee & Ashton, 2008).

The main finding of these lexical studies was that a similar set of six personality factors was found in each of these diverse languages. The English translations of the adjectives that typically had high loadings on a given factor are shown, for all six factors, in Table 3.5.[5] Here are some comparisons of these six factors with the Big Five.

Extraversion, Conscientiousness, and Intellect or Imagination (Openness). Three of the factors obtained from the various languages were nearly identical in content—that is, in the overall meaning of their defining adjectives—to the Extraversion, Conscientiousness, and Intellect or Imagination (a.k.a. Openness to Experience) factors of the Big Five (compare with Table 3.3). Note, however, that the adjectives of the latter factor tended to vary somewhat across different studies. In several cases, this factor included terms suggesting unconventionality, in addition to intellectual or imaginative tendencies.

Agreeableness. Each of the languages also revealed an Agreeableness factor (see Table 3.5) that was similar to the Big Five Agreeableness factor in some ways. For example, adjectives describing gentleness versus quarrelsomeness loaded on this factor in various languages. But this version of Agreeableness was in some ways different from the Big Five version, as we will discuss later.

Emotionality. Across the various languages, a factor called Emotionality (see Table 3.5) was recovered. Notice that in some ways this factor is the same as the Big Five Emotional Stability factor, but is "flipped" to the opposite side of that Big Five factor—

[5] A broadly similar set of six factors has also been found by Saucier (2009) in a review of lexical studies of several languages. Some of the studies of this review included some adjectives that some researchers consider as evaluations (e.g., *awful, impressive*) rather than as personality characteristics. One of the challenges in conducting lexical studies of personality structure is in deciding precisely which adjectives represent personality characteristics and which do not.

Table 3.5 Examples of English translations of adjectives that typically have high loadings on the six factors obtained in lexical studies of personality structure in various languages

Factor	Adjectives
Honesty—Humility	Sincere, honest, faithful/loyal, modest/unassuming, fair-minded versus sly, deceitful, greedy, pretentious, hypocritical, boastful, pompous
Emotionality	Emotional, oversensitive, sentimental, fearful, anxious, vulnerable versus brave, tough, independent, self-assured, stable
Extraversion	Outgoing, lively, extraverted, sociable, talkative, cheerful, active versus shy, passive, withdrawn, introverted, quiet, reserved
Agreeableness	Patient, tolerant, peaceful, mild, agreeable, lenient, gentle versus ill-tempered, quarrelsome, stubborn, choleric
Conscientiousness	Organized, disciplined, diligent, careful, thorough, precise versus sloppy, negligent, reckless, lazy, irresponsible, absent-minded
Intellect/Imagination/ Unconventionality[a]	Intellectual, creative, unconventional, innovative, ironic versus shallow, unimaginative, conventional

[a]Intellect/Imagination/Unconventionality is also known as Openness to Experience.
Based on Ashton, M. C., & Lee, K. (2007). Empirical, theoretical, and practical advantages of the HEXACO model of personality structure. *Personality and Social Psychology Bulletin, 11*, 150—166; Ashton, M. C., Lee, K., Perugini, M., Szarota, P., de Vries, R. E., Di Blas, L., et al. (2004). A six-factor structure of personality-descriptive adjectives: Solutions from psycholexical studies in seven languages. *Journal of Personality and Social Psychology, 86*, 356—366.

that is, to the Neuroticism side. For example, the Emotionality factor includes characteristics such as anxiety, which are also associated with Big Five Neuroticism (i.e., with low Big Five Emotional Stability, as viewed from the opposite direction). But in other ways, this Emotionality factor obtained from many languages is different from the Big Five Neuroticism factor obtained in English.

Fig. 3.1 illustrates the differences between, on the one hand, the original Big Five Agreeableness and Emotional Stability (vs. Neuroticism) factors, and on the other hand, the Agreeableness and Emotionality factors observed in many languages. First, notice that the Big Five Emotional Stability (vs. Neuroticism) factor contains traits such as patience versus irritability. Notice also that the Big Five Agreeableness factor contains traits such as sentimentality versus toughness. But in the lexical studies of many languages, the arrangement of traits within factors is different. Traits of patience versus irritability belong to the Agreeableness factor, and traits of sentimentality versus toughness belong to the Emotionality factor. (The name "Emotionality" is used instead of "Neuroticism" or "low Emotional Stability" for the factor observed in many languages.)

Honesty—Humility. In addition to the differences involving the Agreeableness and Emotionality factors, there was another striking difference between the results obtained

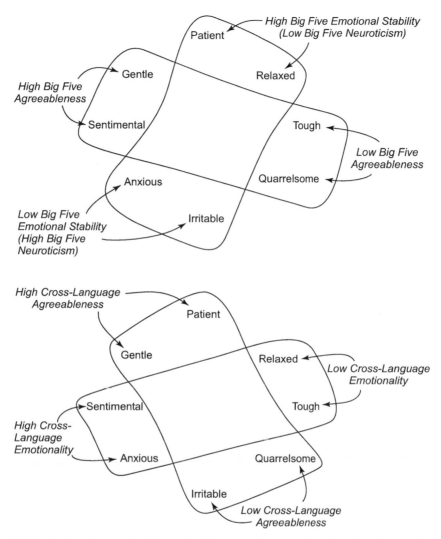

Figure 3.1 Graph showing similarities and differences between the Big Five Agreeableness and Emotional Stability (vs. Neuroticism) factors (top panel) and the cross-language Agreeableness and Emotionality factors (bottom panel). Note that the traits are arranged in the same pattern in the two panels but are grouped differently.

in various languages and those obtained in the earlier English studies. This surprising difference was the consistent finding of a factor that has been called Honesty–Humility. This factor includes traits such as sincerity, fairness, and modesty versus slyness, deceit, greed, and pretentiousness. In the earlier English-language studies, these traits were to some extent located within the Agreeableness factor, but they had fairly small loadings on that factor.

As with the Big Five, the various traits belonging to the same HEXACO factor are correlated with each other (with traits at the same pole being positively correlated and traits at opposite poles being negatively correlated); traits belonging to different HEX-ACO factors tend to be uncorrelated with each other. To summarize people's personalities, you could measure them on a few traits from each of the HEXACO factors.

The finding of a set of six personality factors was an interesting result, but it raises the question of why the entire set of six factors did not emerge in the English language. After all, the English language does have many adjectives to describe a wide array of personality traits, and each of the six factors found in other languages appears to be described by many English adjectives. One possible explanation for the discrepancy is that the studies done in English involved the factor analysis of *clusters* of very similar adjectives, rather than on individual, separate adjectives. As you will recall from the previous section, computers were not fast enough or powerful enough, until quite recently, to factor analyze very large numbers of variables. So, at the time when the English-language studies were conducted, it was necessary to combine similar terms into clusters before performing the factor analysis. For example, Norman (1967) had identified many hundreds of personality terms, but because of limited computing power, he and Goldberg (e.g., Goldberg, 1990) had to condense those terms into 75 clusters of synonyms before performing any factor analyses. After the adjectives had been averaged together into the 75 clusters, then it was possible to do a factor analysis. But for the purpose of finding all of the major dimensions of personality, analyzing the clusters is not as powerful as analyzing the original adjectives themselves.

With modern high-speed computers, it became possible to factor analyze all of the adjectives separately. One study (Ashton, Lee, & Goldberg, 2004) examined all 1700 of the adjectives identified by Goldberg and Norman, and another study (Lee & Ashton, 2008) examined about 450 of the most familiar adjectives from this set. The results of these studies, based on self-rating responses, showed six factors that were similar to those found across the various other languages described previously. Not surprisingly, there were very clear Extraversion, Conscientiousness, and Openness to Experience factors. But also in both studies, there were Agreeableness and "Emotionality" factors similar to those of the various other languages, not to the previous English-language factor. Both studies also found an Honesty—Humility factor similar to those of other languages. So, these results indicated that there was little discrepancy between the results in English and those in other languages: The English language contained all six personality-descriptive factors, but limited computing power had made it difficult to find them until fairly recently.[6]

---

[6] Several years ago, some researchers argued that the various languages did not really show a similar set of six factors, or even five factors (De Raad et al., 2010), but their later analyses (De Raad et al., 2014) confirmed the six-factor solution (see also Ashton & Lee, 2010).

You might wonder whether there could be a set of seven (or even more) personality factors that can be found across languages. Researchers have checked this possibility, but when they have compared the sets of seven factors obtained from different languages, they find that the results differ widely, without any particular set of seven being widely recovered.

3.5.2 The HEXACO Model of Personality Structure

The set of six personality factors that has been observed in studies of many languages has been called the "HEXACO" structure. This label suggests both the number of factors (the Greek prefix "hexa" means six) and also their names: H is for Honesty—Humility, E is for Emotionality, X is for Extraversion, A is for Agreeableness, C is for Conscientiousness, and O is for Openness to Experience. (Note that the last factor is named as in the Five-Factor Model, rather than as in the original Big Five.) For the purpose of measuring these six factors, a questionnaire called the HEXACO Personality Inventory was developed (HEXACO-PI; Lee & Ashton, 2004, 2006). The traits measured within the six broad factors of the revised version of this instrument (Ashton & Lee, 2009a; Lee & Ashton, 2017) are listed in Table 3.6.

As can be seen by comparing this table with Table 3.4, the Extraversion, Conscientiousness, and Openness to Experience factors of the HEXACO-PI-R are largely similar to the same-named factors of the NEO-PI-R. Some differences can be observed, however, in the remaining factors: HEXACO-PI-R Emotionality includes some traits associated with NEO-PI-R Neuroticism, but also some traits not included

Table 3.6 Broad personality factors and narrower personality traits assessed by the HEXACO Personality Inventory—Revised (HEXACO-PI-R)

Honesty—Humility	**Agreeableness**
Sincerity	Forgivingness
Fairness	Gentleness
Greed-avoidance	Flexibility
Modesty	Patience
Emotionality	**Conscientiousness**
Fearfulness	Organization
Anxiety	Diligence
Dependence	Perfectionism
Sentimentality	Prudence
Extraversion	**Openness to experience**
Social self-esteem	Aesthetic appreciation
Social boldness	Inquisitiveness
Sociability	Creativity
Liveliness	Unconventionality

The six headings refer to the six broad factors (i.e., dimensions, domains) assessed by the HEXACO-PI-R; the four names under each heading refer to the four narrower traits (i.e., facets) that form each of the broad factors. The Social self-esteem scale of the HEXACO-PI-R replaced the Expressiveness scale of the original HEXACO-PI.

in Neuroticism. Also, HEXACO-PI-R Agreeableness includes traits associated with NEO-PI-R Agreeableness but also traits associated with low Neuroticism. Finally, HEXACO-PI-R Honesty—Humility includes some traits associated with NEO-PI-R Agreeableness, but also some traits not included in the NEO-PI-R version of Agreeableness.[7]

Do these differences matter? Some investigations have examined whether or not the HEXACO framework can account for some personality traits that are not well accounted for by the Big Five or Five-Factor Model. The results of these studies (e.g., Lee, Ogunfowora, & Ashton, 2005) have suggested that several traits do not fit well within the Five-Factor Model, but do fit well within the HEXACO framework. For example, traits such as physical risk taking and femininity are strongly related to low Emotionality of the HEXACO model, but not to any combination of factors of the Big Five or Five-Factor Model. Similarly, traits such as egotism, manipulativeness, and lack of integrity are strongly related to low Honesty—Humility of the HEXACO model, but less strongly to any combination of factors of the Big Five or Five-Factor Model (see also Gaughan, Miller, & Lynam, 2012). These results suggest that the domain of personality characteristics is more thoroughly summarized by the HEXACO framework than by the five-dimensional framework. However, since the 1980s, hundreds of researchers have measured the Big Five factors in their studies of personality, and those dimensions continue to be studied widely. Therefore, it is worthwhile to study the content of both the Big Five factors and the HEXACO factors, and thus to understand the similarities and differences between the Five-Factor Model and the HEXACO model.

BOX 3.1 Many Traits Are Blends of Two (or More) Factors

When researchers conduct a factor analysis of a set of variables, they use some mathematical procedures to make the results as simple and as easy to interpret as possible. One aspect of this is that the variables tend to be sorted rather neatly into the various factors: Most variables have strong loadings on only one factor, and most factors have strong loadings for a few variables only. But this ideal cannot be achieved completely, because some variables tend to be mixtures, or blends, of two or more factors.

Let us consider a couple of examples, using the set of six factors described previously. Some traits, such as self-confidence, usually have some loadings on the positive pole of the Extraversion factor and also on the negative pole of the Emotionality factor; sometimes the highest loading is on Extraversion and sometimes on (low) Emotionality. This result suggests that self-confidence is a blend of high Extraversion and low Emotionality. As another example,

---

[7] Note that the traits measured by the NEO-PI-R and the HEXACO-PI-R were not meant to be a complete list of all personality traits associated with each factor. Instead, those traits were intended simply as a sampling of several characteristics within each of the factors, and presumably some other traits could have been selected as an alternative way of sampling the content of the factors.

BOX 3.1 Many Traits Are Blends of Two (or More) Factors—cont'd

consider the trait of generosity. This trait usually has some loadings on the positive poles of both Honesty—Humility and Agreeableness, sometimes showing its highest loading on one and sometimes on the other. Thus, generosity appears to be a blend of Honesty—Humility and of Agreeableness.

The preceding examples are described with reference to the six factors observed across many languages, but similar cases can be observed for the loadings of traits within the Big Five framework. In fact, most research on the existence of traits that represent blends of two or more factors has been conducted using the Big Five factors (e.g., Hofstee et al., 1992; Saucier, 1992).

BOX 3.2 Even Bigger Personality Factors?

The Big Five personality factors were generally considered to be uncorrelated with each other. However, some researchers noticed that self-report (or observer report) scales measuring the Big Five actually tended to correlate moderately with each other. This fact led some researchers to suggest that the Big Five could themselves be grouped into two very large factors (DeYoung, 2006; Digman, 1997) or into one even larger factor (Musek, 2007). However, later research showed that some traits within any one Big Five (or HEXACO) factor were uncorrelated with some traits within each of the other Big Five (or HEXACO) factors (Ashton, Lee, Goldberg, & de Vries, 2009). Also, scales measuring the Big Five (or HEXACO) factors can be constructed in such a way that the scales show near-zero correlations with each other. These results would not be possible if the Big Five or HEXACO factors really belonged to just one or two very large factors. Therefore, those one or two very large factors do not actually exist.

3.6 WHAT IT ALL MEANS: A FEW DIMENSIONS, BUT MANY PERSONALITIES

Now that we have described the nature of the major categories of personality traits, it is worth reflecting on why this knowledge matters. Essentially, the results of the lexical studies of personality structure tell us that human personality traits can be classified into six major groups. Therefore, if you could find an individual's overall level of the traits within each group, then these six levels would give you a pretty complete summary of his or her personality. Of course, some of the finer detail would certainly be lost, because any person would show differences among the traits that fall within the same category. (For example, two people might both be fairly high in Extraversion, but one of them might be very outgoing and moderately lively, whereas the other might be moderately outgoing and very lively.) But nevertheless, the six broad personality factors would together account for the important features of personality. Note that, because the six factors are roughly uncorrelated with each other, you would need all six to summarize people's personalities.

It might seem surprising that human personality traits can be summarized by only six groups and, by extension, that people's personalities can be summarized by only these six dimensions. At first, it might even seem preposterous that something as complicated as human personality can be reduced, even in rough outline, to only six broad characteristics. But remember that the finding of six personality factors does not mean there are only six "types" of people. To appreciate this point more fully, let us consider how many different "kinds" of people can be described with these six variables.

First, suppose that, for each factor, we can discriminate among five different levels of the factor. For example, let us say that for Agreeableness, we can divide people up into five levels, say, "very disagreeable," "disagreeable," "average," "agreeable," and "very agreeable." If we do this for each of the six factors, then we could describe $5 \times 5 \times 5 \times 5 \times 5 \times 5 = 15,625$ different kinds of people. And, if we could discriminate with a bit more precision, with seven levels for each factor, then we would be able to describe nearly 118,000 different kinds of people. So, it is possible to explain a great deal of the variety and complexity of human personality with only six basic factors. Again, this is not to say that personality is *completely* accounted for by these factors—instead, the various specific traits within a given factor will provide us with important details about a person's personality—but we can go a long way toward describing someone's personality using only the six broad dimensions.

Another important implication of the results described in this chapter is that there is apparently some similarity across cultures in the nature of the major elements of personality. Recall the languages that were investigated in the lexical studies of personality structure described earlier in this chapter: Even though some of these languages were closely related to each other (e.g., French with Italian, or Dutch with German), other languages were almost completely unrelated to each other (e.g., Hungarian, Korean, and English). Nevertheless, these languages all contained similar sets of personality-descriptive adjectives, and this indicates that people in very different cultures are describing the same major elements of personality. Across these diverse cultures, people talk about personality traits that can be classified within the same six groups, and this result suggests that these six factors represent the basic components of human personality variation. It will be interesting to examine the results of future research involving other languages: For example, it is possible that not all six factors will be obtained from the personality lexicons of languages spoken by very small populations and having an exclusively oral (not written) tradition; some recent research suggests that only two very broad personality dimensions would be found (Saucier et al., 2014).

BOX 3.3 Are There Personality "Types?"

If we consider the many possible combinations of levels of the personality factors, we can describe many distinctly different personalities. But some researchers have suggested that certain combinations of personality trait levels are especially common and therefore make it useful to speak of a few main "types" of people. For example, some researchers (e.g., Asendorpf, 2003) have suggested that there are three such personality types:

1. The resilient type: An all-around well-adjusted person, characterized by a somewhat low level of Big Five Neuroticism (i.e., high Emotional Stability) and somewhat high levels of the other four Big Five factors.
2. The internalizing type: A rather anxious and timid person, characterized by a low level of Big Five Extraversion and a high level of Big Five Neuroticism. (This person is said to "internalize" his or her emotions.)
3. The externalizing type: A rather aggressive and impulsive person, characterized by low levels of Big Five Agreeableness and Conscientiousness. (This person is said to "externalize" his or her emotions.)

The main problem with the idea of three personality types, however, is that these precise combinations are not particularly common. Most people have combinations of personality trait levels that do not fit any of the aforementioned three types (Ashton & Lee, 2009b; Costa, Herbst, McCrae, Samuels, & Ozer, 2002). For example, many people are high in both Extraversion and Neuroticism or low in Agreeableness and high in Conscientiousness. If we try to classify people into a few types, we find that most people just do not fit the descriptions very well. (The same problem still applies even if we look for many more types of people.) And if we try to use personality types to predict people's behavior, the prediction is much less accurate than it is if personality trait levels are used instead (Asendorpf, 2003; Ashton & Lee, 2009b; Costa et al., 2002).

In some sense, the fact that people have so many different combinations of personality trait levels is an unfortunate one for personality researchers: If there were really just a few basic personality types, it would make research much easier. But then again, it would also make personality a lot less interesting.

BOX 3.4 Broad Factors Versus Narrow Traits

The finding that so many personality traits can be classified into six broad categories is important, because it allows us to summarize people's personalities very efficiently, and it gives us some direction for future research about personality. But we should not get too carried away with this result, because it is important to remember that the broad factors are only summaries of many narrower traits that each has some unique aspect that is not shared with the others.

The importance of this fact can be seen when we use personality measurements to predict criterion variables. In many cases, the criteria that we want to predict are likely to be strongly related to some specific narrow trait, but not so strongly related to other narrow traits (even those that belong to the *same* factor as does the one that we expect to be a good predictor). As a result, that specific narrow trait would probably be a more valid predictor of the criterion than would the broad factor that combines this narrow trait with many other narrow traits that

(Continued)

BOX 3.4 Broad Factors Versus Narrow Traits—cont'd

are less relevant to the criterion. That is, if one of the narrow traits within a factor is strongly relevant to a criterion variable, its validity will be weakened by combining it with other narrow traits that are less relevant to that criterion. Consider the following example. Suppose that you are interested in predicting students' levels of academic performance. Presumably, measurements of students' levels of the Conscientiousness factor would be associated with the grade point averages obtained for the students. However, some traits within Conscientiousness, such as achievement motivation, seem likely to contribute especially strongly to academic performance and might be strongly associated with grade point average. In contrast, other traits within Conscientiousness, such as impulse control or neatness, seem less relevant to academic performance and might be only weakly associated with grade point average. Therefore, if we want to predict students' grade point averages, we might be better off measuring students' levels of the narrow trait that seems most relevant to the criterion (in this case, achievement motivation) rather than the broad factor (in this case, Conscientiousness) that contains this trait (Paunonen & Ashton, 2001a, 2001b).

So, despite the importance of the broad factors of personality, we should not forget that the narrow traits that make up those factors are themselves important. By measuring these specific aspects of personality, we can sometimes predict criterion variables more effectively than we could if we were to rely only on a half-dozen major factors.

3.7 SUMMARY AND CONCLUSIONS

We began this chapter with the problem of how to summarize the vast array of personality characteristics in terms of a few major dimensions. By finding the basic personality factors, researchers would be able to measure people's personalities thoroughly (i.e., without missing important characteristics) but without redundancy (i.e., without measuring many very similar characteristics). This in turn would make personality research much easier, and it would also give us a better understanding of the meaning of personality itself.

The process of identifying the major personality dimensions involves a technique called factor analysis, which uses the correlations among variables to categorize them into groups called factors. One of the challenges in trying to find the basic factors of personality is to obtain a set of personality characteristics that represents all of the important aspects of personality. Researchers have accomplished this through the "lexical" approach, which involves identifying the familiar personality-descriptive adjectives of a language. By finding such a variable set, researchers can study the characteristics that the speakers of that language have found to be useful and important for describing personality.

Factor analyses of the personality characteristics identified in lexical studies were first conducted in the English language. Researchers obtained self- or observer ratings of personality, using familiar personality-descriptive adjectives taken from the dictionary. When these adjective ratings were factor analyzed, the results indicated a set of five factors now called the "Big Five." These factors are known as Extraversion, Agreeableness, Conscientiousness, Emotional Stability (vs. Neuroticism), and Intellect/Imagination. The Big Five factors became popular in personality research partly through the "NEO" questionnaires, which measure the characteristics of this "Five-Factor Model." In the Five-Factor Model, the Intellect/Imagination factor is called Openness to Experience.

Beginning in the late 20th century, lexical studies of personality structure have been conducted in many different languages, using much larger sets of adjectives than were used in the earlier research. These studies have recovered a set of six—not just five—factors. Three of the factors are similar to the Big Five Extraversion, Conscientiousness, and Intellect/Imagination (or Openness to Experience) dimensions. Two other factors of the six (Agreeableness and Emotionality) are broadly similar to the Big Five Agreeableness and Emotional Stability factors but differ in some noteworthy ways. Another of the six factors is called Honesty—Humility and is only modestly related to the Big Five factors. This six-dimensional framework is called the "HEXACO" model, and there exists a personality inventory to assess those six factors. Some personality characteristics show considerably stronger relations with the HEXACO dimensions than with those of the Big Five or Five-Factor Model.

Since the 1980s, many researchers have measured personality using the Big Five framework, and today many researchers continue to use that framework or have adopted the newer HEXACO model. By assessing these sets of basic personality dimensions, researchers have been able to examine more efficiently some very interesting questions about personality. How do people's personalities change throughout the life span? How do brain structures and brain chemicals relate to personality? What are the genetic and environmental influences on personality? How did personality variation evolve and maintain itself across human history? How does personality influence important life outcomes? These fascinating questions will be the subjects of the next several chapters of this book.

CHAPTER 4

Developmental Change and Stability of Personality

Contents

Our next topic is that of personality development. In this chapter we will consider how the typical person changes in personality through different stages of life. We will also examine the extent to which people's levels of personality characteristics—relative to those of other people of their own age cohort—tend to be stable across long periods of time. In a separate section, we will investigate the same questions in relation to children's personalities, whose measurement poses some special challenges for the researcher.

4.1 DEFINING CHANGE AND STABILITY

As explained in Chapter 2, the idea of a personality trait is that people differ in their tendencies to show a pattern of related behaviors, thoughts, and feelings. An important part

Individual Differences and Personality
ISBN 978-0-12-809845-5, http://dx.doi.org/10.1016/B978-0-12-809845-5.00004-4

of this idea is that the differences among people are rather stable across fairly long periods of time. That is, personality traits are relatively enduring dispositions, not temporary states. If we say that Cathy is a more talkative person than most, we are saying that, over the long run, Cathy tends to talk more than most people do; we are not merely saying that Cathy has been more talkative today (or this week, or this month) than most other people have been.

But the idea of a trait does not require that an individual's tendencies remain equally strong or weak throughout his or her entire life span. Instead, one can imagine that trait levels could gradually change quite substantially across the years, or even that trait levels might be changed rather suddenly by some major event. In this way, it is conceivable that Cathy might have had a consistent, relatively enduring tendency to be somewhat less talkative than average during her 20s, but that she had a consistent, relatively enduring tendency to be rather more talkative than average during her 40s. But does this actually happen? Do people show important changes throughout their life span in their levels of personality traits?

In an important sense, this question about personality change actually combines two rather different questions. One question is that of how the *average person* changes in his or her levels of various personality traits throughout the life span. The other question is that of how stable are the *differences between people* in their levels of personality traits: that is, in a large group of people of roughly the same age, will the individuals' relative levels of a trait remain consistent across time? Note that even if people on average change a great deal in their trait levels throughout various periods of life, the differences between people might still be rather stable throughout those periods.

One way to understand these two questions is to consider changes in the physical characteristic of height. If we ask whether people's height changes much across the life span, the answer is obviously yes, in the important sense that children generally grow so much taller. But if we ask whether people's height remains stable or consistent in relation to that of other people of the same age, the answer might also be yes (at least to some extent). It is likely that the tallest children of a given age will tend to be taller-than-average adults, even though sometimes a tall child will be overtaken in height by a shorter child who happens to have a later or greater "growth spurt" at some point during adolescence.

In the following sections, we will address both questions about personality development. First, we will examine the differences across periods of the life span in people's average levels of personality traits. Then, we will examine the degree of stability across the years in the differences between people in their personality trait levels. In addressing these questions, we will focus our attention on adulthood and to some extent on adolescence. In a later section of this chapter, however, we will also examine personality during childhood and infancy.

4.2 DEVELOPMENTAL CHANGES IN MEAN LEVELS OF PERSONALITY TRAITS

4.2.1 Cross-Sectional and Longitudinal Studies

We begin by examining how the average (mean) levels of personality traits change across the life span. One way that researchers can get some clues about these changes is to do a *cross-sectional* study of personality trait levels. In a cross-sectional study, researchers measure the personality trait levels of many persons of widely varying ages. The researchers can then compare the average personality trait levels for persons of different ages. One advantage of a cross-sectional design is that it is sometimes fairly easy to get a large sample of people, which helps to give a more accurate indication of any personality differences between people of different ages.

However, one limitation of a cross-sectional study is that we cannot know for certain that a difference between age groups really means a developmental change in the trait. Consider this example: Suppose we conduct a cross-sectional study and find that, on average, older adults have higher levels of a trait than younger adults do. This result might mean that the average level of the trait actually increases as people get older—in other words, that there is a real developmental change in the trait.

But this is not the only possibility. It might mean instead that today's older adults *already* had high levels of the trait long ago, back when they were young adults. That is, the difference between today's older adults and today's young adults might be due to differences between those generations, such as the conditions they experienced when growing up. [These latter effects are called "cohort effects" (or sometimes "generational effects").]

Because of this problem, researchers will sometimes also use another kind of investigation called a *longitudinal* study. In a longitudinal study, researchers measure the personality trait levels of many persons on two or more occasions, usually at least several years apart. The researchers can then compare the personality trait levels of the same persons across those occasions, to find out whether the typical person of a given age has increased or decreased or stayed the same. (As you can imagine, it is more work to conduct a longitudinal study than a cross-sectional study, because in a longitudinal study the researcher must keep track of the participants over a period of many years and measure them on multiple occasions. For this reason, cross-sectional studies are much more common than longitudinal studies.)

By considering the results of a cross-sectional study together with the results of a longitudinal study, researchers can get a clearer indication of any developmental changes in personality trait levels. Recall our earlier example: If a cross-sectional study shows that older people have higher levels of the trait (on average) than younger people do, then this might mean a developmental increase, but it might mean that cohort effects have produced the difference. But suppose that we also have results from a longitudinal study.

If the longitudinal study shows that most people increase in their level of the trait between the two occasions, then this suggests that the age difference in the cross-sectional study really is due to a developmental increase. If instead the longitudinal study shows that most people do not increase, then this suggests that the age difference in the cross-sectional study was not due to a developmental increase, and instead that a cohort effect was responsible.

At this point you might wonder: why not just do a longitudinal study in the first place and skip doing a cross-sectional study? Sometimes that is what researchers do, but a longitudinal study on its own also has some limitations. If a longitudinal study shows that most people's level of a trait has increased, then this might mean a developmental increase—but it might not. The increase could instead be due to conditions or events that people in general have been experiencing between these occasions. [These latter effects are called "historical effects" (or sometimes "period effects").] So, to find out about any developmental changes in people's levels of a trait, it is best to have information from both cross-sectional study and a longitudinal study.

4.2.2 Findings About Age Trends in Personality Trait Levels

Most research on age trends in personality has been based on cross-sectional studies, some of them involving very large samples.[1] As noted earlier, the use of cross-sectional studies alone does not allow us to determine whether age differences are due to developmental change or due to cohort effects. However, when researchers have compared results from cross-sectional studies with results from longitudinal studies, the results have usually been fairly similar, even though not identical. This rough similarity between cross-sectional and longitudinal findings suggests that the age differences revealed in cross-sectional research are likely to reflect (at least for the most part) developmental changes in personality.

The following section summarizes the findings from research on age differences in personality trait levels, for ages ranging from the early teens until the 70s or beyond. The results are organized using the HEXACO framework, but are based on findings from relevant traits of the Big Five as well as the HEXACO dimensions. Note that the results are given for men and women together rather than separately, because the age differences have typically been reasonably similar for men and for women. The results described here are based on self-reports, but when researchers have also examined age trends using observer reports, the findings have generally been similar. And again, because previous findings from longitudinal studies have been fairly similar to those of cross-sectional studies, the results here are interpreted—provisionally—as suggesting developmental change even when based on cross-sectional studies.

---

[1] Not many large-sample longitudinal studies have been conducted, because as noted in the previous section it is difficult and expensive to track many people over many years.

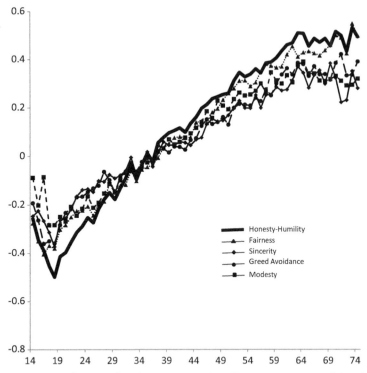

Figure 4.1 Mean z-scores by age for the Honesty—Humility component and its defining facets. *(Reproduced from Ashton, M. C., & Lee, K. (2016). Age trends in HEXACO-PI-R self-reports.* Journal of Research in Personality, 64, *102—111.)*

4.2.2.1 Honesty—Humility

Honesty—Humility decreases during the teens, but after the late teens it increases through late middle age (Ashton & Lee, 2016; Milojev & Sibley, 2017; Sibley & Pirie, 2013). The trends are similar for the various facets of Honesty—Humility (see Fig. 4.1). The average level of Honesty—Humility is about one full standard deviation unit higher among 60-year-olds than among 18-year-olds. Age differences in Honesty—Humility correspond fairly closely, but in the opposite direction, to age differences in crime rates: crime rates are generally highest for persons in their mid-to-late teens and decrease steadily thereafter (see Section 9.7.2 for relations between Honesty—Humility and criminal tendencies).

4.2.2.2 Emotionality

Age differences in Emotionality depend on what facet of that broad factor is considered (see Fig. 4.2). Anxiety tends to decrease substantially after young adulthood, whereas sentimentality (i.e., sensitivity, empathy) tends to increase slightly (Ashton & Lee, 2016).

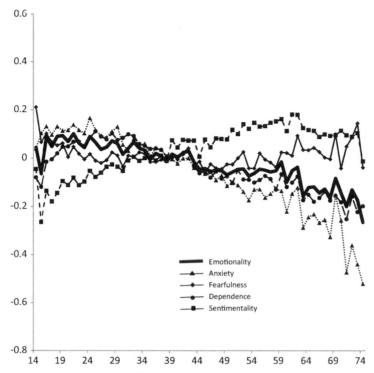

Figure 4.2 Mean z-scores by age for the Emotionality component and its defining facets. *(Reproduced from Ashton, M. C., & Lee, K. (2016). Age trends in HEXACO-PI-R self-reports.* Journal of Research in Personality, *64, 102–111.)*

4.2.2.3 Extraversion

Age differences in Extraversion also depend on what facet of that broad factor is considered (see Fig. 4.3). Social self–esteem and social boldness (i.e., assertiveness, social confidence) tend to increase throughout adulthood, but sociability tends to increase through the teens and then to decrease after the early 20s (Ashton & Lee, 2016; Soto & John, 2012).

4.2.2.4 Agreeableness

Age differences in Agreeableness are generally quite small, although there seems to be a small decrease during the 20s and 30s followed by a small increase in the 40s and later (see Fig. 4.4; Ashton & Lee, 2016). Note that these results are for the HEXACO Agreeableness factor, which involves traits such as patience (i.e., even–temperedness) and forgivingness. For Big Five Agreeableness, which emphasizes traits such as altruism, there tends to be a modest increase throughout adulthood.

4.2.2.5 Conscientiousness

Conscientiousness increases during the teens and early 20s, but thereafter the changes depend on which facet of Conscientiousness is considered (see Fig. 4.5). Prudence

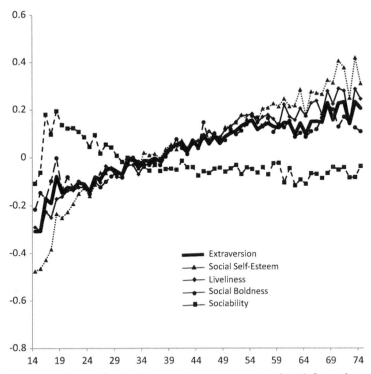

Figure 4.3 Mean z-scores by age for the Extraversion component and its defining facets. *(Reproduced from Ashton, M. C., & Lee, K. (2016). Age trends in HEXACO-PI-R self-reports. Journal of Research in Personality, 64, 102—111.)*

(i.e., cautiousness, impulse control) increases considerably throughout early and middle adulthood, whereas perfectionism stays roughly the same; other facets of Conscientiousness show modest increases (e.g., Ashton & Lee, 2016; Jackson et al., 2009).

4.2.2.6 Openness to Experience

Age differences in Openness have differed across research studies. One recent large-sample study found increases in Openness during the teen years, but also found that changes during adulthood depend on the particular facet of Openness (see Fig. 4.6). Inquisitiveness (intellectual curiosity) and aesthetic appreciation (interest in art and nature) both increase throughout adulthood, but unconventionality decreases (Ashton & Lee, 2016; see also Jackson et al., 2009, for unconventionality).

4.2.2.7 Summary

A couple of main conclusions can be taken from these results. First, the "facet"-level traits that belong to the same factor often differ in the way they change across the life span— even though those traits do tend to go together in persons of any given age. For example,

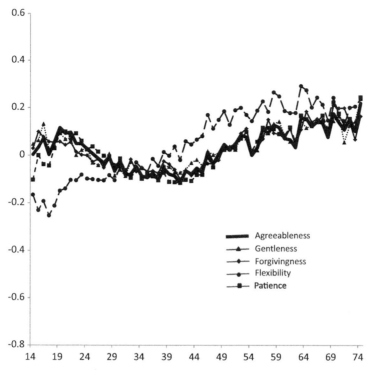

Figure 4.4 Mean z-scores by age for the Agreeableness component and its defining facets. *(Reproduced from Ashton, M. C., & Lee, K. (2016). Age trends in HEXACO-PI-R self-reports.* Journal of Research in Personality, *64, 102–111.)*

one trait belonging to a given factor may increase sharply and another not at all, or one may increase while another decreases. Second, the Honesty–Humility factor (and all of the facet-level traits that belong to it) shows some strong age-related trends, apparently decreasing during the teens and then increasing throughout adulthood.

4.2.3 Why Do Average Personality Trait Levels Change as People Get Older?

Researchers who study developmental change in the average levels of various personality traits have proposed two main reasons for such change: social roles and biological maturation.

According to the hypothesis that social roles are the source of mean-level personality change, people are expected by others to become more responsible and more stable as they get older, particularly as they progress through young adulthood. This expectation follows from the roles that most young adults typically enter, such as working full time for a living, beginning a marriage or other long-term relationship, and beginning to raise a family. According to the social roles hypothesis—often called the social investment

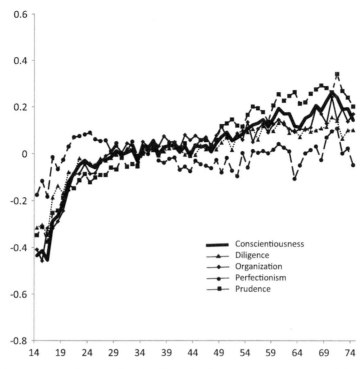

Figure 4.5 Mean z-scores by age for the Conscientiousness component and its defining facets. *(Reproduced from Ashton, M. C., & Lee, K. (2016). Age trends in HEXACO-PI-R self-reports.* Journal of Research in Personality, 64, *102–111.)*

hypothesis (e.g., Roberts, Wood, & Smith, 2005)—people respond to the demands of these roles by developing a more mature personality.

According to the hypothesis that biological maturation is responsible for mean-level personality change (e.g., McCrae & Costa, 1999), people experience genetically based changes in the biological bases of personality (involving the hormones, neurotransmitters, and brain structures described in Chapter 5). This process of biological development presumably has been favored by natural selection because of changes across the life span in the costs and benefits associated with higher or lower levels of a personality trait. (For example, perhaps being low in Honesty–Humility has greater potential payoffs for an 18-year-old than for a 60-year-old; see Box 7.2.)

Which of these hypotheses is correct? It is possible that both causes are responsible for developmental change in personality, but it is not yet clear how much each reason is involved. Some studies suggest that personality trait levels do change as a result of investment in one's career (e.g., Hudson, Roberts, & Lodi-Smith, 2012) or of long-term romantic relationships (see Box 4.1), although other research has found no role for parenthood as a source of personality change (van Scheppingen et al., 2016). However, many personality

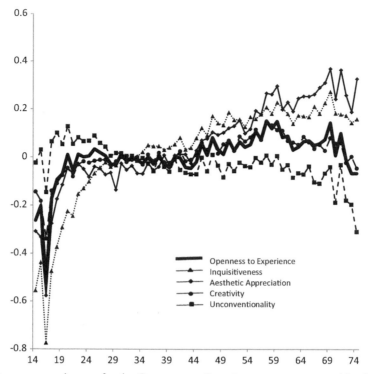

Figure 4.6 Mean z-scores by age for the Openness to Experience component and its defining facets. *(Reproduced from Ashton, M. C., & Lee, K. (2016). Age trends in HEXACO-PI-R self-reports.* Journal of Research in Personality, 64, 102–111.)

traits show steadily changing mean levels over a period of decades rather than relatively abrupt changes during young adulthood—consider the increases in Honesty–Humility, in prudence, in social boldness, or in inquisitiveness, or the decreases in anxiety described earlier in this section. These steady changes might be more consistent with an ongoing pattern of biological maturation than with responses to the social roles of young adulthood.

4.3 STABILITY OF TRAITS ACROSS THE YEARS (AND THE LIFE SPAN)

4.3.1 Stability Across a Period of Several Years During Adulthood

As discussed earlier in this chapter, one important aspect of the idea of a personality trait is that individual differences show some stability over fairly long periods of time. In other words, when we say that people differ in their levels of some personality trait, we are describing differences in an enduring disposition, not just in a temporary state. Consistent with the idea of a trait, several large-scale investigations have shown that there are strong correlations between measurements of people's personality trait levels taken at time intervals several years apart.

Box 4.1 Relationships and Personality Change

Some research studies have been conducted to find out whether certain events or circumstances in life contribute to changes in people's relative positions on various personality traits. One investigation in Germany by Neyer and Lehnart (2007) focused on romantic partner relationships as a possible source of personality change. They examined the changes in young adults' personalities over an eight-year period, typically from their mid-20s to their early 30s. The participants completed self-report personality inventories at the beginning, in the middle, and at the end of the study.

At the start of the study by Neyer and Lehnart, most participants were already in a serious relationship with a boyfriend or girlfriend. During the next 8 years, most of the remaining participants also entered a partner relationship, although some remained single. One interesting finding was that the participants who started out as single but who later entered a partner relationship tended to be higher in neuroticism and in sociability than did those who remained single throughout this period. Neyer and Lehnart suggested that being a rather anxious and sociable person made one more likely to seek out a relationship with a partner.

Another finding by Neyer and Lehnart was that participants who entered a partner relationship tended to become less anxious, less shy, and higher in self-esteem, whereas these changes were not observed among participants who remained single. The researchers suggested that the experience of being in a serious relationship tended to make people feel more secure. (Of course, this would not apply to all partner relationships, but this was the tendency on average.)

Yet another interesting result reported by Neyer and Lehnart involved the participants who were already in a partner relationship at the start of the study. Of these participants, about half were still with the same partner eight years later, and about half were no longer with that partner, having either become single or entered a relationship with a different partner. The researchers found that personality characteristics at the start of the study were unrelated to change in partner relationship. In other words, it was not possible to predict whether or not someone would stay in the same relationship by knowing that person's personality. But the researchers also found that participants who had ended their relationship had become slightly more extraverted, on average, than did those who had stayed in the same relationship.

For example, Costa and McCrae (1988b) studied a sample of nearly 1000 adults, whose ages at the beginning of the investigation spanned a very wide range, from 25 to 84 years. Costa and McCrae obtained self-reports of these adults' personality characteristics on two occasions, 6 years apart. The results showed very strong relations between the level of a given personality trait at the first occasion and the level of the same trait at the second occasion, with correlations averaging over .70 across the various traits measured by Costa and McCrae. This in itself suggests a great deal of stability across these years, but it is especially impressive when one considers the fact that when personality measurements are taken only a few *weeks* apart, correlations are only slightly higher—that is, the test—retest reliability is typically in the .80s (Costa & McCrae, 1992a). In other words, people's levels of personality traits showed almost as much stability across a period of several years as they would across a period of several weeks.

A second study by the same researchers obtained similar results, but this time using observer report data. In this investigation, Costa and McCrae (1992c) obtained observer reports of about 90 adults whose ages ranged from 31 to 57 years at the beginning of the study. The observer reports were provided at two periods, 7 years apart, by close friends of these adults (that is, each participant was rated on two occasions by the same friend). The results were similar to those of the earlier study of self-reports, as the correlations between measures of the same trait across the two occasions again averaged in the .70s. This suggests that personality traits show a high level of stability across a period of several years, regardless of whether the traits were measured by self- or observer report.

One interesting aspect of the results obtained by Costa and McCrae (1988b, 1992c) in both of their investigations was that the stability of personality traits did not depend very much on *which* trait was being considered. Although you might expect that some characteristics would be nearly constant and that some other characteristics would show a fair amount of fluctuation across the years, the results instead showed very similar levels of stability for a wide variety of traits. There was no consistent pattern of higher stability for some traits and lower stability for other traits.

The preceding studies show that adults' personality trait levels show very high stability across a period of several years, at least when the same inventories are used to measure personality at both time intervals. However, similar results are also obtained even when roughly the same traits are measured by the scales of different personality inventories. For example, Ashton and Lee (2005b) examined the relations between scales from two personality inventories—the NEO-PI-R and the HEXACO-PI (see Chapters 2 and 3)—that were administered 9 years apart to a sample of over 600 adults. Despite the use of different inventories and despite this 9-year interval, the respondents' self-reported levels of personality traits were very stable in this sample (see Table 4.1). For several

Table 4.1 Stability of personality trait levels across a 9-year period

NEO-PI-R scale (1994)	HEXACO-PI scale (2003)	Correlation
Order	Organization	.71
Angry hostility	Patience	−.64
Anxiety	Anxiety	.63
Assertiveness	Social boldness	.69
Openness to aesthetics	Aesthetic appreciation	.71
Modesty	Modesty	.55

Results based on self-reports from 655 adults. NEO-PI-R was administered in 1994; HEXACO-PI was administered in 2003. Angry hostility and patience are opposite in meaning, so correlation between those scales is expected to be negative.
Data examined in Ashton, M. C., & Lee, K. (2005b). Honesty—Humility, the Big Five, and the Five-Factor Model. *Journal of Personality, 73*, 1321—1353 using Goldberg's Oregon sample (see Goldberg, 1999).

diverse traits, the correlations between the two measures of essentially the same trait were generally in the .60s. Interestingly, the level of stability was similar regardless of the age of the participants at the time when the first inventory was administered: The correlations across the 9-year period were similar for respondents who were in their 30s, in their 60s, or in between.

4.3.2 Stability Across Longer Periods of Time During Adulthood

The results summarized in the previous section indicate a high level of stability over periods of several years. But they also raise another interesting question: How stable would personality trait levels remain across much longer segments of the life span? Does personality remain stable over periods of, say, 20 years or 40 years? Keep in mind that, even if personality did change substantially over these very long periods, this would not really contradict the idea of a trait. Although traits are viewed as enduring dispositions, it is possible that the strengths of those dispositions would change gradually over the life span: In this way, there would be hardly any noticeable change in an individual's personality over a period of a few years, but nevertheless the individual's personality might show some clear differences across periods of a few decades.

The stability of personality across longer periods of the life span was examined by Costa and McCrae (1992c), who administered self-report personality questionnaires to participants at several points across a period of 24 years. The results showed that the stability of personality across the entire 24-year period, based on the average correlation for the various traits, was very high, at .65. This level of stability was only slightly lower than that observed across a 12-year period, for which the average correlation for the various traits was .70. This result suggests that the stability of personality declines only modestly when longer time intervals are considered. On the basis of similar results, Costa and McCrae have estimated that the stability of personality across a 50-year interval—say, between the ages of 30 and 80 years— would probably be about .60. (Note that this estimate corrects for the fact that the personality scales do not have perfect test—retest reliability even across short time periods.) Other research by the same team (Terracciano, Costa, & McCrae, 2006) suggests that this 50-year stability may be even higher, perhaps .80.

4.3.3 Stability During Adolescence and Young Adulthood

All of the preceding results suggest that there is a fairly high degree of stability in personality, even across very long periods of time. However, those results are all based on samples of people who were at least 25—30 years old at the beginning of the investigations, and therefore had already emerged from young adulthood. But is the long-term stability of personality traits equally strong for young adults or adolescents? Or, instead, is there a greater degree of personality change during those earlier periods of the life span, such that individuals' relative levels of a trait might be more likely to shift?

These questions have been investigated in several studies that have measured the personality trait levels of high school or college students and have then measured those individuals again several years or even several decades later. In one such study, Robins, Fraley, Roberts, and Trzesniewski (2001) obtained self-reports from 270 American students at the beginning of their college career and on their graduation 4 years later. They found that the correlations between levels of a given trait averaged about .60 across this 4-year period. This value is certainly high enough to suggest that traits are rather stable during the college years, but it is also somewhat lower than that observed for older adults. This suggests that personality is undergoing some change during the college-age years, before entering a period of greater consistency later on in adulthood. Another investigation of personality stability during young adulthood was that of Roberts, Caspi, and Moffitt (2001), who examined the personalities over 900 New Zealand young adults who provided self-reports at the age 18 and 26 years. Across this 8-year period, the correlations between levels of a given trait averaged about .55. Thus, these results are broadly similar to those of the Robins et al. study.

Similar results have been observed when personality trait levels have been measured during high school or college, and then measured again during middle age. For example, Finn (1986) found that personality trait levels assessed by self-report in college students were correlated .35, on average, with levels of the same traits when assessed in the same individuals 30 years later. In comparison, levels of the same traits measured originally in 40-year-olds were correlated about .55, on average, with levels of the same traits 30 years later. These results also suggest that personality traits are somewhat less stable during early adulthood than during later adulthood.

When personality is examined still earlier in the life span, at the beginning and end of the teenage years, the levels of stability tend to be somewhat lower than in early adulthood. A study by McCrae et al. (2002) examined self-reports of the Big Five personality traits as provided by 230 American adolescents at two time intervals 4 years apart, when the participants were 12 and 16 years old. The correlations between levels of the same trait across this 4-year interval were generally about .40, although one of the dimensions, Conscientiousness, showed a correlation of about .50. These results suggest that personality is somewhat stable during adolescence, but that it is less stable than during early adulthood or (especially) older adulthood.[2,3]

---

[2] The adolescents of the McCrae et al. (2002) study were selected as part of a search for "gifted" students, so the results might not be typical of those for adolescents in general. On the other hand, the status of these students as gifted suggests that they were probably able to read and understand the personality inventory very well even at the age of 12. Therefore, it is unlikely that any lack of comprehension of the items can explain the somewhat modest level of stability that was observed in this study.

[3] The levels of stability in the studies described in this section are somewhat higher than observed in some earlier studies (see review by Roberts & DelVecchio, 2000). However, many of those earlier investigations were based on personality inventories whose scales are likely to be less reliable and less valid than those used in the studies described above.

Let us summarize all of the preceding results about the stability of personality traits. First, when measured on occasions that are several years apart, personality traits generally show high correlations across those occasions. This indicates that differences among people are, in fact, very stable over these time periods, and are consistent with the idea of a personality trait. Also, when measured across much longer periods of time, such as 20 years or more, the levels of stability are slightly lower, suggesting that there are some changes in personality across the life span despite a fairly high level of long-term stability. Personality stability tends to be higher after young adulthood than during the earlier periods of the life span, when people's relative levels of traits tend to be more changeable.

4.4 PERSONALITY IN CHILDHOOD AND INFANCY: MEASUREMENT AND STRUCTURE

So far in this chapter, our examination of personality change and stability has focused chiefly on adulthood and on adolescence, without considering personality development during childhood or infancy. This is largely because the study of personality during the early years of the life span can present several major challenges to the researcher.

One difficulty is that of obtaining accurate personality descriptions from children. For example, it appears to be only after about the age of 10 years that most children begin to describe themselves and others in terms of personality traits. Prior to that age, many children tend simply to give overall evaluations of themselves and others (i.e., as good or bad) rather than to give descriptions that differentiate between specific traits. A second difficulty is that the self-report personality inventories used with adults generally demand a level of reading comprehension that is not reached until adolescence. As a result, these inventories are unlikely to be useful for making comparisons of mean levels of a personality trait between childhood and adulthood. Finally, a third difficulty emerges when assessing the personality of very young children (or especially of infants), because many of the behaviors and situations in which personality is assessed are not really observed in those children. For example, children who have not yet passed the toddler stage may not yet have well-developed language skills or the complex social interactions that can be observed even in young school-aged children.

Of course, the study of personality in children is still of much interest in spite of the preceding challenges. Investigations of personality change and stability can still be informative, as long as we keep in mind the difficulty of making meaningful comparisons of personality between childhood (especially infancy) and adulthood. In the following sections, we will examine the patterns of change and stability during the early periods of life. But first, let us consider a related question about personality during childhood—specifically, what are the major dimensions of personality during this phase of the life span?

4.4.1 Personality Structure During Childhood

In the earlier sections of this chapter, we discussed the issues of personality change and stability across various stages of adulthood and adolescence. However, we did not examine the topic of personality structure—the number and the meaning of the major dimensions of personality—at these various periods of the life span. There are two simple reasons why this is not really necessary: First, we can use the same personality characteristics to describe differences among the adults (and among the adolescents) of any age group. Second, the correlations among those various personality characteristics are rather similar within any given age group, with the result that personality structure remains pretty much the same across those parts of the life span. Thus, models of the major personality dimensions, such as the Big Five or the HEXACO framework, can be used to summarize personality throughout adolescence and the whole of adulthood.

But if we consider children—especially very young children—it is possible that personality structure could be somewhat different. First, some of the personality traits that describe adults or adolescents might not be applicable to young children. For example, it might not be meaningful to compare 3-year-old children in terms of how philosophical, or how self-conscious, or how pretentious, or how casual they are. Also, it is possible that some of the personality traits that can be applied to children might show patterns of correlations different from those observed within adult samples.

The preceding concerns are reasonable, but the evidence so far suggests that at least during much of childhood, personality structure is similar to that observed during adulthood. For example, factor analyses of teachers' ratings of children's personalities, as assessed using the adjective descriptions developed by Cattell (see Chapter 3), have produced the Big Five factors (Digman & Takemoto-Chock, 1981). These factors have also been obtained in several other analyses of personality characteristics in childhood (see review by Shiner & Caspi, 2003), although the Openness to Experience dimension does not always emerge as strongly as the others (e.g., Halverson et al., 2003). More recently, researchers have developed a version of the HEXACO-PI-R (see Chapter 2) that is suitable for assessing personality in elementary school children. Factor analyses of parents' reports of their children's personalities using this inventory have recovered all six HEXACO factors (Allgaier, Zettler, Göllner, Hilbig, & Trautwein, 2013).

The structure of personality among very young children or among infants is somewhat less clear. When parents or other observers provide ratings of the personality or the "temperament" traits of infants or of toddlers (e.g., Caspi, Roberts, & Shiner, 2005; Rothbart & Bates, 1998),[4] the resulting factors usually include dimensions representing activity level, irritability, fearfulness, positive emotions, attention span or persistence, soothability, and "rhythmicity" (i.e., preferring a clear daily rhythm or routine). Several of these dimensions resemble those obtained in studies of adult personality, such as Extraversion, Conscientiousness, Emotionality, and Agreeableness. But the correspondence is not perfect, because there is no counterpart of Openness to Experience or of Honesty—Humility in these early childhood factors (e.g., Farrell, Brook, Dane, Marini, & Volk, 2014). As noted earlier, some personality traits are difficult to assess at such an early stage of the life span, and some personality traits might not yet exist at that age. Conversely, the activity level, soothability, and rhythmicity factors do not emerge as separate dimensions later in the life span. It appears that at least some of these characteristics tend to join other factors during later periods of the life span; for example, during adulthood, activity level tends to be associated with Extraversion and with Conscientiousness.

4.4.2 Developmental Change in Personality Traits During Childhood

When considering the development of personality during childhood, one interesting issue is that of personality change during these formative years. That is, for any given personality characteristic, do children typically tend to show increasing, decreasing, or stable levels? One study by Lamb, Chuang, Wessels, Broberg, and Hwang (2002) addressed this question by examining the personalities of about 100 Swedish children at various time intervals during a 13-year period. The first personality assessments were made when the children were 2 years old, and further assessments were made at ages 3, 6, 8, and 15 years. All of the assessments were obtained using mothers' reports of their children's personalities in terms of the Big Five personality factors.

Lamb et al. (2002) found that, across the duration of the study, the typical child became lower in Extraversion, higher in Agreeableness, and higher in Conscientiousness. These differences were moderately large, being roughly one standard deviation unit in size. In addition, the children typically became somewhat lower in Emotional Stability between the ages of 3 and 6 years (i.e., during the period when they began school), and most became somewhat lower in Openness to Experience between the ages of 8 and 15 years (i.e., during the period when they reached adolescence).

---

[4] Some researchers use the terms "temperament" and "personality" to refer to two different concepts. According to this view, temperament characteristics are basic emotional tendencies (such as being fearful, impulsive, or energetic), whereas personality characteristics are more complex patterns of behavior that occur only in social contexts (such as being stubborn, hardworking, or unconventional). In this book, we will use the term "personality" to include both kinds of characteristics. However, we will sometimes use the term temperament when researchers have used this term in describing young children (in this chapter) or in discussing the biological basis of personality (in Chapter 5).

It is interesting to speculate on the possible reasons for these patterns of developmental changes. For example, Lamb et al. (2002) suggested that the demands imposed by the educational system tended to make children become more conscientious throughout their childhoods, and perhaps a similar suggestion could be offered for Agreeableness. However, these results are based on only one investigation, and future research will be needed to find out whether the results will apply to children in general. The interpretation of these findings is complicated by the fact that the personality trait scales had low reliabilities during the early periods, especially Extraversion and Openness to Experience. This low reliability might reflect one of the difficulties in examining developmental change in children's personality: Because children's personalities are expressed in terms of different behaviors as they grow older, it might not be possible to assess personality by using reports of the same behaviors at different ages.

4.4.3 Stability of Traits During Childhood

Now let us turn to the question of whether there is personality trait stability throughout childhood: Do children who have high levels of a given characteristic at one age (relative to their same-age peers) tend to maintain those high levels at some later age (again, relative to their same-age peers)? This question was also examined in the study by Lamb et al. (2002), who measured children's personalities at five intervals beginning at the age of 2 years and ending at the age of 15 years. Lamb et al. found that personality was rather stable between adjacent intervals (i.e., between 2 and 3 years old, between 3 and 6 years old, between 6 and 8 years old, and between 8 and 15 years old), with most correlations above .50 for each of the Big Five factors. However, over the much longer period between the beginning and the end of the study—a total interval of 13 years—the children's personalities were less stable, with correlations only about .20 for each of the Big Five factors.

These results probably underestimate the stability of personality trait levels, because the personality assessments of very young children in that study were not very reliable. Nevertheless, there does appear to be some considerable shifting in the relative levels of personality characteristics between toddlerhood and adolescence; for example, a toddler who is relatively talkative (or anxious, or cautious, etc.) might become an adolescent who is relatively quiet (or calm, or impulsive, etc.). The results of the Lamb et al. (2002) study suggest that the changes tend to be gradual, as personality was generally fairly stable across each of the shorter intervals (a few years each) within that study.

More recently, Neppl et al. (2010) reported another study of the stability of temperament or personality in childhood. In this investigation, the authors studied about 250 children in the United States. Parents provided reports of the temperament or personality characteristics of their children first during toddlerhood (2 years old), then during early childhood (3—5 years old), and finally during middle childhood (6—10 years old). The researchers found that stability between toddlerhood and early childhood was moderate (correlations about .35 on average), but that stability between early childhood and middle childhood was rather high (correlations above .60 on average). Taking these results together, the stability between toddlerhood and middle childhood was quite modest, which is consistent with the findings of the study by Lamb et al. noted earlier.

The findings of rather limited stability of personality in childhood raise some interesting questions for future research. For example, do children's early experiences with their peers and their teachers, as encountered in elementary school, have an important influence on the development of their personalities? Or, do the differences in development result mainly from genetic influences that may become stronger at different points during childhood? We will examine some related questions about genetic and environmental influences on personality a bit later in this book, in Chapter 6.

4.4.4 Stability of Traits Between Childhood and Adulthood

Many studies have examined the stability of personality during adulthood, and some studies have examined the stability of personality during childhood. But fewer studies have examined the stability of personality *between* childhood and adulthood.

One research study that did examine this question was that of Hampson and Goldberg (2006). In this investigation, the authors used some data that had been collected in Hawaiian elementary schools, mainly during the early 1960s, by a researcher named John Digman. In Digman's study, the personalities of more than 2000 children of elementary school age were rated by their teachers. When Hampson and Goldberg conducted their research about 40 years later, they were able to locate most of those former elementary school students, who were by now in middle age. The researchers then assessed the personalities of 800 of these people, by obtaining self-reports on personality variables similar to those assessed by teacher ratings during childhood. Hampson and Goldberg interpreted their results in terms of the Big Five personality factors. They found that levels of stability between childhood and middle age were moderate for Extraversion and Conscientiousness (correlations above .25), close to zero for Neuroticism, and in between for Agreeableness and Openness to Experience.

These results suggest that there is only a weak degree of stability between childhood and adulthood in the personality differences among people. However, the true level of stability is likely at least slightly higher than the values mentioned earlier, because of some inaccuracy in the assessment of the children's personalities. The teachers who rated the children might not have been able to observe accurately all aspects of their personalities, and to the extent that the teacher ratings were somewhat inaccurate, this would make the stability appear to be low. (As Hampson and Goldberg noted, this concern about the validity of teacher ratings might be particularly relevant for Neuroticism, which showed essentially a zero correlation between childhood and adulthood.) Still, the findings of this unique study suggest that the stability of personality between childhood and adulthood could be rather weak, and that different aspects of personality might differ in their levels of stability.

The study by Hampson and Goldberg examined a wide array of characteristics, but other studies have focused on one trait only. Huesmann, Dubow, and Boxer (2009) conducted a 40-year longitudinal study that examined the links of childhood aggressiveness with various outcomes in adulthood. When the research participants were 8 years old, their levels of aggressiveness were assessed using a "peer nomination" procedure in which the children were asked to indicate which classmates did a variety of aggressive acts (e.g., pushing and shoving, saying mean things, taking others' possessions). In this way, each child's level of aggressiveness was estimated by taking the overall proportion of times that he or she was nominated by his or her classmates. A similar procedure was used at a follow-up assessment 11 years later, when the participants were 19 years old; at that time, participants also completed some self-report measures of aggressive behavior and aggressive personality characteristics. These latter measures were again used in further follow-up assessments, when the participants were 30 years old and again when they were 48 years old. In this way, the researchers estimated each participant's level of aggressiveness at four time periods across a period of 40 years. (There were over 800 participants in the original sample, representing 38 classrooms. Data from at least two of the four time points was available for most participants, but data from all four time points were available for only about one-quarter of the participants.)

One of the main findings of the Huesmann et al. (2009) study was that levels of aggression were moderately stable across the 40-year period, even though the initial measurements were made when participants were children. The correlation between aggressiveness levels at age 8 and 48 was about .50 (for male participants) or .40 (for female participants). Although some participants were high in aggressiveness at one time point only, most participants tended either to be high in aggressiveness at all four time points or to be low in aggressiveness at all four time points. This finding of fairly high stability for aggressiveness between childhood and adulthood contrasts with the much lower levels of stability found by Hampson and Goldberg.

The other main finding of the Huesmann et al. study was that the participants who were consistently high in aggressiveness across the various time periods tended to show more unfavorable life outcomes in middle age. On average, they were more likely to be arrested, to commit traffic violations, to get divorced, to be depressed, to drink excessively, and to have lower levels of health, occupational attainment, and educational attainment. In contrast, the participants who were high in aggressiveness only at age 8 or only at age 19 years generally did not show higher levels of most of these outcomes; however, the participants who developed a high level of aggressiveness later on (by age 30 years) did show higher levels of several unfavorable outcomes. (In Chapter 9, we will examine the relation of personality to life outcomes in much more detail.)

A study by Mischel, Shoda, and Peake (1988) also focused on a single trait in childhood, that of "delay of gratification." But instead of examining the stability of delay of gratification itself, those researchers tried to find out how delay of gratification in childhood would be related to a variety of characteristics in adolescence. Mischel et al. assessed the willingness of 4- and 5-year-old children to delay gratification, using a behavioral test (i.e., a form of direct observation in an artificial setting). Specifically, the experimenter showed each child two marshmallows (very desirable treats for these children) and told the child that the experimenter had to leave the room. The experimenter also told the child that if he or she could wait until the experimenter came back into the room, then he or she could have both marshmallows, but that he or she could instead decide at any time just to take one marshmallow. The average time taken before a child took a marshmallow was about 9 minutes, but there were large differences between children: Some of them took a marshmallow after only a few seconds, whereas others waited the entire duration of the experimenter's absence (15 minutes). Each child's delay of gratification score was counted as the time taken before he or she took the marshmallow (or before the experimenter returned, in the case of children who waited the full 15 minutes).

Mischel et al. (1988) then assessed the personalities of the participants about 11 years later, when they were 15 years old. For each participant, ratings of a variety of his or her personality characteristics were made by the participant's mother or father (or, in most cases, by both parents). Mischel et al. found that the participants who had longer delay-of-gratification scores as 4- or 5-year-old children tended to be rated by their parents as being more socially competent, more academically competent, more verbally fluent, better able to deal with frustration and stress, and more attentive, playful, and rational. (The correlations for these ratings ranged in size from the .20s to the .40s.) Thus, delay of gratification in childhood was associated with a wide array of characteristics and outcomes in adolescence. These results suggest that delay of gratification might reflect the combined action of several characteristics, including personality dimensions such as Conscientiousness or Emotional Stability as well as intelligence or mental ability.

4.5 SUMMARY AND CONCLUSIONS

In this chapter we considered the patterns of developmental change and stability in personality characteristics. The main points can be summarized as follows. First, with regard to mean-level change in personality trait levels, results from cross-sectional studies have generally been similar to findings from longitudinal studies, and this suggests that the cross-sectional results probably do reflect developmental change in personality. Those results suggest that Honesty—Humility decreases somewhat during the teenage years but then increases throughout adulthood. The results also suggest that for each of the other personality factors, the patterns of age-related change differ for the various "facet" traits within a factor. For example, although most traits within the Extraversion factor increase throughout adulthood, sociability actually decreases somewhat; likewise, although most traits within the Conscientiousness increase throughout adulthood, perfectionism does not.

With regard to the stability of individual differences among adults of the same age cohort, there are generally very strong correlations between levels of any given personality trait at two intervals several years apart. When much longer intervals of two or more decades are considered, these stability correlations become lower, but remain fairly high. In general, individual differences in personality characteristics are more stable after young adulthood (during and after the 30s) than during adolescence or young adulthood.

The study of personality during childhood presents some serious challenges to the researcher. This is particularly true of the earliest years, when the range of behaviors by which children express their personalities is much less varied than it is during later childhood, adolescence, or adulthood. For the same reason, comparisons between personality in early childhood and personality in later periods are difficult to undertake. Research thus far suggests that among children, the structure of personality characteristics is similar to what is observed among adults, but it is not yet clear whether this will be the case among very young children. Little research has been conducted thus far to determine the typical changes in levels of personality characteristics as children develop, but one study has suggested modest decreases in Extraversion and modest increases in Big Five Agreeableness and Conscientiousness during childhood. Results from the same study and from a more recent study suggest that children's personalities, in the sense of individual differences among children of the same age cohort, are fairly stable across a period of a few years, but show only weak stability across the entire span of childhood. Other studies suggest that between childhood and adulthood, the stability of personality trait levels is fairly low; however, some isolated studies of particular traits (e.g., aggressiveness) suggest higher levels of stability. Our knowledge of personality in childhood and its relations with personality in later life remains limited, but will be improved as the results of future investigations become known.

CHAPTER 5

Biological Bases of Personality

Contents

More than 2000 years ago, the philosophers of ancient Greece suspected that personality was influenced by various fluids in the body. Today, researchers have made systematic efforts to understand the biological basis of personality, by studying substances such as neurotransmitters and hormones and also by studying the workings of the brain itself. In this chapter, we will take a quick look at the very early ideas about biological variables thought to underlie personality variation. We will then examine the recent theories that have been proposed to explain how personality variation might be influenced by various substances and brain structures, and we will discuss some of the research that has attempted to evaluate and to refine those theories.

Individual Differences and Personality
ISBN 978-0-12-809845-5, http://dx.doi.org/10.1016/B978-0-12-809845-5.00005-6

5.1 EARLY IDEAS: THE FOUR "HUMORS" AND PERSONALITY

Ancient Greek thinkers believed that one's personality, or temperament, depended on the strengths of various fluids, or "humors," in one's body. According to the Greek physicians Hippocrates and (later) Galen, there were four main humors, each of which was responsible for a particular pattern of personality (and also of susceptibility to disease). One of these humors was blood, an excess of which was thought to produce a very cheerful ("sanguine") temperament. Another was black bile, which in excess was believed to cause a depressive ("melancholic") temperament. An excess of the humor called yellow bile was considered responsible for an angry ("choleric") temperament. And an excess of the remaining humor, phlegm, was seen as the basis of a calm ("phlegmatic") temperament. But there is no evidence that any of these ideas is accurate, and the ancient Greeks themselves did not do any empirical research to find out whether the levels of these bodily humors were actually related to personality characteristics.

Nevertheless, the idea of the four humors or temperaments remained popular during medieval times, and was influential even in the modern era. One researcher who tried to interpret his own observations in terms of the four temperaments was the famous Russian psychologist and physiologist, Ivan Pavlov. Although Pavlov is famous chiefly for his discovery of classical conditioning, he was also interested in temperament. In observing the dogs of his laboratory, Pavlov suggested that there were four basic kinds of temperaments in those dogs, and he believed that there were parallels between dogs and people. According to Pavlov, the four kinds of dogs' temperaments were as follows:

Weak: inhibited, anxious, easily upset (similar to melancholic);

Strong unbalanced: excitable, hyperactive, irritable (similar to choleric);

Strong balanced slow: calm, consistent, not easily aroused (similar to phlegmatic);

Strong balanced mobile: lively, fast, eager (similar to sanguine).

Pavlov did not try to study these four temperament types in people, but in recent decades some researchers have done so, developing self-report questionnaire scales for this purpose (Strelau, Angleitner, Bantelmann, & Ruch, 1990). In general, the results suggest that there is some similarity between the characteristics of Pavlov's temperament dimensions and the characteristics associated with the four humors (Ruch, 1992). However, these results do not provide any indication as to what might be the biological causes of these personality differences. But as we will see later in this chapter, other researchers have proposed some possible biological bases for personality dimensions, and have even conducted experiments to test those hypotheses.

Now that we have considered some of the early history of ideas regarding the biological bases of personality, we can next consider some of the more recent theories and investigations that have dealt with the same topic. In the remainder of this chapter, we will review research on the potential biological causes of personality characteristics, with attention to neurotransmitters, brain structures, and hormones.

BOX 5.1 Physique and Personality

Some early proposals of a biological basis for personality were based on the idea that an individual's physique, or body type, could be related to his or her personality characteristics. In 1925, a German psychiatrist, Ernst Kretschmer, suggested that there were three basic types of physiques: pyknic (fat), athletic (muscular), and asthenic (thin). On the basis of his clinical observations, Kretschmer (1925) suggested that manic-depressive patients tended to have pyknic physiques, and that schizophrenic patients tended to have asthenic physiques. However, Kretschmer did not conduct any research to find out whether or not these observations were accurate, and later research did not support his suggestions (Cabot, 1938).

Nevertheless, some of Kretschmer's ideas were adopted by an American researcher, William Sheldon, who suggested that each person's physique could be described as a combination of the three basic types suggested by Kretschmer. Sheldon (1940) referred to the three physiques as "somatotypes," and used different names for them: endomorph (fat), mesomorph (muscular), and ectomorph (thin). (These names referred to different layers of cells in the human embryo; according to Sheldon, the endomorphic physique emphasized the digestive system, the mesomorphic physique emphasized the circulatory system, and the ectomorphic physique emphasized the skin and the nervous system.) In Sheldon's proposal, an endomorphic physique was associated with traits such as cheerfulness, sociability, relaxedness, love of comfort and luxury, and indulgence in food and drink. The mesomorphic physique, by contrast, was associated with traits such as dominance, activity level, assertiveness, and adventurousness. Finally, the ectomorphic physique was associated with traits such as nervousness, shyness, sensitivity, and intellectuality.

Sheldon did conduct some research to examine the links between somatotype and personality, and he found some extremely strong relations. For example, Sheldon (1942) reported correlations of about .80 between endomorphic physical characteristics and the personality characteristics that were supposed to be associated with endomorphy; similarly strong relations were observed for the other body types and their presumed personality characteristics. These values are amazingly strong and would suggest that the link between somatotype and personality is almost perfect. However, there was a major problem with Sheldon's research: It was Sheldon himself who assessed the personality characteristics of his research participants, after having first observed the body types of those persons. This leaves the possibility that Sheldon's ratings of the participants' personalities might have been influenced by his knowledge of their body type. When this bias is removed, by conducting studies in which the assessments of body type and personality are made by different raters, the relations are much weaker, with correlations only in the .20s (Child, 1950). Thus, it appears that there may be some links between body type and personality, but that these relations are quite modest in size. However, there has been very little recent research on this topic, and it will be interesting to see the results of future studies that might examine the relations of various physical characteristics (height, muscle mass, fat mass, etc.) with the major personality dimensions.

5.2 NEUROTRANSMITTERS

Much modern research on the biological basis of personality has focused on substances known as *neurotransmitters*. These biochemical substances are involved in the communication among nerve cells or *neurons*. Specifically, neurotransmitters can act in such a way as to speed up the communication of messages from one neuron to the next, or to slow down that communication. Because this sending of messages—the "firing" of neurons—is the basis of our emotions, our thoughts, and our behaviors, the levels of the substances that influence these messages might be important in influencing one's personality.

Let us consider for a moment how the neurotransmitters work. First, imagine two neurons, one of which sends (or transmits) messages to the other (see Fig. 5.1). The messages are sent as electrical impulses that travel down a very long, thin segment, called an *axon*, of the sending (or transmitting) neuron. When these impulses reach the end of the axon (called the axon terminal), they then cause some molecules of the neurotransmitter substance to be released from the axon terminal and into the space, called the *synapse*, between the two neurons. These neurotransmitter molecules are then absorbed by the receiving neuron at a segment called the *dendrite*. Depending on which neurotransmitter is involved, these molecules can either facilitate the sending of an electrical impulse by the receiving neuron to the next neuron in the chain, or inhibit the receiving neuron from sending that message.

5.2.1 Cloninger's Theory

In discussing the role of neurotransmitters in personality variation, we will focus on three neurotransmitters that are active in the brain and the spinal cord—the areas known as the *central nervous system*. (Other neurotransmitters are active in the *peripheral nervous system*, which extends throughout all of the remaining parts of the body.) We will discuss these neurotransmitters—dopamine, serotonin, and norepinephrine—in the context of a theory proposed by the American psychiatrist Robert Cloninger (e.g., Cloninger, 1987; Cloninger, Svrakic, & Przybeck, 1993) regarding the relations between neurotransmitters and personality dimensions (see Table 5.1).[1]

5.2.1.1 Dopamine and Novelty Seeking

Dopamine is a neurotransmitter that facilitates the transmission of signals of reward. In other words, dopamine helps your neurons to send messages in response to things that feel pleasurable or exciting. Cloninger has suggested that this neurotransmitter is therefore implicated in personality characteristics related to one's response to pleasure

---

[1] Note that the personality dimensions described by Cloninger do not match those discussed in Chapter 3, such as the Big Five or HEXACO dimensions; instead, Cloninger's dimensions generally represent combinations of two or more of those factors.

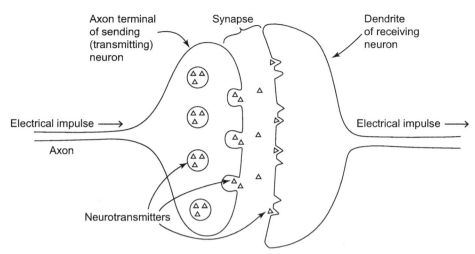

Figure 5.1 *The role of neurotransmitters in nerve cell communication.* An electrical impulse travels through the axon of the sending (transmitting) neuron, stimulating the release of neurotransmitter chemicals into the space between the two neurons (the synapse). The neurotransmitters are then absorbed by the receiving neuron, and make that neuron either more likely or less likely to send an electrical impulse to the next neuron.

Table 5.1 Summary of Cloninger's theory of neurotransmitters and personality

Neurotransmitter	Function of neurotransmitter	Personality dimension
Dopamine	Facilitates response to pleasurable, exciting stimuli	Novelty Seeking (excitability, impulsiveness, extravagance, disorderliness)
Serotonin	Inhibits response to harmful, unpleasant stimuli	Harm Avoidance (worry/ pessimism, fear, shyness, fatigability)
Norepinephrine	Inhibits response to stimuli that have previously been associated with pleasure	Reward Dependence (sentimentality, warm communication, dependence)

According to Cloninger's theory, high levels of dopamine are associated with high levels of Novelty Seeking, high levels of serotonin are associated with low levels of Harm Avoidance, and high levels of norepinephrine are associated with low levels of Reward Dependence.

Based on Cloninger, C.R. (1987). A systematic method for clinical description and classification of personality disorders: a proposal. *Archives of General Psychiatry*, 44, 573–588; Cloninger, C.R., Svrakic, D.M., & Przybeck, T.R. (1993). A psychobiological model of temperament and character. *Archives of General Psychiatry*, 50, 975–990.

and excitement. According to Cloninger, individuals whose dopamine system is very active will tend to have high levels of a personality dimension that he calls "Novelty Seeking"—the tendency to seek pleasure and excitement. This dimension is seen in traits that Cloninger calls *exploratory excitability, impulsiveness, extravagance,* and *disorderliness.*

Conversely, individuals whose dopamine system is very inactive will tend to be low in Novelty Seeking; that is, they will not be particularly motivated to find fun and variety.

When the dopamine system is either extremely underactivated or extremely overactivated, there can be some important effects on levels of Novelty Seeking–related traits. For example, persons who suffer from Parkinson's disease have an extremely inactive dopamine system, and these individuals display a marked lack of interest in new things, in fun activities, or in their environment more generally (and, even more strikingly, they display very slow, uncoordinated movements). At the opposite end, persons who use cocaine feel extremely aroused and stimulated while under the influence of that highly addictive drug, which increases dopamine activity and Novelty Seeking behavior.

5.2.1.2 Serotonin and Harm Avoidance

Serotonin is a neurotransmitter that inhibits the transmission of signals of punishment. In other words, serotonin tends to prevent your neurons from sending messages in response to things that feel harmful or unpleasant. Cloninger has suggested that this neurotransmitter is therefore implicated in personality characteristics related to one's response to pain and anxiety. According to Cloninger, individuals whose serotonin system is very *inactive* will tend to have high levels of a personality dimension that he calls "Harm Avoidance"—the tendency to avoid pain and anxiety. This dimension is seen in traits that Cloninger calls *worry/pessimism*, *fear of uncertainty*, *shyness with strangers*, and *fatigability*. Conversely, individuals whose serotonin system is very active will tend to be low in Harm Avoidance; that is, they will not be particularly motivated to avoid pain and anxiety (at least, not as much as other people are).

The links between the serotonin system and Harm Avoidance can be seen in the effects of antidepressant drugs. These drugs act to keep serotonin molecules in action, allowing those molecules to continue inhibiting the transmission of punishment signals. As a result, persons who take these drugs tend to experience a reduction in negative emotions such as anxiety and depression. (The side effects of those drugs are still being studied, however.)

5.2.1.3 Norepinephrine and Reward Dependence

Norepinephrine, also known as noradrenaline, is a neurotransmitter that inhibits the transmission of signals of *conditioned* reward—that is, of signals in response to stimuli that in the past have been associated with reward. Cloninger has suggested that this neurotransmitter is therefore implicated in personality characteristics related to one's response to people and things that have tended to be associated with pleasure. According to Cloninger, individuals whose norepinephrine system is very *inactive* will tend to have high levels of a personality dimension that he calls "Reward Dependence"—the tendency to develop strong sentimental attachments. This dimension is seen in traits that Cloninger calls *sentimentality*, *warm communication*, and *dependence*. Conversely, individuals whose norepinephrine system is very active will tend to be low in Reward Dependence; that is, they will tend not to develop strong sentimental attachments.

5.2.1.4 Empirical Tests of Cloninger's Theory

In recent years there have been several investigations aimed at testing Cloninger's model of the relations between neurotransmitters and personality. Typically, the strategy used in these studies has been to identify people who have different alleles (varieties) of a gene that influences the activity of one of the neurotransmitters. The people who have one of the alleles are then compared with the people who have a different allele, to find out whether or not there are any differences in the average levels of personality traits that Cloninger has hypothesized to be influenced by these neurotransmitters. According to Cloninger's model, people having different alleles of a gene that regulates a given neurotransmitter should differ in their levels of the personality traits that are hypothesized to be influenced by that neurotransmitter.

So far, the results of these studies have been mixed. Sometimes, the results are consistent with Cloninger's model, but sometimes they are not. One study (Comings et al., 2000) examined a large number of genes, including 7 that influence dopamine, 12 that influence serotonin, and 9 that influence norepinephrine. The results showed that each set of genes tended to be related to more than one of Cloninger's personality dimensions. Overall, Reward Dependence was more strongly related to norepinephrine genes than to the other genes; to a lesser extent, a parallel result was found for Harm Avoidance and serotonin genes. However, Novelty Seeking was not more strongly related to dopamine genes than to other genes. This pattern of results is partly consistent with Cloninger's model, but the correspondences are not as neat as one might have hoped. Nevertheless, Cloninger's theory remains a pioneering attempt to understand the links between neurotransmitter activity and personality.

5.3 BRAIN STRUCTURES

In addition to the study of neurotransmitters, another way to learn about the biological basis of personality is to examine various structures within the brain. Some researchers have suggested that personality might be influenced by the extent to which the brain performs certain functions, each of which would involve some complex interaction among different regions of the brain.

5.3.1 Gray's Theory

One influential theory of the relation between brain structures and personality variation has been the *reinforcement sensitivity theory* of Jeffrey Gray, who conducted much research on the biological basis of animal behavior. Gray (1981, 1987) suggested that certain regions of the brain work together as mechanisms or systems that underlie personality.

According to Gray, differences among people in the activity of these systems are the basis of important personality dimensions. Two of the systems identified by Gray on the basis of his research are called the Behavioral Activation System and the Behavioral Inhibition System. As you will see from the following descriptions, these two systems are conceptually very similar to two of Cloninger's dimensions as described in Section 5.2.

5.3.1.1 The Behavioral Activation System

The Behavioral Activation System, as described by Gray, involves regions of the brain that are responsible for receiving signals from the nervous system which indicate that rewards are being experienced (or are about to be experienced). This system can be called a "go" system, as it encourages the pursuit of rewards, by transmitting signals within the brain to communicate the pleasurable and exciting nature of those rewards. In Gray's model, people differ in the extent to which their Behavioral Activation System, or go system, is sensitive to reward stimuli: The stronger or more sensitive one's go system is, the more one tends to pursue rewards. As a result, people differ in their tendency to be impulsive and to seek pleasure and excitement. This trait of impulsivity, as described by Gray, is therefore similar conceptually to the Novelty Seeking dimension as described by Cloninger (whose work was influenced by that of Gray). The difference between the perspectives of Gray and Cloninger is that Gray focuses more on the role of brain structures in governing these traits, whereas Cloninger focuses more on the role of neurotransmitters (in this case, dopamine). Note, however, that the correlations between scales measuring the Behavioral Activation System and Novelty Seeking are only modest in size (see Carver & White, 1994; Zelenski & Larsen, 1999).

5.3.1.2 The Behavioral Inhibition System

The Behavioral Inhibition System, as described by Gray, involves regions of the brain that are responsible for receiving signals from the nervous system which indicate that punishments are being experienced (or may soon be experienced). This system can be called a "stop" system, as it encourages the avoidance of punishments, by transmitting signals within the brain to communicate the painful and frightening nature of those punishments. In Gray's model, people differ in the extent to which their Behavioral Inhibition System, or stop system, is sensitive to punishment stimuli: The stronger or more sensitive one's stop system is, the more one tends to avoid punishments. As a result, people differ in their tendency to be anxious and to avoid pain and danger. This trait of anxiety, as described by Gray, is therefore similar conceptually to the Harm Avoidance dimension described by Cloninger (partly on the basis of Gray's earlier work). (Scales measuring the Behavioral Inhibition System and Harm Avoidance are fairly strongly correlated with each other; see Carver & White, 1994; Zelenski & Larsen, 1999.) As was the case for the go system earlier, the difference between the perspectives of Gray and Cloninger is that Gray focuses more on the role of brain structures in governing these traits, whereas Cloninger focuses more on the role of neurotransmitters (in this case, serotonin).

5.3.1.3 The Fight-or-Flight System

In addition to the "go" and "stop" systems described, Gray also suggested a third system that is also responsible for an important dimension of personality. The third system proposed by Gray is referred to as a "Fight-or-Flight" system, and involves regions of the brain that are responsible for motivating extreme reactions—fighting and/or fleeing—in response to extremely threatening situations. According to Gray, people differ in the extent to which their "Fight-or-Flight" system is sensitive to these extremely threatening situations: The stronger or more sensitive one's Fight-or-Flight system is, the more ready one is to fight or to flee when an emergency situation arises. (Be careful, because this can be confusing: This third system is *not* a dimension of fighting vs. fleeing, but rather a dimension of *being ready to fight or to flee* in response to extreme dangers.) As a result, people differ in their tendency to show extreme reactions, such as responding aggressively or leaving hurriedly, when confronted with situations that appear potentially threatening. It is possible that low levels of this Fight-or-Flight system might have some link with Cloninger's third dimension, Reward Dependence, which involved traits such as sentimentality, dependence, and warmth. Some researchers have suggested that the latter traits represent a response to threat that is an alternative to Fight-or-Flight (see Taylor et al., 2000), but there is not yet any empirical evidence that traits associated with Fight-or-Flight are negatively related to traits associated with Reward Dependence.

5.3.2 Eysenck's Theory

The theory proposed by Gray was in some ways a modification of an earlier theory by Hans Eysenck. During World War II, Eysenck worked in clinical psychology at military hospitals in England. Based on his observations of individual differences in the personalities of the soldiers whom he treated, he proposed a theory involving two major dimensions of personality, called Extraversion and Neuroticism (Eysenck, 1947). Later, Eysenck added a third dimension, which he called Psychoticism (Eysenck & Eysenck, 1968; Eysenck, 1970), and modified somewhat his ideas regarding the earlier two dimensions. A summary of Eysenck's theory in its revised form is given as follows.

5.3.2.1 Extraversion

Eysenck's observations led him to believe that one of the fundamental differences among people involved the strength of their reactions to stimulation of their senses—in other words, the arousability of their brains. According to Eysenck, some people are very sensitive to stimuli, and, as a result, these people tend to feel uncomfortable with strong sensations, and instead prefer a low level of stimulation. In contrast, Eysenck said, some people are much less sensitive to stimuli, and, consequently, these people tend to feel bored by a low level of stimulation, and instead prefer to experience strong sensations. This dimension of differences was described by Eysenck as Extraversion (versus Introversion). At one extreme, very extraverted people tend to seek stimulation, and therefore enjoy bright colors, loud noises, and other sensations; these extraverts enjoy meeting and interacting with lots of people, for example at parties. At the other extreme, introverted people tend to avoid stimulation, and therefore prefer quieter surroundings; these introverts would prefer to be alone or with a few others rather than to attend parties or other large social gatherings.

Eysenck believed that individual differences in Extraversion were governed by a brain mechanism that he called the ascending reticular activating system (ARAS). In Eysenck's model, this system is located in the brain stem, where the spinal cord meets the brain itself. The ARAS works as a kind of filter that regulates the amount of stimulation that is admitted to the brain from the nervous system, which receives stimulation from the environment. To the extent that one's ARAS admits little stimulation, one feels underaroused and thus seeks stimulation, producing an extraverted personality. Conversely, to the extent that one's ARAS admits a great deal of stimulation, one feels overaroused and thus avoids stimulation, producing an introverted personality.

5.3.2.2 Neuroticism

Eysenck's research also suggested to him that another fundamental difference among people involved the strength of their reactions to stressful stimuli. Eysenck observed that some people are very sensitive to stress, and therefore tend to experience fear and anxiety. At the opposite pole, Eysenck noticed, some people are much less sensitive to stress, and therefore experience rather little fear and anxiety. This dimension of differences was described by Eysenck as Neuroticism (versus Emotional Stability). At one extreme, very neurotic people feel a great deal of worry and nervousness in response to life's problems; at the other extreme, emotionally stable people feel little of the negative emotions that are caused by life's stresses.

Eysenck believed that individual differences in Neuroticism were governed by segments of the brain belonging to what is called the limbic system. One of the functions of the brain's limbic system is to regulate responses to stress. To the extent that one's limbic system tends to be overwhelmed by stressful stimuli, one tends to have a neurotic personality; conversely, to the extent that one's limbic system is able to handle those stresses, one tends to have a stable personality.

5.3.2.3 Psychoticism

Finally, Eysenck also suggested a third major dimension of personality, which he called Psychoticism. According to Eysenck, this dimension included traits such as aggressiveness, manipulation, tough mindedness, risk taking, irresponsibility, and impulsivity versus their opposites.[2] He suggested that high levels of Psychoticism were associated with criminal behavior, but also with various mental illnesses (including manic depressiveness

---

[2] Eysenck here used "impulsivity" in the sense of poor control of impulses. This is different from Gray's use of "impulsivity" as spontaneity or novelty seeking.

and schizophrenia) and even with creativity. As far as the biological basis of the Psychoticism dimension is concerned, Eysenck suggested that persons high in Psychoticism tended to have high levels of the hormone called testosterone (see later in this chapter for a discussion of hormones) and low levels of a substance called monoamine oxidase, which influences the levels of neurotransmitters.

5.3.3 Comparing Gray's and Eysenck's Dimensions

In reading the descriptions of the dimensions proposed by Gray and Eysenck, you might have noticed some strong similarities between them. It was previously believed that the relations between these dimensions were somewhat complicated. Gray (1987) had suggested that Eysenck's Extraversion was a blend of high Impulsivity and low Anxiety, and that Eysenck's Neuroticism was a blend of high Impulsivity and high Anxiety. But more recent research based on self-report scales measuring the two sets of dimensions has suggested that the relations, although not particularly strong, might actually be rather simple: Gray's Behavioral Activation System (i.e., Impulsivity, or the go system) is related to Eysenck's Extraversion, and Gray's Behavioral Inhibition System (i.e., Anxiety, or the stop system) is related to Eysenck's Neuroticism (Carver & White, 1994; Zelenski & Larsen, 1999). With regard to the third dimension, some researchers have suggested that Gray's "Fight-or-Flight" is similar to Eysenck's Psychoticism, but this similarity is more difficult to examine, given the lack of detail about the traits associated with Gray's third dimension.[3]

5.3.4 Empirical Evidence and the Theories of Gray and Eysenck

Many research studies have been conducted to test the theories of Gray and Eysenck. Of these studies, a few have been intended to compare the relative accuracy of the two theories, but the results have not been conclusive (Rusting & Larsen, 1999). Many more investigations have been focused on investigating Eysenck's idea that the Extraversion versus Introversion dimension reflects individual differences in the arousability of the brain. Two of these investigations—one rather simple, and the other more complex—are described next.

One classic study (Eysenck & Eysenck, 1967) was based on the "lemon juice test," in which the researchers dropped small amounts of lemon juice onto the tongues of the research participants, and then measured the amounts of saliva that each participant

[3] In addition to the three-dimensional models of Gray and Eysenck, another set of three biologically based dimensions has been proposed by Tellegen (e.g., 2016). Tellegen's dimensions, which are assessed by the Multidimensional Personality Questionnaire (see Chapter 2), are known as Positive Emotionality, Negative Emotionality, and Constraint. Positive Emotionality is similar to Eysenck's Extraversion and to Gray's Behavioral Activation System. Negative Emotionality is similar to Eysenck's Neuroticism and Gray's Behavioral Inhibition System. Constraint is less clearly related to the third dimensions of Eysenck's and Gray's systems, but has some aspects in common with the low pole of Eysenck's Psychoticism.

produced in response. According to Eysenck's theory, the stimulation produced by the lemon juice would tend to be perceived more strongly by introverted participants than by extraverted participants, and therefore would elicit (on average) more salivation from the introverts than from the extraverts. This is indeed what was found: The participants who were more introverted (as measured by Eysenck's self-report questionnaire) tended to produce the greatest amounts of saliva in response to the lemon juice.[4]

In another study, Geen (1984) identified persons who had above-average levels or below-average levels of Extraversion, on the basis of their self-report questionnaire responses. He then assigned these "extraverts" and "introverts" to complete a learning task while being exposed to noises, and he measured the heart rates of the participants as they performed the task. In this study, some of the participants were allowed to choose the loudness of the noise. According to Eysenck's theory, the more extraverted participants would tend to choose the louder noises, because those persons would prefer the higher level of stimulation provided by loud noise; in contrast, introverted persons would prefer a lower level of stimulation, and hence a quieter noise. Geen's results confirmed this expectation. Moreover, when exposed to their preferred levels of noise, the extraverts and introverts had similar heart rates, which suggested that the quieter noises were as stimulating for introverts as the louder noises were for extraverts.

But there is more to Geen's (1984) study: Some participants did not get to choose the loudness of the noise to which they were exposed while performing the word-learning task; instead, a given loudness level was assigned to them. Some participants were assigned the louder noises (i.e., the levels typically chosen by extraverted persons), and some were assigned the quieter noises (i.e., the levels typically chosen by introverted persons). Note that some of the participants who were assigned loud noises were extraverts, and that some were introverts; similarly, the participants who were assigned quiet noises also represented a mix of extraverts and introverts. Geen measured the participants' heart rates as they performed the task under the noise conditions that they were assigned. According to Eysenck's theory, one would expect that introverts (but not extraverts) would have particularly high heart rates when exposed to loud noises (as a result of feeling overstimulated by the noise), whereas extraverts (but not introverts) would have particularly low heart rates when exposed to quiet noises (as a result of feeling understimulated by the noise).

The results found by Geen (1984) were consistent with this hypothesis. When loud noise levels were assigned, introverted participants had high heart rates, whereas extraverts had heart rates similar to those of participants who had chosen their own noise

---

[4] In the years since the Eysenck and Eysenck (1967) study, some researchers have conducted similar experiments. Sometimes the results have been similar, but sometimes there has been little or no tendency for introverted people to salivate more. In any case, the lemon juice test is unlikely to give a highly accurate estimate of a person's level of Extraversion. To measure people's levels of that trait, a self- or observer report questionnaire scale will be more valid (and less messy) than the lemon juice test.

levels. In contrast, when quiet noise levels were assigned, extraverted participants had low heart rates, whereas introverts had heart rates similar to those of participants who had chosen their own noise levels. Thus, these results suggest that introverts do tend to prefer a lower level of stimulation than do extraverts, and that introverts do tend to react more strongly to a given level of stimulation than do extraverts.

Geen's (1984) study also investigated levels of skin conductance—that is, how well the skin can conduct small amounts of electricity. (The presence of sweat on the skin increases skin conductance, and therefore higher skin conductance suggests more sweating. Because sweating tends to indicate arousal, Geen used skin conductance in assessing how strongly aroused participants were in response to the noise.) The results for skin conductance were parallel to those for heart rate, with introverts showing high skin conductance when noises were loud, and with extraverts showing low skin conductance when noises were quiet. In addition to measuring heart rate and skin conductance, Geen also measured how many trials participants needed to perform the learning task successfully. He found that extraverts performed better than introverts under loud noise conditions (suggesting that the introverts were too highly aroused to perform well), and that introverts performed better than extraverts under quiet noise conditions (suggesting that the extraverts were not aroused highly enough to perform well).

Thus, the results of some laboratory experiments are broadly consistent with Eysenck's theory of the biological basis of Extraversion. However, many other studies have examined the links between Extraversion and the arousal levels of various segments of the brain, and those studies have produced rather complex patterns of results that are only partly consistent with Eysenck's theory (e.g., Zuckerman, 2005). A really clear understanding of the brain structures that underlie personality is yet to be achieved.

5.3.5 Zuckerman's Model

One recent attempt to describe the biological bases of personality characteristics has been that of Marvin Zuckerman (e.g., Zuckerman, 2005; Zuckerman, Kuhlman, & Camac, 1988; Zuckerman, Kuhlman, Joireman, Teta, & Kraft, 1993; Zuckerman, Kuhlman, Thornquist, & Kiers, 1991). In developing his model of the biological bases of personality, Zuckerman did not begin with a theory in which each dimension of personality would be linked directly to a single brain structure or a single neurotransmitter. Instead, Zuckerman and his colleagues conducted factor analyses of a few dozen personality questionnaire scales. Those analyses were based on scales measuring traits that, in Zuckerman's view, would be good candidates to represent basic dimensions of personality or temperament in humans and in other animals. (But recall the problem discussed in Chapter 3: When researchers select sets of personality traits to examine the structure of personality characteristics, some aspects of personality might be over- or underrepresented.)

The results of these analyses (see Zuckerman et al., 1988, 1991, 1993) showed three factors that were similar to Eysenck's Extraversion, Neuroticism, and Psychoticism dimensions. Zuckerman and colleagues also suggested that the scales could alternatively be summarized in terms of five factors: Activity, Sociability, Impulsive Sensation-Seeking, Aggression, and Neuroticism-Anxiety. Some researchers suggested that these five factors could be understood as being combinations of various Big Five factors (Costa & McCrae, 1992a), although the Openness to Experience factor might not be well represented in the "alternative five" factors (see Zuckerman et al., 1993). But in any case, Zuckerman (2005) has suggested that each of the personality dimensions is caused by its own set of complex interactions among brain structures, neurotransmitters, and hormones, and not by any single brain structure or neurotransmitter or hormone. The results of various studies conducted so far—for example, the investigations of neurotransmitter-regulating genes on personality, as described before in Section 5.2.1.4—suggest that the causal bases of personality are indeed likely to be complex. The challenge for future research will be to understand the details of the direct and indirect links between biological variables and personality variables.

BOX 5.2 Some Biological Bases for Conscientiousness?

Some research on the biological basis of personality has been conducted without being based on any theories involving several personality dimensions. For example, some researchers have tried to identify some biological origins of attention deficit/hyperactivity disorder (ADHD). The symptoms of this disorder include inattention, poor impulse control, disorganization, and lack of persistence, and these symptoms correspond closely to the traits that define low levels of Conscientiousness (see Chapter 3). Some of the investigations of ADHD have made use of machines that take pictures of the brain, using a technique called functional magnetic resonance imaging (fMRI). (fMRI measures the activity of various areas of the brain by producing images that show how much glucose is consumed in those brain areas, as glucose is the main "fuel" used by the brain.) Those studies have suggested that adults diagnosed with ADHD show less activity in the areas of the brain that control attention (Zametkin et al., 1990), with the difference between ADHD and non-ADHD adults being more than half of a standard deviation unit in size. Other areas of the brain are also involved in ADHD, and the overall picture is very complex, but these studies suggest that ADHD symptoms—and hence, low levels of Conscientiousness—are associated with reduced activity (i.e., glucose consumption) in regions of the brain responsible for attention. In addition, other studies using fMRI have found that these same areas of the brain tend to be smaller in volume for ADHD-diagnosed people than for people without ADHD (Castellanos et al., 1996).

5.4 HORMONES

Hormones are biological chemicals that are produced in glands of one part of the body, but then transmitted to other parts of the body where they have their effects. Some hormones have effects on the activity of neurons, and thus may influence behavior and personality. Next, we will discuss the possible associations of several hormones—testosterone, cortisol, and oxytocin—with various personality characteristics.

5.4.1 Testosterone

Testosterone is a hormone that is responsible for many of the physical characteristics of men. During the gestation of the fetus, testosterone triggers the development of the male reproductive organs. During puberty, testosterone triggers the development of male secondary sex characteristics, such as hair growth, deepening of the voice, and increased muscle mass. Women do naturally have some testosterone, but men's levels are typically at least 10 times higher. Testosterone is secreted mainly by the testes in men and mainly by the ovaries in women.

Many research studies have examined the question of whether individual differences in testosterone levels—among men and among women—might be related to their personality trait levels. Before we begin reviewing this research, however, there are a couple of important points to note. First, even though testosterone levels tend to be higher in some individuals than in others, those levels can fluctuate across times of day and perhaps as a function of situations, such as competition, sexual activity, and others. Second, it is not only the current levels of testosterone that may influence an individual's personality and behavior, but also the levels of androgens (i.e., testosterone and related hormones) during early periods of development. For example, as we will discuss in Chapter 13, it has been suggested that exposure to androgens during prenatal development is implicated in the development of sexual orientation.

Now back to the question: How do testosterone levels relate to personality trait levels? In other words, do men or women with higher levels of testosterone differ in personality from men or women with lower levels? Several studies have suggested that differences in testosterone levels are associated with differences in behavior, such as rambunctiousness in college fraternity members (e.g., Dabbs, Hargrove, & Heusel, 1996). However, there has been little systematic research aimed at examining testosterone levels in relation to the levels of major personality dimensions. Some recent large-sample research suggests that any links between testosterone and personality may be rather weak: Määttänen et al. (2013) examined testosterone levels and self-reported personality in a sample of about 700 Finnish men, with personality being assessed in terms of Cloninger's dimensions (recall Section 5.2.1). The researchers found that higher levels of testosterone were associated with higher levels of Novelty Seeking, but the association was weak (equivalent to a correlation of about .10). Other personality dimensions were essentially unrelated to testosterone levels. Future research might examine these relations among women as well as among men, and using measures of the Big Five or HEXACO dimensions. But the findings suggest of Määttänen et al. that testosterone levels in adulthood—at least within the ranges that occur naturally among men or among women—are unlikely to be a strong influence on personality trait levels.

5.4.2 Cortisol

Cortisol is a hormone that is released by the adrenal cortex, which is found on the perimeter of the adrenal glands, which in turn are located just above the kidneys. The release of cortisol is triggered by physical or psychological stress. The function of cortisol is to prepare the body for action in response to stress, and among its effects are an increase in blood pressure, an increase in blood sugar, and a suppression of the immune system. As with testosterone levels, researchers have been interested in examining whether individual differences in cortisol levels are associated with personality differences. Some research has suggested that lower cortisol levels may be associated with "callous-unemotional" personality traits in boys but not in girls (Loney, Butler, Lima, Counts, & Eckel, 2006). However, this result remains tentative, as there have not yet been any studies of cortisol/personality links based on large samples and examining the major dimensions of personality.

5.4.3 Oxytocin

Oxytocin is a hormone that is produced in the hypothalamus and released by the pituitary gland. (Both of these glands are located just below the brain, behind the eyes.) In women, oxytocin is released when giving birth, when breastfeeding, and when experiencing orgasm. The psychological effects of oxytocin appear to be associated with emotional bonding, such as that between a mother and her child or between a wife and her husband. Note, however, that men also have oxytocin, and that it may play a similar role in facilitating a man's emotional attachments with his children and with his wife. Because of the role of oxytocin in promoting close attachments with others, researchers have examined whether individual differences in the levels of this hormone are related to personality characteristics.

Some early research (Zak, Kurzban, & Matzner, 2005) suggested that oxytocin levels in the blood were related to trustworthiness and trustingness as assessed in a laboratory decision-making task. However, some subsequent research has not found any association between oxytocin levels and trustworthy or trusting behavior (Christensen, Shiyanov, Estepp, & Schlager, 2014). Thus far, there have not been any large-sample investigations of oxytocin levels in relation to the major personality dimensions.

BOX 5.3 Is Personality Related to Blood Type, Handwriting Style, or Astrological Sign?

Blood type
The possibility of a link between personality and blood type has long been discussed in popular books, particularly in countries of eastern Asia. For example, Furukawa (1930) reported that persons with certain blood types as described by the ABO system tended to have higher levels of certain personality characteristics. In the following decades, several studies reported

BOX 5.3 Is Personality Related to Blood Type, Handwriting Style, or Astrological Sign?—cont'd

links between personality and blood type, although the results tended to be inconsistent. However, several more recent investigations (Cramer & Imaike, 2002; Rogers & Glendon, 2003; Wu, Lindsted, & Lee, 2005) have not found any significant differences between persons having different blood types (i.e., types O, A, B, and AB) in their average self-reported levels of personality characteristics, such as the Big Five dimensions. Thus, the current evidence suggests that there are no strong relations between personality and blood type.

Handwriting style

Possible relations between personality and handwriting style have also received much attention, and in fact "graphology" (the analysis of handwriting) has been used widely as a method of personnel selection by employers in many countries, particularly France and Israel (Edwards & Armitage, 1992). Recently, some efforts have been made to investigate any relations between personality characteristics and features of handwriting. In these studies (e.g., Furnham, Chamorro-Premuzic, & Callahan, 2003; Tett & Palmer, 1997), large samples of participants have had their personalities assessed by self-report questionnaires and have also provided handwriting samples. The handwriting samples have then been evaluated in terms of various features (overall size, size of loops, roundedness versus pointedness, positions and angles of T-crosses, etc.), as judged by individuals who do not know the personality trait levels of the participants. The handwriting features were reliably measured in these studies, as there was a high level of agreement among judges as to the features of a given individual's handwriting. However, there were few significant correlations between those features and any personality characteristics, and those relations often involved features that graphologists had not predicted to be related to personality. Thus, the evidence so far suggests that personality is not strongly related to handwriting features.

Astrological sign

The popularity of horoscopes and of astrology is well known, and one feature of astrology is the idea that persons born at different times of the year will tend to have different personalities, because of the supposed influence of heavenly bodies on these characteristics. A large systematic investigation of the relations between personality and astrological sign was that of Dahlstrom, Hopkins, Dahlstrom, Jackson, and Cumella (1996), who examined the self-report personality characteristics of over 2000 adults whose dates of birth were also recorded. The results showed that there was no relation between astrological sign and any of the diverse personality characteristics that were assessed. That is, persons having a given astrological sign did not differ in their average levels of any traits from persons having any other astrological sign. These results suggest that there are not any strong links between personality and astrological sign. Dahlstrom et al. also examined possible links between personality and the day of the week on which persons were born, and also between personality and the year of birth as given in the Chinese calendar (year of the tiger, year of the snake, etc.). However, the personality characteristics were unrelated both to the day of the week on which persons were born and also to the Chinese calendar year in which persons were born.

5.5 SUMMARY AND CONCLUSIONS

Let us now make a brief overview of the main points of this chapter. First, the idea of a biological basis for personality is very old. Even in the days of ancient Greece, some thinkers speculated that personality might be governed by the amounts of various substances in the body. In modern times, scientists have tried to develop more systematic theories about the biological bases of personality, and to test those theories empirically.

One such attempt to understand the biological origins of personality variation has been that of Cloninger, who proposed that three of the brain's neurotransmitters were involved in influencing three important aspects of personality. In Cloninger's model, dopamine promotes Novelty Seeking, serotonin inhibits Harm Avoidance, and norepinephrine inhibits Reward Dependence. Empirical tests of this model have shown some support for Cloninger's theory, but overall the results have been rather mixed.

Other efforts to determine the biological bases of personality have focused on various structures or regions of the brain. Gray's theory involves dimensions of Impulsivity (roughly similar to Novelty Seeking) and Anxiety (similar to Harm Avoidance), which are thought to be governed by a Behavioral Activation ("go") System and a Behavioral Inhibition ("stop") System, each of which involves its own distinct structures within the brain. An earlier theory by Eysenck was also based on individual differences in the activity of various structures in the brain, and the two original dimensions in Eysenck's theory were similar to the dimensions that were later elaborated by Gray. In Eysenck's system, an Extraversion factor is attributable to individual differences in how easily the brain is stimulated, and a Neuroticism factor is attributable to individual differences in how readily the brain can handle stressful situations. A third dimension was included in both Gray's theory ("Fight-or-Flight") and Eysenck's theory (Psychoticism), but it is not clear how similar those dimensions are to each other or to Cloninger's Reward Dependence dimension. Some empirical tests of the theories of Eysenck and Gray, particularly the aspects of Eysenck's theory concerning Extraversion, have supported some aspects of those theories. More recently, Zuckerman has suggested that the biological bases of personality are likely to be much more complex than might be indicated by the models of Cloninger or Gray or Eysenck.

Other recent research has examined how individual differences in hormone levels are related to personality trait levels. Among the more widely studied hormones have been testosterone, cortisol, and oxytocin, but thus far these hormones have not been found to show more than weak associations with personality trait levels in large-sample studies.

In reading this chapter, you will have noticed that there has already been a great deal of theory and research on the biological bases of personality. But perhaps the most important challenge for future research will be to figure out the complex ways in which each of the major dimensions of personality (see Chapter 3) are influenced by those various biological bases. For example, what exactly are the biological variables that influence levels of a given personality dimension, and how do those variables exert their effects? Now that personality psychologists have identified the major broad factors of personality, research into the biological causes of personality can aim at explaining *how* each of those factors is influenced by the action of various substances and structures.

CHAPTER 6

Genetic and Environmental Influences on Personality

Contents

6.1 THE QUESTION: NATURE VERSUS NURTURE

One of the crucial questions of personality psychology is that of "nature versus nurture": the extent to which personality variation is caused by heredity or by the environment. In other words, do people have different personalities because they inherit different genes from their biological parents, or because they have different experiences during development? In this chapter we will first describe how researchers have tried to answer that

Individual Differences and Personality
ISBN 978-0-12-809845-5, http://dx.doi.org/10.1016/B978-0-12-809845-5.00006-8

question and we will then describe the results that they have obtained. As you will see, the methods for answering this question are rather complex, but in some ways the results have been much less so.

When considering this question of nature versus nurture, it is important to keep in mind that we are asking about the origins of the *variability* or *differences* among persons in certain personality traits, and not of the absolute levels of those traits.[1] Consider an analogy with the physical trait of height: We might ask what proportion of the variability in height among adults is due to hereditary differences, and what proportion is due to environmental differences. But it would not make sense to ask what proportion of a given individual's height is due to heredity or due to environment. For example, we cannot meaningfully say that $x\%$ of your height is due to your genes, and the other $y\%$ is due to your environment; instead, *all* of your height results from a combination of your genes and your environment acting together. Your height (and you) can only exist because your genes and your environment are both operating. But because people *differ* from each other in height, we can try to figure out whether this variation is chiefly due to the *different* genes that people inherit, or chiefly due to the *different* environments that people experience.[2]

6.2 EXAMINING THE SIMILARITY OF RELATIVES

When researchers try to assess the relative importance of heredity and environment in accounting for individual differences, the first step is to figure out how similar are the personalities of people who are related to each other. But this is only the first step, because even if we find that relatives tend to be more similar than different in personality, we do not know *why* they are similar. Maybe the similarity is due to the fact that relatives are biologically related, and therefore have more genes in common than do unrelated persons. Or, maybe the similarity is due to the fact that relatives have lived together over a period of many years, and have had many features of their home environment in common. To find out whether any similarities among relatives are due to heredity or to the environment, we need a way to separate these two kinds of effects.

One solution used by personality researchers has been to study relatives who share *only* their heredity or *only* their rearing environment. For example, they could study biological siblings who have been raised in different households because of adoption, or they

---

[1] In a sense, the expression "nature versus nurture" does not correspond exactly to the contrast between heredity and environment. This is because environmental influences on personality include not only family experiences, but also a variety of other influences that are experienced outside the family. These experiences outside the family are not really "nurture" in the sense of the way a child is raised.

[2] Recall from your high school science classes that genes are the units that carry hereditary information, and are carried on chromosomes. Each person has thousands of genes on their 23 pairs of chromosomes; one chromosome of each pair is inherited from one's mother, and the other from one's father.

could study adoptive siblings who are biologically unrelated. Using this approach, researchers could figure out the relative strength of heredity and environment in influencing the personality similarity of relatives. Another solution, and the one that has been used much more widely, is to study different kinds of biological relatives that have different degrees of relatedness, even if the relatives have lived together; we will examine this approach in detail a bit later on in this chapter.

To calculate the relative influence of heredity and environment, researchers first need to calculate how similar relatives tend to be on a given trait. To do this, the researchers first identify many pairs of a certain kind of relative (e.g., siblings) from many families. Then, the researchers measure the personalities of both members of each pair of relatives. The most common method of measurement has been to use self-report questionnaires, but observer report questionnaires are also used in some studies. (It is important, of course, that the reports be obtained independently; for example, the relatives who provide self-reports should not discuss their responses with each other.)

Next, the researchers calculate how much variance there is altogether in the trait of interest, across all of the people being studied. Finally, they calculate what proportion of that variance is *within* families (i.e., due to differences between the two members of each pair) and what proportion is *between* families (i.e., differences among the pairs, where the score for each pair is the average of the two relatives who are its members). You can see why they do this: If the relatives within each pair tend to be very similar to each other, then the proportion of total variance that is due to within-family differences will be very small, and the proportion of total variance that is due to between-family differences will be very large. In contrast, if the relatives within each pair tend to be quite different from each other, then the proportion of total variance that is due to within-family differences will be much larger, and the proportion of total variance that is due to between-family differences will be much smaller. (The mathematical formulas used for calculating these proportions are based on the technique called analysis of variance, or ANOVA. This technique corrects for the fact that there are many pairs but only two persons within each pair.)

To figure out how similar the relatives tend to be on the trait in question, researchers calculate the proportion of variance due to between-family differences. (Again, when most of the variation is between the families, this means that differences within families tend to be small, which also means that relatives are similar.) This value is called an *intraclass correlation coefficient*, and although it is calculated in a way different from that of the usual correlation coefficient, it has similar properties and can be thought of as the correlation between the relatives on the trait. If relatives tend to be much more similar to each other than to unrelated persons, then the correlation will be high, perhaps above .50. If relatives tend only to be modestly more similar to each other than to unrelated persons, then the correlation will be low, perhaps not much above zero.

The preceding paragraphs have described how researchers can calculate how much relatives tend to be similar on a given trait. But now let us return to the issue of figuring out whether that similarity is due to heredity or due to the environment.

6.3 SEPARATING HEREDITY AND ENVIRONMENT

6.3.1 Examining the Similarity of Identical Twins Raised Apart

One way to estimate the heritable, or genetic, influence on a trait is to evaluate the similarity between biological relatives who have not lived in the same household. In some cases, this has been achieved by studying a very special kind of pair of relatives; specifically, identical twins who were adopted into two different families. If the adoptions take place shortly after birth, before the siblings have had any common experiences in growing up, then we can assume that the similarities between the siblings are due to their genetic similarity rather than due to any environmental similarity.[3]

Now, suppose that we find large numbers of these raised-apart identical twins after they have grown up, and that we measure their personalities. If for example we find that the correlation between identical twins raised apart for a given trait is .60, then this suggests that the identical twins raised apart tend to be a lot more similar to each other than to unrelated persons. This value of .60 would mean that 60% of the variance among people in this trait is due to the variance among people in their genes or heredity.

One useful feature of investigations involving identical twins is that their genetic makeup is truly identical. Even when we consider the genes that differ from one person to the next, fully 100% of the genes of one identical twin are the same as those of the other identical twin of that pair. Therefore, if we find that the correlation between identical twins raised apart for a given trait is (say) .60, we know that this value tells us the full influence of genes on the trait, because this is the amount of similarity that results when all genes are in common.

6.3.2 Examining the Similarity of Other Relatives Raised Apart

The situation is slightly different when we consider relatives who are not identical twins. Suppose that, instead of studying identical twins raised apart, we instead studied fraternal twins raised apart (or nontwin siblings raised apart).[4,5] The important difference here is

---

[3] Actually, this assumption might not be completely accurate, for reasons that you might already have realized. But let us accept this assumption for the time being, and then examine some possible problems a little later on in this chapter.

[4] You might have wondered whether similarities or differences among relatives might seem exaggerated or underestimated depending on whether or not they are of the same sex and age. Researchers can control for sex and age differences by calculating people's personality trait scores relative to other persons of the same sex and age.

[5] Identical twins are twins who developed after a single fertilized egg cell (zygote) divided into two separate embryos. Fraternal twins are twins who developed after two different egg cells were fertilized. Identical twins are therefore called *monozygotic* twins, and fraternal twins are therefore called *dizygotic* twins. Note that fraternal twins are no more genetically similar to each other than nontwin siblings are.

that fraternal twins (as well as nontwin siblings) have, on average, only 50% of their genes in common.[6] Therefore, when we find some similarity in a given trait between these kinds of relatives, we are witnessing the effects of only 50% of the genes. This means that, if we want to know the full effect of genetic influence on the trait, we need to take into account the fact that only half of the genes were involved. The way that researchers do this is straightforward: They double the amount of similarity that is observed between these relatives on the trait in question. For example, suppose that the correlation between fraternal twins on a given trait is found to be .30, indicating that these fraternal twins tend to be somewhat more similar to each other than to people in general. This degree of similarity reflects the effects of only the 50% of genes that fraternal twins (or nontwin siblings), on average, have in common. To estimate the full proportion of variance in this trait that is due to heredity, we must multiply the value of .30 by 2, which gives .60, or 60% due to heredity.

6.3.3 Comparing the Similarities Between Identical Twins and Between Fraternal Twins

You might have noticed that all of the preceding methods involved studying people who had been adopted at a very early age. One practical disadvantage of this method is that it can be somewhat difficult to find large numbers of biological relatives—whether identical twins, fraternal twins, or nontwin siblings—who have been adopted into different families. But there is a way to estimate the influence of heredity on a trait without having to rely only on samples of people who have been adopted. This method is to compare pairs of relatives who are from the same households, but to determine how much *more* similar certain kinds of relatives tend to be, and to examine this in relation to differences in their degree of genetic similarity.

One example of this strategy involves comparing the similarity between identical twins raised together with the similarity between fraternal twins raised together. (Note that, to make meaningful comparisons with identical twins, who are always of the same sex, these analyses typically use fraternal twins who are also of the same sex.) Because, in both cases, we are considering the similarity between relatives raised together, we can assume that the effects of growing up in the same household should affect both kinds of twins equally. Therefore, any "extra" similarity of identical twins, beyond that of

[6] Actually, all human beings have the vast majority of their genes in common with each other. But when we talk about the degree of genetic similarity between two persons, we ignore those genes completely, and focus only on the small fraction of genes (still a large number!) that differ from one person to the next. When studying the effects of heredity on personality, we consider only the genes that do vary from one person to the next, because only these genes can cause personality differences among people. In this sense, it is meaningful to say that two siblings have 50% of their genes in common (or that two unrelated persons have 0% of their genes in common), because we are intentionally putting aside all the genes that everyone has in common.

fraternal twins, should be due to the additional genetic similarity of identical twins, beyond that of fraternal twins.[7]

Let us see how this would work. Suppose we study a large number of *identical* twin pairs (where in every case the twins of a given pair have been raised together), and we find that the proportion of between-family variance—that is, the correlation between identical twins—is .60. Suppose we also study a large number of *fraternal* twin pairs (where again in every case the twins of a given pair have been raised together), and we find that the proportion of between-family variance—that is, the correlation between fraternal twins—is .30. Now, the difference between the correlations for identical twins (.60) and fraternal twins (.30) is .30. This difference is due to the "extra" genetic similarity of identical twins (who are 100% genetically similar) beyond that of fraternal twins (who are 50% genetically similar). Therefore, the difference results from $100 - 50 = 50\%$ extra genetic similarity. To estimate the full impact of heredity on the trait, we therefore need to double the difference between the correlations for the two types of twins: .30 times 2 is .60, so this would give an estimate of 60% genetic influence on the trait.

Notice that in the earlier example, the similarity of identical twins (.60) happened to be exactly twice as great as the similarity of fraternal twins (.30). In this example, then, the estimate of heritability ended up as .60 [i.e., 2(.60−.30)]. But there are some reasons why the similarity of identical twins could actually be considerably more than, or considerably less than, twice as great as the similarity of fraternal twins. Let us consider how this might happen.

6.3.4 Additive and Nonadditive Genetic Influences

First, it is possible that the similarity of identical twins could be *more* than twice as large as the similarity of fraternal twins. For example, instead of observing similarities of .60 and .30, the similarities might be .70 and .30, or .60 and .20. How could the identical twins be more than twice as similar as the fraternal twins on a given personality trait? To understand this, we must first take a brief detour to consider the different ways in which combinations of genes can influence a trait.

Sometimes, the combined effects of two or more genes on personality are very simple, with each gene contributing separately to making one's level of the trait a bit higher or lower. In such a case, there are *additive genetic effects*, because the combined effect of the genes can be estimated simply by adding together their separate effects. For example, suppose that a particular *allele* (i.e., a particular version of a gene) tends to cause higher levels of a trait, and that a person has one out of a possible two copies of this allele. In this case, his or her expected level of the trait would be about halfway between what would be

---

[7] Again, you might have some doubts about this assumption. We will discuss this a bit later on in the chapter.

expected if he or she had neither allele and what would be expected if he or she had both alleles.

Sometimes, however, the combined effects of two or more genes are more complex, being different from what you would expect based on adding the separate effects of the genes. In such a case, there are *nonadditive genetic effects* (also called *multiplicative genetic effects*). For example, suppose that if a person has two very rare alleles, *a* and *b*, then he or she ends up with a higher level of a given trait, but that this happens only if he or she has *both* of those alleles. If, instead, the person has alleles *A* and *b*, or alleles *a* and *B*, or (like most people) alleles *A* and *B*, then he or she will not end up with a higher level of the trait—not even halfway higher. In this case, the influence of alleles *a* and *b* is not additive; instead, the effects depend on the presence or absence of the other allele.[8]

What does this difference between additive and nonadditive genetic influences have to do with the heritability studies comparing identical twins and fraternal twins? Notice that identical twins, who have all of their genes in common, will always have the same combinations of genes. Therefore, any effects on a trait caused by nonadditive genetic influences will affect both identical twins in the same way. But notice that fraternal twins, who have only half of their genes in common, will have the same combinations of genes less than half of the time. If it is a combination of two genes, then the two fraternal twins would have the same combination about one-quarter of the time; if three genes, then one-eighth of the time. Therefore, when nonadditive genetic influences on a trait are important, identical twins will be considerably more than twice as similar as fraternal twins will be. If we see that identical twins are more than twice as similar as fraternal twins, this tells us that nonadditive genetic influences are involved.

6.3.5 Common (Shared) Environment Influences

It is also possible that the similarity of identical twins could be *less* than twice as large as the similarity of fraternal twins. For example, instead of observing similarities of .60 and .30, the similarities might be .80 and .50. How could the identical twins be less than twice as similar as the fraternal twins on a given personality trait?

The reason involves the effects of the rearing environment that is shared by any twins who have been raised together—what is called the *common* or *shared environment*. If one's level of a trait depends on some aspects of the household or family in which one is raised—for example, how wealthy (or educated, or religious, or harsh, or warm) one's

---

[8] When the genes in question are at different places on the chromosomes (i.e., at different *loci*), the nonadditive effect is known as *epistasis*. When the genes in question are different versions (i.e., different alleles) of a gene that is at the same place (i.e., the same *locus*) on the corresponding chromosome, this nonadditive effect involves *recessive* versus *dominant* genes.

parents are—then this should tend to make twins similar to each other. This would apply to both identical and fraternal twins, which means that there would be some similarity for each kind of twins, even apart from any genetic effects. (This is the reason why we estimate heritability by finding the *difference* between the identical twin correlation and the fraternal twin correlation; either correlation on its own could be in part due to the effects of the twins being raised together—that is, of the common environment.)

Suppose, for example, that being raised in the same household tended to make twins somewhat similar to each other, so that the correlation between twins (regardless of whether identical or fraternal) would be .20 higher than would be produced by genetic effects alone. Now, if there were also a genetic influence of (say) .60 on the trait, then the identical twins would have a similarity of .20 + .60 = .80, and the fraternal twins would have a similarity of .20 + .60/2 = .20 + .30 = .50. (Remember that fraternal twins have half of their genes in common, so we only add half of the .60.) In this way, identical twins would be less than twice as similar as fraternal twins.

By comparing the similarity between identical twins with the similarity between fraternal twins, we can figure out how much a trait is influenced by the environment shared between twins. In the above example, if identical twins have a similarity of .80 and fraternal twins have a similarity of .50, then we would find the heritability of the trait (i.e., the genetic effect on the trait) as 2(.80 − .50) = 2(.30) = .60. But recall that in this example the similarity of the identical twins was .80 (not .60) and that the similarity of the fraternal twins was .50 (not half of .60, or .30). This means that the similarity was in each case .20 higher than we would expect based on genetic effects alone. The extra similarity is due to the environment that is shared by, or common to, the two twins of any pair. (Note that if we had found the similarities to be .60 and .30, then this environmental effect would have been zero.)

Another way to estimate the common environment effect on a trait is to measure the similarity between biologically unrelated persons who were raised in the same household. Typically, this means assessing across many families the similarity between biologically unrelated siblings—that is, where one sibling is adopted and the other is not, or where both siblings are adopted but are biologically unrelated to each other. If, for example, the similarity between these biologically unrelated siblings was .30, then this would indicate that the effect of the environment shared by these siblings was .30, because the similarity would be entirely due to the environment.

6.3.6 Unique (Nonshared) Environment Influences

Thus far, when we have discussed the effects of the environment on a trait, we have examined only those aspects of the environment that tend to make siblings similar to each other. Consider two siblings who grow up in the same family or household. Both siblings experience many of the same features of their environment: They will both grow up in a high-income household, or both in a low-income household; they will both be raised in a household with few books, or both in a household with many books; they will both be raised by religious parents, or both by nonreligious parents; they will both be raised by harsh parents, or both by gentle parents. As a result, we might expect that siblings would tend to develop similar levels of some personality traits, and we might even expect that they would tend to develop trait levels similar to those of the parents who raise them. To the extent that this is true, we would expect that even biologically *unrelated* persons would show some similarity in their personality traits after having lived in the same household. (This similarity might be greater for two siblings than for a parent and child, because the two siblings are both raised by the same parents.) Recall that researchers refer to these environmental influences as *shared* or *common*, for the simple reason that these are aspects of the environment that relatives share or have in common with each other. These are also called *between-family* environmental influences, because they differ between families (i.e., from one family to the next). As explained earlier, the influence of the common environment can be estimated by using the results of studies comparing the similarities of identical twins and of fraternal twins, and it can also be estimated by using the results of studies of the similarity between biologically unrelated siblings.

The other kind of environmental influence includes many different features of the environment that differ even for individuals from the same household. For example, two siblings (even two twins) may have different friends, who might influence their personalities in different ways. Or, two siblings might be treated differently by their parents, which might lead the siblings to differ in terms of some personality traits. These environmental influences are called *nonshared* or *unique*, because by definition they are not shared, but are instead unique to each person, even when those persons belong to the same family. These are also called *within-family* environmental influences, because they differ within families (i.e., from one family member to the next.)

Researchers sometimes want to find out how much a *particular kind* of unique environment influence is responsible for differences between siblings in a given trait. To do so, researchers can obtain a sample of many pairs of siblings, and find out whether the siblings who were more different in some aspect of their environment are also more different in the trait being examined. For example, researchers can try to measure (in each of many families) how differently the siblings were treated by their parents, and then find out whether siblings treated more differently are usually more different in the trait. This result could indicate how much the differences between siblings in treatment by their parents are later reflected in personality differences. Similarly, researchers can try to measure (in each of many families) how different were the groups of friends that the siblings had (i.e., the siblings' peer groups), and then find out whether siblings who had more different peer groups are usually more different in the trait. This result could indicate how much the differences between siblings in peer groups are later reflected in personality differences.[9]

We have just discussed how researchers can test for the influence of some *particular aspect* of the unique environment. But in most studies of the genetic and environmental influences on a trait, researchers do not actually do this at all. Instead, they estimate the *overall effect* of unique environment influences—that is, the proportion of variation among people in the trait which is due to the combined effect of all unique environment influences, many of which may be unknown.

To estimate the total effect of the unique or nonshared environment, researchers simply figure out how much variance in a trait is "left over" after genetic influences and common environment influences have been estimated: For example, if 65% of the variance in a trait is due to genetic influences, and if 5% is due to common environment influences, then this leaves 30% to be accounted for by unique environment influences. (This amount might reflect the combined action of many different unique environment influences, each of which may be very small on its own.)

But there is a problem with estimating unique environment effects in this way. The problem is that the proportion of trait variance that remains—after genetic and common environment effects have been accounted for—includes not only unique environment effects, but a couple of other important elements as well.

One part of this "left-over" variance is not really due to the trait at all. Recall that whenever researchers measure people's levels of a trait, the measurements will not be perfectly reliable and will not be perfectly valid. Instead, some of the variance in those measurements will be "error" variance due to the specific items used or the specific occasion (recall Section 1.2.1) and some will be due to response biases (including social desirability or undesirability; recall Section 2.6.4). Because of these imperfections in measurement, the correlations between relatives' scores could be smaller than they would be if the traits were measured with perfect accuracy. This in turn means that the estimates of genetic variance and common environment variance—both of which depend on those correlations—could also be smaller. And as a result, the amount of "left-over" variance—which gets counted as being due to the unique environment—could be larger. Therefore, when researchers estimate the unique environment influence on a trait, some part of that estimate could actually be due to the imperfect measurement of the trait.

[9] You might have noticed one potential complication with this approach. Suppose that researchers find that the siblings who differ more in some aspect of their environment also tend to differ more in some personality trait. This might mean that differences in this aspect of the environment tend to make siblings more different in the trait. However, it might also mean that siblings who differ in this personality trait tend to end up with differences in this aspect of their environment. Therefore, it can be tricky to figure out whether a difference in some aspect of the environment really is a cause—rather than a consequence—of personality differences between siblings.

Another part of the "left-over" variance in the trait is likely due to randomness in development. Even if two people are identical twins (and hence have the same genes), and even if those identical twins are exposed to the same environments, those twins will still differ in the way they develop, just by chance. Development—both before birth and after—is not determined perfectly by genetic and environmental influences; in addition, many small random differences occur, and these can influence people's levels of various physical and psychological traits. Therefore, some of the variation in trait levels not accounted for by genetic and common environment influences—that is, the "left-over" variation attributed to unique environment influences—is actually due to random chance in development.

6.4 THE ANSWERS

6.4.1 Results From Comparisons of the Similarities Between Identical Twins and Between Fraternal Twins

As explained in the previous section, the heritability of a personality characteristic can be estimated in several different ways. Of these various methods, the one that is most frequently used in heritability studies is that of finding how much more similar identical twins are in comparison with fraternal twins. Some particularly well-designed studies using this approach have been conducted by a team of researchers in Germany (Kandler, Riemann, Spinath, & Angleitner, 2010; Riemann, Angleitner, & Strelau, 1997; Riemann & Kandler, 2010). These studies are based on large samples of twins whose personalities were assessed in terms of the Big Five factors using both self-reports and observer reports. In this section, we will discuss the results of this research in some detail. Because the findings from these German twin studies are similar to those obtained elsewhere—even from studies using the other methods—the results provide a good current estimate of the heritabilities of personality characteristics. Note that, because the results as averaged across studies are broadly similar from one personality characteristic to the next, we will discuss the results for personality characteristics in general.

First let us consider the results based on self-report data. Averaging across results for self-reports on the Big Five factors, the mean correlation for identical twins was .54, and the mean correlation for fraternal twins was .27 (based on Riemann & Kandler, 2010; Appendix). This indicates that, on average, the heritability of personality characteristics was about .54 [i.e., 2(.54−.27)]. Note that, on average, the identical twins were twice as similar as the fraternal twins, which suggests that the heritability is additive and that there is no common or shared environmental effect.[10]

---

[10] In principle, it is possible that some effects of nonadditive heritability and of the common environment could both exist, but also could be canceling each other out perfectly, thereby concealing each other. This would be an unlikely coincidence, but it is possible.

Next, let us consider the results based on observer report data. The observer reports in this study were actually the average of reports from two observers, both of whom knew the twin reasonably well. (Each observer gave reports only about one twin of each pair; that is, the observer reports made for one twin were given by two people, and the observer reports made for the other twin of the same pair were given by two other people. The twins did not provide observer reports for each other.)

Averaging across results for observer reports on the Big Five factors, the mean correlation for identical twins was .45, and the mean correlation for fraternal twins was .20 (based on Riemann & Kandler, 2010; Appendix). This indicates that, on average, the heritability of personality characteristics was about .50 [i.e., 2(.45−.20)]. Note that on average, the identical twins were just slightly more than twice as similar as the fraternal twins, which suggests that the heritability is almost all additive and that there is no common or shared environmental effect.

As you can see, the heritability estimates from the self-report data and the observer report data are quite similar. Both results suggest that about half of the variation in personality characteristics is due to genetic variation. All or almost all of that genetic variation is of the additive kind, with little if any being nonadditive. The remaining variation in personality characteristics can be attributed to environmental variation, but because there was no effect due to the common or shared environment, this environmental influence must be of the unique or nonshared variety. (Later in this chapter, we will discuss several aspects of the unique environment that might influence personality.)

The heritability results just described were found by considering the self-reports of personality and the observer reports of personality as two separate sources of information. However, the researchers who conducted these studies have also estimated the heritability of personality when both self-reports and observer reports are considered together. The reason for doing this is that neither self-reports nor observer reports are perfectly reliable or perfectly valid (this is the problem noted in Section 6.3.6 about estimation of unique environment effects). By considering the variance that is shared by the two methods, it is possible to estimate what the heritability of a trait would be if it could be measured with perfect reliability and validity. (The mathematical methods used in these analyses are somewhat complex and are beyond the scope of this book.) When self-reports and observer reports are considered jointly, the results indicate higher levels of heritability than when either method is used alone, averaging nearly .65 across the Big Five factors (Kandler et al., 2010). These findings suggest that the heritability of personality characteristics has been underestimated in most studies that rely on self-reports alone.

Now let us summarize the results. Personality characteristics showed similar and fairly high levels of heritability: When personality characteristics were assessed using either self-reports or observer reports, about 50% of the variation in each characteristic was found to be due to genetic influences. When personality characteristics were assessed using self-reports and observer reports together—focusing on the variance shared by the two methods of measurement—the heritability is found to be even higher, about 65%. In either case, almost all of that genetic variation was additive, and almost none was nonadditive. Of the remaining variation, it appears that all of it is due to unique environment influences, and none of it is due to common environment influences.

6.4.2 Results From Studies of the Similarity Between Relatives

The findings described in the previous section, as based on studies comparing the similarity of identical twins with the similarity of fraternal twins, are consistent with the results of studies that have used other methods to estimate the heritability of personality characteristics.

Table 6.1 shows the correlations that have typically been found between relatives of various kinds for personality trait levels, as assessed mainly by self-report (see reviews by Bouchard & Loehlin, 2001; Loehlin, 2005; Plomin & Caspi, 1999). Because the results have generally been similar regardless of which personality trait is considered, the results are not reported separately by trait. As you can see, the results show that biological relatives tend to be similar in personality, with identical twins being much more similar than other kinds of relatives. Also, the similarity between biological relatives does not depend on whether or not they have been raised together, and adoptive relatives do not tend to be similar in personality. These results indicate a substantial role of heredity in personality variation, but little if any role of the common or shared environment.[11]

Table 6.1 Typical correlations of personality trait levels between relatives of various kinds (in mainly self-report data)

Type of relative	Correlation
Identical twins raised together	.45
Identical twins raised apart	.45
Fraternal twins raised together	.20
Nontwin biological siblings raised together	.20
Parent and biological child (together)	.10—.15
Parent and biological child (apart)	.10—.15
Adoptive siblings	.00—.05
Adoptive parent and child	.00—.05

All values are approximate, being averaged across different traits and different samples of persons.
Bouchard, T.J., Jr., & Loehlin, J.C. (2001). Genes, evolution, and personality. Behavior Genetics, 31, 243—273; Plomin, R.C., & Caspi, A. (1999). Behavioral genetics and personality. In L.A. Pervin, & O.P. John (Eds.). Handbook of personality: Theory and research (2nd ed., pp. 251—276). New York: Guilford; Loehlin, J.C. (2005). Resemblance in personality and attitudes between parents and their children: Genetic and environmental contributions. In S. Bowles, H. Gintis, & M. Osborne Groves (Eds.). Unequal chances: Family background and economic success (pp. 192—207). Princeton, NJ: Princeton University Press.

[11] There are, however, some other psychological characteristics—specifically, some religious beliefs and political attitudes—that do show a stronger influence of the common environment. We will discuss these findings in Chapter 12.

When findings about the heritability of personality characteristics were first reported, the results were very surprising to many people, including many personality researchers. Most people probably would have expected a stronger role of the common environment; instead, however, the results show that differences between family and household environments have little if any influence on people's personality trait levels.[12]

6.5 ASSUMPTIONS UNDERLYING HERITABILITY STUDIES IN GENERAL

In describing the methods and results of investigations of the heritability of personality, we have been making some important assumptions. Let us now consider some of the main assumptions on which heritability studies are based. First, we will consider the assumption that each participant's personality is measured independently, that is, without being influenced by the personality of his or her relatives. Then, we will consider the assumption that there is little or no "assortative mating" for personality—in other words, that parents do not tend to be more similar to each other in personality than two people picked at random would tend to be. These two assumptions apply to all heritability studies of the kinds described so far in this chapter; in a later section, we will consider some assumptions that apply to twin-based heritability studies in particular.

6.5.1 Are Relatives' Personalities Really Measured Independently?

As mentioned earlier in this chapter, one of the assumptions on which heritability studies are based is that the personalities of relatives can be assessed independently. If, instead, one individual's personality might influence the measurements of his or her relative's personality, then this could either inflate or deflate the similarity between those relatives, and thereby distort the results of the heritability study.

But how could this problem of nonindependent measurements happen? Consider, for example, two siblings (or two twins) who complete a self-report personality inventory. It is possible that, when responding to the questions of that inventory, the siblings would tend to compare themselves not to people in general but instead to each other, and thus to give answers that emphasize differences between them. For example, suppose that two brothers both tend to be rather anxious or nervous, but that one is more so than the other. In responding to self-report items about worry and anxiety, the somewhat less anxious brother might be contrasting his tendencies with those of his brother, and

---

[12] You might wonder how it is that biological relatives can be similar in personality given your own observations that such relatives can be much different in their levels of a given personality trait. The answer is that even though the degree of personality similarity between relatives is enough to be scientifically important, it would have to be much, much greater for the differences between relatives to be consistently small. Even in the case of identical twins, the relatively high degree of personality similarity still leaves a lot of room for any given pair of twins to differ widely on some personality traits.

would thereby underestimate his own anxiety level, which would end up causing the researchers to overestimate the difference between himself and his brother. A similar process could also influence the other brother's self-reports, causing him to overestimate his anxiety level and thus again to lead the researchers to overestimate the difference between brothers.

The same lack of independence could occur when an individual's personality is assessed through observer reports. In the previous example, suppose that the mother of the two brothers is instead the one who provides reports of each brother's personality. When describing each brother's personality, she might be considering not how each brother compares with all other boys, but rather how each brother compares with the other. If she thinks of one brother as "the nervous one" and the other as "the calm one," then she might tend to overestimate the anxiety level of the first, and underestimate the anxiety level of the second. As a result, the researchers would conclude that the brothers are less similar in personality than might really be the case.

This tendency to emphasize differences between related persons is called a *contrast effect*, but it is not clear how much these effects really do occur in personality assessments. Nevertheless, it is possible that contrast effects could be stronger for some kinds of relatives than for others. For example, perhaps the relatives of two twins will be less likely to emphasize contrasts between them if the twins are identical rather than fraternal. But it is also possible that contrast effects are not observed at all for some kinds of relatives, or even that instead there is a tendency to emphasize similarities between relatives. Suppose, for example, that two sisters consider themselves to be similar in personality. If the two sisters actually do differ somewhat in a given trait, such as creativity, then perhaps the more-creative sister will underestimate her own level of creativity, and perhaps the less-creative sister will overestimate her own level of creativity, thereby leading the researcher to conclude that the sisters are more similar than they really are. And again, this effect might also be seen in observer reports of the personalities of relatives; for example, if the father of these two sisters tended to see them as being similar to each other, then this might also influence his reports of each sister's level of creativity (or of any other trait), in such a way as to cause researchers to overestimate that similarity. This tendency to emphasize similarities between related persons is called an *assimilation effect*.

How can researchers overcome the potential problems that could be caused by the nonindependence of personality assessments? One solution is that the researchers could assess an individual's personality by obtaining reports from someone who knows that individual well, but who does not know that individual's relative(s) very well. The problem of contrast effects (or assimilation effects) is unlikely to occur if the personality assessments are provided by someone who is not a family member and who is not well acquainted with anyone in the family other than the individual to be assessed.

The German twin studies described earlier in this chapter used methods that were fairly close to those of the above strategy. As you will recall, those studies included both self-reports and observer reports of personality, and the observer reports for each twin of a given pair were provided by two persons who knew him or her very well but who did not know the other twin very well. The findings obtained from these observer reports were similar to those from self-reports, insofar as identical twins were considerably more similar than were fraternal twins, thereby suggesting substantial heritability for the personality characteristics.

Another study that also attempted to overcome the problems of contrast and assimilation effects was an investigation by the same group of researchers (Borkenau, Riemann, Angleitner, & Spinath, 2001) involving participants from the same sample of German twins. In this study, personality was assessed not only using self-reports and observer reports, but also using direct observations made by the experimenters and by students who watched videos of the participants' behaviors. That is, the participants took part in a variety of activities while being observed and being video-recorded by the experimenters. These observations and video recordings allowed the experimenters to make further assessments of the participants' personalities. When making the personality assessments, each experimenter (and each person who later watched the video) was assigned to observe only one member of any twin pair, so that contrast and assimilation effects would not occur.

The results of the Borkenau et al. (2001) study suggested that twins—whether fraternal or identical—were more similar to each other in personality when assessed by experimenters or by video "judges" than when assessed by self-report or observer report; however, this effect was stronger for fraternal twins than for identical twins, thus suggesting that contrast effects are larger in fraternal twins. One important consequence of this result was that fraternal twins were *more than* half as similar to each other as were identical twins, and therefore it did appear that there was some effect of the common environment on personality, perhaps as much as .25. (The effect of heredity was estimated at about .40.) The common environment effect was much higher than in previous studies, and it will be interesting to see if the result is replicated in future studies; if so, it would suggest that earlier investigations had underestimated the effect of the common environment.

Before leaving this section, one other important point should be made about contrast effects and assimilation effects. Even though we have been describing these effects as occurring simply in people's style of responding to personality inventories, it is also possible that these effects could genuinely influence people's personalities. That is, for some characteristics, two siblings (whether twins or not) might really become more different from each other, or they might really become more similar to each other. For example, you can imagine that two twins might diverge in such a way that one becomes "dominant" and the other "submissive"; or, those twins might converge in such a way that both develop higher (or lower) levels of some traits, such as organization or creativity or any others.

6.5.2 Is There Really No Assortative Mating for Personality?

Another assumption on which heritability studies are based is that the parents of the individuals being studied are no more similar to each other in the characteristic of interest than are any two people chosen at random. That is, researchers assume that there is no *assortative mating* for the characteristic, or in other words, that there is no tendency for parents to be similar in their levels of the trait. For example, if researchers study the heritability of Agreeableness by comparing the personalities of many pairs of fraternal and identical twins, the researchers assume that the mothers' and fathers' levels of Agreeableness are nearly uncorrelated—to put it another way, the researchers assume that there is no tendency for the more agreeable mothers to be married to the more agreeable fathers.

Why is this assumption made? Consider what would happen if, at the opposite extreme, mothers' and fathers' levels of a trait were strongly correlated. If this trait were strongly genetically influenced, then every child would inherit roughly the same genetic predisposition for this trait from both parents. Therefore, for this particular trait, it would be as if regular siblings or fraternal twins have much more than 50% of their genes in common with each other. As a result, they would end up being more similar in this trait than would be the case if no assortative mating occurred. Consequently, if researchers estimated the heritability of the trait by studying fraternal twins or nontwin siblings raised apart, those researchers would *overestimate* the heritability if they used the usual method. (The usual method is to double the correlation, but if the siblings have more than 50% of their genes in common, then this will overestimate the heritability.) Or, to take a more common situation, if researchers estimated the heritability of the trait by comparing the similarity of identical twins with that of fraternal twins, those researchers would *underestimate* the heritability if they used the usual method. (The usual method is to double the *difference* between the identical-twin and fraternal-twin correlations; however, if fraternal twins have more than 50% of their genes in common, then this difference will represent the effects of less than 50% of genes, and doubling the difference will underestimate the heritability.)

How accurate is the assumption of no assortative mating? Researchers have studied the extent to which spouses are similar in personality characteristics, but let us save the precise results of those studies until Chapter 9. For now, it is enough to say that the obtained results do not show particularly high levels of assortative mating; that is, in most families, the parents are not so similar in any personality characteristic that this similarity would cause any important distortion of the results of heritability studies. However, the situation is rather different for some other characteristics, such as beliefs, attitudes, and abilities, and we will discuss the implications of this fact in later chapters that deal with those topics.

6.6 ASSUMPTIONS UNDERLYING TWIN-BASED HERITABILITY STUDIES IN PARTICULAR

Now let us consider some assumptions that underlie heritability studies involving twins in particular. First, we will discuss objections to two assumptions related to the study of twins raised apart: one objection is that these twins would share some features of their early environment, and another objection is that the twins might be placed into adopting households that are less varied than households in general are. Then we will discuss an objection to an assumption related to the study of twins raised together, specifically, the objection that identical twins raised together might tend to receive more similar treatment than would fraternal twins (or regular siblings) raised together.

6.6.1 Are Twins' Early Environments Really Separate?

With regard to twins raised apart, you might have wondered whether these twins really have been raised apart for the entire duration of their development. If instead the twins have spent some considerable part of their childhood together before being separated, then this leaves open the possibility that the similarity of the twins' personalities (or any other characteristics) might be due to this common experience rather than to the common genetic background of the twins. In most heritability studies that have been based on twins raised apart, the typical age at which the twins were separated is very young; for example, in one large study, the average age at separation was only 5 months (Bouchard, Lykken, McGue, Segal, & Tellegen, 1990). Thus, although the twins in these studies have usually been separated at a very young age, the fact that they were together for at least a few months means that we cannot automatically rule out the possibility of the shared environment making a contribution to their similarity.

To address the problem that twins raised apart have usually spent at least some time raised together, researchers have done some additional analyses of their data. One way that researchers have tried to find out whether the early time spent together might have increased the similarity of twins raised apart has been to compare the similarity of twins who were separated very early with the similarity of twins who were separated somewhat later. To the extent that the later-separated twins were more similar, this would suggest that the early environment shared by the twins had tended to make them similar to each other. However, the results of analyses using this approach have not shown any substantially greater similarity for the twins who were separated at somewhat later ages, relative to the twins who were separated even earlier (e.g., Bouchard et al., 1990). Thus, this result suggests that the similarity between twins raised apart is not attributable, in any substantial part, to the early time spent together by those twins.

But we are not finished yet with the problem that twins raised apart have actually spent some time together. This is because of the fact that, even if we compare twins who have been separated at birth, we have not in fact eliminated the influence of the common environment on those twins. Can you figure out why this is so? The reason is that the twins would have experienced a common environment during their development in the uterus (womb) of their mother. Because the twins experienced the same uterine (womb) environment, and because their womb environment may have differed from that experienced by other twins developing in the wombs of other mothers, some of the similarity of the twins might be attributable to their experience of a common womb environment. For example, suppose that the mother's level of various nutrients (or various toxins, or various stresses) was different from that of other mothers. These differences might have influenced the development of the twin fetuses of that mother in similar ways, and in ways that would then lead both twins, after being born, to develop personalities different from those of twins who had shared the womb environment of a different mother. As a result, the observed similarities between twins raised apart would be attributable in some part to the common environment that they shared prior to being born.

You might have noticed that the womb environment could also be the source of some unique environment influences, to the extent that the twins might not receive exactly the same levels of nutrients, toxins, hormones, and so on, from the mother's bloodstream. (For an example of how this might work, see Box 6.1). Likewise, womb

Box 6.1 Chorion Type as an Example of Womb Environment Effects on Personality

The *chorion* is the outermost of the two membranes that surround the developing fetus. When two identical twins (i.e., monozygotic twins) are developing in their mother's womb, they might both be inside the same chorion, or each might be inside his or her own chorion. About two-thirds of identical twins have the same chorion (and thus are called *monochorionic* monozygotic twins), and about one-third have their own chorion (and thus are called *dichorionic* monozygotic twins). Because dichorionic monozygotic twins receive nutrients and hormones from the mother through different blood vessels, they might receive different levels of those nutrients and hormones, and thereby show larger differences in personality (and other) characteristics than would monochorionic monozygotic twins, who would be expected to receive nearly the same nutrient and hormone levels.

In one recent study (van Beijsterveldt et al., 2016), researchers obtained self-reports on the Big Five personality factors from a sample of 16-year-old Dutch identical twins, including more than 300 pairs of monochorionic monozygotic twins and more than 200 pairs of dichorionic monozygotic twins. The results showed that the monochorionic monozygotic twins were no more similar (and in fact, actually slightly less similar) than were the dichorionic monozygotic twins. These findings suggest that even though differences in chorion type could in principle be a source of personality variation, they might not actually be responsible for any personality differences.

environment effects might also occur for nontwin siblings and again could represent common or unique environment influences. Siblings who are not twins have also developed within the womb of the same mother, and any features of their mother's womb environment that are *consistent across pregnancies* will represent features of the *common environment* experienced by the siblings. (For example, if a mother smokes during both pregnancies, then both siblings will be exposed to the same smoking-related toxins.) But any features of the mother's womb environment that *change across pregnancies* will represent features of the *unique environment* experienced by the siblings. (For example, if a mother's diet during her first pregnancy differs from that during her second, or if a mother's experience of stress during her first pregnancy differs from that during her second, then the siblings will have been exposed to different womb environments.) In this way, the features of the womb environment can constitute aspects both of the common environment and also of the unique environment.

What is the actual effect of the womb environment on personality? Is the similarity of twins (or of nontwin siblings) raised apart actually due in some degree to the common environment experienced in the same mother's womb? Unfortunately, this question has not yet been addressed in heritability studies involving personality traits, and so it is quite possible that some fraction of the "heritable" influences on personality are instead attributable to the common womb environment experienced by twins. As we will see in Chapter 10 of this book, the contribution of the common womb environment has already been examined in studies of variation in mental abilities. The results of those investigations suggest that the womb environment is responsible for some of that variation.

6.6.2 Are Twins' Adoptive Households Really Very Different?

As described earlier in this chapter, investigations of the heritability of personality characteristics have found very little influence of the common or shared environment. Some of those investigations are based on comparisons of siblings who are biologically unrelated but who were raised in the same family because of adoption. But there is a potential problem here: What if the households that adopt children tend to be rather similar to each other in most ways? For example, if adopting parents in general tend to have fairly high levels of income or education, or to be rather gentle and attentive in their parenting styles, then the relative lack of variation among adopting households would tend to limit the effect of the common environment on personality. In other words, even if personality could be substantially influenced by some aspects of the shared environment—such as socioeconomic status or parenting style—we might never see these influences in a sample of families that are all fairly similar in those respects. We would only notice these influences if the sample of adopting families had a really wide range on these variables, by including families of very low income and educational levels and of very harsh and distant parenting styles. But because of the screening process that is involved in placing children to be adopted (and also because of the characteristics of people who wish to adopt), it may be that these latter families would only rarely adopt children.

One recent study was designed to find out how much less variable adoptive families are, in comparison with families in which children are not adopted (McGue et al., 2007). This study found that adoptive parents had, on average, somewhat lower levels of anti-social behavior and of drug and alcohol abuse—and lower variability in these behaviors—than did nonadoptive parents. The adoptive parents also had slightly higher average levels of socioeconomic status—and less variability in socioeconomic status—than did nona-doptive parents. (In contrast, adoptive parents showed, on average, about the same levels of depression as did nonadoptive parents. Also, adoptive families were about the same as nonadoptive families in the quality of family relationships or the extent of negative peer influences on the children.)

Even though the adoptive parents studied by McGue et al. tended to have low levels of antisocial behavior, some of them did commit considerable amounts of such behavior. McGue et al. examined whether adopted children were more likely to commit antisocial behaviors depending on how much antisocial behavior their adoptive parents committed. (If this relation were found, it would indicate a shared environment effect on antisocial behavior. Note that the adopted children were in their teenage years at the time of the study.) The results showed, however, that antisocial behavior of adopted children was completely unrelated to the antisocial behavior of their adoptive parents. Adopted children whose adoptive parents had high levels of antisocial behavior did not commit any more antisocial behavior than did adopted children whose adoptive parents had low levels of antisocial behavior. These findings suggest that restricted variability among adopting parents does not necessarily lead to an underestimation of shared environment effects on behavior, because those effects are sometimes virtually zero.

Beyond the issue of restricted variability, a related concern about studies based on adoptive families is the possibility that those families may be selected in such a way as to be similar to the biological parents of the children who are to be adopted. For example, perhaps children whose biological parents were from a high socioeconomic status background would tend to be placed into adoptive families having the same background. This is called *selective placement*, and if it were to happen, then it could distort the results of heritability studies in various ways. For example, it could make it appear as though the characteristics of the adopted children were caused by the environment of their adoptive families, even if those characteristics were really caused by genes inherited from biological parents. Or, it could make it appear as though the similarities between identical twins raised apart (but adopted into similar households) were due to genetic similarities, even if the similar household environments were responsible. However, the evidence from adoption studies suggests that there is very little selective placement: On average, the biological parents of an adopted child are only very slightly more similar to the adoptive parents than to parents in the general population (Plomin & DeFries, 1985). Therefore, it is unlikely that selective place-ment has had any important effect on the results of heritability studies.

6.6.3 Are Identical Twins Really Treated Differently by Others?

In many heritability studies, researchers estimate the heritability of a trait by comparing the similarity of identical twins with the similarity of fraternal twins. In those investiga-tions, it is assumed that the greater similarity of identical twins is due to their greater ge-netic similarity, and not due to any greater similarity of their environments. This is called the *equal environments assumption*. But what if this assumption is false? Could it be, instead, that identical twins become very similar to each other because they experience environ-ments that are especially similar? Perhaps the parents of identical twins tend to treat those twins more similarly than they would treat fraternal twins or nontwin siblings, for example, by dressing them in the same sets of clothes, enrolling them in the same activ-ities, or giving them the same birthday presents. And perhaps the extremely similar phys-ical appearance of identical twins leads them to be treated in a very similar way by people in general, including teachers or classmates. As a result of this very similar treatment, perhaps identical twins would become more similar in personality than would be caused by their genetic similarity alone.

Researchers have examined this possibility in two different ways. One way has been to find out whether the similarity of identical twins depends on how similarly their par-ents have treated them. That is, do identical twins whose parents have tried to treat them in very similar ways end up being more similar than do identical twins whose parents have tried to treat them differently? This question was examined by Loehlin and Nichols (1976), who studied a sample of over 300 identical twin pairs in Texas. They found that the similarity of identical twins' personalities was only very slightly related to how similar their experiences had been, in terms of being dressed alike, playing together, or being treated similarly by parents or teachers. Because this similarity of treatment had little effect on the similarity of personality for identical twins, it appears that the greater personality similarity of identical twins, compared with fraternal twins, cannot be attributed to the similar treatment of identical twins.

Another way to examine the possibility that similar treatment might make identical twins more similar than fraternal twins involves an unusual comparison. Specifically, which kinds of twins are more similar: Identical twins whose parents mistakenly believe them to be fraternal twins, or fraternal twins whose parents mistakenly believe them to be identical twins? Answering this question allows us to determine whether the personality similarity between twins depends more on their *actual* genetic similarity (as measured by biological tests of their status as identical or fraternal twins) or on their *perceived* genetic similarity (as indicated by their parents' belief as to their status as identical or fraternal twins)? If actual genetic similarity is the better predictor of personality similarity, then similar treatment is not the source of much of the twins' similarity; but, if perceived genetic similarity is a better predictor, then similar treatment is responsible for much of that similarity. When researchers have examined this question, they have found that similarity of personality (and other) characteristics is greater for identical twins whose parents mistakenly believed them to be fraternal than for fraternal twins whose parents mistakenly believed them to be identical (e.g., Scarr & Carter-Saltzman, 1979). Therefore, these results also indicate that the personality similarity of identical twins is due to genetic similarity, and not due to similar treatment of those twins.

Box 6.2 What About Epigenetic Effects?

Much attention has been given in recent years to *epigenetic effects*, whereby certain genes can be activated or repressed (i.e., "switched on" or "switched off"). Even if two people are identical twins, they will differ in which of their genes are activated or repressed, as these epigenetic changes will depend partly on specific environmental influences and on random chance. If epigenetic changes influence the levels of psychological characteristics, then this influence will be captured (along with other influences) within the estimates of unique environment variance. Thus far, however, it is not known whether or not these epigenetic effects can account for any appreciable amount of variance in personality trait levels.

6.7 EFFECTS OF THE UNIQUE ENVIRONMENT ON PERSONALITY? PARENTAL TREATMENT, PEER GROUPS, AND BIRTH ORDER

Now let us consider some environmental influences on personality. To the extent that the variation in the unique environment contributes to personality variation, which specific features of the unique environment are important? Researchers have suggested several such features, and a few of these have been investigated empirically. Here we will explore some of the most prominent of these possible unique environment influences on personality: parental treatment, peer groups, and birth order.

6.7.1 Parental Treatment and Peer Groups

Loehlin (1997) attempted to determine whether or not differences in personality within twin pairs would be related to differences in parental treatment and to differences in friends. To examine these questions, Loehlin had about 800 pairs of twins (both identical and fraternal) provide self-reports on several variables, including (1) various personality characteristics, (2) any differences between twins in the same family in the way their parents had treated them, and (3) any differences between twins of the same family in their peer groups (i.e., the fraction of friends of one twin who were not friends of the other.)

The results showed that the size of the difference between two twins' personalities (across various traits) was positively, but weakly, correlated with both the amount of difference in parental treatment and the degree of difference in their friendship groups. That is, when two twins had larger personality differences than most other twins did, they also had a slight tendency also to report larger differences in treatment by their parents, and to report more differences in their groups of friends (i.e., fewer mutual friends). Again, these tendencies were rather weak, with correlations only about .15, but they suggest that these aspects of the unique environment—different treatment by parents and different peer groups—might have at least some small influence on differences between twins (or other siblings) in personality.

A possible alternative explanation for the findings is that early personality differences between the twins are actually the cause of differential treatment by parents and of differences in friendship groups. The results of a study by Burt, McGue, and Iacono (2009) show how this might happen. Burt et al. studied about 450 pairs of identical twins at age 14 and again at age 17. They found that twins who engaged in more delinquent or "externalizing" behavior at age 14 tended to have more "deviant" friends at age 17. This relation was stronger than the relation between having deviant friends at 14 and engaging in delinquent behavior at age 17. Therefore, these results suggest that behavior (and personality) tends to influence peer groups more than peer groups influence behavior (and personality).

The preceding findings regarding the effects of one's group of friends on one's personality are important given the increased recent interest in the effects of the peer environment on personality. A researcher named Judith Rich Harris suggested that the peer groups to which one belongs during childhood and adolescence are crucial to personality development (Harris, 1995, 1998). As seen for many variables, such as the prevailing accent, clothing, and music of a given time and place, the influence of one's peer group is obviously strong. Similarly, peer groups also influence norms regarding drug use, sexual activity, delinquency, and other behaviors, so that there can be large differences between communities (or cultures, or generations) in the prevalence of these behaviors. However, in terms of *individual differences* in personality trait levels among people from the same time and place, the evidence so far suggests that the particular group of friends one has can exert only a modest influence, if any.

6.7.2 Birth Order

Another aspect of the unique environment that received a great deal of research attention beginning in the mid-1990s is that of birth order. The idea that there are personality differences between siblings having different birth order positions—first-born, middle-born, last-born, or "only" child—has been around for a long time. In the early 20th century, a theorist named Alfred Adler suggested that first-born children would tend to be insecure due to the unpleasant experience of being "dethroned" from their favored position by the arrival of a younger sibling. Adler also suggested that last-born children would, by virtue of being the "baby" of the family, tend to be rather spoiled. He suggested that middle-born children would be better adjusted, because their experiences of dethronement and of spoiling would be less strong than those of their other siblings.

More recently, a researcher named Frank Sulloway argued that first-born and later-born siblings would tend to develop different personalities. Sulloway (1995, 1996) believed that differences would emerge in several aspects of personality, as described in terms of the Big Five framework: For example, he believed that the later-born siblings would have higher levels of Agreeableness and lower levels of Conscientiousness than would the earlier-born siblings. However, he suggested that the largest differences would be found in the Openness to Experience factor, where later-born siblings would be expected to have higher levels than would first-born siblings. Sulloway suggested that younger siblings would need to develop a more creative, unconventional, risk-taking personality to find areas in which they could excel and thereby impress their parents. This diversity of interests was necessary for younger siblings, Sulloway suggested, to avoid direct competition with their older siblings, who would (during childhood) tend to be smarter and stronger by virtue of their age.

Sulloway (1995, 1996) supported these arguments with a wide range of historical evidence, including the records of the votes and decisions made by first-born and later-born politicians and judges, and the theories and writings of first-born and later-born scientists and intellectuals. However, there has also been much criticism of this evidence (Townsend, 2000), and several empirical tests of the theories have shown mixed results. Studies in which first- and later-born siblings are directly compared with reference to each other (e.g., by asking which sibling is more rebellious) generally do find that the later-born siblings tend to be rated as having higher levels of traits related to Openness to Experience (Paulhus, Trapnell, & Chen, 1999). But, on the other hand, studies in which the personalities of first- and later-born siblings are measured by self- and observer report questionnaires have generally found very weak results, with virtually no difference between them on the Openness to Experience factor (Jefferson, Herbst, & McCrae, 1998). These latter results, which represent the most direct way of assessing the size of the personality differences between siblings, suggest that the effects of birth order on personality are quite small. It may be that the effects observed in some studies of birth order and personality have capitalized on "contrast effects" (as described earlier in this chapter) that are especially strong when personality reports ask the respondent to make direct comparisons between siblings.

Box 6.3 Identifying Specific Genes That Influence Personality: Molecular Genetic Studies

As noted in Chapter 5, some studies have examined the role of specific genes in influencing personality. In these investigations, the researchers have identified different alleles (i.e., different gene variants at the same place, or locus) that influence the levels of some neurotransmitter substance. The researchers have then compared the personalities of people who have those different alleles to find out whether those people differ in their levels of characteristics thought to be influenced by that neurotransmitter. The results of some early studies suggested that a gene called DRD4 (which influences dopamine levels) was related to the trait of novelty seeking (Benjamin et al., 1996) and that a gene called 5-HTTLPR (which influences levels of serotonin) was related to the traits of harm avoidance and Neuroticism (Lesch et al., 1996). However, results from many subsequent studies have found that any such links are quite weak (Munafo et al., 2009; Munafo, Yalcin, Willis-Owen, & Flint, 2008). These latter findings reflect the fact that any reasonably common single gene is likely to have only a weak effect on personality; instead, the genetic influences on any given personality characteristic are likely to be attributable to the total effects of a very large number of genes (e.g., McCrae, Scally, Terracciano, Abecasis, & Costa, 2010).

6.8 SUMMARY AND CONCLUSIONS

In this chapter, we have examined the methods used by researchers to find out the extent to which differences in people's personalities are due to genetic (heritable) differences or due to environmental differences. Let us briefly review the main points.

First, psychologists use several methods to examine the heritability of a trait—that is, the extent to which variation in the trait is due to genetic variation. These methods generally involve determining the extent to which relatives have similar levels of a personality trait. The researchers try to separate the effects of heredity and environment in several ways, such as by comparing relatives who have been raised apart (e.g., twins adopted into different households), or by comparing relatives who have more genes in common with relatives who have fewer genes in common (e.g., identical twins versus fraternal twins). Research on the heritability of personality is based on many assumptions, which researchers have attempted to verify; some of the questions associated with these assumptions are complex and have not yet been fully resolved, but the basic results obtained in heritability studies are probably fairly accurate.

The results of heritability studies suggest that there are fairly strong genetic influences on personality characteristics, regardless of which characteristics are considered. These genetic influences are nearly all additive rather than nonadditive, and they appear to account for nearly two-thirds of the variation in personality trait levels. In contrast to the strong genetic effects on personality, the effects of the common environment—that is, features of the household that are shared among siblings—on personality characteristics appear to be very weak. Instead, environmental effects on personality chiefly involve the unique environment—that is, experiences that are different for each sibling of the same family. Some research has examined the possibility that birth order, parental treatment, and peer relationships may be important aspects of the unique environment, but the relations between these variables and personality have been rather weak.

6.9 APPENDIX: DIFFICULTIES IN SEPARATING THE EFFECTS OF HEREDITY AND ENVIRONMENT

As described in this chapter, researchers have devised some creative and useful ways of separating the influences of genetic variation and environmental variation on personality variation. But in some sense these effects cannot be so easily divided, because it is possible that genetic and environmental influences can combine in complex ways, or that genetic and environmental influences would "go together" in some circumstances. These interactions and correlations between heredity and environment add some interesting complications to the study of genetic and environmental influences on personality, and this appendix gives a brief summary of these genotype—environment interactions and correlations.

6.9.1 Genotype—Environment Interactions

In the previous sections, we have described the role of genetic and environmental variation as if each aspect contributed independently to personality variation. For example, we have assumed that a given environmental situation would tend to influence everyone in the same way. This might well be the case for many aspects of the environment: Perhaps poor nutrition would make all children grow up to be shorter than they would otherwise be, or perhaps exercise would make all adults stronger than they would otherwise be. In some cases, however, the situation might be more complicated than this: It is possible that the same environment will influence people's levels of a given characteristic in different ways, depending on their genetic characteristics (i.e., their genotype). This is known as *genotype—environment interaction*.

It is not hard to imagine plausible examples of genotype—environment interactions. Suppose that two children grow up in a household in which one of the parents is very overprotective. If one child has a genetically based inclination to enjoy being protected, then perhaps he or she would accept and encourage the parent's overprotectiveness, and thus grow up to be a rather risk-averse, dependent person. However, if the other child has a genetically based inclination to dislike being protected, then he or she may try to escape from the parent's overprotectiveness, and grow up to be a daring, independent person. Or, consider another example, in which a parent is very domineering. A child with a genetic tendency to be somewhat submissive might grow up to be very submissive as a result of consistently accepting domination by the parent. However, a child with a genetic tendency to be somewhat rebellious might grow up to be very rebellious as a result of consistently resisting domination by the parent. Of course, genotype—environment interactions can involve aspects of the environment other than those provided by parents: For example, children with different genetic tendencies might react very differently to the same opportunities for playing sports, for playing a musical instrument, or for playing video games. Similarly, children with different genetic inclinations could react very differently to the influence of "delinquent" peers: One child might be very easily influenced, but another might not be.

Genotype—environment interactions can influence the estimates of genetic influence that are obtained from heritability studies. Because these interactions will make people different from each other whenever those people differ *either* genetically *or* in their environments, any such interaction will tend to make all relatives less similar to each other than would be the case if that interaction did not exist. As a result, estimates of heritability based on correlations between relatives (e.g., siblings or twins raised apart) will tend to be lower when genotype—environment interactions are operating on a characteristic. However, heritability estimates based on *differences between* the correlations between relatives (e.g., identical twins relative to fraternal twins) will not be affected, because both correlations will be lowered by the interactions.

This raises the question of how important these genotype—environment interactions actually are. Do these interactions have strong influences on many characteristics? The methods used to study these questions are very complex, but the research on this topic suggests that genotype—environment interactions are usually not very strong (e.g., Plomin, DeFries, & Fulker, 1988).

6.9.2 Genotype—Environment Correlations: Passive, Reactive, and Active

As described in the previous section, a genotype—environment interaction occurs whenever the same environment has different influences on people's characteristics depending on the genetic differences among those people. But genotype—environment interactions are not the only way in which the effects of heredity and environment can combine in complex ways to influence individual differences in characteristics. Another phenomenon involves the tendency for people with different genetic tendencies to experience different environments, which then in turn have different influences on the characteristics of those people. In other words, your genetic tendencies might actually cause you to be exposed to some kinds of environments more than other kinds, and the differences between those environments might then influence the development of your personality characteristics. This is known as *genotype—environment correlation*.

Genotype—environment correlations can occur in three different ways. One kind of genotype—environment correlation happens when the environment experienced by children is influenced by their parents' genetic predispositions, which are also inherited by those children. For example, suppose that two parents have a genetic tendency to be very athletic. As a result, those parents might be enthusiastic sports participants, and might thereby raise their child in a very sports-oriented home environment. In this way, the child inherits both a genetic tendency to be athletic as well as an environment that tends to promote athletic ability. This kind of situation is called a *passive genotype−environment correlation*, because the children inherit this combination of genes and environment "passively," not as a result of their own behavior.

A different kind of genotype−environment correlation happens when children experience different environments depending on other people's reactions to the children's different genetic tendencies. Let us consider athletic ability as an example once again. Suppose that a child inherits a genetic tendency to be very athletic. The adults who interact with the child—including his or her parents, teachers, and coaches—might then react to his or her natural talent by providing the child with additional opportunities for playing and practicing sports. This highly sports-oriented environment might then contribute, along with the child's natural athletic talent, to the development of a very high level of athletic ability. This kind of situation is called a *reactive genotype−environment correlation*, because other people's reactions to the child's genetic tendencies end up influencing the environment that the child experiences. (A reactive genotype−environment correlation is sometimes known as an *evocative genotype−environment correlation,* because it is as if the child's genetic tendencies evoke the environment that the child experiences.)

Finally, another kind of genotype−environment correlation happens when children themselves seek out a particular kind of environment as a function of their own genetic tendencies. Continuing with our athletic ability example, consider a child who inherits a genetic predisposition to be highly athletic. As a result of his or her talent, this child might find sports participation to be very satisfying, and he or she might therefore seek many opportunities to play and practice various sports. This very sports-oriented environment might then cause the child's athletic ability to develop still further, beyond even what his or her genes alone would have caused. This kind of genotype−environment correlation is called an *active genotype−environment correlation*, because the child actively chooses environments as a function of his or her genetic predispositions.

When considering genotype−environment correlations, keep in mind that these correlations could be either positive or negative. In the preceding examples, we have described situations in which the genotype and environment are correlated positively, but it could work the other way around. Consider the example of the reactive genotype−environment correlation that was mentioned earlier. It is possible that a child with a genetic tendency to be high in athletic ability would cause his parents and other adults to react by providing a very sports-oriented environment; if this happened frequently, then the genes for athletic ability and the environment for developing that ability would be positively correlated. But imagine that a child has a genetic tendency to be low in athletic ability. It is possible (although not likely) that this could also lead the child's parents to provide a sports-oriented environment, as a way of improving the child's athletic ability. If this were to happen frequently enough, then the genes for athletic ability and the environment for developing that ability would be negatively correlated, because genes for *low* ability are causing an environment that develops *higher* ability.

The possibility of genotype—environment correlations leaves us with the question of whether these influences actually have an important influence on individual differences in various characteristics. Researchers who study the genetic and environmental influences on characteristics (e.g., Plomin et al., 1988) have found some evidence of genotype—environment correlations, but these correlations have been fairly weak.

To sum up, the study of genetic and environmental influences on personality is made more complicated by the difficulty in separating the effects of genes and environment. Rather than only acting additively and independently, the genetic and environmental influences may interact with each other and may be correlated with each other. Thus far, however, research findings have not shown especially strong effects of these genotype—environment interactions and genotype—environment correlations on individual differences in personality trait levels.

CHAPTER 7

The Evolutionary Function of Personality

Contents

Like the human body, human behavior has been influenced by the process of evolution by natural selection. In this chapter, we will begin with a brief summary of how evolution works and then turn to the question of how personality variation has evolved. In doing so, we will consider the ways by which evolution can act to preserve the differences among people in personality, and we will consider the advantages and disadvantages—from an evolutionary standpoint—that are associated with high and low levels of each personality dimension.

Individual Differences and Personality
ISBN 978-0-12-809845-5, http://dx.doi.org/10.1016/B978-0-12-809845-5.00007-X

7.1 THE IDEA OF EVOLUTION BY NATURAL SELECTION

One of the cornerstones of modern biology is the concept of evolution by natural selection, as discovered by Charles Darwin (Darwin, 1859).[1] Briefly, the idea of evolution by natural selection can be summarized as follows:

1. individuals differ in various characteristics;
2. these characteristics are to some extent transmitted directly—through reproduction itself—from parents to offspring; and
3. some characteristics are associated with greater numbers of surviving offspring (i.e., with *reproductive success*); therefore,
4. across generations, those characteristics will become more widespread among the individuals of the population.

Because of (4), there will sometimes emerge large differences between two populations of individuals that were originally a single population, but that have been divided or separated for a long period of time. For example, suppose that one group of individuals has moved out of its original range to a different region and later becomes permanently isolated from the group of individuals who stayed behind. As a result of being separated and of inhabiting different environments (in which different characteristics may be associated with reproductive success), the two groups may then change in very different ways as the generations pass. After a very long time, the two groups might become so different from each other that they would no longer be able to interbreed, even if they were to be reunited in the same location. At this point, two different "species" would have emerged from the single, original species that had once existed.

In this chapter, however, our focus is not on the evolution of separate species, but instead on how individual difference characteristics have evolved within the human species. To understand how evolution by natural selection can apply to human characteristics, let us consider each of the preceding four steps in turn, focusing on variation among people.

1. *Individual Differences among People.* First of all, it is obvious that for many characteristics, there are important individual differences among humans of any population: We vary in physical characteristics such as body size and proportions, and we vary in psychological characteristics such as our shyness, impulsiveness, and aggressiveness.
2. *Inheritance of Characteristics.* Next is the question of whether or not these characteristics are transmitted from parents to offspring. The answer, as reviewed in Chapter 6, is that to an important extent, those characteristics are indeed transmitted via heredity. For an array of psychological (and physical) traits, the variation that exists within a population is typically due in large part to additive genetic variation. For personality

---

[1] The principle of evolution by natural selection was also discovered independently by another biologist, Alfred Russel Wallace. However, Darwin provided a much more detailed and thorough explanation of this theory.

traits, recent evidence (see Chapter 6) suggests that perhaps more than 60% of the variability that exists in a population is due to genetic differences that are passed directly from parents to offspring. Given that variation in traits is often rather large, this means the amount of variation due to heredity can be important.[2]

3. *Characteristics Associated with Reproductive Success.* The next issue is whether or not the variation in some characteristics can be associated with survival and, ultimately, with reproductive success. That is, are some levels of a trait better, or more "adaptive," from the point of view of increasing one's likelihood of having surviving offspring? On the one hand, it is clear that some varieties of a trait are indeed more adaptive and others less so; for example, some alleles (i.e., variants) of some genes are associated with fatal childhood diseases. But, on the other hand, it is not as obvious as to whether or not the different varieties, or levels, of characteristics that show *normal* variation— that is, variation among basically healthy individuals—are also associated with different levels of reproductive success in a given environment. This is a big and tricky question, and we will discuss it in detail in the next section; for the moment, however, let us assume that reproductive success does sometimes depend in part on the characteristics one inherits.[3,4]

4. *Changes across Generations in Levels of Characteristics.* The final issue is whether or not population-level differences can emerge as a result of the accumulated action of evolution over many generations. Suppose that in a given environment, people's levels of reproductive success did depend, at least in some small part, on their levels of some heritable characteristic. For example, perhaps people with higher levels of a given characteristic tended to have more surviving offspring, on average, than did people with lower levels. In this way, each generation would show a small increase in the

---

[2] In case you are wondering where these variations actually come from, they emerge as a result of genetic mutations—that is, as a result of changes in the genes that carry the instructions to produce the many features of our bodies. Although these "mistakes" in the genetic code often produce changes that are disastrous for an individual's chances of survival and reproduction, they sometimes produce changes that actually improve those chances.

[3] Individual differences in characteristics might influence reproductive success in two distinct ways. First, one's level of a characteristic might improve (or undermine) one's reproductive success by making one more (or less) able to deal with the natural environment, for example, by getting food or by avoiding predators. Alternatively, it might operate by making one better able to obtain a mate, whether directly (by being more attractive to mates) or indirectly (by defeating one's rivals in confrontations). Darwin referred to the environment-related mechanism as natural selection and to the mating-related mechanism as sexual selection. For the sake of simplicity, we will use the term "natural selection" to refer to both of them together.

[4] The idea of evolution by natural selection does not suggest that people (or any other organisms) are consciously trying to improve their reproductive success. The idea instead is that people (or other organisms) inherit physical and psychological characteristics that have tended to promote reproductive success, within the environments in which their evolution occurred. For example, human evolution has not necessarily selected individuals who have a drive to want as many children as possible, but it has tended to select individuals who are interested in sexual intercourse and who are motivated to care for their children. These latter drives have tended to promote reproductive success in most environments that our ancestors inhabited.

average level of that characteristic. If this tendency persisted for many generations, then it could result in a rather large change in the average person's level of the characteristic. But if instead the association between this characteristic and reproductive success tended to change from one generation to the next—such that (for example) reproductive success was sometimes associated with higher levels and sometimes associated with lower levels—then the average level might show little or no net change over the generations. (But as we will see in the following section, *variation* in the characteristic might still be maintained.)

7.2 WHY ARE WE NOT ALL THE SAME? FLUCTUATING OPTIMUM AND FREQUENCY DEPENDENCE

7.2.1 Several Reasons Why Variation Does Not Go Away

For many characteristics, the forces of selection tend to eliminate all variation, by favoring a single solution that is apparently the "best" that can be easily achieved. For example, virtually every healthy human is born with two eyes, two ears, two arms, and two legs. This is presumably because having two of these organs simply worked much better for the extremely distant ancestors of all modern humans, in terms of facilitating survival and reproduction, than did having one or three of those organs.

But there are also many characteristics for which the forces of selection have apparently preserved a great deal of variation. In addition to the obvious physical differences between men and women, there is also a great deal of variation among people of the same sex (and the same age) in basic physical characteristics such as height and body build, as well as in the psychological characteristics that are the topic of this book. But the existence of so much variation in these various traits raises the question of *how* that variation has been maintained over the course of human evolution: Why has it not been eliminated? Why is there not a single "ideal" level for each trait—such as height, body build, or any personality trait—for every adult of a given sex and age?

There are several possible reasons why variation has been maintained in many characteristics (see also Buss & Greiling, 1999, for a detailed discussion that includes some additional reasons not examined here). Some of these reasons do not involve any particular advantage or disadvantage to having a higher or lower level of a given trait.

1. One possibility is that the variation is simply unimportant, in the sense that it has no consequences for survival and reproduction. As a result, new mutations that increase or decrease levels of a trait will persist in the population and will increase *variation* in trait levels.

2. A related possibility is that new mutations do cause variation away from an ideal level of a trait and thereby reduce reproductive success, but that natural selection does not remove these mutations quickly enough to eliminate variation in the trait.

3. Another possibility involves the importance of variation in combating infections by parasites. Researchers have pointed out that parasitic infections tend to spread less quickly when the individuals of a species are different from each other in various ways. According to this idea, sexual reproduction evolved because it produces offspring who differ from each other and from their parents, and this variation helps to slow the spread of parasitic infections. (That is, parasites need to "learn" how to defeat the defenses of each individual in a species that reproduces sexually. By contrast, asexual reproduction produces individuals who are genetically identical, so parasites can infect all individuals as soon as they can infect one.) In this way, differences between individuals in various characteristics are merely due to the importance of sexual reproduction in preventing parasitic infections.

However, it is unlikely that the above explanations can fully account for the wide individual differences in personality characteristics which have been maintained over a long period of time. Next we consider some ways in which trait variation could be maintained for reasons that involve advantages or disadvantages associated with higher or lower levels of a given characteristic.

7.2.2 Fluctuating Optimum: Ideal Levels of a Characteristic Vary Across Places and Times

If a characteristic is important to survival and reproduction, why would variation in that characteristic be maintained across long periods of time? Why would one "ideal" level of the trait not simply displace all the others? Researchers have proposed two main reasons, which are likely to operate in combination.

One reason is that the ideal level of the characteristic might differ depending on environmental conditions that change from one time and place to another. If the ideal level varies from one generation or from one region to the next, then these changes would help to maintain variation between individuals in the characteristic. Depending on when and where a group of people was living, the people with high levels might have better reproductive success, or the people with low levels might have better reproductive success. If a group of people moved from one place to another, the ideal level of any given trait would probably shift somewhat, according to changes in various features of the environment, such as the climate and vegetation. Or, if they stayed in the same place for long enough, the ideal level of the same characteristic would also be likely to shift somewhat, again according to any changes in features of the environment. As a result of this *fluctuating optimum* level of the characteristic, the variation in the characteristic would tend to be maintained even over very long periods of time.[5] The average level

---

[5] Actually, for the trait variation to persist across generations, some conditions might need to be met, such as migration of some individuals between different regions, and the occasional emergence of new mutations. But we will assume that these conditions are at least sometimes met.

of the trait would gradually shift up or down within a given population, in response to the features of its current environment, but the amount of *variation* in those levels would not be reduced very much.

As a possible example of the way in which the fluctuating optimum could operate, consider the characteristic of "parental investment." Suppose that there are some partly heritable differences among the individuals of a given animal species, such that some individuals tend to have many offspring (but give little parental care to those offspring), whereas other individuals tend to have few offspring (but give much parental care to those offspring). During times when there is abundant food, the individuals who have many offspring (but who give little parental care) will probably have better reproductive success, because those many offspring are likely to survive even without any help from their parents and will therefore become more numerous than the offspring of other individuals. But in times when food shortages occur, the individuals who have few offspring (but who give much parental care) will probably have better reproductive success, because those few offspring have a good chance of surviving due to their parents' assistance, while the offspring of other individuals may nearly all die (or at least fail to reproduce). Depending on changes across times and across places in the abundance of food, either high or low parental investment may be favored, with the result that the population of the species would tend not to become uniformly high or low with regard to this characteristic.[6]

7.2.3 Frequency Dependence: The Advantages of Doing What Others Are Not Doing

Along with the "fluctuating optimum" reason described before, a second reason why the variation in a characteristic would persist is that there might never be a *single* ideal level of a characteristic, but rather an ideal *balance* of different levels of a characteristic. Suppose that nearly everyone had a high level of a characteristic. If so, perhaps the few people who had a low level of that characteristic would be more successful. Conversely, if nearly everyone had a low level of a trait, then perhaps the few people who had a high level of that trait would be more successful. As a result of this process, which is similar to one that biologists call *frequency-dependent selection*, we might see a rough balance in the population between people who have higher and lower levels of the characteristic.[7]

---

[6] Note, of course, that over long periods of time, there might be an overall trend in one direction or another, with the possible result that the species eventually *would* show a major increase or decrease in its level of a trait.

[7] Specifically, this is *negative* frequency-dependent selection, because individuals having a given level of a trait become less successful when there are more of them in the population. If instead the individuals having that level of the trait become more successful when there are more of them in the population, then there is *positive* frequency-dependent selection. Positive frequency-dependent selection eliminates trait variation.

As a hypothetical example of the way in which frequency dependence could operate, consider the color of feathers in a species of bird. Suppose that there are partly heritable differences among the males of a given bird species in the color of their feathers, and that the females of this species prefer to mate with males who have a rare color. If so, then a lone blue male among a group of many green males would be more likely to reproduce successfully, and blue males would become more frequent in the next generation. But over the generations, the advantage of being blue would decrease, because this color would no longer be so rare and hence would no longer be so attractive to females. Eventually, when blue males became as common as green males, there would be no advantage at all, and the two colors would balance each other out. (Note that if one color had an advantage in some other way, such as for avoiding predators, then the "balance" would not be 50–50 but would instead favor a higher proportion of that color.)

7.2.4 "Personality" Variation in Nonhuman Animals: Examples of Fluctuating Optimum Levels and Frequency-Dependent Selection

Scientists have observed some cases of fluctuating optimum levels and frequency-dependent selection in the behavior of various species of animals. Here are two examples, both involving species of fish (see also Nettle, 2006).

Trinidadian guppies differ from one another in how bold or timid they are (O'Steen, Cullum, & Bennett, 2002). Guppies that live below waterfalls are at risk from other species of fish that eat the guppies. In these areas, guppies tend to be rather timid, avoiding exposure to predators. In contrast, guppies that live above waterfalls are at much less risk of being eaten, as there are few predators in those areas. These guppies tend to be rather bold. The timidness or boldness of guppies is heritable: When guppies from both downstream and upstream areas are bred and raised in the laboratory, the "downstream" guppies are better at avoiding predators than are the "upstream" guppies. Now, if the guppies are exposed to a different level of predation (for example, if researchers introduce predators into a predator-free stream or move guppies into a stream having fewer predators), then the average level of boldness or timidness in the guppy population evolves accordingly: When predation is heavy, timid guppies are more likely to survive and reproduce, and when predation is light, bold guppies are more likely to survive and reproduce. (Presumably, timid guppies are at a disadvantage when there are few predators, perhaps by being less effective in finding food and mates.) Thus, Trinidadian guppies provide an example of fluctuating optimum levels of a characteristic.

Males of the bluegill sunfish follow one of two "strategies" of reproduction (Gross, 1991). Some males build nests after having delayed their reproduction for some time, and then fertilize the eggs deposited into the nests by females; because the nest-building males provide parental care for the eggs, these males are said to follow the parental strategy. Other males mature more quickly and, instead of building nests, sneak into the nests of other males and fertilize the eggs there; this is called the cuckolding strategy. When few males follow the cuckolding strategy, those males are successful—it is easy for them to find nests and deposit sperm there—so the number of cuckolding males increases in the next generation. But when many males follow the cuckolding strategy, those males are less successful—there are too few nests for all of the cuckolding males—so the number of cuckolding males decreases in the next generation. In this way, a balance is established between the numbers of parental and cuckolding males. Thus, bluegill sunfish males provide an example of frequency-dependent selection.

BOX 7.1 Games as Simulations of Frequency-Dependent Selection

One way that researchers examine the process of frequency-dependent selection is to create "games" that simulate, in a simplified way, the processes that maintain variation between individuals through many generations.

One of these games is called the *hawk–dove game* (e.g., Maynard Smith & Price, 1973). Imagine that people compete for resources. There are two kinds of competitors: "Dove" people compete only mildly, whereas "hawk" people compete much more intensely. Both hawks and doves compete as individuals, not as teams.

When two doves compete with each other for some resource, one of them will give up fairly quickly. (Each dove has roughly the same chance of winning, because they are assumed to be similar in their ability to compete.) The winning dove thus gains the resource, but the losing dove suffers little cost from the competition.

When a hawk competes with a dove, the dove always gives up quickly and therefore the hawk always wins. In this way, there is little cost to the dove, but the hawk always gains the resource. This means that if a few hawks entered a population of doves, they would be very successful. By beating the doves in the competition for resources, the hawks would be more likely to survive and reproduce. Over the generations, the proportion of hawks would increase.

You might think that eventually the hawks would completely replace the doves. But this is not what would happen. Consider what happens when a hawk competes with a hawk. Both hawks compete intensely, each refusing to give up until they have really no chance of winning. (At the start of the game, each hawk has roughly the same chance of winning, because they are assumed to be similar in their ability to compete.) The hawk that wins will gain the resource, but the hawk that loses will suffer a very large cost from the competition (through injury and wasted energy), and to some extent so will even the winning hawk.

What this means is that when hawks are consistently competing with each other (rather than with doves), they incur heavy costs over the long run—costs that exceed the value of the resources that they compete to gain. Therefore, in a population full of hawks, a dove would actually have better chances of surviving and reproducing than would the hawks, simply by avoiding the costs of competition that are suffered by the hawks.

So, hawks do better than doves when there are very few hawks, but doves do better than hawks when there are very few doves. This eventually leads to a kind of balance between "hawk" people and "dove" people. The exact proportion of hawks and doves would depend

BOX 7.1 Games as Simulations of Frequency-Dependent Selection—cont'd

on the benefit of gaining the resource and on the cost of intense competition. But the main point is that individuals representing both of these opposite "strategies" would remain in the population. Both hawks and doves would persist over the long term.

Now consider a different game, which we will call the *lion—jackal game*. This game is mathematically equivalent to the hawk—dove game, but it involves different behaviors on the part of the two strategies.

"Lion" people actively try to find resources. They thereby gain the benefits of finding resources, but they also pay the costs of seeking them (probably through energy expended or injuries sustained). "Jackal" people do not bother to look for resources, so they do not pay any costs. But they do consume resources obtained by lions, so they gain benefits without paying costs. (Suppose, for example, that lions tend to obtain large amounts of food that they cannot eat all by themselves, which means that there are lots of left-overs for jackals.)

If a few jackals were to enter a population consisting only of lions, those jackals would therefore have better chances of surviving and reproducing than would the lions. Over the generations, the proportions of jackals would increase.

But this increase would only go so far. If the proportion of jackals became very high, then there would no longer be enough left-over resources to support all of them. (Remember that jackals do not actually get resources for themselves; they just wait around for lions to find resources, and then consume the left-overs.) The lions would actually do better in these circumstances, because they at least get the benefit of consuming the resources they find.

The result, as in the case of the hawk—dove game, is a balance between the two kinds of people: Jackals do better than lions when there are few jackals, but lions do better than jackals when there are few lions. The exact proportions depend on the benefits of the resources and the costs of seeking them, but the important point is that both "lion" people and "jackal" people would remain in the population.

Obviously, these games greatly oversimplify the way that people (or any other organisms) actually behave. But even though the assumptions of these games are not strictly true, the games still show us the basic reasons why variation in some aspects of behavior would never be eliminated.

7.2.5 The Operation of the Fluctuating Optimum and Frequency Dependence: Genetic and Developmental Routes

When we think about the role of frequency dependence and of the fluctuating optimum, it is useful to keep in mind two different ways in which both of those mechanisms preserve trait variation. One way is by favoring the reproductive success of individuals who have a *genetic inclination to have a particular level of the trait*. Sometimes, individuals who are genetically inclined to have high levels of a trait will be favored, and sometimes, individuals who are genetically inclined to have low levels of a trait will be favored. But over the long run, the mechanisms of the fluctuating optimum and of frequency dependence tend to produce roughly equal levels of reproductive success for individuals whose genes tend to produce very different levels of the trait. As a result, heritable variation in the trait is maintained.

A second way by which these mechanisms can operate (and one that can occur alongside the first) is by favoring the reproductive success of individuals *whose genetic inclination is more flexible, allowing the development of* either *a high* or *a low level of the trait,* depending on experiences early in life. That is, some individuals have genes that allow either a fairly high or a fairly low level of the trait to be developed, depending on experiences during development that indicate the optimal level of the trait in the current environment. In many environments, these individuals would be able to adapt successfully by developing a level of the trait that is suitable for that environment. (For example, suppose that in a given species of animals, individuals who have heavy fur are more likely to survive and reproduce in cold climates, but that individuals who have lighter fur are more likely to survive and reproduce in hot climates. If some individuals inherit genes that allow them to develop *either* heavier fur *or* lighter fur, depending on the temperatures that they experience while developing, then those individuals would be likely to survive and reproduce successfully in either type of climate.) The reproductive success of these individuals would then preserve the genes that allow an individual to develop a different level of the trait in response to cues from his or her environment.[8]

7.3 ADAPTIVE TRADE-OFFS BETWEEN HIGH AND LOW LEVELS OF THE HEXACO PERSONALITY FACTORS

We now consider the question of what costs and benefits might be associated with high or low levels of each dimension. In other words, what are the "trade-offs" involved for each personality factor, as judged in terms of how a high or a low level might influence one's chances of survival and reproductive success? These advantages and disadvantages are discussed below (and summarized in Table 7.1) for each of the six HEXACO factors as described in Chapter 3. Keep in mind that this discussion does not necessarily apply to the situation that currently exists in modern societies. Instead, it is meant to apply to the situations that existed in the prehistoric and historic environments in which evolution by natural selection would have operated on our ancestors.

---

[8] However, these individuals would probably not be able to develop quite as high or quite as low a level of the trait as would individuals whose genetic predispositions are to be high only or to be low only. As a result, in the more extreme environments, the more developmentally flexible individuals would not be quite as successful as the more specialized individuals (see Wilson, 1994).

Table 7.1 Summary of theoretical interpretations of HEXACO personality factors

Factor	Interpretation	Benefits of high levels?	Costs of high levels?
Honesty—Humility	Reciprocal altruism (fairness)	Gains from cooperation (mutual help and nonaggression)	Loss of potential gains that would result from exploitation of others
Agreeableness (versus Anger)	Reciprocal altruism (tolerance)	Gains from cooperation (mutual help and nonaggression)	Losses due to being exploited by others
Emotionality	Kin altruism	Survival of kin (especially offspring); personal survival (especially as it favors kin survival)	Loss of potential gains associated with risks to self and kin
Extraversion	Engagement in social endeavors	Social gains (i.e., friends, mates, allies)	Energy and time; risks from social environment
Conscientiousness	Engagement in task-related endeavors	Material gains (i.e., improved use of resources), reduced risks	Energy and time
Openness to Experience	Engagement in idea-related endeavors	Material and social gains (i.e., resulting from discovery)	Energy and time; risks from social and natural environment

Ashton, M. C., & Lee, K. (2001). A theoretical basis for the major dimensions of personality. *European Journal of Personality*, *15*, 327–353; Ashton, M. C., Lee, K., & Paunonen, S. V. (2002). What is the central feature of extraversion? Social attention versus reward sensitivity. *Journal of Personality and Social Psychology*, *83*, 245–252; Ashton, M. C., & Lee, K. (2007). Empirical, theoretical, and practical advantages of the HEXACO model of personality structure. *Personality and Social Psychology Bulletin*, *11*, 150–166.

7.3.1 Honesty—Humility

The traits that belong to the Honesty—Humility factor include sincerity, fairness, modesty, and lack of greed. A common element of these traits seems to be a tendency not to exploit or take advantage of others: For example, a sincere person tends to avoid manipulating or deceiving others, a fair person tends to avoid cheating or stealing from others, a modest person tends not to feel entitled to exploit others, and a person who is not greedy tends not to feel tempted to gain at others' expense.

As explained in this way, the potential costs and benefits of having high or low levels of Honesty—Humility might be imagined (see Table 7.1). A person with a very high level of Honesty—Humility would be unwilling to exploit others even if he or she could surely get away with doing so; therefore, such a person would forgo any of the gains that might be had by taking advantage of others. But, on the other hand, a person high in Honesty—Humility would not create any victims, and therefore would avoid the risk of retaliation (including withdrawal of future cooperation) by those victims. At the opposite end of the dimension, a person with a very low level of Honesty—Humility would sometimes gain by exploiting others, but would sometimes lose the potential gains from future cooperation with others, because those exploited persons would be likely to retaliate by ending their cooperation.

BOX 7.2 Age Differences in Honesty—Humility

Recall from Chapter 4 the finding that on average, people's Honesty—Humility levels appear to decline during the teen years and then to increase throughout most of adulthood, such that 60-year-old persons average about one full standard deviation unit higher than 18-year-old persons (e.g., Ashton & Lee, 2016; Sibley & Pirie, 2013). These age differences in Honesty—Humility probably reflect developmental changes that would have evolved through natural selection.

As explained in this chapter, higher (versus lower) levels of Honesty—Humility are interpreted as a reluctance (versus a willingness) to exploit others. According to this view, the lower levels of Honesty—Humility observed at the beginning of the adult years could reflect a tendency, throughout the human evolutionary past, for the potential gains from exploiting others to be especially high at the beginning of adulthood. During that period of the lifespan, competition for mates, status, and resources is especially intense, and the "payoffs" for gaining at the expense of others are potentially very high. In contrast, the potential gains from exploiting others (relative to the gains from cooperating with them) are probably smaller in later adulthood.

Note that the intensity of intrasexual competition (i.e., competition among members of the same sex) tends to be stronger for men than for women. This difference reflects the fact that a man who successfully outcompetes his rivals can potentially have many more offspring than a woman can, because of the obvious differences in men's and women's reproduction. Consistent with this fact, the average level of Honesty—Humility among 18-year-old men is about one-half of a standard deviation below that among 18-year-old women; in contrast, these sex differences are only about half as large among persons in their 60s and 70s. But the fact that women also show fairly large age differences in Honesty—Humility (though not as large as those shown by men) is consistent with some considerable intrasexual competition among young women, as those who obtained the most desirable mates and the most resources would have tended to have more surviving children and grandchildren.

None of this, of course, justifies the exploitation of others, regardless of one's age. Even when one is in late adolescence or early adulthood, basic notions of right and wrong—not to mention the law—still apply.

7.3.2 Agreeableness

The traits that belong to the Agreeableness factor include forgivingness, gentleness, flexibility, and patience. A common element of these traits seems to be a tendency to continue cooperating (or to resume cooperating) with others who might have exploited one in some way: For example, a forgiving person tends not to hold a grudge for past injustices, a gentle person tends not to retaliate harshly, a flexible person tends to cooperate despite some degree of unfairness, and a patient person tends not to become angry at the first sign of exploitation.

As explained in this way, the potential costs and benefits of having high or low levels of Agreeableness might be imagined (see Table 7.1). A person with a very high level of Agreeableness would be likely to continue cooperating with others even when it is likely that he or she is being exploited; therefore, such a person would incur some costs due to this tolerance of being taken advantage of by others. But, on the other hand, a person high in Agreeableness would gain from future cooperation with someone who might not *really* have been trying to exploit him or her (it is not always obvious, after all), or who might usually be cooperative rather than exploitative. At the opposite end of the dimension, a person with a very low level of Agreeableness would sometimes gain by avoiding being exploited by others, but would sometimes lose some potential gains that would be obtained by cooperating with others who usually are rather cooperative.

BOX 7.3 Honesty–Humility and Agreeableness in the Dictator Game and the Ultimatum Game

Some recent studies (Hilbig, Zettler, Leist, & Heydasch, 2013; Thielmann, Hilbig, & Niedtfeld, 2014) have examined people's self-reports of Honesty–Humility and Agreeableness in relation to their behavior in two games that are designed to assess the two kinds of cooperative or reciprocally altruistic tendency. These two games are called the *dictator game* and the *ultimatum game*.

In the dictator game, two players who do not know each other are given an amount of money. One player is randomly given the role of "proposer" (who can divide up the money between the two persons in whatever way he or she chooses) and the "responder" (who gets no choice in the matter). When the dictator game is played only once (and hence with no possibility that the responder will get a turn as the proposer), the proposer can take most or even all of the money without any risk of being punished by the responder. The proportion of money allocated to the responder thus indicates the proposer's tendency to be fair toward the other person—in other words, to avoid exploiting another person even when this could easily be done. Therefore, the proportion of money given to the responder is expected to be related to Honesty–Humility: Persons higher in Honesty–Humility would presumably be more likely to divide the money fairly.

(Continued)

BOX 7.3 Honesty—Humility and Agreeableness in the Dictator Game and the Ultimatum Game—cont'd

In the ultimatum game, there is an important difference in the rules: The responder may reject the proposer's division of the money, in which case neither player gets any money at all. In this way, if the responder considers the proposer's division of the money to be unfair, the responder can punish the proposer. The (maximum) proportion of money that the responder will allow the proposer to give to himself or herself thus indicates the responder's tendency to tolerate unfair treatment by another person. Therefore, the proportion of money that the responder allows the proposer to keep (i.e., without rejecting this division) is expected to be related to Agreeableness: Persons higher in Agreeableness would presumably be more likely to accept a somewhat unfair division of money.

In both of these studies (Hilbig et al., 2013; Thielmann et al., 2014), behavior in the two games was related modestly but in the expected way with self-reports on Honesty—Humility and Agreeableness. In the dictator game, the proposers who divided the money more fairly tended to be higher in Honesty—Humility than were the proposers who divided the money more selfishly; in the ultimatum game, the responders who would accept divisions that were less fair to them tended to be higher in Agreeableness than the responders who would not accept those divisions. Thus, the results were consistent with the theoretical interpretations of these two dimensions.

7.3.3 Emotionality

The traits that belong to the Emotionality factor include fearfulness, anxiety, dependence, and sentimentality. A common element of these traits seems to be a tendency to promote the survival of oneself and one's kin: For example, a fearful person tends to avoid physical dangers, an anxious person tends to worry about potential harms, a dependent person tends to seek help and support in times of need, and a sentimental person tends to feel a sense of empathy and attachment toward one's family and friends. As explained in this way, the potential costs and benefits of having high or low levels of Emotionality might be imagined (see Table 7.1). A person with a very high level of Emotionality would gain in several ways: By avoiding harm to oneself and one's kin, by gaining help for oneself and one's kin, and by being motivated to help one's kin. But, on the other hand, a person high in Emotionality would also lose out on potential gains from any endeavors that involve some threats to the well-being of oneself or one's kin. A person with a very low level of Emotionality would (along with his or her kin) be more likely to experience death or serious injury but would potentially enjoy greater gains as a result of exposing oneself and one's kin to various dangers.

BOX 7.4 Sex Differences in Personality Traits: The Emotionality Factor

For most personality traits, there are only small differences between the average man and the average woman. But some moderately large differences are observed on the Emotionality dimension: More than 70% of women (but less than 30% of men) have an above-average level of Emotionality; conversely, more than 70% of men (but less than 30% of women) have a below-average level of Emotionality. This sex difference in the Emotionality factor—typically at least one full standard deviation unit in size—might be explained by the interpretation of Emotionality as a dimension that influences kin altruism (Ashton & Lee, 2007; see Section 7.3.3).

There are several reasons why we might expect kin altruistic tendencies to be stronger on average in women than in men. Consider the case of parenting: Having a child imposes a heavier biological cost on women than on men, because it is women who undergo pregnancy, childbirth, and breastfeeding. Also, a woman can be certain as to which children are her biological children and which children are not, whereas this is not always the case for a man. And throughout the human evolutionary past, the survival of a child has depended more heavily on the survival of its mother than of its father.

Several researchers have explained sex differences in Emotionality-related personality traits in terms of kin altruism and "investment" in one's children. For example, fearfulness of physical dangers (Campbell, 1999) and willingness to ask others for help (Taylor et al., 2000) are likely to improve the chances of personal and offspring survival, and feelings of emotional attachment and empathy are likely to motivate one to care for one's children. All of these tendencies are associated with the Emotionality factor of personality.

7.3.4 Summary for Honesty—Humility, Agreeableness, and Emotionality: Altruism Versus Aggression

Notice that each of the three characteristics described above is thought to involve some trade-off between behavior that is altruistic (or nonaggressive) and behavior that is nonaltruistic (or aggressive). In other words, higher levels of these three dimensions are associated with the tendency to help other individuals (or to avoid harming them), as opposed to the tendency to harm other individuals (or to avoid helping them).

In the cases of Honesty—Humility and Agreeableness, the form of altruism that is involved is called *reciprocal altruism* (e.g., Trivers, 1971), because the benefit to the altruistic individual comes from the *reciprocation* of that altruism by the other individual. Although reciprocal altruism can be beneficial for both individuals, it can break down. As described earlier, a person low in Honesty—Humility will try to exploit the other person. Similarly, a person low in Agreeableness will be too quick to decide that the other person is exploiting him or her (see also Perugini, Gallucci, Presaghi, & Ercolani, 2003).

In the case of Emotionality, the form of altruism that is involved is called *kin altruism* (e.g., Hamilton, 1964), because the benefit to the altruistic individual comes from the fact that the other individual is likely to be his or her kin. When those kin are one's own children, then the benefit to one's own reproductive success is obvious. But note that there can also be benefits to an altruistic individual even when he or she helps kin who are *not* his or her own children: Whenever one helps *any* genetic relative to improve his or her chances of survival and reproduction, this might *indirectly* improve one's own reproductive success, because the children of that relative will also carry one's own genes.

According to these explanations, an individual who tends to be very altruistic would be expected to have high levels of Honesty—Humility, Agreeableness, and Emotionality; conversely, a person who tends to be very aggressive would be expected to have low levels of all three of those dimensions. Some evidence suggests that this is indeed the case: In lexical studies of personality structure, adjectives suggesting an overall altruistic tendency (*sympathetic, softhearted*, etc.) tend to divide their loadings across these factors, and questionnaire scales assessing altruistic (versus aggressive) tendencies show moderate correlations with each of the three dimensions (e.g., Lee & Ashton, 2006).

7.3.5 Extraversion

The traits that belong to the Extraversion factor include social self-esteem, social bold-ness, sociability, and liveliness. A common element of these traits seems to be a tendency to engage actively in *social* endeavors: For example, a person with high social self-esteem feels that he or she is popular, a socially bold person tends to lead others and to state opin-ions, a sociable person tends to make friends and to interact frequently with them, and a lively person tends to exhibit cheerfulness and enthusiasm. As explained in this way, the potential costs and benefits of having high or low levels of Extraversion might be imag-ined (see Table 7.1). A person with a very high level of Extraversion would tend to gain and hold the attention of other people, and would thereby have an advantage in gaining friends and allies, and also in attracting desirable mates. But, on the other hand, a person with a high level of Extraversion would also expend a great deal of energy by engaging actively in social endeavors, and that person might also be the target of some hostility from other people, who might resent the attention being paid by others to that person.

7.3.6 Conscientiousness

The traits that belong to the Conscientiousness factor include organization, diligence, perfectionism, and prudence. A common element of these traits seems to be a tendency to engage actively in *task-related* endeavors: For example, an organized person tends to arrange his or her physical surroundings, a diligent person tends to work hard and long, a perfectionistic person pays thorough attention to details, and a prudent person thinks through options carefully. As explained in this way, the potential costs and benefits of having high or low levels of Conscientiousness might be imagined (see Table 7.1). A person with a very high level of Conscientiousness would tend to perform many important tasks efficiently and accurately, and would thereby potentially gain material advantages. (In earlier times, "material advantages" would mean a better food supply, better clothing and shelter, and better safety from impending dangers; nowadays, material advantages would mean earning, saving money, and staying healthy.) But, on the other hand, a person with a high level of Conscientiousness would also expend a great deal of energy by engaging actively in task-related endeavors, and these endeavors might not always yield worthwhile rewards.

7.3.7 Openness to Experience

The traits that belong to the Openness to Experience factor include aesthetic appreciation, inquisitiveness, creativity, and unconventionality. A common element of these traits seems to be a tendency to engage actively in *idea-related* endeavors: For example, an aesthetically appreciative person tends to contemplate artistic or natural beauty, an inquisitive person tends to search for understanding of the human or natural world, a creative person tends to generate new ideas and new solutions, and an unconventional person tends to be receptive to people and ideas that are new or strange. As explained in this way, the potential costs and benefits of having high or low levels of Openness to Experience might be imagined (see Table 7.1). A person with a very high level of Openness to Experience would tend to discover, learn, and invent new things that would then be useful in social- or task-related endeavors. But, on the other hand, a person with a high level of Openness to Experience would also expend a great deal of energy by engaging actively in idea-related endeavors. Moreover, these endeavors might also involve some risks, to the extent that one's new ideas and discoveries are mistaken or dangerous or might elicit hostility from more conventional persons.

7.3.8 Summary for Extraversion, Conscientiousness, and Openness to Experience: Engagement in Areas of Endeavor

Thus, the three personality dimensions of this second set are all associated with some contrast between high and low levels of engagement, but each within its own area of endeavor. That is, higher levels of each of these three dimensions are associated with being, in some sense, more "activated" or "involved." There is not yet any biological evidence to show whether or not this is in fact the case, but it will be interesting to see the results of future research studies that examine the biological bases of the Extraversion, Conscientiousness, and Openness to Experience factors. Presumably, such investigations could test the idea that each of these three dimensions involves a greater intensity of some kind, such as (perhaps) the energy consumption of the body or brain.

BOX 7.5 Adaptive Trade-offs from the Perspective of the Big Five Personality Dimensions

The discussions given earlier and in Table 7.1 regarding the adaptive trade-offs of personality variation were described in terms of the six HEXACO personality dimensions. However, these trade-offs can also be considered from the perspective of the Big Five personality dimensions (Nettle, 2006) (For further interesting discussions, see also Buss, 1996; Hogan, 1996; MacDonald, 1995).

Recall from Chapter 3 that the Big Five factors of Extraversion, Conscientiousness, and Openness to Experience are very similar to the same-named factors of the HEXACO model. Therefore, interpretations of the costs and benefits for any of these factors should be applicable regardless of which model is considered. In general, the discussion of these factors as given by Nettle (2006) is similar to that given in this chapter (see also Ashton & Lee, 2001, 2007; Ashton et al., 2002). But some of the potential costs and benefits suggested by Nettle for these factors are different from those discussed here. For example, Nettle suggested that high levels of Openness to Experience tend to be attractive to potential mates, but that high Openness is also associated with increased risk of some mental disorders, particularly schizophrenia and other delusional disorders.

With regard to the Big Five Agreeableness factor, Nettle's (2006) interpretation is similar to the interpretations that are given in this chapter (and in Ashton & Lee, 2001, 2007) for the HEXACO Agreeableness and Honesty—Humility factors. For Big Five Neuroticism (i.e., low Emotional Stability), Nettle suggested that high levels have some benefits, such as avoidance of dangers as well as competitive success, but also some costs, such as the illnesses and relationship problems caused by excessive stress. The suggestion that Neuroticism is associated with avoidance of dangers is consistent with the interpretation of Emotionality as given here, but the suggestion about Neuroticism and competitive success is not. In any case, the interpretations proposed by Nettle provide some interesting hypotheses regarding the costs and benefits of the Big Five personality factors.

7.4 CROSS-GENERATIONAL AND CROSS-NATIONAL DIFFERENCES IN MEAN LEVELS OF PERSONALITY TRAITS

As described in this chapter, the mechanisms of frequency dependence and the fluctuating optimum have different implications for variation across times and places in the mean levels of personality traits. Frequency dependence tends to make the mean levels similar, whereas the fluctuating optimum tends to make the mean levels different according to the conditions in a given time and place.

One way to compare the relative influence of these mechanisms is to examine how much variation there is between generations and between countries in the average levels of various personality traits. If the differences are large, then the fluctuating optimum would appear to be the stronger influence, but if the differences are small, then frequency dependence would appear to be stronger. However, there are some complications in comparing mean levels of personality traits across generations or across countries.

One complication involves the self-report questionnaire scales that are often used in measuring personality. When a person provides self-reports on the items of these scales, his or her responses are likely based to some extent on comparisons between him or her and the other members of his or her society. This tendency to judge one's own personality in comparison with the other people of one's society might conceal any differences between generations or between countries (Perugini & Richetin, 2007). For example, in a country of very quiet people, the average person might *not* describe himself or herself as being particularly quiet, because he or she seems average within that society; the same pattern would be observed for the average person in a country of very noisy people. As a result, there might appear to be no difference between the two countries when self-report questionnaire scales are considered, even though an outside observer would notice that the people of one country were much quieter than the people of the other country.

Another complication involving comparisons of the mean levels of personality traits across generations or across countries is due to people's "styles" of responding to personality questionnaire scales. If there are differences between generations or between countries in the tendency to give socially desirable responses to self-report (or observer report) statements (recall Box 2.3), then this might give the appearance of differences in personality even if these do not really exist. For example, if people in one country tend to give less socially desirable responses than do people in other countries—independently of any real differences in behavior—then the people of that country will appear to be different in personality from the people of other countries, even though there might not be any real difference. One case of this has been observed already: McCrae, Yik, Trapnell, Bond, and Paulhus (1998) found that Chinese immigrants to Canada tended to give less socially desirable self-reports (and also less socially desirable observer reports) than did Canadian-born people of Chinese ancestry.

Keeping these warnings in mind, it is still interesting to note the findings so far regarding differences in mean personality trait levels between countries and between age cohorts. Evidence from self-report (and observer report) personality questionnaires suggests that differences between most countries in the average levels of various personality characteristics are rather small. Even when countries with the highest and lowest levels of various traits are considered, the differences are usually not much more than one standard deviation unit in size (see McCrae, 2002, p. 112). Moreover, the differences that are observed tend not to correspond to commonly held perceptions or stereotypes of national differences in personality: For example, the commonly held stereotype that Canadians are much more agreeable than Americans is not supported by actual self-report personality data, which shows no such difference (McCrae & Terracciano, 2006). One broad pattern of findings is that persons from Western countries tend to have higher levels of Extraversion, on average, than do people from Asian or African countries; however, there is some evidence that when people from the latter countries immigrate to the West, their levels of Extraversion tend to increase (McCrae et al., 1998).

With regard to differences between generations, Twenge (2000, 2001) has reported that American college students became considerably more anxious and more extraverted between the 1960s and 1990s, with increases of nearly one standard deviation unit. However, other researchers using sophisticated statistical methods in samples of adults have found almost no generational differences (Terracciano, McCrae, Brant, & Costa, 2005).

Taken together, the results described above suggest that cross-national and cross-generational differences in average personality trait levels are usually not very large. This in turn suggests, at least tentatively, that variation in personality trait levels is not chiefly due to fluctuations across places and times in the optimum levels of those traits, and that frequency-dependent selection may be the more important mechanism.

BOX 7.6 Personality in Nonhuman Animals

Just as people differ from one another in their behavioral tendencies, so might the animals of any other species. Some interesting questions in personality psychology involve personality in nonhuman animals. For example, there is the practical question of how accurately we can assess personality trait levels in the individuals of another species. The answer to this question might depend on which species and which trait are being considered—perhaps there are some traits that are easily measured in another species, but other traits that hardly seem to apply at all. And we might wonder whether or not the major personality dimensions as observed in humans would also be found in other species, especially the species that are our closest relatives and the species whose behavior seems most complex.

Many researchers have already attempted to examine personality in nonhuman animals. In several research studies, persons who are familiar with individual animals have provided personality trait ratings of those animals. For example, in a given investigation, dog owners might rate the personalities of their dogs, or zoo veterinarians might rate the personalities of the chimpanzees they look after. To help the person making the ratings of an animal, the traits may be listed as single adjectives along with definitions relevant to the behavior of the species being studied. These investigations have shown fairly good agreement between independent raters as to which individual animals have higher versus lower levels of a given trait. In fact, levels of agreement are comparable to those obtained in ratings of individual humans' personality trait levels (Gosling, Kwan, & John, 2003; King & Figueredo, 1997). Also, in some studies, the behavior of individual animals is directly observed in experimental tests—for example, observing dogs as they run with their owners, show affection to their owners, meet new persons, or perform obedience tasks such as "sit" and "stay". Results of such studies indicate that these observed behaviors tend to be correlated with the personality trait ratings of the animals (Gosling

BOX 7.6 Personality in Nonhuman Animals—cont'd

et al., 2003; Pederson, King, & Landau, 2005). These findings are obtained even though the behavior is observed in only one situation and even though a single testing session is somewhat unreliable.

Some researchers have examined the factor structure of personality trait ratings of animals, to determine how much the factor structure obtained from ratings of individual animals resembles or differs from the human factor structure (e.g., Weiss, Adams, Widdig, & Gerald, 2011). However, one difficulty in these comparisons is that the meanings of trait ratings may not be the same for people as for animals. For example, King and Figueredo (1997) pointed out that when someone refers to a chimpanzee as "lazy", it suggests lethargy but not avoidance of work, whereas the latter is often implied when a person is called "lazy". Another difficulty is that samples are (understandably) small, due to the challenges of finding individual animals to be observed; these low sample sizes leave open the possibility that results will differ from one species to another simply by random chance.

The results of these studies suggest that most of the Big Five factors actually can be recovered in studies of various primate species. However, the Conscientiousness factor has not emerged clearly in nonhuman primate species other than chimpanzees. This result has led some researchers to suggest that the Conscientiousness dimension has only recently emerged in the human evolutionary past (e.g., Weiss et al., 2011), at some time when humans and chimpanzees had a common ancestor, but after the time when they shared a common ancestor with gorillas (and, further back, with orangutans). However, the absence of a clear Conscientiousness factor in these studies might simply be due to the fact that the variable sets did not contain many traits that are good examples of Conscientiousness. (Even in chimpanzees, the Conscientiousness factor does not closely resemble the one found in humans.) It is not known whether the six HEXACO factors would be recovered in these primate species, as the studies of this research program (which were started before the HEXACO model was widely known) were based on sets of traits that were selected to measure the Big Five.

Future research in primates might help to show how "old" the various personality dimensions are, and future research in other animals with complex social behavior (e.g., cetaceans such as whales or dolphins; see, e.g., Highfill & Kuczaj, 2007) might help to show whether these dimensions have emerged in other evolutionary lines.

7.5 SUMMARY AND CONCLUSIONS

In this chapter, we summarized the process of evolution by natural selection, and then discussed why the variation among people in personality trait levels has been maintained. Two main reasons why this variation has not disappeared were described in some detail: First, the ideal levels of characteristics tend to vary across different times and places (the "fluctuating optimum"); and second, when most people have a high level of a characteristic, there may be advantages to having a low level, and vice versa ("frequency dependence").

Each of the major dimensions of personality can be discussed in terms of the likely advantages and disadvantages associated with higher or lower levels. These trade-offs can be summarized as follows. For Honesty—Humility, high levels allow gains from cooperation, whereas low levels may provide gains by exploiting others. For Agreeableness, high levels allow gains from cooperation, whereas low levels may prevent losses that would result from being exploited by others. For Emotionality, high levels reduce risks of harm to one's kin (both directly and by avoiding harm to oneself), but low levels allow potential gains associated with those risks. For Extraversion, Conscientiousness, and Openness to Experience, high levels may produce social or material gains from "investing" one's time and energy in social, task-related, or idea-related endeavors, respectively; however, low levels avoid the energy costs and in some cases the risks associated with those endeavors.

CHAPTER 8

Personality Disorders

Contents

8.1 THE IDEA OF A PERSONALITY DISORDER

In previous chapters, we considered personality variation as if all levels of all personality characteristics were equally adaptive. From an evolutionary perspective, this is probably almost accurate: The fact that higher and lower levels of a given characteristic have persisted for so long suggests that they might be equally successful in promoting survival and reproduction.

Individual Differences and Personality
ISBN 978-0-12-809845-5, http://dx.doi.org/10.1016/B978-0-12-809845-5.00008-1

But in another important sense, the different levels of personality characteristics are far from being equally adaptive. If we consider the influence of an individual's personality on his or her own well-being—or on the well-being of persons who interact with him or her—then some personalities clearly seem better than others, and some personalities seem downright harmful. This is certainly the view held by people who work in mental health settings, such as psychiatrists and clinical psychologists, who believe that extreme levels of some personality characteristics are maladaptive enough to result in *personality disorders*. In this chapter, we will describe in some detail the meaning of a personality disorder as currently understood by psychiatrists and clinical psychologists.

Mental health professionals view personality disorders as stable and enduring patterns of thought, feeling, and behavior—that is, as personality traits—that emerge in adolescence or early adulthood, that deviate from the norms of one's culture, that are pervasive and inflexible across many aspects of one's life, and that lead to distress or impairment (American Psychiatric Association, 2013). The last of these aspects of personality disorder is especially important, insofar as a "disorder" of personality must involve some negative consequences for the functioning and the happiness of the individual or of others around him or her.

In this chapter, we will begin by describing the 10 personality disorders that are included in the reference book used by North American psychiatrists and clinical psychologists—the *Diagnostic and Statistical Manual of Mental Disorders*, Volume 5 (DSM-5; American Psychiatric Association, 2013). These 10 personality disorders (see Table 8.1) are classified into three groups or clusters according to the similarity of their symptoms. We will describe these clusters later in the chapter, but as we will also note, there are some problems with these groupings.

Before we begin describing the disorders, one note of caution: when reading about these disorders, you may notice that some of the descriptions are reminiscent of your own personality or of the personalities of people you know well. Keep in mind that this will be true of virtually everyone, because most of the disorders involve characteristics that are found to varying extents in most people. It is only when these tendencies are especially extreme, and interfere with the person's functioning, that a personality disorder would be diagnosed. For most disorders, only about 1% or 2% of the population would be diagnosed as having the disorder, and even for the most common disorders the rate would be about 4% (Mattia & Zimmerman, 2001). In total, less than 15% of the population would be diagnosed as having one or more of the 10 disorders listed in the DSM-5. To be diagnosed with a personality disorder, one would need to be diagnosed with several of the specific symptoms—usually most of the symptoms—that are associated with that disorder.

Table 8.1 Brief descriptions of the *Diagnostic and Statistical Manual of Mental Disorders*, Volume 5 personality disorders

Cluster and disorder	Description
Cluster A ("odd, eccentric")	
Schizoid	Extreme detachment and lack of interest in social or personal relationships
Schizotypal	Discomfort in close relationships, combined with eccentric behaviors and thoughts
Paranoid	Extreme distrust and suspiciousness of others
Cluster B ("dramatic, emotional, erratic")	
Antisocial	Disregard for and violation of the rights of others
Borderline	Extreme impulsivity and instability of relationships, self-image, and emotions
Histrionic	Excessive attention seeking and exaggerated expression of emotions
Narcissistic	Excessive sense of self-importance and entitlement
Cluster C ("anxious, fearful")	
Avoidant	Extreme shyness, low self-esteem, and fear of rejection
Dependent	Excessive need to be taken care of, with submissive and clinging behavior
Obsessive compulsive	Excessive preoccupation with order, perfection, and control

Based on American Psychiatric Association. (2013). Diagnostic and Statistical Manual of Mental Disorders: DSM-5. Washington, DC: American Psychiatric Association.

8.2 THE DSM-5 PERSONALITY DISORDERS

8.2.1 Schizoid

Schizoid personality disorder involves an extreme degree of detachment from social relationships and a very limited expression of emotions in interpersonal settings (American Psychiatric Association, 2013). Schizoid individuals are not interested in family relationships, friendships, or sexual relationships, and instead prefer almost always to be alone. This social isolation is accompanied by emotional detachment, as the schizoid person expresses no affection for others and is indifferent to their praise or criticism. Even in the nonsocial settings that are preferred by the schizoid individual, he or she feels little joy or pleasure.

8.2.2 Schizotypal

Like the schizoid personality disorder described previously, the schizotypal personality disorder also involves detachment from social relationships. But schizotypal personality disorder also involves an extreme discomfort with such relationships, and a pattern of odd thinking and eccentric behaviors (American Psychiatric Association, 2013). For example, the schizotypal individual may have unusual "ideas of reference," whereby he or she perceives a special personal meaning in everyday events or objects (e.g., billboard signs, television commercials, etc.). Similarly, schizotypal persons tend to be highly superstitious or fascinated with the paranormal, and may even have bizarre perceptual experiences, such as "seeing" things happening far away. The overall behavior and appearance of the schizotypal person is generally considered by others to be extremely odd, peculiar, or eccentric.

8.2.3 Paranoid

The paranoid personality disorder shares many features with the schizoid and schizotypal disorders, but is characterized by an especially strong suspiciousness of others' motives and by a sense of being persecuted (American Psychiatric Association, 2013). Paranoid individuals suspect without good reason that others are trying to harm, deceive, or exploit them, and tend to dwell on doubts about the loyalty of those around them (this often includes suspicions about a spouse's possible sexual infidelity). They are quick to take offense or to feel insulted even in response to actions or comments that may be entirely innocent, and they tend to hold grudges against those perceived as causing harm.

8.2.4 Antisocial

The hallmark of the antisocial personality disorder is a tendency to disregard and to violate the rights of others (American Psychiatric Association, 2013). Antisocial individuals are very deceitful, repeatedly lying to others and "conning" them for personal gain, and feel no remorse for the harm their actions have caused to others.[1] The antisocial person tends to be aggressive (e.g., committing assaults and getting into fights), to be irresponsible (e.g., failing to hold a job or to pay debts), and to be impulsive and reckless (e.g., doing dangerous activities that put others at risk).

8.2.5 Borderline

Borderline personality disorder involves extreme instability in one's own self-image and in one's relationships with others, along with extreme impulsivity in various contexts (American Psychiatric Association, 2013).[2] The borderline individual has intense and unstable "love/hate" relationships with others, and tends to worry frantically about the

---

[1] Many people use the word *antisocial* to describe people who are unsociable, but psychologists instead use it to describe people who harm others.

[2] The name *borderline* refers to the earlier idea among psychiatrists that this disorder was close to the boundary with disorders in which the individual suffers from delusions or hallucinations.

possibility of being abandoned. There is a pattern of impulsive behavior—including drug and alcohol abuse, eating binges, spending sprees, or sexual escapades—and also of self-harming behaviors, including self-mutilation or suicide attempts. The borderline person tends to be extremely moody and temperamental, and has little sense of personal identity or of meaning in life.

8.2.6 Histrionic

The histrionic personality disorder is characterized by an exaggerated display of emotions and by excessive attention seeking (American Psychiatric Association, 2013). Histrionic individuals have an intense need to be the center of attention, such that they feel uncomfortable when not the focus of others' attention. They use their physical appearance to draw attention, and have a seductive, sexually provocative style. Histrionic persons also have an overly dramatic, exaggerated style of expressing their emotions, yet those emotions are shallow and rapidly changing. They tend to be suggestible or easily influenced by others, and tend to consider casual acquaintanceships as being much closer relationships than is actually the case.

8.2.7 Narcissistic

The narcissistic personality disorder involves "grandiosity"—a tendency to consider oneself as a superior individual who deserves the admiration of others—and a selfish lack of concern for others' needs (American Psychiatric Association, 2013).[3] Narcissistic persons see themselves as being entitled to special treatment and admiration, and generally have an arrogant style, often exploiting others and failing to appreciate others' needs. The narcissistic person tends to fantasize about having high status and to envy those who are highly successful.

8.2.8 Avoidant

The avoidant personality disorder is defined by social inhibition and shyness, by feelings of inadequacy, and by oversensitivity to possible negative evaluation (American Psychiatric Association, 2013). Avoidant persons have such strong fears of criticism, disapproval, and rejection that their social interactions are severely restricted: They are unwilling to participate socially unless certain of being liked, and tend to avoid work activities that involve interpersonal contact. In general, there is a sense of low self-esteem and of inferiority along with an extreme sensitivity to embarrassment, criticism, and rejection.

Avoidant personality disorder shares the symptom of lack of social contact with schizoid and schizotypal disorders, but the reasons for that lack of contact are very

---

[3] The name of this disorder comes from Narcissus, a figure in Greek mythology who fell in love with his own image as reflected by a pool of water.

different: The avoidant person wants social contact but is afraid of rejection, whereas the schizoid or schizotypal person is completely indifferent to such contact.

8.2.9 Dependent

The dependent personality disorder is characterized by an excessive need to be taken care of and by submissive, clinging behavior and fears of separation (American Psychiatric Association, 2013). Dependent individuals require a great deal of advice and reassurance even in making everyday decisions, and lack the confidence to undertake projects on their own. They need other people to take responsibility for important features of their lives, and feel unable to take care of themselves when alone. Dependent persons often go to great lengths to maintain the support and nurturance of others—for example, by volunteering to do unpleasant tasks, or by avoiding any expression of disagreement. If a close relationship ends for some reason, the dependent person may desperately seek a new one.

8.2.10 Obsessive Compulsive

The main features of obsessive-compulsive personality disorder involve preoccupation with orderliness, perfection, and control (American Psychiatric Association, 2013). The obsessive-compulsive person tends to be so preoccupied with details (e.g., lists, schedules) that the entire point of an activity is lost. Similarly, individuals who have an obsessive-compulsive personality may be so concerned with attaining perfection and following specific rules that they fail to complete their tasks or projects, and fail to delegate any tasks to others. A person who has an obsessive-compulsive personality tends to put work ahead of personal relationships and to be highly stubborn and inflexible. There is a tendency to hoard money unnecessarily (rather than spend it) and to hoard objects unnecessarily (rather than discard them).

Note that obsessive-compulsive *personality* disorder is not the same as the condition known simply as obsessive-compulsive disorder; the latter condition involves repeated behaviors such as hand washing, counting, or tapping and is not classified as a personality disorder. (The two conditions, however, tend to be related.)

8.2.11 Classifying the DSM-5 Personality Disorders: Clusters A, B, and C

The DSM-5 personality disorders are usually classified into three groups or "clusters." This categorization is not based on results of factor analytic studies, but rather on clinicians' views of the similarities of content among some of the disorders. (As we will discuss later in this chapter, the dimensions that emerge when personality disorder symptoms are factor analyzed are apparently somewhat different.) The three DSM-5 clusters of personality disorders are called cluster A ("odd and eccentric"), cluster B ("dramatic and erratic"), and cluster C ("anxious and fearful"). The disorders that have been categorized within each cluster are listed as follows (see also Table 8.1).

Cluster A contains the schizoid, schizotypal, and paranoid personality disorders. The disorders classified within this cluster are described as the odd or eccentric disorders, because the behavior of persons diagnosed with these disorders seems strange or unusual.

Cluster B contains the antisocial, borderline, histrionic, and narcissistic personality disorders. The disorders classified within this cluster are described as the dramatic and erratic disorders, because the behavior of persons diagnosed with these disorders seems impulsive and unstable.

Cluster C contains the avoidant, dependent, and obsessive-compulsive personality disorders. The disorders classified within this cluster are described as the anxious and fearful disorders, because the behavior of persons diagnosed with these disorders seems motivated by anxiety and fear.

8.2.12 Problems With the DSM-5 Personality Disorders

The system of personality disorders described in the DSM-5 has been a convenient guide for mental health professionals, but there have been some serious criticisms of this system. Let us consider several difficulties that have been particularly prominent.

1. *Symptoms of a given disorder do not necessarily* "go together." One problem with the various personality disorders of the DSM-5 classification is that, for several disorders, there are some symptoms that do not really show much tendency to co-occur. In other words, for several disorders, there are some symptoms that are just about unrelated to each other: a person with one symptom is no more likely than anyone else to have another symptom. One example of this involves obsessive-compulsive personality disorder, for which some symptoms, such as rule following and tidiness, are not correlated with other symptoms, such as stubbornness and obstinacy. In addition, it is possible in some cases that two persons diagnosed with the same disorder might not have any symptoms in common.

2. *Two disorders may have overlapping symptoms, and may tend to be diagnosed together.* Not only do the symptoms of a given disorder not necessarily "hang together" in the sense of being likely to co-occur, but there are some symptoms that tend to co-occur despite being listed in different personality disorders. For example, the conning and deceitful behavior that characterize antisocial personality disorder tend to be observed in the same persons who also show the grandiosity and sense of entitlement that characterize narcissistic personality disorder. As a result of this problem, many persons are diagnosed with two or more personality disorders at the same time. This "comorbidity" (i.e., joint occurrence of two or more disorders) is frequently observed for several pairs of personality disorders, including schizoid and schizotypal, or avoidant and dependent, or histrionic and borderline. The substantial overlap in the symptoms associated with the various disorders thus tends to make the system inefficient.

3. *"Clusters" of disorders do not match factor analysis results.* A related shortcoming of the DSM system is that the three "clusters" do not necessarily correspond to the factors that are obtained when personality disorder—related traits are factor analyzed. As we will discuss later, factor analyses of such traits have usually produced dimensions quite different from the clusters that have been proposed to summarize the DSM disorders.

4. *A personality disorder should be seen as a continuum, not as a category.* One problem with the DSM approach to disorders has been that it conceptualizes disorders as categories: Either you have the disorder, or you do not have it, depending on whether you are observed to show a certain number of the features of the disorder. Most researchers believe instead that having a personality disorder is a matter of degree, so that some people may have slight indications of a disorder, whereas other people may have a severe case.

8.3 AN ALTERNATIVE SYSTEM FOR PERSONALITY DISORDERS

Because of the problems with the DSM personality disorders as described in the previous section, some researchers have begun to develop a new system of classifying and diagnosing personality disorders.

Originally, this new system was supposed to replace the one described earlier in this chapter when the DSM-5 was published, but the American Psychiatric Association ultimately decided to keep its earlier system and to include the new system only as a topic for further study. This decision was based largely on concerns raised by clinicians who were more comfortable with the earlier system, despite its shortcomings.

We will now consider the new system for personality disorders that had been proposed for the DSM-5. According to this new system, there are two essential features of a personality disorder: impaired personality functioning and the presence of pathological personality traits. Let us consider each of these features in turn.

8.3.1 Impaired Personality Functioning

Problems in personality functioning are divided into two kinds: those involving the "self" and those that are interpersonal. Each of these kinds of problems is further divided.

8.3.1.1 "Self" Problems (Identity and Self-Direction)

"Self" problems involve impairment in one's identity and one's self-direction.

Identity problems:
- A person might not have a sense of himself or herself as a unique person, if he or she identifies too strongly with some other person(s), or alternatively if he or she is too much concerned with being independent of certain others.

- A person might have self-esteem that is highly unstable, being easily threatened by negative experiences, or might have a distorted appraisal of his or her strengths and weaknesses.
- A person might not be able to regulate his or her emotions or even to recognize what emotions he or she experiences.

Self-direction problems:
- A person might not be able to set realistic or meaningful goals in his or her life.
- A person might lack any internal standards for behaving prosocially, and thus miss out on opportunities for fulfillment from cooperation with others.
- A person might be unable to reflect constructively on his or her own experiences or motivations.

8.3.1.2 Interpersonal Problems (Empathy and Intimacy)
Interpersonal problems involve impairments in empathy and intimacy.

Empathy problems:
- A person might be unable to understand the experiences or motivations of other people.
- A person might be unable to understand or unwilling to consider the perspectives of others.
- A person might have little understanding of how his or her own behavior affects others.

Intimacy problems:
- A person might be lacking in positive, sustained relationships with people in general.
- A person might be unable to engage in close, caring relationships with any other persons.
- A person might be unwilling or unable to cooperate with others.

Table 8.2 describes the self- and interpersonal functioning of two hypothetical patients, one of whom shows no impairment at all (and hence no personality disorder), and one of whom shows extreme impairment. (Note that many patients would have intermediate levels of impairment.)

8.3.2 Pathological Personality Traits

The particular problems of self- and interpersonal functioning that a person might show will depend on his or her levels of various personality traits. The proposed new system recognizes 25 specific personality traits (called "trait facets") as being potentially patho-logical or maladaptive, when an individual shows a high level of the trait. There is nothing special about the number 25—the researchers could have identified more traits (by dividing some of the listed traits) or fewer traits (by combining some of those that

Table 8.2 Descriptions of self and interpersonal functioning in patients showing no impairment and extreme impairment in personality functioning

---

Hypothetical patient with no impairment of personality functioning

---

1. Self
   A. Identity
      Experiences self as unique; understands boundaries between self and others
      Has stable self-esteem and accurate self-appraisal
      Can experience and regulate a range of emotions
   B. Self-direction
      Sets and pursues reasonable goals (short- and long term), based on reasonable assessment of own abilities
      Uses prosocial standards of behavior to attain fulfillment in various areas of life
      Can reflect constructively on own experiences
2. Interpersonal
   A. Empathy
      Able to understand the motivations and experiences of others
      Able to understand and appreciate the perspectives of others
      Is aware of effect of own actions on others
   B. Intimacy
      Has multiple positive, long-term relationships with others in personal and community life
      Participates in caring, close, reciprocal relationships
      Seeks cooperation and mutual benefit in relations with others; responds flexibly to others

---

Hypothetical patient with extreme impairment of personality functioning

---

1. Self
   A. Identity
      Lacks sense of unique self; has confused boundaries with others
      Has distorted self-image that is easily threatened by interactions with others; confused self-appraisal
      Emotions inappropriate to context
   B. Self-direction
      Goal-setting ability severely limited (unrealistic or incoherent goals)
      No internal standards of behavior; genuine fulfillment not possible
      Unable to reflect constructively on own experience; may not recognize own motivations
2. Interpersonal
   A. Empathy
      Unable to understand the motivations and experiences of others
      Does not consider others' perspectives
      Social interactions perceived as confusing, disorienting
   B. Intimacy
      Limited desire for affiliation; negative interactions with others
      Relationships viewed solely in terms of ability to provide pleasure or pain
      Social behavior not reciprocal, focused only on basic needs

---

Based on descriptions proposed for the DSM-5. The descriptions shown reflect only the "no impairment" and "extreme impairment" levels, but there are also levels in between representing mild, moderate, and serious impairment.

were similar). But the set of 25 was meant to be reasonably convenient for the purpose of describing patients in terms of traits that might be pathological (Krueger et al., 2011; Krueger, Derringer, Markon, Watson, & Skodol, 2012).

The 25 maladaptive traits, listed in Table 8.3, are classified into five broad dimensions, also called "domains." This arrangement is very similar to those that are used for personality traits in general, based on the results of factor analyses. To see this similarity, compare the list of traits in Table 8.3 with those for the NEO Personality Inventory—Revised (Table 3.4) and for the HEXACO Personality Inventory (Table 3.6). As explained later, several of these domains are similar to factors of the Big Five or the HEXACO framework (Ashton, Lee, de Vries, Hendrickse, & Born, 2012).

Table 8.3 The *Diagnostic and Statistical Manual of Mental Disorders*, Volume 5 proposed personality trait domains (dimensions) and their defining traits

---

Negative Affectivity
    Emotional lability (frequent mood changes, intense emotional reactions)
    Anxiousness
    Separation insecurity (fears of separation from close others)
    Perseveration (continuing a behavior that is no longer effective)
    Submissiveness
    Hostility
    [a]Restricted affectivity (emotional coldness)
Detachment
    Withdrawal
    Anhedonia (lack of enjoyment or pleasure)
    Intimacy avoidance (avoidance of close or romantic relationships)
    Depressivity
    Suspiciousness
Antagonism
    Manipulativeness
    Deceitfulness
    Grandiosity (feelings of entitlement and superiority)
    Attention seeking
    Callousness
Disinhibition (vs. Compulsivity)
    Irresponsibility
    Impulsivity
    [a]Rigid perfectionism
    Distractibility
    Risk taking
Psychoticism
    Unusual beliefs and experiences (bizarre thoughts, "hearing things," "seeing things")
    Eccentricity (perceived as odd or unusual)
    Cognitive and perceptual dysregulation (feeling disconnected from own thoughts and body)

---

[a]Indicates that lower levels of this trait are associated with higher levels of the other traits within the same domain.

The Negative Affectivity domain involves intense and frequent experience of negative emotions. This domain is very similar to Neuroticism in the Big Five or Five-Factor Model system. It also has some similarity with several of the HEXACO factors, including Emotionality, low Extraversion, and low Agreeableness. (Notice that one of the traits within this domain—restricted affectivity—is intended to represent a pathologically low level of this dimension.)

The Detachment domain involves withdrawal from social interactions and from other people. This domain is similar to the low pole of Extraversion (i.e., to the introverted end of the dimension) in both the Big Five and the HEXACO model.

The Antagonism domain involves acting in ways that create difficulties for other people. This domain is fairly similar to the low pole of the Big Five Agreeableness dimension. However, because Antagonism emphasizes traits such as manipulativeness, deceitfulness, and grandiosity, it is also quite similar to the low pole of HEXACO Honesty—Humility. (The proposed system does not have a separate domain that corresponds to low Agreeableness of the HEXACO model.)

The Disinhibition domain involves behaving on impulse, without thinking of consequences. This domain is reasonably similar to the low pole of Conscientiousness in both the Big Five and the HEXACO model. (Notice that one of the traits within this domain—rigid perfectionism—is intended to represent a pathologically low level of the Disinhibition dimension. The opposite pole of DSM-5 Disinhibition is called Compulsivity.)

The Psychoticism domain involves unusual, bizarre thoughts and perceptions. This domain has only limited similarities to the factors of the Big Five or the HEXACO model. The perceptual distortions associated with this factor (e.g., feeling disconnected from one's body, feeling that one's thoughts are controlled by others, etc.) do not have any direct counterpart in models of normal personality variation. However, the traits of eccentricity or oddness are somewhat related to Openness to Experience (and to low Conscientiousness) in the Big Five and the HEXACO model.[4]

To measure the set of 25 maladaptive personality traits, researchers have developed a self-report questionnaire (Krueger et al., 2012). In several research studies, the scales on that questionnaire have shown strong convergent validity correlations with other self-report personality scales assessing normal or pathological traits. In addition, self-reports on the new questionnaire scale have shown moderately high convergent validity correlations with observer reports provided by persons closely acquainted with the target person (Markon, Quilty, Bagby, & Krueger, 2013). One limitation of the questionnaire

---

[4] Note that this "Psychoticism" factor is different from the Psychoticism dimension proposed by Eysenck, as described in Chapter 5. Eysenck chose the label "Psychoticism" because he believed that the traits of his factor (such as aggressiveness and impulsiveness) were related to truly psychotic symptoms, such as hallucinations and delusions. But the dimension proposed by Eysenck was not actually defined by those psychotic symptoms.

assessing these maladaptive traits is that the scales contain items that are very undesirable statements, with very few reverse-keyed items. As a result, the scales are influenced strongly by self-report response styles such as desirability (see Section 2.6.4 and Box 2.3) and acquiescence (see Section 2.4), and there are fairly high correlations between scales that measure theoretically unrelated traits (Ashton, de Vries, & Lee, 2016); that is, discriminant validity is somewhat limited.

8.3.3 Diagnosing Personality Disorders in the Proposed New System

A clinician—that is, a psychiatrist or a clinical psychologist—who adopts the proposed new system may use several sources of information to assess whether or not a patient has a personality disorder. The clinician may conduct a structured interview (an interview designed specifically to assess certain characteristics) with the patient and perhaps with other persons who know the patient well. The clinician may also observe the patient's behavior directly or consult various records of the patient's behavior. By gaining this information, the clinician has some basis for evaluating the severity of any impairments in personality functioning as well as the severity of any pathological personality traits.

The proposed new system of personality disorder diagnosis includes specific rating forms for this purpose. The form that is used for rating impairment of personality functioning asks the clinician to rate each of the problems in personality functioning on a scale from 0 (no impairment at all) to 4 (extreme impairment). Most people would probably be rated as 0 on the four listed problems in personality functioning, although many others would be rated as 1 on at least some of the problems, or perhaps even a 2. But scores of 3 or 4 would be considered as indicating a personality disorder.

Likewise, the form that is used for rating pathological personality traits also involves ratings on a multipoint scale. However, the ratings on this DSM-5 form range from 0 (very little or not at all descriptive) to 3 (extremely descriptive). On this form, scores of 0 or 1 are not considered to indicate a personality disorder, but scores of 2 and especially 3 are interpreted in this way.

To diagnose a patient as having a personality disorder, a clinician must first determine that the patient is showing significant impairment in functioning (both "self" and interpersonal functioning) as well as pathological personality traits (whether a whole domain of traits, or various traits from different domains). The important point is that both of the essential features of a personality disorder—impaired personality functioning and pathological personality traits—must be present for the disorder to be diagnosed.

In addition to these two essential features, other criteria must also be met if a personality disorder is to be diagnosed. First, the impaired personality functioning and pathological personality traits must be relatively stable across time and consistent across situations. This is actually a rather obvious requirement; the problems described earlier would not be "personality" problems at all if they did not meet these specifications.

Also, the impaired personality functioning and pathological personality traits must not be considered as normal for the person's stage of development or for the society and culture from which the person comes. For example, a level of impulsivity or irresponsibility that would be pathological in an adult might be rather normal in a 5-year-old child. Similarly, a lack of stability in self-esteem or identity that would be pathological in a middle-aged adult might be rather normal in an adolescent. Likewise, a level of submissiveness that would suggest a personality disorder for a woman in a modern society might be fairly common among women in societies in which women are oppressed; in this case, the problem would not be one of the woman's personality.

Finally, the impaired personality functioning and pathological personality traits must not be due to the effects of some substance, such as a medication or some "recreational" drug, and not due to any medical condition, such as a serious head injury.

In the proposed new system, a clinician can distinguish between patients having more severe or less severe cases of personality disorder by considering the severity of the patients' impairments in personality functioning and also the severity of patients' pathological personality traits. In addition, a clinician can distinguish between many different varieties of personality disorder, by considering which pathological personality traits are shown by a given patient. (Any two patients might have similar levels of some pathological personality traits, but those patients are likely to differ in levels of other pathological personality traits.)

8.4 ORIGINS OF PERSONALITY DISORDERS: DEVELOPMENTAL CHANGE AND STABILITY, BIOLOGICAL BASES, HEREDITY AND ENVIRONMENT, AND EVOLUTIONARY FUNCTION

As discussed earlier, personality disorders can be understood, to a large extent, in terms of the same personality characteristics that all people exhibit to differing degrees. That is, most personality disorder symptoms correspond to extreme levels of various personality traits—levels that cause problems for the individual and for others. There are a few personality disorder symptoms that are exceptions. For example, self-harming behaviors (associated with Borderline personality disorder) and major perceptual distortions (associated with Schizotypal personality disorder) seem to be expressed only in a small percentage of people. But for the most part, personality disorders represent maladaptive levels of the same personality dimensions that differentiate people in general. As a consequence of this fact, any questions that we might have about the nature of personality disorders will have essentially the same answers as do questions about the nature of personality more generally. For example, the development, biological bases, the genetic and environmental origins, and the evolutionary adaptive functions of personality disorders can be understood simply by referring to the results for normal variation in personality characteristics, as summarized in Chapters 4—7.

However, some specific remarks are warranted regarding the causes of Borderline and Schizotypal symptoms. Even though Borderline symptoms show rather high heritability (probably at least .40; e.g., Boomsma et al., 2009), it is commonly thought that these symptoms are also caused, at least in part, by various kinds of trauma during childhood, such as being sexually or physically abused. Several studies have shown that the frequency of childhood sexual or physical abuse is higher in Borderline patients than in other persons. However, the link is not extremely strong, as many Borderline patients do not have any history of being abused, and most persons who are abused as children do not develop Borderline symptoms (see review by New, Triebwasser, & Charney, 2008); one review of studies estimated the correlation between childhood abuse and later Borderline diagnosis at less than .30 (Fossati, Madeddu, & Maffei, 1999). Moreover, this link might reflect genetic tendencies, if parents who have Borderline symptoms tend both to mistreat their children and to transmit their personality characteristics genetically. Nevertheless, some studies do suggest that a history of childhood abuse does add independently to the likelihood of developing Borderline symptoms.

Although many researchers are highly skeptical about the meaningfulness of distinct personality disorder "types," there is some evidence that the Schizotypal disorder approaches being a true type. Meehl (1990) and Lenzenweger (2010) have estimated that about 10% of persons have a genetic tendency toward an abnormal pattern of brain functioning, which can produce schizotypal symptoms depending on a person's social learning experiences when growing up. (For a smaller fraction of those persons, additional stresses might bring about full-blown schizophrenia in young adulthood.) According to Meehl and to Lenzenweger, about 90% of the population has no liability whatsoever toward the development of schizotypal symptoms; in this sense, the Schizotypal disorder is not really dimensional. (By contrast, with the other disorders, all persons could hypothetically have at least *some* chance of developing some symptoms, with the likelihood depending on their levels of the relevant personality characteristics.)

8.5 TREATMENT OF PERSONALITY DISORDERS

Personality disorders can be difficult to treat, for at least two reasons. One reason is that the disorders are based not on some external conditions that can be easily modified, but rather on the individual's own personality characteristics, which tend to be rather stable across long periods of time and across different circumstances. Nevertheless, some features of personality disorders involve specific dysfunctional behaviors, which might be reduced or eliminated through certain forms of treatment.

A second reason for the difficulty of treating personality disorders is that some disorders are based on personality characteristics that make an individual less likely to be a

cooperative patient: consider the extreme emotional reactions of the Borderline personality disorder, or the deceitfulness of the antisocial personality disorder.

Despite these difficulties in treating personality disorders, some forms of treatment
have shown at least modest success in reducing the problematic thoughts, feelings, and
behaviors associated with those disorders. Here, we will consider three psychological
approaches to the treatment of personality disorders, as well as drug-based (psychobiological) approaches to treatment.

8.5.1 Psychodynamic Psychotherapy

In psychodynamic psychotherapy (e.g., Shedler, 2010), the clinician tries to help the
patient to express his or her emotions, including emotions that he or she might find trou-
bling or distressing. The clinician also tries to help the patient identify recurring patterns in
his or her behavior and to examine the important relationships and interpersonal experiences in the patient's life. An overarching aim of this approach is to encourage the patient
to speak freely about what is on his or her mind, including dreams and fantasies. By helping the patient to reflect on and explore his or her mental life, the therapist aims to
improve the patient's self-understanding and thereby improve his or her functioning.

8.5.2 Cognitive Behavioral Therapy

As applied to personality disorders, cognitive behavioral therapy (CBT) (e.g., Beck,
Freeman, & Davis, 2004) is based on the idea that personality disorders involve dysfunctional views about oneself, about the surrounding world, or about the future. The clinician who uses some form of CBT aims to understand the irrational beliefs that a patient
holds and to show the patient that those views are maladaptive. For example, a patient
who has Avoidant personality disorder might have highly unrealistic perceptions about
his or her own inferiority, about other people's readiness to criticize and reject him or
her, and about the possible negative consequences of social interaction. The clinician
would try to get the patient to realize that these perceptions are both inaccurate and
harmful, and then try also to change those perceptions (e.g., by showing the patient
that he or she is not inferior, that other people are not generally so critical and rejecting,
and that even unpleasant social interactions are not so disastrous).

8.5.3 Dialectical Behavior Therapy

Dialectical behavior therapy (DBT) (e.g., Linehan & Dexter-Mazza, 2008) was developed specifically as a treatment for patients having Borderline personality disorder.
This approach to therapy is aimed at making the patient more aware of what he or
she is currently thinking and feeling, and to get the patient to reflect on and accept those
thoughts and feelings openly and without judgment. By developing "mindfulness" in this
way, the patient finds it easier to handle the thoughts and feelings that often cause much
distress. In conducting DBT, the clinician tries to avoid conflict with the patient; rather

than criticizing the patient for having certain feelings or for behaving in certain ways, the clinician points out that those feelings and behaviors might be maladaptive for the patient. The clinician can then try to help the patient to develop responses that are more adaptive.

Some research studies have been aimed at evaluating the effectiveness of these psychological methods of treating personality disorders. A review of this research suggests that all three of the aforementioned methods of therapy have been found to be moderately effective in improving personality disorder symptoms, but that there is not yet enough evidence to make clear recommendations about which therapy is most effective for treating any given disorder (Tyrer & Bateman, 2004a).

8.5.4 Psychobiological Treatments

Some researchers have suggested that personality disorders can be understood in terms of imbalances of chemical substances in the brain. Siever and Davis (1991) discussed the possible biological bases of various kinds of personality disorder symptoms, and suggested that certain kinds of drugs could counteract the underlying imbalances and thereby reduce the symptoms. A review of research studies on the effects of drug treatment for personality disorders (Tyrer & Bateman, 2004b) has indicated modestly positive results. Some antidepressant and mood-stabilizing drugs had helped in managing Borderline symptoms, and some antipsychotic drugs (which reduce delusions and hallucinations) had helped in managing Borderline and Schizotypal symptoms.

8.5.5 Treatment of Antisocial Personality Disorder

In describing treatment of personality disorders, the antisocial personality disorder warrants some special mention. An important problem in treating persons with this disorder is that many of those persons will be motivated to appear as though they have been "cured" of their tendency to exploit others ruthlessly. For example, criminal offenders might try to obtain early release from their imprisonment by declaring that they now understand the wrongness of their actions and that they now feel remorse for the harm that they have caused. But such declarations are likely to be cynical, being calculated to deceive the clinicians and the members of the parole board.

Research on treatment for antisocial persons has indicated that several approaches do not work (Harris & Rice, 2006). For example, some studies have examined a form of psychodynamic group therapy (a "therapeutic community") intended to develop feelings of empathy and responsibility toward one's peers. When used in treating criminal offenders, this form of therapy has been found to show different results depending on the characteristics of the offender: the likelihood of future violent offending is decreased in nonpsychopathic offenders, but is actually *increased* in psychopathic offenders. (Psychopathic criminal offenders are those who show many of the characteristics of the DSM-5 antisocial personality disorder, whereas nonpsychopathic criminal offenders show few of those characteristics; see also Section 9.7.2.) Harris and Rice (2006) suggested that this therapy tends to improve offenders' skills in understanding other people's emotions and in describing emotions; for nonpsychopathic offenders, these skills promote prosocial, noncriminal behavior, but for psychopathic offenders, these skills promote confidence and competence in exploiting others. Moreover, antisocial offenders simply "play along" with the clinicians by pretending to develop greater emotional depth.

Similar results have also been reported in studies of CBT for antisocial offenders. Harris and Rice (2006) reviewed several investigations in which cognitive behavioral programs were applied to criminal offenders. The common result of those studies was that the more psychopathic offenders showed the poorest outcomes, having the highest rate of violent reoffending; this occurred even though clinicians reported that the more psychopathic offenders *appeared* to be showing the greatest improvement.

Harris and Rice (2006) suggested that the most successful method for treating antisocial persons who have already committed serious crimes—and who are thus at high risk of committing more such crimes—is to make it in the person's own self-interest to avoid exploiting other people. By showing antisocial persons that criminal acts lead to imprisonment, and by showing them ways to get what they want without harming others, those persons may be less likely to commit further crimes. This approach does not involve any attempt to change the personality of the antisocial person; instead, it is aimed at reducing the gap between that person's self-interest and the society's expectations of acceptable behavior. Presumably, such treatment would have to be maintained on an ongoing basis.

8.6 SUMMARY AND CONCLUSIONS

In this chapter, we have surveyed the topic of personality disorders, beginning with an explanation of the concept of personality disorder itself. According to the DSM-5 (American Psychiatric Association, 2013), an individual may have a personality disorder when he or she exhibits patterns of behavior that deviate from the norms of his or her culture, that are pervasive and inflexible across many aspects of his or her life, and that lead to distress or impairment. To be considered as personality disorders, these patterns of behavior must emerge in adolescence or in adulthood.

The DSM-5 currently lists 10 personality disorders, which are grouped into three "clusters." Within cluster A (the "odd, eccentric" disorders) are the schizoid, schizotypal, and paranoid personality disorders. Cluster B (the "dramatic, erratic" disorders) contains the borderline, histrionic, narcissistic, and antisocial personality disorders. Within cluster C (the "anxious, fearful" disorders) are the avoidant, dependent, and obsessive-compulsive personality disorders.

Many researchers believe that the DSM-5 system has serious shortcomings. For example, the symptoms of a given disorder often do not appear together, whereas the symptoms of different disorders often do. Moreover, the grouping of personality disorders into clusters does not closely match observed results. Also, although the DSM-5 treats disorders as categories (i.e., a person either is or is not diagnosed as having a given disorder), the evidence indicates that these disorders are dimensions rather than categories.

Some researchers have proposed a new system for classifying and diagnosing personality disorders. This system, which is based on assessment of impaired personality functioning and pathological personality traits, was originally meant to replace the set of 10 personality disorders, but it was ultimately included in the DSM-5 only as an idea for further study. Impaired personality functioning involves problems both with the self (one's identity and self-direction) and with interpersonal interaction (empathy and intimacy). Pathological personality traits are very diverse and can be categorized into domains resembling the major dimensions of normal personality. In using the new system to diagnose a patient, the clinician rates the severity of impairment exhibited by the patient, considering the various forms of self and interpersonal functioning and their impairment. The clinician also diagnoses the patient by assessing the patient's levels of the various pathological personality traits.

To a large extent, questions about the biological bases, the genetic and environmental origins, and the evolutionary adaptive functions of personality disorders will have answers similar to those found for normal variation in personality characteristics. Possible exceptions include some of the features of Borderline and Schizotypal personality disorders.

Treatment of personality disorders is difficult, but several methods of psychological therapy have shown at least some success, including psychodynamic therapy, CBT, and DBT. Some drug-based therapies have also shown modest success.

CHAPTER 9

Personality and Life Outcomes

Contents

9.1 DOES PERSONALITY MATTER IN LIFE?

One of the most interesting issues in personality psychology is the extent to which personality characteristics can influence important features of people's lives. Intuitively, it seems likely that some life outcomes would depend in part on a person's levels of various personality traits. That is, most people would probably expect that an individual's personality could influence a variety of important "results" in his or her life, such as his or her marriage partner and marital satisfaction, friendships and other peer relationships, achievement at school and work, health and longevity, law–abidingness or criminality, or overall life satisfaction.

But is this actually true? It is clear that many life outcomes will be influenced heavily by situations and circumstances that can arise almost at random. For example, even if personality might influence health or wealth, there are many illnesses and many financial

Individual Differences and Personality
ISBN 978-0-12-809845-5, http://dx.doi.org/10.1016/B978-0-12-809845-5.00009-3

difficulties that can afflict people regardless of their personality. So, how much—if at all—does personality relate to these various life outcomes? In this chapter, we will discuss the research that personality psychologists have undertaken in their efforts to answer this question.

9.2 RELATIONSHIPS AND MARRIAGE

Romantic relationships are obviously an important aspect of most people's lives, and the role of personality in those relationships is a fascinating topic. Here we will consider two fundamental questions about personality and relationships: First, do spouses tend to be similar or dissimilar in their personality characteristics? Second, in what ways are the personality characteristics of spouses associated with the satisfaction they have with their marriage? (The same questions also apply to romantic partners other than spouses and to romantic relationships other than marriage, but for the sake of brevity we will use "spouse" and "marriage.")

Several investigations of the personalities of spouses have generally yielded similar results. In these investigations, the couples have typically participated in the research project at the researchers' laboratory; the usual procedure has been to have spouses seated at separate desks when completing the questionnaires, to ensure that their responses—both self-reports and spouse reports—are independent and frank.

9.2.1 Are Spouses Similar in Personality?

To find out whether spouses tend to be alike or different in personality, researchers calculate correlations between spouses on each of various personality characteristics. For example, consider a personality dimension such as Extraversion. Researchers examine whether husbands who have high self-report scores on Extraversion tend to be married to wives who also have high self-report scores on Extraversion, by calculating the correlation between the self-report scores of husbands and wives. (In other words, the correlation is calculated as if "husband Extraversion" and "wife Extraversion" were two variables being measured for the same person.) A large positive correlation would indicate strong similarity, and a strong negative correlation would indicate strong dissimilarity.[1]

At this point, you might want to try to guess at the results: Do you expect that spouses would tend to have personalities that are similar ("like marries like") or dissimilar ("opposites attract")? Well, for most personality characteristics, there is not much

---

[1] Sometimes, researchers will also examine the similarity of spouses by repeating the aforementioned analyses using the spouses' observer reports of each other. For example, in the case of Extraversion, they would examine whether husbands who have high scores on Extraversion as indicated by their wives' spouse reports tend to be married to wives who also have high scores on Extraversion as indicated by their husbands' spouse reports.

similarity or much dissimilarity: on average, spouses tend to be slightly similar to each other, but only very slightly. In two very large studies (Humbad, Donnellan, Iacono, McGue, & Burt, 2010; McCrae et al., 2008), the correlations between wives' personality trait levels and husbands' personality trait levels were mainly positive but small, usually ranging between .00 and .25. These results indicate that the personality of one spouse usually gives very little clue as to the personality of the other spouse: On average, husbands and wives tend to be only slightly similar in personality.

Now, this conclusion refers to personality traits rather than to other psychological characteristics, such as mental abilities, religiosity, and political attitudes. As we will see in Chapters 10 and 12, there tends to be much more similarity between spouses on these other psychological characteristics.

9.2.2 Marital Satisfaction

As described earlier, spouses tend overall to be only slightly similar to each other in personality characteristics. But there remains the important question of how these variables are related to marital satisfaction. Can we predict one's level of marital satisfaction from the personality of one's spouse? From one's own personality? From the similarity (or the difference) between oneself and one's spouse?

A review of research on the links between personality and marital satisfaction was reported by Malouff, Thorsteinsson, Schutte, Bhullar, and Rooke (2010). They reviewed several previous studies containing 19 samples and nearly 4000 participants in total. Across these studies, participants' self-ratings of marital satisfaction were examined in relation to their spouses' self-reported personality trait levels, which were assessed in terms of the Big Five factors. The results showed that higher marital satisfaction was associated with having a spouse who was higher in Emotional Stability (i.e., lower in Neuroticism), higher in Agreeableness, and higher in Conscientiousness. (The correlations were only modest, about .22, .15, and .12, respectively; they would be somewhat stronger if marital satisfaction and personality were measured with higher reliability and validity.) The traits that were associated with marital satisfaction were the same for husbands as for wives.

The review by Malouff et al. examined how marital satisfaction is related to the personality trait levels of one's spouse. But it is also interesting to find out how marital satisfaction is related to one's own personality trait levels, because we might expect that some people's personalities would tend to make them happier with their marriages. One study examined this issue by administering short measures of marital satisfaction and short self-report Big Five personality scales to large samples of married couples from the United Kingdom and Australia (Dyrenforth, Kashy, Donnellan, & Lucas, 2010). Dyrenforth et al. found that people who reported higher marital satisfaction tended to be higher in Agreeableness, Emotional Stability, Conscientiousness, and

Extraversion. The associations were not very strong (about .20 for Agreeableness and weaker for the other factors) but would be somewhat stronger if marital satisfaction and personality traits were assessed using longer scales. In any case, though, the results suggest that people with more agreeable personalities—and to some extent, more stable, conscientious, and extraverted personalities—tend to be happier in their marriages. This result probably means that such people tend to be more easily satisfied with their marriages, but it also might mean that such people actually tend to get better marriages, by eliciting more "positive" behaviors from their spouses. This latter possibility seems plausible given the typical finding that people with agreeable, stable, conscientious personalities tend to have spouses who are happier in their marriages (recall the Malouff et al. review described earlier.)

Dyrenforth et al. (2010) also considered the extent to which marital satisfaction was related to similarity (or dissimilarity) between spouses. It is possible that marital satisfaction might depend not only on one's own personality and on one's spouse's personality considered separately, but also on the similarity (or difference) between the spouses on various personality characteristics. One might expect that spouses would feel greater marital satisfaction to the extent that they are similar in some characteristics, or to the extent that they are different in some characteristics. However, Dyrenforth et al. found that marital satisfaction was nearly unrelated to the size of the differences between one's own personality trait levels and those of one's spouse. In other words, marital satisfaction was about the same regardless of whether the spouses were similar or opposite in their levels of a given personality trait.

9.3 FRIENDSHIPS AND OTHER PEER RELATIONSHIPS

9.3.1 Are Friends Similar in Personality?

In recent years, researchers have begun to study the question of whether friends tend to be similar or opposite to each other in their personality characteristics. If you think of various friendships that you have observed (whether your own friendships or those of other people), you can probably think of some cases where two friends were very similar in some aspect of personality, and you can probably think of some cases where two friends were quite opposite in some aspect of personality. But researchers have tried to find out whether there is any tendency, across many people, for friends to be similar or opposite in the various personality dimensions. If we "average out" across many friendships, maybe we would find that friends are usually similar in some personality traits, or opposite in some other personality traits.

One investigation examined the personalities of several hundred pairs of college students, where each pair consisted of two friends who provided personality self-reports as well as observer reports of the friend's personality (Lee et al., 2009). The results showed the usual finding of strong agreement between a person's self-reports and the observer reports about that person by his or her friend (correlations around .50; recall Section 2.6.1). But Lee et al. also compared each person's self-report with his or her friend's self-report, to find out whether friends tended to be similar or opposite in personality. The results showed that for four of the six HEXACO personality dimensions, there was no tendency on average for friends to be either similar or opposite: The correlations between friends' self-reports were close to zero. In other words, if you knew one friend's level of a given personality dimension, this would not give you any idea about the other friend's level of that dimension.

But for two of the HEXACO factors—Honesty—Humility and Openness to Experience—friends on average were somewhat similar in personality. (Specifically, the correlation between friends' levels on each of these dimensions was about .25.) This means that there is some tendency for people to form or maintain friendships with people whose levels of Honesty—Humility and Openness to Experience are similar to their own. However, this tendency is not very strong, so there will still be many cases where two friends are much different from each other on these dimensions of personality.

Because the Lee et al. study included both self-reports and observer reports, the researchers could also examine another question: Do people *perceive* their friends as having personality trait levels similar (or opposite) to their own? More precisely, does a person's self-report tend to be similar (or opposite) to the observer report that the person provides for his or her friend? (If you are getting confused, see Fig. 9.1 to keep track of these different relations involving self- and observer reports.) The results indicated that for four of the six HEXACO personality dimensions, there was no such "perceived" similarity—and no perceived dissimilarity either: the correlations were close to zero. But for Honesty—Humility and Openness to Experience, people's self-reports tended to be similar to the observer reports they provided about their friends. (Specifically, the correlation of self-reports with observer reports about the other person were around .40.) This means that people seem to perceive themselves and their friends as having similar personality trait levels, but only for the Honesty—Humility and Openness to Experience dimensions.

Notice that the correlations for perceived similarity in Honesty—Humility and Openness to Experience (about .40) were larger than the correlations for "actual" similarity in these dimensions (about .25). This means that although friends tend to be somewhat similar to each other in these two dimensions, they tend to perceive even more similarity than actually exists. It is as if people notice the similarity between themselves and their friends on these two dimensions, but also overestimate that similarity.

Why do friends tend to be similar (and to see themselves as similar) in Honesty—Humility and Openness to Experience, but not in the other dimensions of personality? Lee et al. suggested that friends often share the same *values*—the same views about how one ought to live and relate to other people. (This is not a suggestion that friends must be

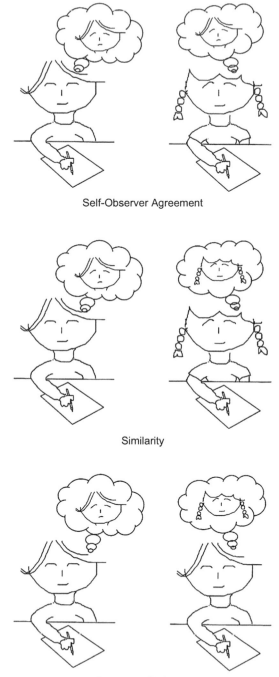

Self-Observer Agreement

Similarity

Perceived Similarity

Figure 9.1 Self-observer agreement, similarity, and perceived similarity in personality reports. *(Lee, K., & Ashton, M.C. (2012). The H factor of personality: Why some people are manipulative, self-entitled, materialistic, and exploitive—and why it matters for everyone. Waterloo, ON: Wilfrid Laurier University Press. Reproduced by permission of Wilfrid Laurier University Press.)*

consciously choosing one another on the basis of their values. The idea instead is that people with similar values are just likely to get along better—to be "on the same wavelength"—even if they never actually discuss their values.) The researchers also suggested that Honesty—Humility and Openness to Experience are probably the aspects of personality that are most strongly related to people's values.

To test this explanation, Lee et al. also obtained self-reports and observer reports of personal values from each pair of friends. The results showed that friends were somewhat similar in their values, and that friends also perceived each other's values as similar to their own. As for the personality characteristics, "perceived" similarity was greater than "actual" similarity. Also, values were more strongly related to Honesty—Humility and Openness to Experience than to the other dimensions of personality. (For example, people who valued power and money tended to be low in Honesty—Humility, and people who valued independence and creativity tended to be high in Openness to Experience.) Therefore, the results supported the idea that friends tend to be similar (and to perceive themselves as even more similar) in the aspects of personality that are related to their values.

To summarize, the findings of Lee et al. suggest that for most aspects of personality, friends are neither similar nor opposite in personality. But for the dimensions of Honesty—Humility and Openness to Experience, there is some tendency for friends to be similar to each other. For these same two dimensions, friends seem to perceive each other as having personality trait levels similar to their own; however, this "perceived" similarity between friends overestimates the actual similarity between them. One likely reason for the similarity between friends in these two personality dimensions is that these dimensions are related to people's values about how to live and relate to other people. Apparently, people tend on average to have friends whose values are similar to their own, and the personality dimensions that are most relevant to people's values are Honesty—Humility and Openness to Experience. Of course, many variables influence which people become friends, and personality traits (or values) are probably not the main influence on friendship formation, especially in the short term and especially when people live in a small social circle. But apparently, personality traits do matter in the process of forming and maintaining friendships.

9.3.2 Personality and Other Peer Relationships

Recently, researchers have begun to study systematically the relations of personality characteristics with general social relationships, whether in childhood, adolescence, or adulthood.

Some studies have examined these questions by investigating the behaviors of children who differ in the extent to which they are liked and disliked by their peers. One large-scale review of such studies (Newcomb, Bukowski, & Pattee, 1993) organized the results in such a way as to show the behavioral differences between children who were classified into one of five groups: Specifically, Newcomb et al. compared "average" children with children who are identified either as *popular* (i.e., liked by many other children, disliked by few other children), *rejected* (i.e., disliked by many, liked by few), *neglected* (i.e., liked by few, disliked by few), or *controversial* (i.e., liked by many, disliked by many).

Newcomb et al. (1993) found that, across these many studies, popular children tended to be low in aggression and high in sociability, whereas rejected children showed an opposite pattern, being high in aggression and low in sociability. Children in the neglected category tended to be low in both aggression and sociability, but children in the controversial category were opposite, tending to be high in both aggression and sociability. These results suggest that sociability is associated with being liked, and that aggression is associated with being disliked. (However, these results on their own do not necessarily indicate that these characteristics are the *cause* of other children's liking and disliking, as opposed to being the *consequence* of being liked or disliked by other children.)

One study examined the links between personality and social status within samples of college students (Anderson, John, Keltner, & Kring, 2001). Anderson et al. obtained self-reports on the Big Five personality factors from students in a fraternity, in a sorority, and in a mixed-sex dormitory. In addition, the researchers also assessed the "social status" of each student in these groups, by obtaining peer (observer) ratings of each student's prominence, influence, and respect within the group. In all three samples, Anderson et al. found that Extraversion was positively related to social status, with a correlation of about .40 both among men and among women. Interestingly, similarly strong relations were found—but only among men—for Emotional Stability and for physical attractiveness. The authors suggested that the toughness associated with Emotional Stability is admired by men more than by women, and that physical attractiveness—which is usually associated with positive perceptions by others—might elicit mixed reactions among women more than among men. (That is, a woman's attractiveness might be a source of some antagonism from other women.) The other Big Five personality characteristics were unrelated to social status, but the authors suggested that different results might be observed in groups that are not purely "social" in their purpose. For example, one hypothesis is that Conscientiousness would be related to social status in groups of workers.

9.4 HEALTH-RELATED OUTCOMES

An important goal for researchers in health psychology and personality psychology is to identify individual difference characteristics that are associated with mortality, with illness, and with behaviors that put one's health at risk. Many such investigations have now been conducted, and some clear patterns of results have emerged.

9.4.1 Substance Use

First, let us consider personality characteristics that might predict the use of substances such as tobacco products, alcohol, and various illegal drugs. One obvious hypothesis is that traits related to high levels of the Conscientiousness dimension, such as self-discipline and impulse control, would predict how well a person *would resist temptations* to smoke, to get drunk, and use other kinds of drugs. An additional hypothesis is that traits suggesting low levels of Big Five Emotional Stability (i.e., high Neuroticism), such as anxiety, moodiness, and irritability, would predict how much a person *would be tempted* to use these drugs as a way of temporarily controlling these negative emotions.

The links between personality and substance use were examined in a large-scale study by Elkins, King, McGue, and Iacono (2006). Those researchers obtained self-reports on various personality traits from about 1000 17-year-olds, roughly evenly divided between the sexes. In addition, Elkins et al. also interviewed the participants to determine the extent of their use of tobacco, alcohol, and illicit drugs. These interviews were conducted both at the time of the personality assessment (when the participants were 17 years old) and again 3 years later (when the participants were 20 years old). On the basis of the interviews, some participants were identified as having nicotine dependence, some as having an alcohol use disorder, and some as having a drug use disorder. By the time the participants were 20 years old, about 30% were diagnosed as nicotine dependent, about 30% were diagnosed with an alcohol disorder, and almost 20% were diagnosed with a drug use disorder. (Some participants, of course, could have two or even all three of these disorders, so the majority of participants had no disorders at all.) For each disorder, almost half of the diagnoses had occurred at the time of the first interview.

How did personality relate to these substance use disorders? The results were similar for all three kinds of disorders: In each case, the participants who had been diagnosed with substance use disorders averaged about half or two-thirds of a standard deviation unit lower in Conscientiousness-related traits than did those who were not diagnosed. In addition, substance use disorders were also associated with traits involving low Emotional Stability (such as irritability, anxiety, and moodiness), but the relations were somewhat weaker than for Conscientiousness. Other personality traits generally showed rather weak relations with substance use disorder symptoms.

One interesting feature of the results obtained by Elkins et al. (2006) was that, even among 17-year-olds who did not have a substance use disorder, there were higher average levels of Conscientiousness and Emotional Stability among those who continued to have no substance use disorder 3 years later than among those who did develop such a disorder during that interval. This suggests that personality was actually predictive of substance use problems, and not merely a consequence of these problems.

The results of Elkins et al. (2006) are consistent with those obtained in a review of earlier studies that had investigated the relations between Conscientiousness-related traits and health-related behaviors. Bogg and Roberts (2004) reviewed dozens of earlier investigations that together involved tens of thousands of participants. They found that traits belonging to the Conscientiousness factor, especially self-control, were correlated negatively with excessive alcohol use and with illegal drug use (both correlations about $-.25$) and, to a lesser extent, with tobacco use (correlation about $-.15$). Thus, the finding of moderate negative relations between Conscientiousness and substance use appears to be consistent.

The relations between personality characteristics and substance use raise the question of how personality might be associated with success in quitting—that is, in ceasing the use of tobacco, alcohol, or other drugs. One study of over 1600 elderly Americans (Terracciano & Costa, 2004) found that, on average, those who had never smoked (about 50% of the sample) were more than half of a standard deviation unit higher in Conscientiousness (and in Emotional Stability) than were those who were still smokers (about 7% of the sample). The remaining participants—those who had quit smoking—had levels of these personality characteristics that were about halfway in between those of the other two groups. Similarly, a much smaller study of about 70 alcohol-dependent patients (Bottlender & Soyka, 2005) found that most had emerged successfully from a 1-year treatment program, but that those who had relapsed tended to be lower in Conscientiousness (and in Emotional Stability) than those whose treatment had succeeded. Results such as these suggest that the high levels of self-control that are associated with Conscientiousness and Emotional Stability may contribute to success in quitting smoking or in quitting drinking. (Note, however, that some of successful patients were low in Conscientiousness and in Emotional Stability.)

9.4.2 Longevity

Given that substance use problems are harmful to one's health, the finding that personality is related to substance use raises the possibility that personality would also be related to health and even to longevity. That is, if some personality characteristics are associated with avoidance of substance abuse—or with engaging in health-promoting behaviors more generally—then persons with high levels of those characteristics might, on average, tend to be healthier and more long-lived than persons with lower levels. One obvious challenge in testing this hypothesis, however, is that a very long time is needed to conduct investigations: It would be necessary to measure personality in healthy young people, and then wait several decades to observe whether personality was predictive of health problems and of early mortality. Fortunately, some researchers have been able to address this question by identifying older adults who had participated in studies of personality decades earlier, during their childhood or adolescence. Using these "archival" data, the researchers have examined the relation between personality characteristics and later health outcomes.

One investigation of the relations between personality and longevity (Friedman et al., 1993) used personality data that were obtained in a very early study of gifted children in California (Terman, 1925). Terman's study was designed to examine the characteristics of children who obtained very high scores on intelligence tests, and it involved the assessment of those children in terms of personality and other characteristics. Ratings of the personality characteristics of the children were provided by their teachers during the 1921–22 school year, when the children were about 11 years old. In 1986, over 60 years later, Friedman and colleagues were able to obtain records of which participants had died and which were still alive. These records—obtained from about 1200 persons—allowed the researchers to examine how childhood personality was related to longevity.

The results obtained by Friedman et al. (1993) showed that childhood personality was indeed related to longevity. In particular, two groups of characteristics were predictive of mortality rates. First, a group of traits that Friedman et al. called "conscientiousness" or "social dependability" was associated with longer life spans.[2] This relation was moderately strong: When the researchers compared persons who were low in dependability (i.e., in the bottom quarter of the sample) with persons who were high in dependability (i.e., in the top quarter of the sample), they found that the low-dependability persons had about a 35% greater chance of dying before the age of 70 than did the high-dependability persons. Also, a group of traits involving cheerfulness and optimism was associated with longevity, but in the negative direction: Persons high in cheerfulness had about a 35% higher chance of dying before the age of 70 than did persons low in cheerfulness. (Note, however, that even among the persons who were low in dependability or high in cheerfulness, most were still alive at the age of 70.) Several other personality traits were unrelated to longevity.

Friedman et al. (1993) examined possible reasons why these traits would be related to longevity. With regard to dependability, Friedman et al. suggested that perhaps the more dependable persons would be less likely to engage in an array of health-damaging behaviors, such as smoking, heavy drinking, overeating, or careless risk-taking. In a later study, Friedman et al. (1995) investigated these possibilities, by obtaining information from the participants (or from their surviving relatives) about the drinking habits, smoking history, and body weight of the participants. The results showed that low dependability was associated with smoking and drinking (although not with obesity), and that smoking and drinking were associated with earlier death. However, these relations were not strong enough to explain the link between dependability and longevity. In other words, the

---

[2] Actually, this group of traits is not the same as Conscientiousness as described in earlier chapters, but is instead more like a blend of Conscientiousness, Agreeableness, and Honesty—Humility. When the personality scales were constructed, in the early 1920s, researchers had not yet identified the major dimensions of personality, so the scales were not constructed in such a way as to correspond directly to each of those dimensions individually.

tendency for dependable persons to live longer could only be explained in small part by their lower likelihood of smoking or of heavy drinking. This leaves open the question of why dependability is associated with longevity, but Friedman et al. suggested that dependable persons might have been better able to handle life's stresses, by virtue of being better prepared, or might have developed better networks of social support with their spouses, relatives, and friends. Also, it is possible that dependable persons took better care of their health in many subtle ways other than merely by not smoking or not drinking to excess.[3]

As for the link between cheerfulness and earlier death, the same team of researchers also examined possible explanations for this result (Martin et al., 2002). The relations of cheerfulness with smoking and heavy drinking were fairly weak, and therefore the relation between cheerfulness and earlier mortality was not attributable in any important part to these behaviors. A possible remaining explanation (Friedman et al., 1993) is that perhaps cheerful persons tend to be overly optimistic about their health prospects, and therefore tend to neglect any health problems that might be developing. However, it was not possible to test this hypothesis using the data that were available from these participants. The reasons for the link between cheerfulness and mortality are of some interest, because intuitively it might seem more likely that cheerful people would live longer.[4] Future studies will be able to examine this question in more detail.

In fact, some further data on the relation between childhood personality and longevity are currently being collected, and results will become available during the next few decades. One large-scale project (Hampson, Goldberg, Vogt, & Dubanoski, 2006) has been examining the health-related outcomes of about 1000 persons in Hawaii. These participants were born during the 1950s, and their personalities had been rated by their elementary school teachers during a research project conducted mainly during the early 1960s (recall Section 4.4.4). [Unlike the participants whose longevity was examined by Friedman et al. (1993), the participants of this Hawaiian investigation represented a wide range of intellectual ability, rather than only the very high levels.] When Hampson et al. began obtaining health-related information from these participants during

---

[3] Also considered by Friedman et al. (1995) was the possibility that persons having higher levels of dependability would be especially unlikely to die of certain specific causes. The more common causes of death that could be examined in this study were cancer, heart disease, and injuries. The results showed that, for each of these causes of death, the high-dependability persons were less likely to have died by age 70 than were the low-dependability persons. Thus, the difference in death rates for persons with different levels of dependability was not attributable to any single cause of death.

[4] The results of one small-scale investigation suggest that cheerfulness might actually be positively related to longevity. Danner, Snowdon, and Friesen (2001) examined the handwritten autobiographies of 180 Roman Catholic nuns, as written when the nuns were applying to their convent, at about 22 years of age. Danner et al. found that the nuns whose autobiographies showed more positive emotional content—presumably reflecting an upbeat and cheerful disposition—tended to live longer: Over three-quarters of those who were above average in positive emotions lived to be at least 85 years old, whereas only half of those who were below average in positive emotions lived to that age.

1999–2000, nearly all were still alive. It has not yet been possible to study the relations between personality and longevity in this sample, but the links between personality and some health-related behaviors and outcomes have been examined. Thus far, the relations between personality and various health-related outcomes—including smoking, drinking, obesity, and self-rated health—have been rather weak (Hampson et al., 2006), although this may reflect in part the limitations of the teacher ratings of personality. But in light of the results obtained by Friedman et al. (1993), it is plausible that some of the personality characteristics will ultimately be associated, at least modestly, with longevity among the participants of the Hawaiian sample.

Other research on personality traits as predictors of longevity has been based on personality assessments made when the participants were already adults. Terracciano, Löckenhoff, Zonderman, Ferrucci, and Costa (2008) used self-report personality data from a sample of over 2000 adults, and examined personality trait levels in relation to longevity. (By the time that Terracciano et al. conducted the study, about 40% of the original participants had died, on average about 18 years after their personality assessment.) Terracciano et al. found that participants who were higher in Conscientiousness, in Emotional Stability, and in activity level tended to live longer on average. For each of these aspects of personality, the average difference in longevity between persons one standard deviation unit above the mean and persons one standard deviation unit below the mean was about 2 or 3 years. Thus, there was a modest but meaningful difference in longevity depending on people's levels of these traits. Terracciano et al. also examined whether higher levels of these personality traits were associated with longevity through a lower likelihood of smoking or of being obese. However, they found that greater longevity of people with higher levels of these personality traits was not due to reduced rates of smoking or obesity. As with the findings of Friedman et al., it seems that the links of personality with longevity do not mainly involve just one or a few particular causes of death.

9.4.3 Heart Disease (and "Type A" Personality)

Heart disease is one of the leading causes of death in modern societies, and the idea that personality may be implicated in heart disease has a long history (see Smith & Ruiz, 2002). In the early 20th century, the Canadian physician William Osler suggested that persons who have a keen and ambitious disposition, and seem always to be moving at full speed, were more likely to be afflicted with heart disease (Osler, 1910). About half a century later, a more fully developed variant of this idea was proposed by Friedman and Rosenman (1959), who identified a set of several characteristics as potential risk factors for heart-related illnesses. These characteristics—including competitiveness, impatience, excessive job involvement, hostility, and time urgency—were collectively described as the "Type A" behavior pattern, which contrasted with the opposite pattern known as "Type B." (Note, however, that people do not divide neatly into two "types" on these characteristics. As with other aspects of personality, most people have intermediate levels, with fewer people having very high or very low levels.)

By the 1980s, several studies had shown that Type A characteristics—as typically assessed through structured interviews between physician and patient—were associated with increased probability of heart disease, equivalent to a correlation coefficient of about .20 (e.g., Cooper, Detre, & Weiss, 1981; Miller, Smith, Turner, Guijarro, & Hallet, 1996). However, it was primarily the hostility aspect of the Type A syndrome—not the various other characteristics—that was responsible for the relation with heart disease. In some studies, persons with higher levels of (self-reported) anger or hostility have shown rates of heart disease several times higher than do persons with lower levels of those traits (see review by Williams, 2010). Some other research has indicated that heart disease is also associated with the personality characteristic of dominance, perhaps even more strongly than with hostility (e.g., Houston, Babyak, Chesney, Black, & Ragland, 1997; Whiteman, Deary, & Fowkes, 2000).

This raises the question of *why* a personality characterized by "hostile dominance" would be at higher risk of heart disease (see, e.g., Smith & Spiro, 2002). One possibility is simply that the biological causes of hostility and dominance also influence heart disease risk, but the mechanism by which this would occur is not known. It is also possible that hostile, dominant people have poorer health habits, but this might not entirely account for the link with heart disease. Still another possible reason is that hostile, dominant people tend to create more stress for themselves by getting into conflicts with others, and also tend to receive less stress-reducing social support from others. Currently, the most widely accepted hypothesis is that persons who are high in hostility and dominance have greater physiological reactions to stress than do other persons, with greater increases in blood pressure, heart rate, and levels of stress-related hormones and neurotransmitters. These reactions in turn tend to damage the blood vessels, thereby increasing the risk of heart disease.

9.5 ACADEMIC PERFORMANCE

Among the important outcome variables that might be predicted by personality are those involving effectiveness, achievement, or performance: What are the personality characteristics of a high-performing worker or of a high-performing student? Of course, one's personality characteristics are unlikely to be the only determinants of performance. For example, one's level of raw ability is likely to be an important contributor to performance, as is one's interest in specific courses of study or specific job tasks. But it still seems plausible that general behavioral tendencies—that is, personality characteristics—would also predict performance at school or on the job. Many investigations of the links between personality and performance have now been conducted, and reviews of these studies show some fairly consistent results. We will now discuss these findings, beginning with the prediction of academic performance, followed by the prediction of job performance.

A recent review of the relations between personality and academic performance summarized over 100 studies involving tens of thousands of students. Poropat (2011) found that, among the Big Five personality factors, Conscientiousness was the strongest and most consistent predictor of academic performance. The average correlation between Conscientiousness and grade point average was about .25, which indicates a moderate tendency for high-Conscientiousness students to perform better in school than low-Conscientiousness students. Poropat's review showed that the relation between Conscientiousness and academic performance was similar across different levels of education; that is, it was about the same in elementary school, in high school, and in college. The link between Conscientiousness and grade point average is hardly surprising because the characteristics that make up the Conscientiousness factor—traits such as self-discipline, organization, and diligence—seem likely to contribute to academic performance through greater effort, efficiency, and attention to detail, both in completing course work and also in studying for examinations. [One particular aspect of Conscientiousness—that of achievement motivation—appears to be an even better predictor of grade point average than is the broad Conscientiousness factor (Paunonen & Ashton, 2001a, 2001b); recall Box 3.4.]

Broad personality factors other than Conscientiousness did not show such consistent relations with academic performance in Poropat's (2011) review. But one interesting finding involved differences between levels of schooling: At the elementary school level, academic performance was associated not only with Conscientiousness but also with Agreeableness, Emotional Stability, Extraversion, and Openness to Experience, with correlations in each case around .20. But beyond the elementary school level, these other factors were no longer substantially related to academic performance; at the college level, none of the correlations reached .10 (except that for Conscientiousness, as noted in the previous paragraph). This pattern of results might be explained in part by changes in grading across levels of school. In elementary school, a teacher's grading of student performance might be influenced by the desirable (or undesirable) personality characteristics of the student, but in high school (and especially in college) these influences are presumably much weaker.

9.6 JOB PERFORMANCE

In comparison with the number of studies examining personality and academic performance, there have been many more studies of the relations between personality and job performance. In fact, since the early 1990s, several reviews of this research have been published (e.g., Tett, Jackson, & Rothstein, 1991), summarizing the results obtained in dozens of previous investigations. But before we discuss those results, we should briefly address the question of how job performance is measured.

9.6.1 How to Assess Job Performance?

In contrast to the situation in school settings—where course grades provide a ready indicator of performance—it is not always obvious how to assess job performance. One approach is to use some objective records of productivity. To take a few examples, one could count the number of customers served by a cashier, the number of pieces produced by a machine operator, the number of scientific articles published by a university professor, and the number (or dollar value) of houses sold by a real estate agent. (Similarly, one could also keep track of the number of *counterproductive* actions, such as latenesses, days absent, rule violations, safety violations, lost merchandise, and even thefts and violent acts.) The objectivity of using such records is an advantage, but is not easily applied to some jobs; for example, it is not clear how a productivity "count" could be used to evaluate the performance of a nurse or a personnel manager or an engineer. Moreover, even when such counts can be made, they may fail to capture important aspects of job performance.

Another approach to the assessment of job performance is to obtain supervisors' evaluations—or sometimes even coworker evaluations—of employee performance, using a rating scale (e.g., from 0 to 10), a ranking system (e.g., from best to worst employee), or some combination thereof. This method has the advantage of being widely applicable across jobs, although it does depend on the more subjective judgment of the persons who assess job performance. But in any case, studies of the relations between personality and job performance have shown relatively little difference between the results obtained on the basis of objective "counts" or of subjective ratings (Nathan & Alexander, 1988), or have shown some tendency for the subjective ratings to be more easily predicted (Barrick & Mount, 1991; Tett et al., 1991).

9.6.2 The Role of Conscientiousness

Now let us consider what those results have shown, first from the perspective of the broad dimensions of personality. When findings are averaged across studies that have reported the correlations between employees' personality self-reports and measures of their job performance, the most consistent finding is that the Conscientiousness dimension is positively correlated with job performance (e.g., Hurtz & Donovan, 2000; see also Barrick & Mount, 1991; Tett et al., 1991). This is exactly what one would expect, given that the personality traits belonging to the Conscientiousness factor are the same traits that describe one's style of working, for example being organized, disciplined, thorough, careful, and diligent. However, the strength of the relations between Conscientiousness and job performance is rather modest, typically about .20 (Hurtz & Donovan, 2000), even when corrections are made for the less-than-perfect reliability of job performance measures.

The validity of Conscientiousness in predicting job performance, although not very strong, appears to be rather general across a variety of occupations. In contrast, some other dimensions of personality are related to performance in some particular categories of occupations or in some aspects of any given job. For example, Big Five Agreeableness shows modest positive correlations with performance in customer service jobs, and Extraversion and Emotional Stability both show modest positive correlations with performance in sales and managerial jobs (Hurtz & Donovan, 2000). Similarly, Agreeableness is related to getting along with coworkers, Extraversion is related to showing leadership on the job, and Emotional Stability is related to better management of job stress (Hogan & Holland, 2003). But in general, it is the Conscientiousness factor of the Big Five that is the best predictor, *across* occupations, of *overall* job performance.

The finding that Conscientiousness shows positive correlations with job performance raises the possibility that Conscientiousness might also lead to higher levels of income and of occupational status. That is, if people who have high levels of job performance tend on average to receive more raises and promotions (or tend on average to be more successful as self-employed persons), then we might expect that people who have higher levels of Conscientiousness would tend to earn higher incomes and higher levels of job status.

Some research by Sutin, Costa, Miech, and Eaton (2009) has investigated this possibility, examining personality in relation to income, job prestige, and job satisfaction in a sample of 700 persons. They found that persons who were higher in Conscientiousness and in Emotional Stability (i.e., lower in Neuroticism) tended to have slightly higher incomes and also slightly better job satisfaction. However, the correlations were quite weak (only about .10), which suggests that the link between personality and occupational success is a modest one at best.

BOX 9.1 Counterproductive Behavior at Work: A Person-by-Situation Interaction

Zettler and Hilbig (2010) examined counterproductive behaviors—such as stealing from work, showing up late, being rude to coworkers, and other acts—in a sample of employees. The researchers wanted to understand how personality characteristics would be related to counterproductive behavior. To find out, they asked the employees to give anonymous self-reports about their personality, about their workplace, and about their counterproductive behavior at work. The findings of Zettler and Hilbig showed, not surprisingly, that employees who were high in Honesty—Humility generally engaged in little counterproductive behavior. In contrast, employees who were low in Honesty—Humility did a lot more counterproductive behavior.

But Zettler and Hilbig noted that this finding only applied to some of the low-Honesty—Humility employees. It depended on whether the employee worked in a place where there was a

(Continued)

BOX 9.1 Counterproductive Behavior at Work: A Person-by-Situation Interaction—cont'd

lot of "organizational politics"—for example, where employees could get ahead simply by agreeing with the boss or by having the right network of allies. Employees who were low in Honesty—Humility did a lot of counterproductive behavior if they worked in places that were very "political," but not if they worked in places that were not so political. Presumably, workplaces with more organizational politics tend to make employees feel that self-serving behaviors (including some counterproductive acts) are normal and that punishment for those behaviors is less likely. In such a workplace, employees low in Honesty—Humility are therefore likely to act on the temptation to commit counterproductive behaviors, but employees high in Honesty—Humility remain untempted. The researchers noted that these findings were an example of a person-by-situation interaction: In one situation, the personality characteristic of low Honesty—Humility was expressed through counterproductive behavior, but in another situation, it was not.

9.6.3 Integrity Tests

Some moderately strong relations with job performance have also been obtained for instruments that are called *integrity tests*. Integrity tests are self-report questionnaires that are intended to assess a potential (or current) employee's level of honesty and dependability, and thus to predict his or her tendency to refrain from counterproductive behavior (rule breaking, theft, loafing, etc.), as well as his or her likely level of overall job performance. These instruments were used by employers as a means of selecting employees as early as the 1950s, but they became widely used during the 1980s, by which time it was already estimated that 5000 employers were using these tests in the United States (Sackett & Harris, 1984).

Integrity tests are usually divided into two main types: *overt* and *personality-based* tests. Overt integrity tests ask the job applicant to indicate whether he or she has committed various dishonest acts, such as stealing from previous employers, shoplifting, and various other criminal activities and counterproductive workplace behaviors. In addition, overt integrity tests often ask the respondent to indicate his or her attitudes and opinions about such acts. Personality-based integrity tests, by contrast, are more similar in content to typical self-report personality inventories. In principle, these tests may be somewhat more "subtle" in the sense that respondents might not know that the employer is attempting to assess integrity. However, the items of these personality-based tests are often obviously meant to assess socially desirable or undesirable characteristics.

Do integrity tests successfully predict employees' performance and behavior on the job? Van Iddekinge, Roth, Raymark, and Odle-Dusseau (2012) reviewed over 100 previous studies of the relations between employees' integrity test scores and job performance as rated by supervisors. They found that higher scores on integrity tests were modestly related to better job performance, with a correlation of about .15. (This is slightly lower than the correlation of about .20 yielded by the Conscientiousness factor in the review by Hurtz and Donovan mentioned earlier.) Van Iddekinge et al.'s study also reviewed previous findings about the relation between integrity test scores and counterproductive behavior on the job, whether as assessed through self-reports or through employer records. They found that integrity test scores were negatively related to both measures of counterproductive behavior, but more strongly to self-reported counterproductivity (correlation about −.40) than to employer records of counterproductivity (correlation about −.15). It is not clear which of these two results is more accurate, as each method of measuring counterproductivity is imperfect: On the one hand, employer records presumably miss many incidents of counterproductivity, but, on the other hand, an applicant who exaggerates his or her integrity will likely also downplay his or her counterproductive behavior. The results of Van Iddekinge et al.'s review suggest that integrity tests could be of at least some modest value to employers in selecting employees who will perform well on the job and refrain from counterproductive behavior.

9.6.4 The Problem of Faking

When reading the previous section, you might have been surprised to learn that integrity tests (or other measures of personality) could show even a modest level of validity for predicting job performance. Many people find it almost difficult to believe that these instruments can predict job performance at all, because it seems very likely that job applicants would "fake" their self-report responses in such a way as to make a good impression on a prospective employer. In particular, it may seem strange that job applicants would admit, for example, to having stolen from a previous employer or to being an irresponsible or lazy or deceitful person.

Apparently, people do tend to fake to some extent—or at least tend to be rather generous in giving themselves the benefit of the doubt—when taking integrity tests or personality inventories in personnel selection settings. One study tried to assess the extent of faking (also called "response distortion") by comparing the self-report personality scores of two groups of people (Rosse, Stecher, Miller, & Levin, 1998). One group consisted of current employees who knew that their responses were being obtained for research purposes only and would not be seen by their employers. The other group consisted of job applicants who were applying for jobs similar to those of the current employees; these job applicants knew that their responses could be used by the employer to decide which applicants to hire. Note that there is no particular reason that there would be any systematic differences in personality trait levels, on average, between the employees and the applicants. Therefore, if the applicants showed much higher scores on socially desirable characteristics, this would suggest some degree of faking. This is exactly what Rosse et al. found: Across a variety of socially desirable characteristics, the self-report scores of the job applicants were, on average, nearly one standard deviation unit higher than were the self-report scores of the current employees. This suggests a fairly strong degree of response distortion among the applicants.

Despite this response distortion among job applicants, however, the fact that integrity tests and personality inventories have at least some validity in predicting job performance suggests that the *differences* among people in their scores are still somewhat meaningful, and give a somewhat accurate reflection of their *relative* levels of integrity and related traits. Presumably, though, the validity of these instruments would be improved if faking could be entirely prevented. Several methods for reducing or detecting faking by job applicants are currently being used or investigated.

For example, one method is to include some items that ask about moral lapses that presumably *everyone* has committed; persons who claim *not* to have performed these behaviors are then identified as having faked their responses. Scores on "faking scales" consisting of these items can be used to disqualify applicants or to "correct" their scores on the other scales, to estimate their real levels of various traits. Although such faking corrections are widely used, there are serious doubts about their effectiveness (Goffin & Christiansen, 2003). For example, as noted in Box 2.3, persons who really are highly virtuous might obtain high scores on scales intended to detect faking.

Some evidence in support of this possibility comes from a study in which participants were instructed to complete various self-report scales—including an integrity test and a scale designed to detect faking—as if they were applying for a job (Cunningham, Wong, & Barbee, 1994). The participants had volunteered for the study in exchange for monetary payment, but at the end of the study, each participant was "accidentally" overpaid by the researchers, who were actually recording whether or not each participant would give back the extra money. Cunningham et al. found that participants with higher scores on the faking scale were actually *more* likely to pay back the extra money than were persons with lower faking scores. (Participants with higher integrity test scores were also more likely to pay back the extra money than were participants with lower integrity test scores, and the integrity test scores correlated positively with the faking scale scores.)

Other methods that have been examined as potential ways to reduce faking include the use of time limits on applicants' responses (Holden, Wood, & Tomashewski, 2001) and the use of items that require respondents to indicate which of several equally desirable (or undesirable) statements describes them most accurately (Jackson, Wroblewski, & Ashton, 2000). Another potentially promising way of overcoming the problem of faking will involve the use of non–self-report methods of assessing personality. All of the results described earlier were derived from self-reports, but it is possible that observer reports from persons who would have little reason to "fake" on behalf of the applicant—for example, previous employers or coworkers—would show higher levels of validity in predicting job performance. In fact, some evidence suggests that personality ratings from coworkers or supervisors can be at least as valid in predicting job performance as are personality self-ratings on the same characteristics (Mount, Barrick, & Strauss, 1994). Future research on personality and job performance is likely to involve a greater focus on observer reports, and not just self-reports, of personality.

9.7 LAW-ABIDINGNESS VERSUS CRIMINALITY

Criminal and other unethical activities cause enormous harm to their victims and to society at large, and researchers have investigated the personality variables that are associated with these activities. Of course, differences among people in the commission of criminal or unethical acts are likely to be due in considerable part to situational variables. For example, a person who would commit a crime under some circumstances—for example, when influenced by a particular social group, or when exposed to a particular temptation or provocation—might not commit a similar crime under other circumstances. But people do differ in the basic inclination to abide by the laws and behave ethically, and personality is a plausible basis for these differences.

Many investigations of the links between personality and criminal activities are based on self-reports of both kinds of variables. When assessed under anonymous conditions—that is, when respondents perceive no risk of any punishment for admitting to unethical or illegal actions—such studies will likely provide a fairly accurate indication of the relations between personality and crime. However, other investigations have used non-self-report methods of assessment, and in this section we will discuss results based on both types of studies.

9.7.1 The Role of Self-control

One hypothesis about the personality basis of criminal activity comes from the work of two sociologists, Michael Gottfredson and Travis Hirschi. Considering crime as "acts of force or fraud undertaken in pursuit of self-interest" (Gottfredson & Hirschi, 1990, p. 15), those researchers tried to identify the crucial difference between criminals and noncriminals. According to those researchers, the critical variable is a lack of self-control: Criminals tend to act impulsively, failing to delay gratification and instead seeking immediate pleasure even at the risk of later punishment or other negative consequences. Gottfredson and Hirschi suggested that criminals are no more *motivated* to commit crimes than are noncriminals. That is, these researchers argued that noncriminals have the same selfish impulses that criminals have but are better able to inhibit those impulses and delay gratification, choosing to cooperate and to work rather than to commit acts of force or fraud.

The description of self-control as given by Gottfredson and Hirschi (1990) is actually a bit more complicated than the preceding description, and there are some difficulties in measuring this variable (Marcus, 2004). But some research does give some interesting tests of the self-control hypothesis. For example, one study examined self-reports of personality and of criminal behavior among adolescents and university students in Spain (Romero, Gómez-Fraguela, Luengo, & Sobral, 2003). The researchers assessed several personality traits that are thought to be relevant to poor self-control, including impulsive risk taking, preference for simple tasks, self-centeredness, preference for physical activities, and volatile temper. In addition, Romero et al. also obtained self-reports for several delinquent or criminal activities, representing categories of vandalism, theft, aggression, general rule breaking, academic dishonesty, and illegal drug use.

The results of the Romero et al. (2003) study showed that overall delinquent behavior was most strongly related to the characteristic of impulsive risk taking, with correlations averaging in the .40s across the two samples. (Other traits showed more modest relations and tended to be associated with specific kinds of delinquent acts. For example, self-centeredness and volatile temper both correlated in the .20s with aggressive acts.) Thus, the results of this study suggest that the willingness to take risks and the tendency *not* to inhibit one's impulses together have an important influence on criminal activity. Given that impulsive risk seeking is probably the trait that is most relevant, conceptually, to the construct of low self-control, these results do seem to be consistent with the hypothesis proposed by Gottfredson and Hirschi (1990).

9.7.2 Psychopathy

In contrast to the hypothesis of Gottfredson and Hirschi (1990), some other ideas about the links between personality and criminal behavior do include a role for differences in the *motivation* to commit crime, in addition to a role for lack of impulse control. For example, researchers have long observed that an important difference among criminals— even among the serious offenders called *psychopaths*—is that some have very poor self-control, whereas others are more coolly calculating and rational. Karpman (1948) used the term "primary psychopath" to refer to the latter kind of criminal and called the former kind of criminal the "secondary psychopath." Consistent with this view, subsequent researchers who studied the personality characteristics of criminals found that those characteristics form two broad factors (e.g., Harpur, Hare, & Hakstian, 1989; Levenson, Kiehl, & Fitzpatrick, 1995) that show only modest positive correlations with each other. One group of characteristics, representing primary psychopathy, includes manipulation, deceit, grandiosity, callousness, and selfishness, whereas the other group of characteristics, representing secondary psychopathy, includes impulsivity, irresponsibility, lack of planning, and poor self-control.

In some studies, researchers have examined the relations of primary psychopathy and secondary psychopathy with criminal or delinquent behavior in samples of people, such as college students, who are generally not convicted criminals. These studies, based on anonymous self-reports, indicate that both sets of characteristics—primary and secondary psychopathy—are positively correlated with delinquent activities, such as thefts, vandalism, driving while intoxicated, and others (Levenson et al., 1995; McHoskey, Worzel, & Szyarto, 1998). These links are moderately strong, with correlations reaching the .40s, and suggest that both primary and secondary psychopathy should be considered when predicting criminal or delinquent behavior. That is, a person's likelihood of committing crimes depends both on how much he or she fails to control impulses, and also on his or her level of manipulativeness and selfishness.

The distinction between primary and secondary psychopathy has some interesting implications. One of these involves the behavior of persons who have high levels of one aspect of psychopathy, but low levels of the other. (Because the two kinds of psychopathy have moderate positive correlations with each other, such persons will be somewhat unusual, but not particularly rare.) Consider a person who has high levels of primary psychopathic traits (such as deceitfulness, grandiosity, and selfishness) but low levels of secondary psychopathic traits (such as impulsivity and irresponsibility). Such a person will likely cause many difficulties for other people, by being exploitative and manipulative of others. However, such a person might be careful enough and self-controlled enough to avoid committing acts that would lead to criminal convictions (or at least to avoid committing such acts when he or she would be caught). Conversely, consider a person who has low levels of primary psychopathic traits but high levels of secondary psychopathic traits. Such a person would be unlikely to harm others deliberately while pursuing some selfish goals, yet he or she might nevertheless get into trouble with the authorities, for example, by impulsively committing a crime in response to some sudden provocation or some sudden temptation.

More recent work (e.g., Williams, Paulhus, & Hare, 2007) has suggested that the two broad aspects of psychopathy can each be divided into two parts, giving four parts altogether. These four parts represent (1) a manipulative, "conning" style of interaction with others; (2) a callous insensitivity to others' concerns; (3) an erratic, uncontrolled, impulsive lifestyle; and (4) a pattern of antisocial behavior or criminal activity. As you would expect, these different aspects of psychopathy are strongly related to basic personality dimensions. All four parts are related to low Honesty—Humility; in addition, callousness is related to low Emotionality, and erratic lifestyle is related to low Conscientiousness (Gaughan, Miller, & Lynam, 2012).

Psychopathy has recently been studied along with two other, related traits: Machiavellianism (a cynical tendency to pursue one's interests by manipulating others) and narcissism (an inflated view of one's own importance, with a sense of entitlement and willingness to exploit others).[5] These overlapping constructs of psychopathy, Machiavellianism, and narcissism are sometimes called the "Dark Triad" (Paulhus & Williams, 2002).

Studies examining the links of the Dark Triad characteristics with the major personality factors have found that all three are strongly negatively correlated with the HEXACO Honesty—Humility factor. In addition, each of the three Dark Triad characteristics has some unique associations with other HEXACO personality factors (see Lee et al., 2013): Psychopathy is related to low Conscientiousness and low Emotionality, Machiavellianism is related to low Agreeableness, and Narcissism is related to high Extraversion

BOX 9.2 Do Guilt-Prone People Make Better Workers?

Some recent research has investigated the personality trait of *guilt proneness* in relation to a variety of behaviors, including those in the workplace (Cohen, Panter, Turan, Morse, & Kim, 2015; Cohen, Wolf, Panter, & Insko, 2011). As conceptualized in this research, guilt proneness refers to a tendency to feel guilty when one commits some ethical wrongdoing, not a general tendency toward feelings of depression or low self-esteem. Guilt proneness is mainly related to the HEXACO Honesty—Humility and Conscientiousness factors.

Persons with higher levels of self-reported guilt proneness have been reported by their coworkers (in anonymous surveys) to commit fewer counterproductive or deviant acts (such as theft) and to commit more "good citizenship" acts (such as helping coworkers). In Cohen et al.'s (2015) data, coworkers reported about five times as many deviant acts by workers with guilt proneness scores in the bottom quarter of the sample as by workers with guilt proneness scores in the top quarter. The coworkers also reported about 50% more "good citizenship" acts by workers with high guilt proneness than by workers with low guilt proneness.

In addition, guilt proneness has been related to behavior in negotiations (Cohen et al., 2015, 2011). Specifically, persons higher in guilt proneness report being much less willing to engage in unethical negotiation behaviors, such as making false promises or misrepresenting one's position. When placed in actual negotiation scenarios, persons higher in guilt proneness have been reported by their negotiation counterparts to engage in fewer of these unethical behaviors.

Why is guilt proneness related to ethical behavior, whether on the job or elsewhere? A likely reason is that guilt-prone people anticipate the guilt that they would feel after behaving unethically, and therefore avoid the unethical action.

---

[5] Machiavellianism is most commonly measured using scales developed by Christie and Geis (1970). This construct is named after Niccolo Machiavelli, an Italian political philosopher of the late 15th and early 16th centuries, who advised rulers to use deceptive and ruthless tactics as a way to maintain and expand their personal power. Narcissism, as noted in the description of narcissistic personality disorder (Chapter 8), is named after a character in an ancient Greek myth who spent time admiring his own reflection in a pool of water.

9.8 LIFE SATISFACTION

Another important variable that might be predicted by personality is that of life satisfaction—a person's subjective evaluation of his or her own life. What aspects of one's personality can predict one's satisfaction with life? Of course, one's life satisfaction at any given time is likely to depend on many variables that may be unrelated to one's personality. For example, the recent death of a loved one, the recent diagnosis of a serious illness, or the recent loss of a job would likely tend to lower one's current level of life satisfaction a great deal. Conversely, one's current level of life satisfaction is likely to be higher than usual if one has recently fallen in love or if one has recently achieved some much-desired success.

However, there is evidence of some substantial stability to individual differences in life satisfaction: Even though one's level may rise or fall substantially in response to important events, some people tend to be more satisfied with life than others do, even across long periods of time (e.g., Diener, 2000). For example, one study of American college students obtained correlations above .50 between life satisfaction levels measured 4 years apart. Moreover, in one recent investigation of a sample of Dutch identical twins, fraternal twins, and nontwin siblings, life satisfaction was found to have a substantial genetic influence, showing a heritability of almost .40 (Stubbe, Posthuma, Boomsma, & De Geus, 2005). Thus, even though one's level of life satisfaction will increase or decrease in response to important life events, there is still a tendency for some people to be consistently more satisfied with life than others are. This leaves open the possibility that personality characteristics might be related to life satisfaction.

One study of American college students (Furr & Funder, 1998) examined the relations of a variety of personality traits with life satisfaction. Furr and Funder found that life satisfaction was associated with self-reports of several personality traits: it showed a positive correlation with self-esteem (about .60) and also with cheerfulness (about .40) and with assertiveness and sociability (both above .30). In addition, life satisfaction showed negative correlations with depressiveness (about −.50) and with anxiety (about −.30) and anger (about −.30). When these traits are considered in terms of the Big Five framework, the results show that life satisfaction is most strongly associated with high levels of Extraversion and of Emotional Stability. (In addition, life satisfaction also showed modest positive correlations, in the .20s, with Big Five Agreeableness and Conscientiousness.) The results were generally similar even when personality was assessed by reports from the participants' parents and friends, although the correlations were weaker.

The findings of the study by Furr and Funder (1998) suggest that an individual's satisfaction with life is to some considerable extent a function of his or her personality. In particular, persons who have a general disposition to feel positive emotions (e.g., cheerfulness, confidence) tend to have high life satisfaction; conversely, persons who have a general disposition to feel negative emotions (e.g., low self-esteem, depression, anxiety, anger) tend to have low life satisfaction. Note that these two dispositions are related independently to life satisfaction: If a person has a tendency to feel *both* positive and negative emotions rather strongly (or to feel both positive and negative emotions rather weakly), then he or she will likely have a roughly average level of life satisfaction (see Larsen & Diener, 1987; Tellegen, Watson, & Clark, 1999). (Interestingly, women on average have a slight tendency to feel both positive emotions and negative emotions more strongly than do men; these tendencies apparently "cancel each other out," leaving virtually no difference between men and women in the average levels of life satisfaction.)

BOX 9.3 Self-Esteem, Narcissism, and Aggression

How does self-esteem relate to aggressive and criminal behaviors? Are violent acts more likely to be committed by people who view themselves very negatively, or by people who view themselves very positively? To understand the relations between self-esteem and aggressive actions, it is important to understand that having low self-esteem is not exactly the opposite of having excessively high self-esteem. For example, a person who is narcissistic (see Chapter 8) tends to be conceited and arrogant, but such a person might also tend to have some feelings of inferiority or worthlessness. Similarly, even if a person rarely (if ever) feels inferior or worthless, he or she might not be at all conceited or arrogant. Therefore, it is important to consider low self-esteem and narcissism as two different traits— not as opposite ends of the same trait—when considering the relations of self-esteem with aggressive behavior.

When researchers have studied aggression in relation to both of these traits, they have found that aggression is associated both with low self-esteem and also with narcissism (Donnellan, Trzesniewski, Robins, Moffitt, & Caspi, 2005; Paulhus, Robins, Trzesniewski, & Tracy, 2004). When both traits are considered together, their ability to predict aggressive tendencies is better than that of either trait alone. That is, the people who are most likely to commit aggressive acts are those who are susceptible to feelings of worthlessness and inferiority, but who are also inclined to have a conceited, arrogant sense of superiority over others. Conversely, the people that are least likely to commit aggressive acts are those who have adequate self-esteem (i.e., who do not feel inferior or worthless) without being narcissistic (i.e., without being self-important).

In a sense, it is not really surprising that life satisfaction tends to be high among people who feel positive emotions strongly and also among people who tend *not* to feel negative emotions strongly. Not only will these tendencies influence the way one evaluates one's life as a whole, but they may also influence the *experiences* one has in life: For example, a person who feels more positive than negative emotions may behave in such a way as to elicit more favorable reactions from others, and thus to develop better relationships and career outcomes. One question of interest for future studies will be to examine whether other personality traits can predict future life satisfaction many years later. For example, as found by Furr and Funder (1998), college students who are high in Conscientiousness traits have a slight tendency to be currently more satisfied with life, but it is also possible that Conscientiousness could also predict future life satisfaction, if traits such as organization and self-discipline tend to produce more favorable life events that improve various outcomes in one's life.

BOX 9.4 Personality and Life Satisfaction: The Role of Culture

A study by Schimmack, Radhakrishnan, Oishi, Dzokoto, and Ahadi (2002) examined the link between personality and life satisfaction in several cultures. They hypothesized that in every culture, persons with higher levels of the Big Five Extraversion and Emotional Stability (i.e., low Neuroticism) factors would tend to have higher levels of life satisfaction. However, they also hypothesized that this relation would be stronger in "individualist" cultures (where people are encouraged to be independent and to pursue their own goals) than in "collectivist" cultures (where people are encouraged to be obedient and to pursue the goals of their groups).

Schimmack et al. assessed personality and life satisfaction in people from two relatively individualist countries (the United States and Germany) and in people from three relatively collectivist countries (Japan, Ghana, and Mexico). Their results showed that within all five countries, people who were higher in Extraversion and Emotional Stability tended to report more satisfaction with life. (This relation was due to the fact that these persons generally experienced positive emotions much more than negative emotions, a situation that usually makes people feel satisfied with their lives.) However, the link between personality and life satisfaction was somewhat stronger in the individualist countries than in the collectivist countries.

What this result means is that in individualist countries, people's relative levels of life satisfaction depend more strongly on their personality differences than is the case in collectivist countries. Apparently, in individualist cultures, life satisfaction depends a great deal on the emotions one feels, which in turn depend on personality; in collectivist cultures, by contrast, life satisfaction is not so strongly tied to one's emotions, so personality is less strongly involved in life satisfaction. This raises the question of what else influences life satisfaction in collectivist cultures, and this will be an interesting topic for future research.

9.9 SUMMARY AND CONCLUSIONS

The relations between personality and the important life outcomes considered in this chapter can be summarized briefly as follows (see Table 9.1).

First, there is only a slight tendency for spouses to be similar in personality; on average, a given husband and wife are likely to be only a little more similar to each other than to

Table 9.1 Summary of relations between personality characteristics and important life outcomes

Life outcome variable	Associated personality characteristics
Marital satisfaction (one's partner's satisfaction)	high Agreeableness high Emotional Stability high Conscientiousness
Marital satisfaction (one's own satisfaction)	high Agreeableness high Emotional Stability high Conscientiousness high Extraversion
Popularity/Status with peers (young adults)	high Extraversion (men and women) high Emotional Stability (men only)
Substance use	low Conscientiousness low Emotional Stability
Longevity	high dependability (and high Conscientiousness) high Emotional Stability high activity
Heart disease	high hostility/anger, high dominance
Academic performance	high Conscientiousness (especially achievement motivation)
Job performance	high Conscientiousness high integrity
Law-abidingness	low impulsivity/secondary psychopathy (and high Conscientiousness) low exploitativeness/primary psychopathy (and high Honesty–Humility)
Life satisfaction	high Extraversion high Emotional Stability high self-esteem high cheerfulness low depressiveness

See text for sources and for sizes of correlations. Names of Big Five or HEXACO factors are capitalized; names of more specific traits are in lower case.

any other person. (As we will see in later chapters, though, there does exist some strong similarity between spouses for some other psychological characteristics.) However, marital satisfaction is modestly related to some aspects of personality: on average, people who are higher in marital satisfaction (1) tend to have spouses with higher levels of Big Five Emotional Stability, Agreeableness, and Conscientiousness, and (2) tend to have higher levels themselves of those same factors, as well as Extraversion.

With regard to peer relationships, research findings among college students suggest that, on average, friends tend to be somewhat similar to each other in their levels of

Honesty—Humility and Openness to Experience, and that friends perceive themselves as being even more similar in those aspects of personality than they really are. Also among college students, popularity has been found to be associated with Extraversion and also (for male college students only) with Emotional Stability and physical attractiveness. Other research has shown that children who are popular with their peers tend to be sociable and nonaggressive.

In the domain of health-related behaviors and outcomes, personality has been found to predict substance use, longevity, and heart disease. Persons with lower levels of Conscientiousness and of Emotional Stability are more likely to smoke and to abuse alcohol or illicit drugs. Conversely, people with higher levels of those traits (and of activity) tend to live longer on average. Higher risk of heart disease has been found to be associated with personality traits of hostility (or anger) and dominance.

Performance in school and on the job is also associated with personality characteristics. The best predictors of academic performance are traits associated with the Conscientiousness factor, particularly achievement motivation. These Conscientiousness-related traits are also modestly related to predicting job performance across the various types of jobs, as are the characteristics measured by integrity tests, which are associated with both Conscientiousness and the HEXACO Honesty—Humility factor.

Research on personality and law-abidingness has focused on low self-control as an important predictor of criminal activity. Other research has suggested that criminal activity is associated not only with traits of poor impulse control, but also with traits of willingness to exploit and manipulate others for personal gain. The distinction between manipulation of others and poor impulse control is roughly the same as that between primary and secondary psychopathy.

Finally, persons' ratings of their overall life satisfaction are associated with traits involving Extraversion and Emotional Stability, such as self-esteem, cheerfulness, and lack of anxious or depressive tendencies. This result suggests that people differ in their underlying tendency to feel satisfied with their lives, as these traits represent a tendency to feel positive emotions and also a tendency not to feel negative emotions.

Taken together, the findings described in this chapter suggest that personality does play a significant role in predicting important life outcomes. Those outcomes are certainly not influenced solely (or even primarily) by personality, but many of the important "results" of people's lives are at least partly a function of their personality characteristics.

CHAPTER 10

Mental Ability

Contents

Individual Differences and Personality
ISBN 978-0-12-809845-5, http://dx.doi.org/10.1016/B978-0-12-809845-5.00010-X

10.1 THE DOMAIN OF MENTAL ABILITY

The topic of this chapter is mental ability—an area of human individual differences that is usually considered to be separate from that of personality. When we discuss personality variation, we are describing differences among people in their *typical behavioral tendencies*—that is, the ways they generally act, think, and feel in various situations. For example, we might try to find out how much different persons tend to socialize, to become angry, to learn new things, or to feel afraid. But when we discuss variation in mental abilities, we are not describing differences among people in these "styles" of behavior; instead, we are describing differences among people in their *maximum performance* in producing correct answers to various problems or questions. For example, we might try to find out how well different persons are able to understand written paragraphs, to solve arithmetic problems, or to figure out directions on a map.

In this chapter, we will explore several important questions about human mental abilities. In many ways, these questions are similar to those that we have addressed throughout this book in the context of personality variation. We will begin with the issue of the structure of mental abilities: Is there a general tendency for some people to be "smarter" than others across the full array of intellectual tasks? Or, is there a tendency for some people to be "smart" at some intellectual tasks and for other people to be "smart" at other such tasks?

After discussing the structure of mental abilities, we will consider a series of questions about the nature of mental ability. How do levels of mental ability change throughout the life span, and how stable are individual differences in mental ability across long periods of time? What are the biological variables that underlie variation among people in mental ability? Is this variation mainly attributable to genetic or to environmental differences? To the extent that the environment is involved, which aspects have the strongest impact on mental abilities?

We will then move on to the question of whether mental abilities have any important influences on real-life outcomes: Do scores on mental ability tests predict academic performance? Do they predict job performance? Health and longevity? Being a good citizen? Whom one marries?

Next, we will examine the sometimes complex ways in which mental abilities are related to several other variables. For example, some aspects of mental ability are substantially related to certain personality characteristics, whereas other aspects are not. Similarly, some aspects of mental ability show large differences between the generations and large changes throughout the life span, whereas other aspects do not.

Finally, we will also consider some alternative ideas about mental ability that have achieved some popularity among the general public, such as the "triarchic theory of intelligence," the "theory of multiple intelligences," and "emotional intelligence."

But before we address these many questions, we should take a moment to clarify what we mean by "mental abilities." This is important, because if we want to study and to measure mental abilities, we will need to decide exactly what is included (and what is not included) within this domain. Generally, researchers who study mental ability have agreed that this domain should be assessed by tasks whose difficulty is due to their demands on mental processes, such as reasoning, understanding, imagining, and remembering. For example, the difficulty in understanding a written paragraph, in solving an arithmetic problem, or in figuring out a route on a map is in each case due to the demands placed on thinking-related skills. The researchers in this field have also agreed that the domain of mental abilities should *not* be assessed by tasks whose difficulty is due in part to their demands on physical skills or on sensory abilities. For example, the difficulty in throwing a javelin, in tying a knot, in hearing a very high-pitched sound, or in seeing a very dim light is in each case largely due to the demands these tasks place on physical or sensory abilities.

Besides focusing on tasks that assess purely mental abilities, researchers in this field also restrict their investigations to tasks that demand skills that are roughly equally familiar to all persons. For example, a test of arithmetic problem solving might be used, because almost everyone is familiar with these problems (at least after middle childhood); however, a test of calculus problem solving would not be used, because most people are not familiar with these problems. Similarly, a mental abilities researcher might measure reading comprehension in a language that was fully familiar to all of the research participants (assuming, of course, that they had all learned to read), but not in a language that some participants had studied and others had not. Fig. 10.1 shows several examples of tasks that are used in tests of various mental abilities.

Also, there is one other point to mention before we examine in depth the topic of mental abilities. You might have noticed that, in the preceding paragraphs, the word "intelligence" has not been used, even though the topic considered here is frequently described by that term. The reason for referring to this domain as "mental ability" rather than "intelligence" is that this avoids raising the (rather meaningless) question of what intelligence "really" is. Frequently, when scientists describe mental abilities research with the word intelligence, many people object that this domain is not necessarily the same thing as intelligence. They might argue that intelligence is not really about solving the problems given on intelligence tests, many of which are either school-like tasks or artificial puzzles. They might suggest instead that intelligence is about achieving success in the competitive struggles of "real life" or (alternatively) about living in harmony with other people and with the natural surroundings. Perhaps you will agree with this objection, or perhaps you will disagree; but to avoid a pointless debate about the meaning of a word, we should make it clear that what we are trying to investigate is mental ability as described earlier—that is, the capacity to solve problems that demand thinking-related skills. After reading the summary provided in this chapter about the nature of mental abilities, their causes, and their consequences for the real world, you might think about whether or not you would describe those abilities as "intelligence." But let us put this aside for now and begin discussing what scientists have learned about individual differences in mental ability.

10.2 THE STRUCTURE OF MENTAL ABILITY: ONE DIMENSION OR MANY?

Consider the four tasks that are shown in Fig. 10.1. These four tasks are all parts of a widely used intelligence test called the Multidimensional Aptitude Battery (MAB; Jackson, 1984a). The first task is a test called Vocabulary, which asks respondents to identify which of several alternative words is closest in meaning to the given word. In the second task, called Arithmetic, respondents must figure out how to solve an arithmetic problem and then correctly perform the needed calculations. The third task is called Spatial; this particular spatial test asks respondents to consider a given two-dimensional shape and to indicate which of several alternative shapes would match the given shape if it were rotated (without having to be flipped over). In the fourth task, called Picture Arrangement, respondents must figure out which sequence of comic strip panels would make the most meaningful story.

Consider these four tasks, and ask yourself this question: Would most people who perform well at one of these tasks also perform well at the others, or would there be essentially zero correlations between levels of performance on the tasks? For example, do you believe that people with better verbal ability (measured by the Vocabulary task) would also have better ability in social interpretation (measured by the Picture Arrangement task), or not? Also, do you believe that people with better quantitative reasoning ability (measured by the Arithmetic task) would also have better ability in spatial orientation (measured by the Spatial task), or not? If you believe that there exists a *general* mental ability—an overall tendency to be "smart"—then you would expect all of the correlations to be positive. On the other hand, if you believe that there are several completely independent mental abilities—several completely different kinds of being "smart"—then you would expect the correlations to be close to zero. Later in this chapter, we will summarize the actual correlations among these tasks, as based on the scores of thousands of high school students who have taken the tests. But now let us examine the history of research on this question of the structure of mental abilities.

It was only in the late 19th century that scientists began the systematic study of mental ability. Some early researchers, such as James McKeen Cattell (in the United States) and Francis Galton (in England), believed that individual differences in intellectual abilities could be understood as the result of individual differences in various physical or sensory abilities. Therefore, they tried to determine whether the latter abilities—for example,

Vocabulary: Choose the alternative from A to E that is nearest in meaning to the word given.

Simple

A. hard   B. easy   C. example   D. the same   E. useful

Arithmetic: Solve the following problem.

If it costs $8 for two students to go to the theatre, how much will it cost for three students?

A. $10   B. $16   C. $12   D. $4   E. $6

Spatial: Choose one figure to the right of the vertical line which is the same as the figure on the left. One figure can be turned to look like the figure on the left; the others would have to be flipped over.

A.   B.   C.   D.   E.

K | Ʞ ⋏ K ⋏ Ʞ

Picture Arrangement: Look at these pictures. Put them in the right order so that they will tell a story.

1.

2.

3.

4.

A.	1	2	4	3
B.	2	3	1	4
C.	1	4	3	2
D.	4	1	3	2
E.	4	3	2	1

Figure 10.1 *Example items from four mental ability subtests of the Multidimensional Aptitude Battery. (Jackson, D.N. (1984a).* Multidimensional aptitude battery manual. *Port Huron, MI: Research Psychologists Press. Reproduced by permission of SIGMA Assessment Systems, Inc. P.O. Box, 610984, Port Huron, MI 48061-0984.)*

lung capacity, grip strength, hearing acuity, or reaction time—would discriminate between persons who were believed to differ in intelligence. However, these researchers did not measure mental abilities directly.

The first researcher to develop tasks assessing mental abilities was Alfred Binet. His work was part of an effort by the French government to improve the educational system by helping teachers to identify which children were mentally disabled, so that these children could be given their own educational curriculum. Binet developed a variety of tasks that he used in measuring the mental ability of children—he used the word "intelligence"—and many of these really did demand mental abilities, such as thinking with numbers, words, and shapes. Binet's tests were rather successful in their intended purpose and went on to be used in revised form in many other countries even to the present day. However, Binet himself did not try to examine empirically the major scientific questions about the nature of mental abilities, such as the crucial issue of whether there is a single major dimension of mental ability, or whether there are instead several independent varieties of mental ability.

10.2.1 Spearman and the *g* Factor

This question of the structure of mental abilities was investigated by Charles Spearman. An engineer by training, Spearman served for 15 years in the British Army, and then in 1897 began studying psychology in Germany under the supervision of Wilhelm Wundt—the first psychologist to conduct experimental research. At the same time, Spearman was also influenced by the work of Francis Galton—the first psychologist to study individual differences. Spearman became interested in the nature of mental ability, and he began to study it systematically when he returned to England, using students in English schools as his research participants.

At first, Spearman did not measure mental ability directly; instead, he examined students' grades in school, which he believed to be a reasonably good indicator of their mental ability. To determine whether or not there was a single mental ability that was responsible for students' performance across their courses, Spearman calculated correlations among the grades in various courses.[1] His results—as published in his classic article (Spearman, 1904)—showed that grades in the various courses tended to be substantially positively correlated with each other. For example, most students who achieved high grades in arithmetic also achieved high grades in Latin, and most students who achieved low grades in geometry also achieved low grades in French. This result suggested to

---

[1] In fact, this was the first time that *anyone* had calculated correlations: It was Spearman himself who invented the correlation coefficient, to express how strongly (or weakly) different abilities were related to each other. Spearman's form of the correlation coefficient was calculated using individuals' ranks on the variables, rather than their actual scores. Nowadays, researchers usually use a form of the correlation coefficient, developed by Karl Pearson, that is based on individuals' scores rather than ranks.

Spearman that students' grades in these various courses were largely a reflection of the students' differing levels of a single, general mental ability. In other words, the fact that grades in each course were related to grades in every other course indicated that grades in every one of those courses were assessing something in common—presumably, a general, all-around academic ability.

In subsequent research (e.g., Spearman, 1927; Spearman & Jones, 1950), Spearman investigated this question by testing students directly on a variety of tasks intended to assess different aspects of mental ability. (This was an important step, because it could have been the case that students' grades were due not only to a general dimension of mental ability, but also to a general dimension of academic motivation, or to some other source.) Again, he found that students' scores on these various tasks tended to have substantial positive correlations with each other. For example, students who performed well at understanding the meanings of proverbs usually also performed well in identifying which of several shapes was unlike the others; similarly, students who performed poorly in solving arithmetic problems also performed poorly in figuring out analogies between various pairs of words. These results therefore confirmed the findings based on school grades, suggesting again that a general mental ability was at work: The correlations among the various tasks indicated that performance on each task was influenced by a general mental ability.

Spearman's finding of positive correlations among the diverse mental ability tasks was important, given that it indicated the existence of a single, major dimension of mental ability. (Like Binet, Spearman did not hesitate to refer to mental ability as "intelligence," and he described this dimension as "general intelligence.") But this was not the only noteworthy aspect of his findings. Another important finding was that some tasks tended to show rather high correlations with the various other tasks, whereas other tasks tended to show rather low correlations with the various other tasks. This result led Spearman to suggest that performance on the former tasks was very strongly influenced by general mental ability; how well someone did on those tasks was a fairly good indication of their overall level of mental ability. Conversely, performance on the latter tasks was not so strongly influenced by general mental ability; how well someone did on those tasks was not such a good indication of their overall level of mental ability. As a way of summarizing the extent to which each task was correlated with the other tasks, Spearman used factor analysis (actually, he invented factor analysis, just as he invented the correlation coefficient). When Spearman factor analyzed the correlations among the various subtests, he obtained one factor of general mental ability. The tasks that tended to correlate strongly with other tasks showed high loadings on that factor, and the tasks that tended to correlate weakly with other tasks showed lower loadings on that factor. Spearman referred to this factor as *g*, using the letter "g" to represent "general intelligence," and this abbreviation is still used today. The loadings of the various tasks on this *g* factor were described as the "*g*-loadings" of the subtests, and this terminology also remains in use to this day.

At this point, you might be wondering about the kinds of tasks that showed higher and lower *g*-loadings—that is, you might wonder *which* tasks were the best indicators of general mental ability (or, to use Spearman's term, general intelligence). For example, do *g*-loadings depend on the content of the task, such as whether it uses numbers or words or shapes? Or, do *g*-loadings depend on the kind of mental process demanded by the task, such as whether it requires reasoning or memory or perception? By comparing the *g*-loadings of the various tasks, Spearman was able to answer these questions.

First, Spearman found that the content of the task did not matter. Among the most highly *g*-loaded tasks, some tasks were based on verbal content, others were based on numerical content, and still others were based on spatial or figural content. Among the tasks with low *g*-loadings, again there were some verbal tasks, some numerical tasks, and some spatial or figural tasks. Spearman considered this to be an important result, and he referred to it as "the principle of the indifference of the indicator." What he meant by this was that the content of the task (i.e., the indicator) was unimportant (i.e., indifferent) in determining whether the task would show a high *g*-loading or a low *g*-loading.

Second, Spearman found that the mental processes involved in the task did matter. Among the tasks with high *g*-loadings, Spearman found that most of these tasks involved reasoning in some form or other. For example, he found high *g*-loadings for tasks in which respondents had to figure out an analogy between two pairs of words, or the next number in a series of numbers, or the shape that was different from the other shapes in a group. In contrast, Spearman found that the tasks with low *g*-loadings involved simpler mental processes that were more automatic or involved following rules. For example, he found relatively low *g*-loadings for tasks involving *spelling* of words (rather than *comprehension* of word meanings), *calculation* of numbers (rather than *solving problems* involving numbers), or *simple comparison* of shapes (rather than *figuring out* how shapes were alike or unalike).

As was the case for Spearman's finding of "the principle of the indifference of the indicator," Spearman thought that the finding of high *g*-loadings for reasoning-based tasks was very important. In fact, he suggested that these reasoning tasks had some important similarities that generalized across the different kinds of content used by those tasks. According to Spearman, the highly *g*-loaded tasks mostly involved a process that he described as the "eduction of relations and correlates." (Note that the word is "eduction" without an "a"; it is not "education.")

As an example of this process of educing relations and correlates, consider the verbal analogy problem shown in Fig. 10.2: "cat is to dog as kitten is to... ?" In solving this problem, you need to "educe" the *relation* between a cat and a kitten—that is, a kitten is a young cat—and then to "educe" the *correlate* of this relation for a dog—that is, a

Verbal Analogies	*Number Series*	*Matrices*	
cat is to dog as kitten is to ?	1 3 5 7 ?	XOX	OXO
		I O I	?

Figure 10.2 *Examples of mental ability tasks requiring the eduction of relations and correlates.* In each task, the respondent must find the answer by educing (inferring) the relations between the given parts of the item, and then educing (inferring) the missing part. See text for further explanation.

young dog is a puppy. Similarly, consider a number series problem such as the one shown in Fig. 10.2, in which you need to figure out which number continues the series 1, 3, 5, 7, … . To solve this, you need to educe the relations between the numbers (in this case, each number is two larger than the number to its left), and then educe the correlate of this relation for the next number of the series (here, a number two greater than 7 is 9).

The same steps are involved in tasks such as matrix reasoning problems (also shown in Fig. 10.2), in which you must notice the pattern of shapes within each cell of the matrix, figure out how the pattern of shapes changes from one cell to the next, and then apply this rule to figure out the pattern of shapes for the missing cell. Spearman's students, including one named John Raven, developed a test of this type (e.g., Raven, 1941), which they intended to be a very highly *g*-loaded task. The items of the Raven's Matrices test are somewhat different from that shown in Fig. 10.2, but the basic principle is very similar. (All of the examples in Fig. 10.2 are easy ones, but as you can imagine, other items of these kinds can be very difficult.)

As we have discussed so far, Spearman discovered some important facts about human mental abilities. One important finding was his discovery of the positive correlations among all the diverse tasks assessing different aspects of mental ability, a fact that indicated the existence of a general factor of mental ability, or *g*. Another important result was that some of these tasks tended to show strong correlations with most other tasks (and thus had high loadings on the *g* factor), whereas other tasks tended to show weaker correlations (and thus had lower *g*-loadings). Finally, Spearman also found that highly *g*-loaded tasks could have any kind of content (i.e., numbers, words, shapes), but that those tasks frequently demanded reasoning of some kind, often involving the process of "educing relations and correlates."

Now, back to the question that we asked earlier in this chapter: The first four tasks shown in Fig. 10.1 are all positively correlated with each other; that is, persons who do very well on one task are likely to perform well on another task also. All of the six correlations among these four tasks are roughly similar in size, ranging from .24 to .42 as found in a large sample of over 3000 high school students (Jackson, 1984a). If these four abilities are then factor analyzed, all four tasks show moderately high loadings on a *g* factor. This result is thus a nice illustration of Spearman's finding that a dimension of general mental ability is involved even in tasks that appear to be very different from each other.[2]

10.2.2 Group Factors

As discussed in the preceding section, Spearman showed that people who did well on one mental ability task tended to do well on other mental ability tasks. These positive correlations between mental ability tasks suggested a single underlying factor that Spearman called "*g*", for general intelligence. Tasks differed in how much they correlated with various other tasks: Some tasks tended to show higher correlations than others did, and therefore the former tasks were more "*g*-loaded" (i.e., depended more on *g*) than the latter tasks. But tasks of quite different kinds could be highly *g*-loaded, especially if they involved reasoning in some form.

Spearman also found, however, that if two tasks had similar content or demanded similar mental processes, they would tend to be strongly correlated with each other, even if those tasks did not correlate strongly with various other tasks. For example, two tasks that both involved generating words (such as listing rhymes or synonyms for a word) would tend to correlate more highly with each other than with other kinds of tasks. Likewise, two tasks that both involved imagining shapes—or perceiving symbols, or remembering numbers, and so on—would also tend to correlate more highly with each other than with other kinds of tasks.

Spearman and his students realized that, to account for all of the correlations between mental ability tasks, it was necessary to have some factors additional to *g*. Even though the *g* factor could fully account for the correlations between tasks that were quite different in their content or mental processes, it could only partly account for the correlations between tasks that were very similar in their content or mental processes. They proposed that there were also several smaller factors, each of which would account for the part of the correlation between tasks which was not accounted for by *g*. Each of these smaller factors would apply to a particular group of related tasks, and thus were called "group" factors. Some of the main group factors proposed by Spearman's students were those for verbal, spatial, perceptual, and memory abilities (e.g., Holzinger & Swineford, 1939; see also Gustafsson, 2002).

10.2.3 Thurstone and Several Primary Factors

After Spearman's work was published, other researchers also began to investigate the structure of mental abilities. Some of the largest and most influential investigations

---

[2] The correlations are actually somewhat higher when these abilities are measured by similar tasks that do not involve multiple-choice responses, but instead use a one-on-one interview-style testing format.

were those of an American psychologist, Louis Thurstone. Like Spearman, Thurstone had originally been trained as an engineer before studying psychology. For a short time in 1912, Thurstone worked as an assistant to the famous inventor, Thomas Edison.

Much of Thurstone's research was motivated by his view that one could identify several very distinct kinds of mental ability. That is, Thurstone believed that it would be possible to identify several important factors of mental ability, by factor analyzing a very large and diverse battery of mental ability tasks. In collaboration with his wife—a psychologist named Thelma Gwinn Thurstone—and some assistants, Thurstone created dozens of tasks intended to assess a wide variety of abilities. After administering those tasks to large numbers of students at the University of Chicago, Thurstone (e.g., 1938) conducted factor analyses on the students' scores on those tasks.[3] But unlike Spearman, Thurstone interpreted the results in terms of several factors, not just one "*g*" factor of general mental ability. After several investigations, Thurstone concluded that there were at least seven important factors (he called them "primary factors") of mental ability:

Verbal Fluency (ability to produce many words related to a given category);
Verbal Comprehension (ability to understand many words, on their own or in the context of a written passage);
Numerical Facility (ability to work quickly with numbers);
Spatial Visualization (ability to imagine shapes from different perspectives);
Memory (ability to remember strings of information or paired associations);
Perceptual Speed (ability to notice quickly the similarities and differences between objects or symbols); and
Reasoning (ability to infer patterns, similar to "eduction of relations and correlates").

As noted by Thurstone, two tasks measuring any one of these factors could correlate particularly strongly with each other and more strongly than with tasks measuring other mental abilities. Thurstone therefore suggested that one could use a set of several factors to account for the relations between mental ability tasks.

At first, Thurstone viewed the various primary mental ability factors as being independent of each other. However, he noticed that tasks loading on one factor tended to be positively correlated with tasks loading on other factors. In other words, people who were above average in the tasks belonging to one primary mental ability also tended to be above average in the tasks belonging to another primary mental ability. These correlations were not very large in Thurstone's original sample of students from the University of Chicago, but this was partly because those students were mostly very smart, and

---

[3] The University of Chicago students who participated in Thurstone research were impressed by the variety and interestingness of the mental ability tasks he had given them. According to Thurstone (1938), at the end of the last testing session the students actually stood and applauded him and his assistants. The students had participated in exchange for information about their profile of mental abilities and suggestions regarding the kinds of work that would be best suited to their own profile.

therefore there was not much room for some students to do much better than others across all of the tasks. But in any sample of people who differed more widely in mental ability—for example, students from a typical elementary school or high school—the correlations were considerably larger.

In recognition of the fact that the primary mental ability factors were correlated, Thurstone suggested that the primary mental ability factors could themselves be factor analyzed. In this way, those factors would give one broad factor that was similar to the *g* factor proposed by Spearman. One way to think of this is that each of the primary mental ability factors had something in common with one another—with that common element being basically a *g* factor—and each had something separate from the others.

10.2.4 Conclusions About the Structure of Mental Abilities

What all of this means is that by the 1940s, researchers were reaching some fairly similar conclusions about the structure of mental abilities. Spearman had started out with the idea of a *g* factor to account for the correlations between very different tasks; later on, he and his students proposed additional "group" factors to account for the fact that a given group of similar tasks would show particularly high correlations with each other. Thurstone had started out with the idea of several "primary mental ability" factors to account for the high correlations between tasks that were similar; soon thereafter, he realized that those factors were themselves correlated and proposed that they could be factor analyzed to produce one large factor roughly equivalent to *g*. Basically, both research teams had concluded that individual differences in mental abilities could be summarized with one large general factor plus several additional, smaller factors (see Fig. 10.3 for a diagram based on Thurstone's conceptualization).

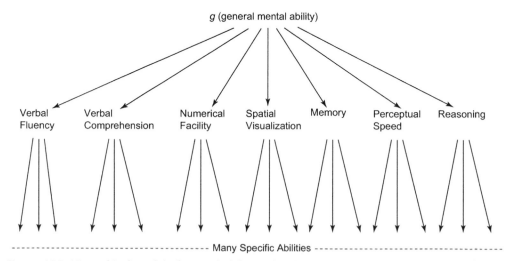

Figure 10.3 *Hierarchical model of mental abilities, showing Thurstone's primary mental abilities as group factors at middle level.*

In accounting for the differences between people in mental ability, the general factor seems to be more important than the several smaller factors (i.e., the group factors or primary mental abilities). Even when tests are quite different in their content or in the mental processes they demand, there is still a fairly strong tendency for persons who are better at one test to be better at the others as well. In a typical diverse battery of mental ability tests, the general factor usually accounts for a large amount of the variability between persons, and for most of the variability accounted for by all factors combined. And as we will see later in this chapter, the overall score based on a variety of mental ability tasks (which is a good approximation to the g factor) is a predictor of many important outcome variables, such as academic performance, job performance, health, law-abidingness, and others.

Nevertheless, the smaller mental ability factors also have an important role. Among people of roughly similar overall ability, patterns of relative strength and weakness in different areas of ability can be important for predicting success in different areas of work or of study. (For example, among persons of very high overall mental ability, those who have better quantitative than verbal ability are more likely to obtain a patent, and less likely to write a book, compared with those who have better verbal than quantitative ability; see Park, Lubinski, & Benbow, 2007.) And as we will see later in this chapter, the various aspects of mental ability show different patterns of change as people get older.

At this point it is useful to discuss how g and other factors of mental ability are related to scores on well-known "IQ" tests. Most IQ tests consist of several diverse subtests that assess different aspects of mental ability. Scores on these subtests are combined to produce an overall IQ score, as well as scores on a few groups of closely related subtests (much like group factors or primary mental abilities). Individuals' overall IQ test scores are usually very strongly correlated with their levels of g, and for the purposes of this chapter we can treat "IQ" as an approximation to g. As noted in Chapter 1, most IQ tests are designed so that the average score is 100, and so that the standard deviation of scores is 15. An individual's IQ score is generally calculated in comparison with people of roughly his or her own age.[4]

In the following sections, we will consider some important questions about the nature and origins of individual differences in mental ability, as represented by scores on IQ tests. How do mental ability levels change throughout the life span? How stable are individual differences in mental ability? What are the biological bases of mental ability? Also, are those

---

[4] The label "IQ" stands for "intelligence quotient," a term that describes the method that was formerly used to calculate children's IQ scores: In the early days, those scores were computed by taking the child's "mental age"—as based on comparison of his or her test score to that of the average child of various other ages—and dividing this by the child's real, "chronological age," and multiplying the result by 100. As used in this chapter, the term "IQ test" refers to a published mental ability test whose validity has been established in empirical research studies. One can find on the internet many tests that are claimed to be IQ tests but that have not been validated in this way.

differences due mainly to hereditary variation or to environmental variation? And how—if at all—do individual differences in mental ability relate to important life outcomes?

10.3 DEVELOPMENTAL CHANGE AND STABILITY IN MENTAL ABILITY

Now let us consider the development of mental abilities—particularly the *g* factor—across the life span. First, we will examine the ways in which the typical person changes in his or her levels of mental abilities and then we will examine the extent to which individual differences in overall IQ—that is, differences among people of the same age cohort—are stable across long periods of time.

10.3.1 Developmental Changes in Mean Levels of Mental Ability

When considering the changes in a typical person's level of mental ability across the life span, we consider individuals' absolute levels of mental ability, rather than levels in comparison with other people of the same age. The clearest findings from research on this question will probably seem rather obvious: On average, people's levels of mental ability increase rapidly through childhood and continue to increase in late adolescence and then decrease during old age. But the changes that occur *in between* the early and late stages of life—that is, between late adolescence and late middle age—are not so clear.

Some indication of age-related differences in mental ability come from the data collected by IQ test publishers in establishing the norms for their tests. Data of this kind have been analyzed by Wisdom, Mignogna, and Collins (2012) for the Wechsler Adult Intelligence Scale—IV (WAIS-IV; Wechsler, 2008). Wisdom et al. compared the mean scores on the various subtests of the WAIS-IV for persons belonging to age groups ranging from 16—17 to 85—89 years old. The pattern of age-related differences varied from one subtest to another:

> For subtests assessing verbal ability, middle-aged adults (in their 40s, 50s, and 60s) averaged somewhat higher than did younger adults, but older adults (in their 70s and 80s) averaged about the same as did younger adults. A similar pattern was observed for the subtest that measures arithmetic problem-solving, but the difference between middle-aged and younger adults was smaller, and younger adults averaged slightly higher than did older adults.

> For subtests assessing spatial ability and perceptual speed, young adults averaged highest, middle-aged adults averaged somewhat lower, and older adults averaged much lower. A similar pattern was observed for memory subtests, but the differences were smaller.

Note that these differences between age groups do not necessarily represent the patterns of how people's levels of mental ability change with age. Because these results are based on test scores of a large group of people who were tested only once (i.e., a *cross-sectional* research design—recall Section 4.2.1), it is possible that the differences between age groups are due to causes other than age-related changes. For example, the differences might be due to the different experiences of people born in different decades; this latter kind of effect is called a *cohort effect*, because it involves differences between birth cohorts.

One way of finding out whether age-related differences are due to age-related change, as opposed to cohort effects, is to use a *longitudinal* research design, in which the same persons are tested on two or more occasions at least several years apart (recall Section 4.2.1). If on average people's scores change between occasions, then this suggests that real age-related changes are at work. However, when using longitudinal designs in studying mental abilities, there is the potential problem that people's scores might improve simply because they have become more familiar with the tasks that are administered. Researchers try to control for these *practice effects* (or *retest effects*) when comparing people's scores across two occasions.[5]

As you can see, figuring out the real pattern of age-related changes in mental abilities is quite complicated. Based on the evidence available so far, it seems that most kinds of mental abilities do decline in old age. However, there is disagreement among researchers as to whether some kinds of abilities (such as spatial ability, perceptual speed, and short-term memory) begin to decline in early adulthood or only at the beginning of old age. Some researchers argue for an early onset of decline in these abilities (e.g., Salthouse, 2009; see also Tucker-Drob & Salthouse, 2011), but other researchers argue for a much later beginning to the decline (e.g., Nilsson, Sternäng, Rönnlund, & Nyberg, 2009; Schaie, 2009).

10.3.2 Stability of Mental Ability Across the Life Span

Regardless of any changes in the people's average levels of mental abilities across the life span, there is also the question of whether or not *individual differences* in mental abilities are stable. As we discussed in Chapter 4 with regard to personality traits, the people of a given age cohort could undergo developmental changes in their levels of characteristics yet still show the same relative standing in comparison with each other. With regard to mental abilities, the research evidence is clear: There does appear to be a high level of consistency across the life course in relative levels of mental ability, at least after late childhood.

Perhaps the most striking evidence on this point comes from a study by Deary, Whiteman, Starr, Whalley, and Fox (2004), who administered an intelligence test to a sample of over 500 elderly Scottish adults. All of these participants—who were 79 or 80 years old at the time of testing—had taken the very same intelligence test nearly seven

---

[5] Another difficulty, even in longitudinal studies, is that changes in people's test scores might be due not just to age-related changes or to practice effects, but also to changes in conditions across time periods. For example, suppose that some new technology tends to develop people's skill in certain kinds of thinking regardless of their age, and therefore tends to improve virtually everyone's scores on certain kinds of tests. Any effects of this kind are called *history (or period) effects* (recall Section 4.2.1), and (as with practice effects) they might make it harder to detect any declines in mental ability that occur due to aging.

decades earlier, when they were 11-year-old elementary school students. Deary et al. found that the participants' scores at 79 or 80 years of age averaged about one standard deviation unit higher than their scores at 11 years of age; interestingly, this suggests that the growth in mental ability during and after adolescence was much greater than any decline in mental ability due to aging. But in spite of the increase in mental ability between 11 years of age and adulthood, the *differences among the participants* in mental ability remained remarkably stable across this interval of almost seven decades: The correlation between test scores at 11 years old and test scores at almost 80 years old was about .65. Thus, the smartest 80-year-olds had usually been among the smartest 11-year-olds, and vice versa.

10.4 BIOLOGICAL CORRELATES OF MENTAL ABILITY

Given that people differ in their levels of mental ability, the obvious question arises as to the biological basis of those individual differences. What is it about people's brains that make some of them smarter than others? As recently as the 1990s, there was relatively little research aimed at answering these questions (Vernon, 1991), but lately there have been many more investigations on this topic. In this section, we will consider some of the biological characteristics that have been examined as potential correlates—and as indicators of the potential causes—of individual differences in mental ability.

10.4.1 Brain Size

If you try to think of some biological variable that might explain how smart people are, the one that comes to mind most readily is probably the size of the brain. In fact, the possibility that bigger brains are smarter brains seems almost *too* obvious, and many people seem to think that this idea has long since been refuted by psychologists. But what is the evidence regarding the links between brain size and IQ?

To answer this question, we first need to know how these variables are measured. We have already discussed the measurement of mental ability, but this leaves the question of how brain size can be measured. Until the late twentieth century, it was difficult for researchers to obtain a precise estimate of the brain sizes of their research participants. As a result, researchers who wanted to find the relation between brain size and IQ had to rely on measurements of head size—which is substantially (but not perfectly) correlated with brain size—rather than of brain size itself. They did this in the simple way that you might imagine, by using tape measures or calipers to measure the perimeter or the width and length of people's heads.

Since the 1980s, however, researchers have been able to measure the brain size of living persons in a much more direct way, by using a technique called magnetic resonance imaging—the MRI scan. An MRI scanner uses magnets and radio waves to produce accurate images of the brain, which allows researchers to measure brain volume. By

2015, this method had been used in more than 140 samples involving a total of over 8000 research participants (see Pietschnig, Penke, Wicherts, Zeiler, & Voracek, 2015). Across these samples, the average correlation of brain size with IQ is positive but modest, about .24 (Pietschnig et al., 2015). Thus, there is a clear tendency for individuals with larger brains to have higher IQs, but that tendency is not strong.[6]

The link between brain size and IQ is obviously not strong enough to let you guess a given person's IQ accurately based on his or her brain size. But it is interesting to consider why it is that—on average—people with larger brains tend to have somewhat higher IQs. It is possible, of course, that having a larger brain tends to make people a little bit smarter, because a larger brain would tend to have more of the neurons that process and transmit information. Many researchers strongly suspect that this is the main reason for the link between brain size and IQ. But it could also be that being smarter would actually cause some increases in brain size, or that some other variable (such as the health of the brain) would cause greater brain size and higher IQ at the same time.

More recently, some research studies have investigated whether other brain measurements—besides the overall volume of the brain—could also be related to mental ability. One large study using MRI scans of the brains of over 600 persons in their 70s (Ritchie et al., 2015) examined several brain measurements in relation to scores on mental ability tests. Ritchie et al. found that mental ability scores were related to overall brain volume but that even when overall brain volume is taken into account, those scores were also modestly related to two other measurements. One was the thickness of the cerebral cortex (i.e., the large outermost layer of the brain), such that persons with a thicker cerebral cortex tended to have higher mental ability scores. (This result makes sense given that the cerebral cortex includes areas that are important for thinking.) Another was the amount of the brain that showed evidence of minor damage, such that persons with less damaged area tended to have higher mental ability scores. (Note that this kind of damage might not be related so much to mental ability in younger persons, simply because young people will not yet have accumulated much damage.) Future work will likely uncover additional brain measurements that are associated with mental ability.

10.4.2 Reaction Time

Another possible biological basis for individual differences in mental ability is the speed with which the brain can process information (an idea that goes back to the nineteenth century). One variable that potentially indicates this mental speed is *reaction time*. Measurements of reaction time involve assessment of how quickly a person can respond to a stimulus—for example, the time taken to release a button in response to a flash of light.

---

[6] This tendency would not apply in the case of persons who have the genetic developmental disorder called megalencephaly, in which the brain is abnormally large. Persons with megalencephaly tend to have low IQs as well as some motor and speech impairments.

Note that the response required in a reaction time task does not demand any complex thinking processes such as those demanded by actual tests of mental ability.

Typically, a reaction time task of the kind used by mental ability researchers would work as follows. The research participant sits in front of a table on which there are several computerized features, including a lightbulb (currently turned off) and a "home" button (where the participant's hand is resting). The task of the research participant is to watch the lightbulb for a flash of light, and then to react as quickly as possible, by moving his or her hand from the home button to another button located in front of the light. The researcher can then measure, using an electronic sensor under the home button, the duration of time that elapsed between the onset of the flash of light and the removal of the participant's hand from the home button. This time interval is the reaction time of the participant.[7] (See Fig. 10.4 for examples of reaction time tasks.)

Some reaction time tasks are more complicated than the basic task described previously, which is known as a "simple" reaction time task. A variation known as a "choice" reaction time task uses not one but several lightbulbs, any one of which might suddenly be turned on (see Fig. 10.4). This task is difficult, because the participant must pay attention to more than one light and also because the participant must "choose"—based on which light does actually flash—the correct direction in which to move his or her hand. Yet another variation is known as the "odd–man–out" reaction time task, in which there are several lightbulbs in front of the participant, three of which will suddenly flash together (see Fig. 10.4). In this task, two of those three flashing bulbs are next to each other, but the third (the "odd–man–out") is separated from them by one or more nonflashing bulbs; the job of the participant is to move his or her hand toward the button that is immediately in front of the "odd–man–out" bulb.

Note that, when reaction times are measured using tasks such as these, each participant would be measured on several attempts for each task. This allows a reliable average score to be calculated for each participant on each reaction time task, which in turn allows a meaningful examination of correlations between reaction time and other variables, such as mental ability test scores. The correlations between IQ and reaction time are often around −.30 (for simple reaction time tasks) or stronger (for choice reaction time tasks) (e.g., Deary, Der, & Ford, 2001; Johnson & Deary, 2011; Luciano et al., 2004). (Apparently, the more complicated reaction time tasks are slightly better indicators of mental ability than are the simpler varieties.) These correlations indicate that longer (slower) reaction times are associated with lower scores on tests of mental ability, and they support the idea that the speed of the brain and nervous system is part of the basis for the *g* factor of mental ability (see, e.g., Detterman, 1987).

---

[7] Some researchers measure reaction time as the total time elapsed between the onset of the flash of light and the arrival of the participant's hand at the button where the light flashed. When reaction time is measured in this way, it therefore includes the time taken to move one's hand from the home button to the other button.

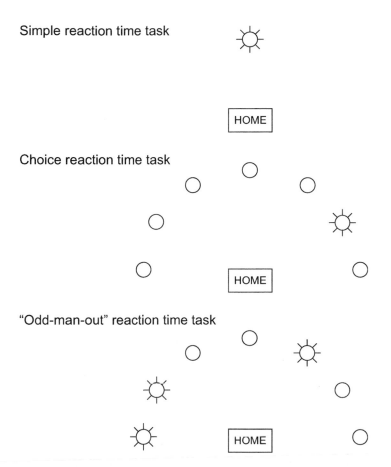

Figure 10.4 *Reaction time tasks.* In each of the tasks, the respondent begins with his or her hand on the "home" button. When one or more of the lights flashes, he or she must move his or her hand as quickly as possible toward one of those flashing lights, according to the specific instructions of the task. In the simple reaction time task, there is only one light. In the choice reaction time task, any one of several lights might flash, and the respondent must move toward the light that does flash. In the "odd-man-out" reaction time task, three lights will flash (two adjacent and one other) and the respondent must move toward the other light.

10.4.3 Inspection Time

Another way of measuring the speed of the brain is to assess the length of time that a stimulus must be present before the brain can notice that stimulus. The tasks that measure this duration are known as *inspection time* tasks, and they typically work as follows. A participant watches a blank screen on which two vertical lines are suddenly flashed for a brief interval, and then covered up by a "mask" pattern that eliminates afterimages remaining in the eyes. One of those two vertical lines is much longer than the other, and the participant's task is simply to decide which line is the longer one (see Fig. 10.5). This is an easy task, except that, if the interval during which the two lines are flashed is extremely short, then the participant may no longer be able to tell which line was the longer one. As

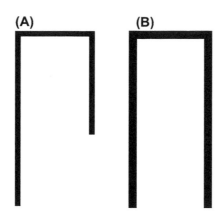

Figure 10.5 *Inspection time task.* Vertical lines are flashed for a brief period of time (A), then immediately covered by a mask (B). The participant's task is to indicate which line in (A), left or right, was longer. As the interval becomes very short, it becomes difficult to judge which line was longer (sometimes the longer line is on the left; sometimes on the right).

the presentation interval becomes very short, the participant begins to make some mistakes, and if the interval becomes shorter still, the participant reaches a point at which he or she is basically guessing. The interesting feature of the inspection time task is that people differ widely in how long this "inspection time" interval must be for them to judge accurately which line is longer. This result was expected by researchers who have suggested that inspection time should be a good indicator of the basic speed of the brain, which in turn is likely to be an important basis of *g*.

Investigations of the relations between inspection time and IQ have generally found moderately strong links, with correlations typically in the −.30s (Grudnik & Kranzler, 2001; see also Johnson & Deary, 2011; Luciano et al., 2004). This means that people who have longer inspection times (i.e., people who need a longer exposure time to be able to judge the line lengths) tend to have lower scores on mental ability tests. This result is particularly interesting, insofar as the inspection time task is very basic, requiring only the very simple decision as to which of two lines is longer. This supports the idea that mental speed, as measured by these inspection time tasks, is implicated in the *g* factor (e.g., Nettelbeck, 1987).[8]

10.4.4 Other Biological Correlates

Researchers have also examined several other biological variables that might underlie individual differences in IQ, including the following.

---

[8] Inspection time and reaction time tend to be modestly associated with each other, with correlations around .20 (Luciano et al., 2004) or in the .30s (Johnson & Deary, 2011). These modest correlations suggest that the two tasks are assessing distinct aspects of mental speed.

Nerve conduction velocity: the speed with which the brain and nervous system can transmit electrical impulses. One way to measure this speed is to record how quickly a person's brain responds to a flash of light (the response is measured using electrodes placed on the person's scalp). Another way involves measuring the speed of the nervous system outside the brain, for example, by applying a mild electrical stimulus to the skin of a person's wrist and then timing how quickly the nervous system impulses travel to the elbow.

Brain waves (averaged evoked potentials): various features of the brain waves (i.e., changes in electrical potential) that occur in response to a stimulus (e.g., a clicking sound or a flashing light). Researchers use a technique called electroencephalography (EEG), which involves electrodes placed on a person's scalp, to measure the latency (speed), frequency, amplitude (size), and complexity of the brain waves that arise in response to a stimulus.

Brain glucose metabolism: the rate at which the brain consumes glucose (i.e., a simple form of carbohydrate that provides energy). Researchers can measure this speed of metabolism in a given person by using a brain-scanning technique called positron emission tomography (PET).

For all of the above variables, associations with IQ have differed across studies, probably in part because of differences in methods and in part because of very small sample sizes. In general, there may be some tendency for higher-IQ persons to have faster nerve conduction velocity, to have shorter brain wave latency (i.e., faster brain waves), and to consume less glucose during a given cognitive task (see, e.g., Vernon, Wickett, Bazana, & Stelmack, 2000). However, the inconsistency of these associations makes it difficult to estimate their real size.

10.5 GENETIC AND ENVIRONMENTAL INFLUENCES ON MENTAL ABILITY

In Chapter 6, we discussed the methods by which researchers can estimate how much of the variation among individuals in any given trait is attributable to genetic (heritable) variation, and how much is attributable to environmental variation. As noted in that chapter, research on the genetic and environmental origins of personality variation has suggested that, across various personality traits, nearly two-thirds of the variation is due to heritable differences. Of the remaining variation, it is the unique or nonshared environment (i.e., aspects of the environment that differ between individuals within the same family) that is the predominant influence on personality, rather than the common or shared environment (i.e., aspects of the environment that differ between families). But what is the situation for mental abilities? Are the results similar to those observed for personality characteristics?

10.5.1 Genetic Influences

The heritability of mental ability has been a widely studied topic for several decades. As has been the case for investigations of the heritability of personality, these studies have made use of various research designs, based on participant samples consisting of identical versus fraternal twins, of twins or other siblings raised apart, or of adoptive siblings raised together. The results of these studies have been fairly consistent and can be summarized rather briefly.[9,10] However, as we will discuss next, there is typically a substantial difference between results based on data from adults and results based on data from children. (Note that when these investigations are conducted, differences due to age are controlled by calculating individuals' levels of mental ability relative to the levels of other people of the same age.)

When studies using mental ability test scores from children are considered, the heritability of mental ability is typically found to be about .40, and the effect of the common or shared environment is found to be almost as strong, about .35. In contrast, when studies using mental ability test scores from adults (or older adolescents) are considered, estimates of the heritability of mental ability are much higher, typically about .65, whereas estimates of common or shared environment effects are much lower, probably under .20 (see review by Haworth et al., 2010). These findings indicate that differences among children in their levels of mental ability are attributable almost as much to their common environment—that is, to features of their family or household circumstances— as to their genetic inheritances. However, the findings also suggest that as children grow up, the differences among them in mental ability become less strongly related to the features of their common environments, and more strongly related to their genetic inheritances. In other words, the effect on one's mental ability of the family or household in which one is reared tends to become less important as one grows up, so that by adulthood one's level of mental ability is heavily dependent on one's genetic characteristics. It is as if one's level of mental ability—relative to that of other persons of the same age—can be raised (or lowered) during childhood by a particularly good (or poor) home environment, but then gradually returns to the level that one's genes tend to produce.

The aforementioned findings are based mainly on samples of participants who belong to the broad middle class of modern Western countries. There is some evidence, though, that the heritability of IQ tends to be somewhat lower (at least until young adulthood, and perhaps beyond) when studies are conducted using participants of less enriched environments, such as those in economically underdeveloped countries or in the lowest socioeconomic classes of some Western countries (see review by Nisbett et al., 2012). One recent study (Tucker-Drob & Bates, 2016) found that in the United States, additive

---

[9] These studies exclude persons who have a severe intellectual disability caused by brain damage or by abnormalities of the genes or chromosomes (e.g., persons with Down's syndrome).

[10] As will be discussed later in this chapter, there is some assortative mating—that is, a tendency for spouses to be similar to each other—for some aspects of mental ability. When calculating estimates of the heritability of intelligence, researchers take this assortative mating into account. As noted in Section 6.5.2, one assumption made in conducting heritability studies is that there is no assortative mating, but researchers can make adjustments in their calculations when assortative mating does occur.

genetic influences had a weaker influence on IQ among persons of low socioeconomic status than among persons of high socioeconomic status. (Interestingly, Tucker-Drob and Bates did not find this effect in western European countries or in Australia, where socio-economic status differences tend to be smaller.) The above findings suggest that when-ever the heritability of IQ is discussed, it is important to consider the ages of the persons being examined as well as their socioeconomic status and their country.

BOX 10.1 The Reasons for Within-Group Differences Might Not Be the Reasons for Between-Group Differences

When considering differences in average IQ test scores between groups of people—for example, different social classes, ethnic or racial groups, sexes, or generations—it is important to keep in mind that the reasons for those between-group differences might not be the same as the reasons for differences within groups.

For example, differences in mental ability between your generation and your great-grandparents' generation probably are not due in any large part to genetic differences, even though the differences in mental ability among persons within either generation probably are due in some large part to genetic differences. Instead, the differences between the gener-ations are likely to be due to some environmental variables (changes in the educational system, in family sizes, in technology, in recreational activities, in nutrition, etc.) that differ greatly between generations but that do not differ so much among persons within a given generation.

Likewise, genetic influences are responsible for much of the variation among people *within* a country (or an ethnic group) in their levels of mental ability, but those influences might not be responsible for differences *between* countries (or ethnic groups) in their peoples' average levels of mental ability. Instead, differences between countries in education, technology, nutrition, or other variables might be responsible for the differences in average mental ability levels. Related to this point, differences between US ethnic groups in average IQ scores have been decreasing in recent decades (e.g., Dickens & Flynn, 2006). It remains possible that differences between groups in average IQ scores could have a partly genetic basis, but in any case, the variation in people's IQ scores is much larger within groups than between groups, so a person's IQ cannot be accurately estimated from his or her group membership.

In considering the preceding findings about the heritability of mental ability, there are some important points to keep in mind. One issue is that of additive and nonadditive genetic variance, which we discussed in Section 6.3.4 in the context of personality char-acteristics. As you will recall from that section, the effects of genes on characteristics can be *additive* (whereby the combined effects of genes are simply the sums of the separate effects of each gene) or *nonadditive* (whereby the combined effects of genes are different from what would be expected based on the separate effects of each gene). When genetic influences are entirely additive, the similarity of identical twins raised apart is about twice that of fraternal twins raised apart, because identical twins have twice as many genes in common as do fraternal twins. However, when genetic effects are partly nonadditive, the similarity of identical twins raised apart can be much more than twice that of fraternal twins raised apart; this is because identical twins have all combinations of genes in common, whereas fraternal twins have few combinations of genes in common. (Even if you share about 50% of your genes with someone, you will share much less than 50% of your combinations of genes with that person, because *any* difference between the two of you will mean a different combination. But if you have 100% of your genes in common with someone, then you must also have 100% of your combinations of genes in common with that person.)

What is the relative contribution of additive and nonadditive genetic influences to mental ability differences in adults? Results from many research studies conducted to date suggest that both influences are implicated (e.g., Devlin, Daniels, & Roeder, 1997): Overall heritability is estimated at about .50, with additive genetic influences contributing about .35 and nonadditive genetic influences the remaining .15. (You might have noticed that the total heritability estimate of .50 is lower than that mentioned earlier in this section. The reason for the difference involves the influence of the womb environment, which is our next topic.)

BOX 10.2 Using Genomes to Calculate Genetic Similarity—and Heritability

A relatively new approach to calculating the heritability of characteristics allows researchers to avoid the assumptions that underlie the twin- and adoption-based studies described in Chapter 6. This new approach involves comparing the entire genomes of persons and is called Genome-wide Complex Trait Analysis (GCTA). Researchers who use this new method can take a large group of people, none of whom are relatives of one another but all of whom belong to the same ethnic group, and calculate the genetic similarity of each pair of persons. (If you pick two people at random, you will be slightly more genetically similar to one than to the other.) Researchers using this approach have found that unrelated persons who are more genetically similar tend to be more similar in IQ, thus supporting the findings from twin-based studies. However, the heritability estimates from GCTA studies are somewhat lower than those from twin-based studies, partly because the GCTA approach captures only additive genetic effects and partly because very rare genes have not yet been examined in these studies (e.g., Plomin et al., 2013).

10.5.2 Womb Environment Influences

The logic of heritability studies is fairly straightforward, but there is an important way in which those investigations may overestimate the heritability of characteristics, including mental ability. The problem involves the role of the womb environment, which we discussed in Section 6.6.1 in the context of personality characteristics. Recall that heritability studies often use research designs that compare twins or siblings who have been raised apart; in this way, any similarity between twins or siblings cannot be attributed to the environment in which they were raised. However, this similarity might not be due entirely to the genetic relatedness of the twins or siblings; instead, it might be due in part to various features of the womb environment, such as the nutrients, toxins, and hormones to which the developing fetus is exposed. Because these aspects of the womb environment differ between mothers, and even between pregnancies of the same mother, it is possible that some part of the "genetic" influence on traits (including mental ability) is not genetic at all, but instead due to the womb environment.

Some research has tried to separate womb environment influences from genetic influences. For example, if one compares *fraternal twin* pairs with *nontwin sibling* pairs, any extra similarity of fraternal twins over that of nontwin siblings might be due to variation between pregnancies in the womb environment, because only the twins developed in the same womb *during the same pregnancy*. (Keep in mind that age differences in mental ability are statistically controlled in these studies and will not affect the results.) Similarly, if one compares *nontwin sibling* pairs with *parent–child* pairs, any extra similarity of siblings over that of parent–child pairs might be due in large part to variation between mothers in the womb environment, because only the siblings developed *within the same mother's womb*. One investigation that examined womb environment effects (Devlin et al., 1997) used these approaches and found that the influence of the womb environment on mental ability was about .20 when fraternal twins were considered, and .05 when nontwin siblings were considered. As a result, the authors suggested, the heritability of mental ability was lower than generally considered, probably not more than .50.

One particular kind of womb environment effect involves the chorion type of identical twins (see Box 6-1 for an explanation of chorion type). A study by Jacobs et al. (2001) examined this possibility of chorion type effects on mental ability, by comparing the mental ability test scores for identical twin pairs who were monochorionic (i.e., monochorionic monozygotic twins) and for identical twin pairs who were dichorionic (i.e., dichorionic monozygotic twins). The results indicated that both kinds of identical twins were very similar in their levels of mental ability, but that the dichorionic twins did show somewhat less similarity than did the monochorionic twins, at least in some aspects of mental ability. This suggests that differences in chorion type—and the associated differences in prenatal nutrition—might have at least some effect on the development of the fetus.

10.5.3 Nutrition

Although the genetic influences on personality are substantial, there are also many environmental variables that are known to influence mental ability. For example, IQs are lower among children who have experienced fetal alcohol poisoning, lead poisoning, severe malnutrition, or brain damage (e.g., Neisser et al., 1996). These problems are relatively rare within the broad middle classes of economically developed countries, within which most investigations of mental ability have been conducted. However, given that there is still an extremely wide variation in mental ability within those samples, this leaves us with the question of which aspects of the environment contribute to the variation in mental ability among healthy people in prosperous societies. Here we will consider several nutrition-related variables, each of which has been suggested to have lasting influences on IQ—influences thought to persist even in late adolescence or in adulthood.

One aspect of the early environment that has been shown to be associated with mental ability even in adulthood is breastfeeding. This link is illustrated by the results of a study by Mortensen, Michaelsen, Sanders, and Reinisch (2002), who investigated the intelligence test scores of nearly 1000 young Danish men and women. The researchers compared the intelligence test scores of adults who, as infants, had been breastfed for different periods of time (as recalled by the mothers of those persons). Mortensen et al. found that longer duration of breastfeeding was associated with higher levels of mental ability. Even when the researchers made statistical adjustments for differences in socioeconomic status and other variables, the difference was still substantial: Persons who had been breastfed as infants for more than 6 months scored about 6 IQ points (about 0.4 standard deviation units) higher, on average, than did persons who had been breastfed for less than 1 month. These results suggest that breastfeeding may provide better nutrition to the developing infant, and thereby contribute to intellectual development. (Alternatively, it is possible that the mother—infant contact associated with breastfeeding, or some other variable, would be responsible for any such effect.)

But there is also an alternative interpretation of the findings of Mortensen et al. (2002): Perhaps mothers with higher levels of mental ability are more likely to breastfeed and also more likely to have children who inherit those high levels of mental ability. In this way, the relation between breastfeeding and mental ability might not be a causal link, but instead a reflection of the fact that smarter mothers tend both to breastfeed and also to have smart children. This hypothesis was tested by Der, Batty, and Deary (2006), who examined the mental ability test scores of over 5000 young adults and of the (more than 3000) mothers of those young adults.

The results obtained by Der et al. (2006) indicated that young adults who had been breastfed as infants scored about 4 IQ points (more than one-quarter of a standard deviation unit) higher than did young adults who had not been breastfed as children. However, it was also found that the mothers with higher IQ scores were more likely to have breastfed their children than were the mothers with lower IQ scores. When the researchers controlled for the IQ scores of the mothers, they found that the difference was less than 1 IQ point, which is very small. In other words, smarter mothers were more likely to breastfeed and were also more likely to have smarter children, but breastfeeding itself did not contribute much to mental ability test scores. For example, in families in which a mother breastfed one child and did not breastfeed another child, there was typically no difference in mental ability test scores between those children. Thus, the findings of Der et al. suggest that breastfeeding might not contribute to higher levels of mental ability, at least when the infant was born at full term and at normal body weight. (It is still possible that breastfeeding would contribute to mental ability when premature or low birth weight infants are considered.)

Since the publication of the Der et al. study, several other studies have reported results suggesting that breastfeeding does contribute to children's later mental ability (e.g., Kramer et al., 2008). However, these studies did not involve comparisons between children who were breastfed and their siblings who were not breastfed, so the results do not directly contradict those reported by Der et al. For the time being, an effect of breastfeeding on mental ability remains a possibility but is not established.

In addition to a possible role for nutrition during infancy, there is also the possibility that nutrition during gestation—that is, before birth—could be responsible for some of the variation among people in mental ability. Perhaps the levels of nutrients obtained by the developing fetus are associated with higher levels of intelligence in adulthood; this might be the case even when we consider societies in which very few pregnant mothers suffer from malnutrition. This possibility is supported by several lines of evidence involving the relations between birth weight (a plausible indicator of prenatal nutrition) and later intelligence test scores. One finding is that children who had a low birth weight (below about 2500 g or 5.5 pounds) average about half of a standard deviation lower than do children of normal birth weight (Aylward, Pfeiffer, Wright, & Verhulst, 1988). But relatively few babies have low birth weights, and many of those babies are born prematurely, which raises the possibility that premature birth, rather than low birth weight itself, is partly responsible for the lower intelligence test scores. However, it has been observed that twins—who as fetuses must share the nutrients available in the womb— have tended on average to have lower intelligence test scores than do their nontwin siblings, with a difference of about 5 IQ points, or one-third of a standard deviation unit (Ronalds, De Stavola, & Leon, 2005). (Some more recent research indicates that the IQ disadvantage of twins has now been eliminated, at least in some countries; e.g., Calvin, Fernandes, Smith, Visscher, & Deary, 2009.)

The results described thus far in this section have examined the possibility that the levels of some nutrients during early childhood (or even in the womb) could influence later levels of mental ability. Some recent research has also tested the hypothesis that nutrient levels in adulthood may be associated with changes in levels of mental ability. One such investigation used data from the Scottish mental ability survey discussed earlier in this chapter. Starr, Pattie, Whiteman, Whalley, and Deary (2005) found that persons with lower blood levels of vitamin B_{12} had a somewhat higher risk of a relative decline in mental ability between childhood and old age. These results do not establish that low B_{12} levels cause a cognitive decline, but they do raise the possibility.

10.5.4 Birth Order

For decades, researchers have noted a small but consistent link between birth order and mental ability: On average, first-born children have slightly higher IQs as adults than do their siblings who were the second-born children, who in turn have slightly higher IQs as adults than do their siblings who were the third-borns, and so on. (Of course, these results are only averages; there will be many families in which the last-born child has a higher IQ, as an adult, than does the first-born child.)

One possible explanation for the link between birth order and mental ability involves biological influences. For example, if the mother's womb environment becomes less favorable with each pregnancy, then this might slightly hinder brain development in later-born children.

Another possibility is that early-born children experience a better social environment for intellectual development than do later-born children. For example, consider first-born children: Before the birth of their siblings, they have the undivided attention of their parents; later, they may benefit intellectually by the process of teaching their younger siblings. In contrast, last-born children never have the undivided attention of their parents and may thereby receive less intellectual stimulation; moreover, they do not have the opportunity to teach a younger sibling. These differences in intellectual stimulation—particularly that due to parental attention—might be enough to account for the small difference in mental ability (a few IQ points) between first-borns and later-borns.

One very large study was conducted to test these explanations of the relation between birth order and IQ. Kristensen and Bjerkedal (2007) examined IQ test data from over 240,000 men who had served as conscripts in the Norwegian armed forces. The researchers compared the IQs of young men who were the first-born, second-born, and third-born children in their families. To compare the "biological" and "social" explanations, they also examined the results separately for men who had had an older sibling who died during infancy.

If the relation between birth order and mental ability were due to biological factors in pregnancy, then men who were first-borns would on average have higher IQs than would men who were second-borns, *even in cases where a second-born's older sibling had died during infancy*. (According to the biological hypothesis, men who were second-borns would have the same IQs on average regardless of whether their older sibling had survived or not, because the effects of the mother's first pregnancy would occur in both cases.) But if instead the relation between birth order and mental ability were due to social factors in childhood, then men who were first-borns would on average have IQs no higher than those of men who were second-borns but whose older sibling had died during infancy. (According to the social hypothesis, men who were second-borns would have lower IQs on average if their older sibling had survived than if their older sibling had died during infancy, because only in the former case would the intellectual stimulation of the second-borns be reduced.)

Kristensen and Bjerkedal (2007) compared the IQs of men in these various categories, controlling for other variables such as parents' education and mother's age. They found that first-born men had IQs about three points higher on average than did second-born men whose older sibling had survived. However, the researchers also found that first-born men did not have higher IQs on average than did second-born men whose older sibling had died during infancy; instead, the IQs were equal. Kristensen and Bjerkedal found a similar pattern of results when they compared second-born men (those whose older sibling had survived) with third-born men: The third-born men whose older siblings had both survived had lower IQs on average than did second-born men, but the third-born men who had an older sibling who had died during infancy had IQs equal on average to those of the second-born men.

These results thus support the social hypothesis of the birth order/IQ association, not the biological hypothesis. That is, the link between birth order and mental ability is likely due to the differences in intellectual stimulation experienced by early-born and later-born children. Apparently, growing up with older siblings tends to interfere with intellectual development, although the size of this effect is quite small.

10.6 EVOLUTIONARY FUNCTION OF MENTAL ABILITY

Let us now turn to the question of why the heritable differences among people in mental ability have persisted across the generations. One potential reason involves new genetic mutations. Presumably, many genetic mutations could have some influence on brain functioning, and because the brain already works very well, any given mutation is much more likely to disrupt brain functioning than to improve it. Mutations that disrupt brain functioning (and hence mental ability) will tend to become less frequent across generations, due to natural selection. But because new mutations arise with each generation, there will never be an elimination of all the mutations that reduce mental ability. And, if people differ in the number of mutations they carry (in their "mutational load", as biologists call it), then this will make people differ in mental ability. Therefore, differences among people in their mutational loads may be responsible for some of the variation in mental ability, and for the persistence of that variation across generations.

Other reasons for the persistence of heritable variation in mental ability across evolutionary time involve the fact that higher levels of mental ability can carry costs as well as benefits. A high level of mental ability will likely help one to meet the challenges of survival and reproduction and parenting, but it also comes with some biological costs. For example, the larger brain associated with higher levels of ability consumes more energy while at rest, requires a longer time to grow to maturity, and increases the risk of complications during childbirth. These disadvantages may tend to reduce the chances of survival and reproduction, thereby "canceling out" the advantages that would be provided by a larger, more able brain. In addition, there may be some genes that increase mental ability while simultaneously causing some disease or other disadvantage that would tend to balance out or even outweigh the advantages of higher mental ability levels.

If there are both advantages and disadvantages associated with higher levels of mental ability, then the persistence of variation in the genetic basis of mental ability is not so surprising. But depending on various features of a given environment—features that might fluctuate across different times and places (recall Section 7.2.2)—it is possible that higher levels of ability would have had more advantages than disadvantages overall, or vice versa.

Some researchers have suggested that patterns of sex differences in mental abilities can be understood in terms of selection pressures that acted differently on men and women during prehistoric times. Specifically, men tend to average somewhat higher than do women in some aspects of spatial ability (especially those that require visualizing objects in three dimensions), whereas women tend to average somewhat higher than do men in some aspects of memory and of perceptual speed (i.e., noticing subtle differences between similar-looking objects); see Halpern (1997). (These differences are moderately large in size, sometimes favoring the higher-scoring sex by about one standard deviation unit.) One possible explanation for these differences is that they have resulted from selection for abilities required by the tasks that men and women tended to do during prehistoric times. According to this view, spatial visualization was needed for the mostly male task of hunting (which required spatial ability for weapon making and for tracking game), whereas perceptual speed and memory were needed for the mostly female task of gathering (which required perception and memory for distinguishing between similar-looking plants).[11]

10.7 MENTAL ABILITY AND LIFE OUTCOMES

You have probably already heard many arguments about the issue of whether or not IQ test scores are related to "success in the real world" or even to academic achievement. Let us now look at the evidence regarding the relations between IQ and a variety of important outcomes, such as academic achievement, job performance, occupational status, health and longevity, law-abiding behavior, and marriage.

---

[11] For overall IQ, the average scores of men and of women (or of boys and of girls) are approximately the same. However, men and boys tend to show wider variation in IQ scores than do women and girls. For example, in a study of 80,000 11-year-old Scottish school-children (Deary, Thorpe, Wilson, Starr, & Whalley, 2003), there was no difference between boys and girls in their mean IQ test scores, but there were more girls than boys at the middle levels of ability, and more boys than girls at both the high and low extremes. Among children with scores in the top 1% of the whole group, nearly 60% were boys and slightly more than 40% were girls, but among children with scores in the bottom 1%, again almost 60% were boys and a little more than 40% were girls. That is, boys and girls showed the same average IQ, but boys' IQs were more variable.

10.7.1 Academic Achievement and Performance

First, let us consider academic achievement. Most people would probably expect that scores on mental ability tests would be at least somewhat predictive of success in school. Still, one can ask whether or not those tests really are associated with grade point average and with the attainment of diplomas and degrees. The answer, as found consistently in hundreds of research studies over the past century, is that mental ability does have a fairly strong relation with academic achievement. But the strength of that relation varies somewhat depending on how academic achievement is measured.

When large groups of students are tested for general mental ability, their resulting IQ scores tend to be correlated rather substantially with their grades in school. For example, among elementary school students, this correlation is often about .50 or .60 (e.g., Kaufman, 1979). What this tells us is that a high level of general mental ability is an important advantage in completing schoolwork successfully. Of course, IQ is not the only reason why students differ in their school grades: A correlation of .50 leaves a great deal of room for other variables, such as the motivation and effort of the student, to have major influences on school performance. Nevertheless, it is clear that, on average, students with higher IQs tend to do better in school.

The relation between IQ and school performance, as just described, is based on grades assigned by teachers to their students. As you will recall from your own days in elementary and secondary school, those grades are generally based on students' performance on tests, on assignments of various kinds, on classroom presentations and participation, and even on the teacher's perceptions of "attitude and effort." But some components of student grades—such as participating enthusiastically, making entertaining presentations to the class, handing in nicely decorated assignments, or just simply being well behaved—might not have much to do with actual academic achievement. To the extent that this is the case, we might expect that the correlation between IQ and school grades would underestimate the strength of the link between IQ and real academic achievement.

The best way to check this possibility is to find the correlation between IQ tests, on the one hand, and tests of academic achievement, on the other. In this way, we can see the extent to which students' levels of general mental ability really are associated with their mastery of course material. The results of many previous studies indicate that IQ is even more strongly related to academic achievement, as measured by actual tests, than to school grades. When tests of general mental ability and tests of academic achievement have been administered to large groups of students, the correlations tend to be in the .60s or even the .70s (e.g., Deary, Strand, Smith, & Fernandes, 2007).

The results as just summarized indicate that IQ is a very important predictor of academic achievement, particularly in the sense of acquiring a real understanding of course material, as assessed by standardized tests. But this might make you wonder whether the correlation between these tests might simply be due to some obvious similarities between them. In other words, could it be that the tests of general mental ability are simply measuring the same abilities as those measured by the tests of academic achievement, with the same kinds of test questions?

The answer to this question has two parts. First, there are some important differences between the tests that measure general mental ability and the tests that measure academic achievement. Tests of general mental ability involve questions that are not based directly on what is learned in school, or on a particular course of study; instead, the questions require problem solving or information of a general nature. In contrast, tests of academic achievement involve questions that are associated with the curriculum as taught in school, with a focus on specific skills that are practiced at certain grade levels. So, in this sense, the relations between IQ and academic achievement cannot be attributed to the similarity of the tests that measure these two variables.

On the other hand, however, there is still some similarity of content between tests of general mental ability and tests of academic achievement. In considerable part, the IQ tests do involve working with numbers and words, as do the tests of academic achievement. This leads to the question of whether the mental ability tests can still predict academic achievement even when the mental ability tests are based on tasks that do not involve working with numbers and words. That is, could nonverbal tests of mental ability also predict performance on academic achievement tests (consider, e.g., the spatial or picture arrangement tasks of Fig. 10.1, or the matrix reasoning task of Fig. 10.2)? Again, the answer from previous research has been clear: Even the nonverbal IQ tests do correlate moderately strongly with academic achievement tests. However, the correlations of nonverbal tests with achievement are typically around .40 (e.g., Sattler, 1988), which are lower than the correlations produced by tests that do involve words or numbers. This suggests that some part of the relation between mental ability tests and tests of academic achievement is due to the specific elements that the two kinds of tests have in common. In large part, though, the relation is due to a real association between *general* mental ability and mastery of the school curriculum.

Before leaving the topic of IQ and academic performance, there is one other finding to mention. In the preceding sections, we discussed how IQ was related to school grades and to achievement test scores. But a related question involves the relation between IQ and educational attainment, in the sense of "how far" one progresses in school: To what extent does IQ predict whether one will drop out of high school, as opposed to obtaining a high school diploma, or continuing on to obtain a college or university degree, or even a professional or graduate degree? Again, the correlations observed in many investigations have generally been rather strong, typically about .55 (Neisser et al., 1996). Moreover, this correlation is observed even when IQ is measured during elementary school, when no one has yet dropped out. This means that the correlation is not simply due to an influence of staying in school on one's level of IQ. Thus, IQ has an important link with educational attainment: Although general mental ability is certainly not the only variable that determines how far one will pursue one's education, it is clearly an important predictor.

Most people would probably not be surprised to learn that high scores on tests of mental ability are associated with high levels of academic achievement. But many people would likely expect that academic achievement would be the *only* important variable predicted by those tests. However, a wide range of evidence indicates that mental ability tests (and particularly the *g* factor that is the main common element of those tests) measure something that is far broader than simply the ability to perform well in school. Instead, scores on mental ability tests show moderately strong correlations with a diverse array of important variables. One such variable is job performance.

10.7.2 Job Performance, Occupational Status, and Income

What is it that makes some workers better at their job than other workers? For many jobs, of course, specific training and expertise is critically important, and a worker who does not have that training and expertise will simply be unable to perform satisfactorily. But beyond this rather obvious point, what characteristics of workers are associated with better work? As we have seen in previous chapters, personality plays some role in job performance: Workers who are disciplined, organized, and diligent tend to do their jobs effectively and thoroughly, and workers who are honest and trustworthy tend to be "good citizens" on the job—a crucial consideration for many employers.

In addition to personality, however, there is also a role for raw *ability* to perform tasks well. Depending on the job, of course, the kind of ability that is needed may vary: Some jobs demand a strong back, some jobs demand nimble fingers, and so on. But almost all jobs involve at least some element of solving problems, making decisions, and learning the "tricks" of doing the job well. And this is exactly where the potential influence of mental ability comes into play: If IQ tests really do mainly represent a general mental ability (rather than just a narrow talent for taking tests), then workers who have high levels of mental ability will likely be better able to solve problems, make decisions, and "learn the ropes" of their jobs. Those abilities, in turn, should mean a higher level of job performance.

This leads us to our next question: To what extent does IQ actually correlate with job performance? Recall from Section 9.6.1 that, when researchers or employers want to assess job performance systematically, they have different ways of doing so. Sometimes they use some objective index of productivity, such as an actual measurement of the amount or accuracy of the completed work. But for many jobs, it is not so easy to measure performance directly, and instead the main measure of job performance is a rating by the worker's supervisor(s). In any case, regardless of the precise way in which job performance is assessed, there is a consistent finding: IQ is correlated positively with job performance. That is, smarter workers tend on average to be better workers. This finding is one of the best established results in the social sciences, being based on reviews of hundreds of studies involving tens of thousands of workers across virtually all jobs and across a wide variety of settings (Hunter & Hunter, 1984; Schmidt & Hunter, 2004).

As you might expect, the importance of IQ as a predictor of job performance depends a great deal on the nature of the job. For some kinds of work, the cognitive elements are not so complex, and the element of problem solving, decision making, or rule learning is not so important. But for other kinds of work, the ability to make difficult decisions, solve complicated problems, and learn subtle "rules of thumb" is in constant demand. Typically, the correlation between IQ and job performance is rather modest, generally around .20, for those jobs that have relatively simple cognitive demands. Thus, for jobs that mainly involve a simple task (which is not to say an easy task!) that is repeated with little variation, higher levels of IQ translate into slightly better (but only slightly better) job performance. But this correlation increases as jobs become more complicated, and for those jobs that are the most cognitively demanding, the correlations often reach the .50s. Thus, for more complex jobs that require a great deal of thinking, a higher level of IQ translates into considerably better job performance; in fact, for the most complex jobs, a reasonably high level of IQ is almost a necessity for really good performance.

Related to the topic of IQ and job performance is the question of how IQ relates to various indicators of occupational achievement, such as the "status" of one's occupation and the income one earns. These variables, of course, depend in part on many variables other than one's level of mental ability (or, for that matter, how diligently one works). Even if we consider people who are equally smart and equally hardworking, we will find that some people deliberately seek out jobs that have high status and pay, whereas other people do not. And, many features of a given situation—economic conditions, "office politics," family connections, family responsibilities, and so on—will also influence the occupational status and income that individuals ultimately obtain. But in spite of these other important influences, there is still some room for IQ to influence occupational achievement (e.g., Jencks, 1979; Neisser et al., 1996): The correlations are typically about .50 for occupational status (as rated on scales used by social scientists) and about .40 for income.

When discussing the relation between IQ and occupational achievement, there is one possible problem, however. If we find a correlation between the IQ factor and occupational achievement (i.e., status and income), it might mean that being smart helps one to get ahead in the world of work. But it might reflect something rather different: Perhaps people who are born into the higher classes of society tend to get better jobs and incomes simply by virtue of their social class, and at the same time tend to do better on mental ability tasks because of educational and environmental advantages when growing up. So, how can we figure out which of these possibilities gives the better explanation of the link between IQ and occupational achievement?

One way to do this is to use a statistic called a *partial correlation*, which allows the researcher to see how much two variables are correlated when the influence of a third variable is statistically removed. In this case, this means finding the correlation of IQ with status or with income, but then adjusting that correlation to control for the fact that both of those variables are related to the socioeconomic status at which a person started. (This is equivalent to finding the correlation between IQ and occupational status among people who have all started out with the same level of socioeconomic status in childhood.) When this procedure is applied, it is typically found that the correlations of IQ with these aspects of occupational achievement become weaker, but remain in the .30s (based on Jencks, 1979; Neisser et al., 1996) or even in the .40s (Deary et al., 2005). This indicates that, for the most part, the link between mental ability and occupational achievement reflects a moderately strong tendency for smarter people to gain higher-status jobs and higher incomes. Of course, these numbers will depend on the level of social mobility in a society; from one generation to the next it may become easier or harder for persons of low socioeconomic status to reach higher levels of occupational achievement.

10.7.3 Longevity and Health

Are higher levels of mental ability associated with better health and a longer life span? One might expect that persons with higher IQs would tend to make better health-related decisions and would also benefit from other variables associated with higher IQ, such as improved socioeconomic status. Medical researchers have long noted an association between socioeconomic status and health, but recently it has been suggested that this association reflects, in part, the influence of IQ on both of these variables (e.g., Gottfredson, 2004).

One of the largest investigations to examine the links between IQ and longevity was based on the longitudinal study (described earlier in this chapter) of Scottish people who had taken an intelligence test when they were 11 years old. Whalley and Deary (2001) examined the childhood mental ability scores of nearly 2800 people in relation to records of which of those people had died and at what age. The analyses showed that there was a substantial link between IQ and longevity within both sexes. Of women whose intelligence test scores as 11-year-olds had been in the top quarter of the sample, about 70% survived to the age of 75 years; for women whose scores had been in the bottom quarter of the sample, the proportion was only 45%. Among men, about 50% of those who had scored in the top quarter survived to the age of 75, versus only about 35% of those who had scored in the bottom quarter. (The somewhat smaller difference between higher-IQ and lower-IQ men, compared with that between higher-IQ and lower-IQ women, was due to the higher death rates of higher-IQ men during World War II; apparently, the higher-IQ men were more likely than lower-IQ men to have been killed during that war, probably because men who had lower IQs were not selected for military service.)

In examining the relations between childhood IQ and longevity, Whalley and Deary (2001) also considered the possibility that this relation might have been due to the effects of the socioeconomic status or social class in which the participants were raised. Therefore, the researchers examined records of the participants' social class during childhood, as measured by the father's occupational status and by the overcrowdedness of the neighborhood in which the children grew up. But Whalley and Deary found that these variables could not explain the relation between mental ability and longevity. That is, even among children who grew up in a similar neighborhood and had fathers of similar occupational status, the children with higher IQs tended to live longer than did the children with lower IQs.

One question that arises from the results of Whalley and Deary (2001) is that of *why* IQ tends to be associated with longevity. Several plausible explanations can be considered (Gottfredson & Deary, 2004). One possibility is that lower IQ in childhood could be due to some health-related problems that arise in childhood (or even before birth) and then ultimately lead to premature death. A similar possibility is that lower IQ in childhood could itself indicate that the body and brain are not functioning well overall (even apart from any specific illnesses), and hence predicts a lower likelihood of surviving to old age. Another possible explanation is that lower IQ is associated with a tendency to adopt unhealthy rather than healthy behaviors, with the consequence of increased risk of injury or death. Yet another possible explanation is that lower IQ is associated with a greater likelihood of experiencing unhealthy environments, such as hazardous or stressful occupations.

It is not yet known how well each of these explanations can account for the link between mental ability and longevity. Some evidence does suggest, however, that the third explanation is at least partly responsible. In the Scottish study, participants with higher IQs were more likely to have quit smoking than were participants with lower IQs and (probably as a result) were less likely to have died of lung cancer. This would only explain a small part of the relation between IQ and longevity, but other differences in behavior between high-IQ and low-IQ participants might also exist. For example, a study of Australian army veterans found that men who were low in IQ were several times more likely than were men high in IQ to have died in motor vehicle accidents (O'Toole & Stankov, 1992). (Of course, motor vehicle accidents depend not only on one's own driving but also on other factors, including other drivers; higher IQ can only predict a somewhat decreased risk of accident involvement.)

Other research shows a link between mental ability and understanding of health information and health risks. Cokely, Galesic, Schulz, Ghazal, and Garcia-Retamero (2012) found that people with higher levels of mental ability—especially "numeracy" (i.e., comprehension of basic probability and statistics)—were better able to understand information about various health and medical risks.[12] Gottfredson (2004) documented

---

[12] Some findings by Cokely et al. (2017) suggest that decision-making skill—in health-related settings and more broadly—is related to general mental ability but is more strongly related to a (moderately g-loaded) ability called statistical numeracy. Other evidence also suggests that statistical numeracy can be substantially improved by appropriate teaching; in this way, persons can develop better decision-making skills even if they do not possess particularly high levels of general mental ability (Cokely et al., 2017).

results of several previous studies in which researchers assessed patients' "health literacy" (i.e., knowledge and understanding of health-related information), which is strongly related to mental ability. Those studies show that patients with low levels of health literacy tend to misunderstand doctors' instructions, to take medication incorrectly, to have higher rates of hospital admissions and to have lower levels of self-rated health. (These relations persist even when socioeconomic status is controlled.) Thus, it appears that at least part of the link between IQ and health, and between IQ and longevity, is attributable to the relation of IQ with behaviors that influence health.

10.7.4 Law-Abidingness Versus Criminality

Crime rates differ widely across different times and different places, for a variety of reasons that are studied by social scientists. But at the level of *individuals*—that is, if we ask which persons in a given group or a given society are more likely to commit crimes—one clear finding is that there are some significant links between crime and low IQ. On average, persons convicted of criminal offenses score almost two-thirds of a standard deviation unit below average on tests of mental ability (Hirschi & Hindelang, 1977; Wilson & Herrnstein, 1985). But this result raises an interesting question: Is it the case that persons who *commit crimes* have lower IQs, or is it instead merely the case that persons who *get caught for committing crimes* have lower IQs?

The evidence suggests that the former is true. One study of about 650 New Zealand teenagers (Moffitt & Silva, 1988) obtained intelligence test scores, anonymous self-reports of delinquent behavior, and police records of arrests and other interventions for delinquency. In this way, the researchers identified three subsets of youths within this sample: A subset of 40 youths who had been in contact with the police because of delinquent behaviors; another subset of nearly 70 youths who had admitted committing equally serious delinquent acts but who had avoided contact with the police; and a final (much larger) subset of youths who had no police contact and no serious self-reported delinquency. Both of the delinquent groups averaged about one-half of a standard deviation lower in intelligence test scores than did the nondelinquent group; there was very little difference between the group that had had police contact and the group that had committed delinquent acts without coming to the attention of the police. Thus, the results of Moffitt and Silva suggest that the lower IQs among persons arrested for crimes are a reflection of a difference between persons who commit and persons who do not commit crimes, not merely of a difference between persons who are caught and persons who are not caught for committing crimes.

Another issue in interpreting the relation between IQ and law-abiding behavior is that of socioeconomic status. Given that lower socioeconomic status tends to be associated, to some extent, with higher rates of crime and with lower IQs, you might wonder whether the negative relation between IQ and crime is attributable simply to low socioeconomic status. In other words, perhaps there is no relation between low IQ and crime if we consider only persons who have grown up in households of equal socioeconomic status.

However, the evidence suggests that this is not the case; instead, persons with higher IQs tend to commit fewer crimes even when socioeconomic status is held constant. One investigation that showed this result was reported by Moffitt, Gabrielli, Mednick, and Schulsinger (1981), who studied a sample of over 4500 young men in Denmark. Of those men, nearly 8% had been convicted of one criminal offense, and another 5% had been convicted of two or more criminal offenses. Using records of these men's socioeconomic status and intelligence test scores as collected years earlier, Moffitt et al. found that the number of criminal offenses was correlated, weakly, with lower socioeconomic status ($r = -.11$), but somewhat more strongly with lower IQ ($r = -.19$). When Moffitt et al. controlled for socioeconomic status by calculating a partial correlation (see description earlier in this chapter), number of offenses was still related to lower IQ ($r = -.17$). This means that even when we consider people who come from households having the same level of socioeconomic status, there is still a modest tendency for those who have lower levels of mental ability to be more likely to commit crimes.

Although the preceding results indicate an association between criminal activity and lower IQs, it is important to keep in mind that this does not mean that persons with high IQs do not commit crime at all. Even though high-IQ individuals are less likely to commit crimes, there is some indication that those who do so tend to "select" crimes that have a higher probability of payoff and a lower probability of arrest. Moreover, there are some "white-collar" crimes—such as large-scale corporate fraud or government corruption—that presumably are committed mainly by high-IQ persons, because only persons with rather high levels of mental ability are able to achieve the positions in which one has the opportunity to commit those crimes.

Why is that persons with higher IQs tend to be more law-abiding? One possibility is that the cost/benefit ratio of criminal activity is higher for persons who have high IQs, because those persons have better chances for educational and occupational success. In contrast, persons with lower IQs may become frustrated by their somewhat poorer prospects for achieving success (Hirschi & Hindelang, 1977). But, more generally, it may also be the case that high-IQ persons are more likely to recognize that committing a crime carries rather high risks of serious penalties and to judge the potential gains from crime as being insufficient to justify those potential losses.

10.7.5 Marriage: Assortative Mating

Another socially important variable associated with mental ability is that of marriage, or more specifically that of who marries whom. A consistent finding in several studies of the characteristics of spouses is that there is a tendency for spouses to be similar in some—but not all—aspects of mental ability; in other words, some aspects of mental ability do show substantial "assortative mating."

For example, in a study of married couples, Watson et al. (2004) examined spouses' scores on two mental ability tasks—a vocabulary test and a matrix reasoning test. Interestingly, even though vocabulary and matrix reasoning tend to be correlated with each other (both are strongly *g*-loaded tests), they revealed quite different results when correlations between spouses were considered. On the one hand, wives' and husbands' levels of vocabulary showed a fairly strong positive correlation, about .45. But, on the other hand, wives' and husbands' levels of matrix reasoning were correlated only about .10. This result is consistent with previous findings, in which spouses have tended to show quite similar levels of verbal comprehension ability, but no particular similarity in mathematical reasoning ability (e.g., Botwin, Buss, & Shackelford, 1997).

Why should it be the case that spouses tend to be similar in verbal abilities, but not so similar in (equally *g*-loaded) nonverbal reasoning abilities? One likely explanation—as you might guess—is that two people will tend to have more rewarding conversations if they have similar levels of verbal ability, but that similar levels of nonverbal or mathematical reasoning ability are unlikely to contribute in an important way to any aspect of relationship quality.

10.8 NOT ALL *G*-LOADED TASKS ARE THE SAME

The topic of the previous section was the link between mental abilities—especially overall scores on IQ tests—and various important life outcomes. As discussed earlier in this chapter, one of Spearman's important discoveries was that many very different tasks—for example, verbal knowledge, spatial visualization, or numerical reasoning—could all be good measures of *g*, and that a combination of such tasks would provide an excellent approximation to *g*. Most IQ tests represent such combinations of tasks.

But it is not necessarily the case that all mental ability tasks, or even all mental ability tasks that have high *g*-loadings, will show the same pattern of relations with other variables, such as personality characteristics, or gender, or age. Instead, one task may correlate rather strongly with one of those variables, whereas another task—even a task with the same loading on the *g* factor—may be roughly uncorrelated with the same variable. In fact, we have already discussed an interesting example of this situation: Recall that husbands and wives tend to be rather similar to each other in their levels of verbal ability (which is highly *g*-loaded), but little tendency to be similar in their levels of nonverbal or mathematical reasoning (which are also highly *g*-loaded). In the following section, we will describe some ways in which different kinds of mental ability—even highly *g*-loaded abilities—show quite different relations with other important variables.

10.8.1 Novel Versus Familiar Tasks: Fluid and Crystallized Intelligence

One widely recognized difference among mental abilities involves the extent to which they involve "novel" versus "familiar" tasks. One way to think of this distinction is that the novel tasks tend to resemble puzzles or riddles, whereas the familiar tasks tend to resemble tests of the kind given in schools (even if the content of such tasks differs from that of school tests). For example, novel tasks would include tests such as Raven's Matrices and also tests such as "Similarities" (in which the respondent must identify the most important similarity between two elements, such as a banana and an orange). In contrast, familiar tasks would be tests of mathematical thinking (e.g., solving problems that require the use of some basic concepts in arithmetic or geometry) and of vocabulary or general knowledge.

This distinction between novel and familiar tasks was first discussed by Raymond Cattell, the same researcher who had conducted some early lexically based studies of personality structure (see Section 3.3.2). Cattell (e.g., 1971; Horn & Cattell, 1966) described the novel tasks as indicators of *fluid* ability and the familiar tasks as indicators of *crystallized* ability. These descriptions were based on Cattell's view that the novel tasks required a "fluid" or flexible response to a new situation, whereas the familiar tasks required the use of some "crystallized" or well-learned skills or knowledge.

The distinction between these two types of tasks is one that makes sense intuitively. However, when mental ability tests are factor analyzed in such a way as to produce two or more factors, those factors do not correspond perfectly to the division between novel and familiar tasks. In many cases, one factor includes tests that are verbal in content, regardless of whether those tasks are somewhat novel (e.g., similarities) or highly familiar (e.g., vocabulary); one or more other factors contain tests that are numerical or spatial in content, again regardless of the novelty or familiarity of the tasks. So, the difference between fluid and crystallized ability, as originally described by Cattell, is not always supported empirically.

10.8.2 Generational Changes in Mental Abilities: The Flynn Effect

Nevertheless, there are some ways in which the difference between fluid and crystallized abilities is meaningful. One striking case of this involves the ways in which people's performance on mental ability tasks has changed over the decades and generations. In many different countries, people today score much better on mental ability tasks than people did a few generations ago. When overall scores are calculated across a wide range of mental ability tests, people of a given age group (say, 18-year-olds, for example) in the year 2000 scored about one full standard deviation higher than did people of the same age group in 1950. This means that if we could put the 18-year-olds from 1950 and from 2000 together, then about 70% of the 18-year-olds from 2000 would score above the average for the combined group on overall mental ability, but only 30% of the 18-year-olds from 1950 would do so. Clearly, this is a large increase.

But the strange thing about these increases is that they differ greatly depending on the kind of mental ability test. On some tests, people's scores have shown huge increases—in some cases, two standard deviations between 1950 and 2000—whereas for other tests, people's scores have shown little if any increase. The largest increases have occurred only on the more novel kinds of mental ability tests, such as Raven's Matrices, which assess fluid intelligence (e.g., Flynn, 2006).[13] In contrast, there have been very small increases (almost no increase at all) on kinds of mental ability tests that involve familiar content, such as Arithmetic (i.e., solving math problems) or Vocabulary, which assess crystallized intelligence (Flynn, 2006). It is not clear why this pattern of increases has emerged, but a plausible reason has been proposed by James Flynn, the researcher who documented the improvements in test scores (Flynn, 1984, 1987). (This increase is now known as the "Flynn effect.") He has suggested that in modern times, people have been doing more and more of the kind of novel thinking that is used in puzzle-solving tasks, and hence have been getting better at those tasks; in contrast, he has noted, people have not really had any greater exposure to the tasks involving skills or knowledge similar to what is taught in school, because these tasks were already highly familiar even decades ago.

This explanation probably makes sense to you, but in one way it is quite surprising. When you consider people of the same age who are tested at the same time, the difference between novel (fluid) and familiar (crystallized) tasks is sometimes almost impossible to notice when considering people's scores on those tests. In other words, if you and your former high school classmates had all taken some mental ability tests on a given day, some people would have tended to do better than others across the various tests, regardless of whether those tests were puzzle-like tasks as opposed to school-like tasks. But, if the class from 50 years earlier had taken the same tests, that class would likely have performed far below your class on the puzzle-like tasks, yet about the same as your class on the school-like tasks. So, the distinction between novel and familiar tasks—between fluid and crystallized intelligence—can potentially be very important when we consider differences between groups of people who have grown up in rather different environments or at very different times. This occurs even though the distinction between those tasks is not so important when we consider differences within a group of people who have grown up in roughly the same environment at the roughly same time.

10.8.3 The Flynn Effect: Are People Really Getting Smarter?

The fact that mental ability test scores have increased raises a fascinating question: Are people really smarter now than they were a generation or a century ago? On the one hand, it appears that they are not smarter, because the increases are not general to *all*

---

[13] Flynn (2006) also reported large increases for the Similarities subtest, but Kaufman (2010) has argued that these increases are actually due to changes in the way that this subtest is administered and scored, not due to real improvements in performance.

mental ability tasks. For example, important abilities such as mathematical problem solving and verbal comprehension (vocabulary) have not shown much improvement during the past several decades. But, on the other hand, it appears that in one sense people *are* smarter, because they do have a much better ability to solve unusual problems that have a puzzle-like aspect to them.

Some researchers have suggested that the increase in mental ability test scores means that nowadays, more people should be capable of completing a college education than was the case in previous generations. However, the increase in mental ability test scores does not apply to the mental ability tasks that are most relevant to higher education, such as tasks involving verbal comprehension or mathematical problem solving. The fact that scores on these kinds of tasks have shown little change among young adults suggests that the aptitude for advanced-level education is not much greater among today's young adults than it was among the young adults of a generation or more ago.

Nevertheless, Flynn (2006) has suggested that the increases in mental ability test scores could have other implications for a modern economy and society. According to Flynn, improvements in the mental abilities required for tasks such as Raven's Matrices have allowed people to adapt to (and to produce) the rapid changes during recent decades in technology, in the workplace, and in social relationships. For example, Dickens and Flynn (2001) pointed out that people now operate many more (and more complicated) appliances in the home and that more people now work in managerial or technical occupations. They also suggested that people's conversation tends to be more sophisticated than in the past; likewise, Flynn (2006) noted that the plots of television dramas have become more complex.

The history and the geography of the Flynn effect are not yet fully understood. Because mental ability tests have only been administered for a little over 100 years, researchers do not know when the increases in test scores would have begun. Most researchers think that the improvements on fluid ability tasks probably began not very long before the tests were invented. But, at some point in the past, the Flynn effect probably also involved crystallized ability tasks, because before the beginning of public education, many people would have lacked even basic skills in reading and arithmetic. This also raises the question of how the Flynn effect might operate in countries that have only recently seen increases in basic education. Perhaps those countries are currently experiencing improvements not only in fluid abilities (due to changes in technology and society) but also in crystallized abilities (due to increased literacy and numeracy).

10.8.4 Reasoning With Numbers and Shapes Versus Understanding Verbal Concepts: Different Relations With Personality

As mentioned in the preceding section, factor analyses of mental ability tests often show a distinction between tasks that involve an understanding of verbal concepts and tasks that involve reasoning with numbers or with shapes and spaces. These factors tend to be correlated with each other—as always, there is a *g* factor of general intelligence—but still, some people are relatively strong in one factor or relatively weak in another. Notice that the numerical and spatial tasks both involve a kind of "mathematical" thinking, such as that used in arithmetic (numerical) or geometry (spatial). In contrast, the verbal ability tasks—such as vocabulary or similarities—instead require an understanding of some concept that is usually not very "mathematical," but instead involves events, places, people, living things, or substances.

This distinction between the "math reasoning" abilities (both numerical and spatial) and the "understanding of verbal concepts" abilities is revealed in a very interesting way—specifically, in the relations of those abilities with personality characteristics. For the most part, personality is not much related to mental abilities: Most of the major dimensions of personality as described earlier in this book are more or less uncorrelated with mental abilities (e.g., Ashton, Lee, Vernon, & Jang, 2000; Noftle & Robins, 2007). In other words, people who are "smarter," as assessed by mental ability tests, do not differ much in personality from people who are less smart.[14]

But there is one important exception to this finding: For some kinds of mental ability, higher scores tend to be obtained by people who have higher levels of the personality traits associated with Openness to Experience, especially intellectual curiosity. Specifically, intellectually curious people tend to have higher levels of verbal ability than do people who are not so intellectually curious. In some studies, the relation has been rather strong, with correlations of more than .40 between inquisitiveness and tests of vocabulary or general knowledge. In contrast, however, intellectually curious people are about the same as less inquisitive people when it comes to spatial or numerical abilities, as intellectual curiosity shows weaker correlations, only about .10, with tests that involve reasoning with shapes and numbers (Ashton et al., 2000). The pattern is observed for the SAT subtests that are taken by high school students in the United States: Openness to Experience correlates almost .30 with the SAT Verbal subtest, but only about .05 with the SAT Mathematical subtest (Noftle & Robins, 2007; see also Ackerman, Bowen, Beier, & Kanfer, 2001).

So, why does this difference exist? Why is intellectual curiosity related rather strongly to verbal ability, but not so much to numerical or spatial ability? One likely explanation is that people who are intellectually curious are exposed to—and thereby learn—many words and facts through reading and listening on a range of topics. Conversely, people who are less inquisitive generally have less exposure to various facts and words, and thus tend not to develop such a deep and broad understanding of those concepts. But

---

[14] There is essentially a zero correlation between Conscientiousness and mental ability (e.g., Noftle & Robins, 2007). Even though both Conscientiousness and mental ability are positively related to performance in school and at work, they are unrelated to each other: Knowing a person's level of mental ability does not tell you anything about that person's level of Conscientiousness, and vice versa. But if you know a person's levels of mental ability and of Conscientiousness, you are likely to predict his or her school and job performance better than with either one alone.

this effect of intellectual curiosity does not apply to the kind of numerical or spatial thinking required in solving mathematical problems: Apparently, intellectual curiosity may help one to learn words or facts, but it does not develop one's ability to solve problems that are of a numerical or spatial kind.[15]

10.9 ALTERNATIVE IDEAS ABOUT MENTAL ABILITY

This chapter has described the current state of knowledge in the field of mental abilities research, as revealed by many hundreds of empirical studies conducted since the early twentieth century. But although the summary presented here represents the views shared by the large majority of researchers in this field, there are some contrasting ideas about the nature of mental abilities, and some of these ideas have become very popular in the media, in schools, and in the general public. In this section, we will take a look at some of these popular alternative views about the nature of mental abilities.

10.9.1 Gardner's "Theory of Multiple Intelligences"

Since the 1980s, a very popular perspective on mental abilities has been the "theory of multiple intelligences," as promoted in a series of books by Howard Gardner. Gardner (1983, 1999) has suggested that the g factor of mental ability is not particularly important for real-world outcomes, and that this factor emerges mainly because virtually all mental ability tests use a verbal format, which gives an advantage to people who are good at verbal skills.

Gardner has suggested that there are eight distinct kinds of intelligence: linguistic, logical—mathematical, spatial, musical, bodily—kinesthetic, interpersonal, intrapersonal, and naturalistic. The meaning of the first four of these "intelligences" is close to what is suggested by their names, as these refer to abilities in thinking with words, numbers, shapes, and musical sounds, respectively. Bodily—kinesthetic intelligence involves motor coordination, both at the level of the whole body (as in sports or in dancing) and also at the level of the hands or fingers (as in using small tools or instruments). *Inter*personal intelligence refers to the ability to understand social situations and the behavior of other people, whereas *intra*personal intelligence refers to the ability to understand one's own behavior, thoughts, and feelings. Finally, naturalistic intelligence involves the ability to classify elements in the natural world (e.g., different species of animals or plants) according to the important similarities and differences among them.

The popularity of Gardner's model may be due in part to the very appealing idea that everyone has his or her own pattern of strengths or weaknesses. This emphasis on this

---

[15] Actually, Openness to Experience does correlate modestly with performance on some nonverbal tests, at least when the content of those tests is novel or unusual to the persons taking the test. People high in Openness to Experience tend to perform better on tasks that seem unfamiliar and strange, probably because those tasks strike them as interesting rather than intimidating.

diversity of abilities is in many ways more satisfying than is the idea that people differ in a major factor of general intelligence, or *g* (which is approximated by overall IQ scores). Notice, however, that several of the abilities considered by Gardner are not purely *mental* abilities, which have generally been the focus of other researchers. That is, most researchers in the field of mental abilities have excluded from their investigations those abilities that involve motor skills (as in bodily—kinesthetic intelligence), sensory acuity (as in musical intelligence), or personality tendencies (as in interpersonal and especially intrapersonal intelligences). This is not to say that these abilities are unimportant or uninteresting—obviously, these abilities play a major role in many human activities and would be a worthwhile topic of study—yet their nonmental aspects tend to make them less relevant to the study of purely mental abilities.

What is the empirical evidence for Gardner's theory? There is not really any empirical evidence of the kind based on factor analysis, partly because Gardner has not developed tests to measure these various abilities. But measures of many of Gardner's intelligences are substantially correlated with each other and have strong loadings on the *g* factor of general intelligence. Recall that in Fig. 10.1 we showed several tests of mental ability; these tests happen to represent (in terms of Gardner's theory) the linguistic, logical—mathematical, spatial, and interpersonal forms of intelligence. As mentioned earlier in this chapter, those tests show moderate positive correlations with each other, and all of them show fairly high loadings on *g*. In addition, tests of naturalistic intelligence—for example, tests in which the respondent must decide which of several diagrams best represents the relations among various categories of objects—also correlate strongly with other mental ability tasks, and thus also load on the *g* factor (Visser, Ashton, & Vernon, 2006).

Now let us consider the other abilities described by Gardner. With regard to intrapersonal intelligence, it is very difficult to measure this form of ability, so its relations with other mental abilities are not really known. One recent attempt to assess the self-knowledge involved in intrapersonal intelligence was moderately successful, and suggested that this ability was only modestly related to the *g* factor (Visser et al., 2006); hence, this ability might be considered as a separate talent of its own. As for musical intelligence, some studies have suggested that it correlates modestly with other mental abilities, and hence is moderately loaded on the *g* factor. Other data suggest that composers and performers of classical music often have very high levels of mental ability; some research suggests that the basic abilities to judge pitch and rhythm are apparently somewhat associated with *g* but are partly a separate talent in their own right (Lynn, Wilson, & Gault, 1989). Finally, measures of bodily—kinesthetic intelligence tend to be correlated modestly with mental abilities, and hence have relatively low loadings on *g*. (Interestingly, the "athletic" physical skills involving the whole body are almost uncorrelated with the "dextrous" physical skills involving the hands and fingers, which suggests that there are actually at least two basic kinds of bodily—kinesthetic talent; Visser et al., 2006.)

To sum up, the evidence from empirical studies of mental abilities largely contradicts Gardner's theory of multiple intelligences. First, the "intelligences" that involve purely mental abilities—linguistic, logical—mathematical, spatial, naturalistic, and interpersonal—are all substantially correlated with each other: People who are strong at one of these abilities tend to be strong at the others also. This indicates the existence of a factor of general mental ability that cuts across some very different kinds of mental ability tasks. (Moreover, this *g* factor cannot be explained by the "verbal" content of the tests used in assessing those abilities, because many of the spatial and logical—mathematical ability tasks are nonverbal in format.) Finally, with regard to the "intelligences" that are not purely mental, but instead have some sensory or physical aspect as well, these abilities are only modestly associated with *g*, but the nonmental aspects of these abilities suggest that they are better understood as separate talents—for example, musical, athletic, or manual—rather than as aspects of mental ability or intelligence.

10.9.2 Sternberg's "Triarchic Theory of Intelligence"

Another popular theory of intelligence is the "triarchic theory" proposed by Robert Sternberg. Sternberg (1985) has suggested that there are three fundamental aspects of mental ability, which he describes as *analytic intelligence*, *creative intelligence*, and *practical intelligence*. In Sternberg's framework, analytic intelligence corresponds closely to the kind of ability that is highly valued in school settings—that is, an ability to think logically and critically. In contrast, creative intelligence represents the ability to formulate new ideas and to gain original insights into problems. Finally, practical intelligence represents the ability to solve problems in the context of everyday life, and thus involves a kind of "street smarts" or a common-sense understanding of how the world works.

To evaluate the triarchic theory, it is necessary to find some way first to measure the three intelligences, and then to find the extent to which they are distinct from each other and the extent to which they can predict important criterion variables. Following Sternberg's theory, it should be possible to obtain reliable measurements of all three of his proposed aspects of intelligence. In addition, those three variables should be only weakly correlated with each other. Moreover, each aspect of intelligence should predict its own distinct set of outcomes—for example, analytical intelligence should predict academic performance, creative intelligence should predict actual creative accomplishments (e.g., in artistic endeavors or in making innovations of some kind), and practical intelligence should predict "real-world" successes (e.g., in job performance or in dealing with everyday financial or social situations).

Sternberg and his colleagues have attempted to measure practical intelligence in a variety of settings, typically by assessing the extent to which persons in a given occupation have managed to learn the best ways to succeed within their careers and organizations (e.g., Sternberg et al., 2000). For example, Sternberg has developed tests to measure the extent to which people in various lines of work—including business managers, bank managers, army officers, university professors, and insurance salespersons—have figured out the "unwritten rules" or "tacit knowledge" of how to get ahead. Generally, these tests ask respondents to rank-order the usefulness of many possible actions that could be taken, in various job-related situations, to improve the chances of career advancement. The respondents' rankings of those actions can then be compared with the typical rankings as provided by people who have achieved a high level of success within the occupation in question—that is, by experts. Respondents whose rankings are most similar to those of the typical successful person are thus showing a high level of tacit knowledge, or of practical intelligence.

In some studies, Sternberg and his colleagues have reported some success for the tests of practical intelligence that they have developed for the occupations just listed (Sternberg et al., 2000). That is, according to Sternberg and colleagues, those persons who perform well on these tests—in the sense of giving answers similar to those rated as good answers by experts in the specified job—tend to have higher levels of variables related to job performance. (However, Gottfredson (2003) has suggested that the positive results reported by Sternberg and colleagues may be due in part to selective reporting—that is, of drawing attention only to the results that support the validity of tacit knowledge tests.) The finding of a link between "practical intelligence" tasks and job performance is actually similar to a well-established finding in industrial psychology. Researchers in that field have found that "situational judgment tests"—tasks that measure something very similar to "tacit knowledge" of Sternberg's practical intelligence—are moderately related to job performance (see McDaniel & Whetzel, 2005). But situational judgment tests are also related to IQ and to experience for the specific type of work in which those tests are designed. In other words, one's level of "situational judgment" or "practical intelligence" in a particular area is due partly to one's level of IQ and partly to one's level of experience in that area.

In addition to developing tests of practical intelligence that are specific to a particular job, Sternberg has also constructed measures of practical intelligence that involve questions of a more general nature (Sternberg, 1993). Those questions ask the respondent to choose the best solutions to various "real-life" problems involving, for example, awkward social situations, "best-buy" purchasing decisions, and finding one's way using a map. Sternberg developed his test of practical intelligence as part of an instrument that also included tests of analytical and creative intelligence. The availability of this test has thus allowed some investigation of the relations among the three kinds of intelligence, and of the extent to which the three are independent of each other.

A study by Koke and Vernon (2003) measured analytical, creative, and practical intelligence in a sample of 150 college students, using the intelligence test developed by Sternberg. In addition, Koke and Vernon also administered another well-known intelligence test (specifically, the Wonderlic Personnel test), and obtained records of the students' examination grades in a first-year psychology course. The results of this study showed that the three aspects of intelligence were substantially correlated with each other, with correlations ranging from about .35 to .50. This result indicates that people with high levels of analytical intelligence tend also to have high levels of creative intelligence and of practical intelligence, and vice versa. In addition, all three aspects of intelligence—not just analytical intelligence—correlated substantially (in the .30s and .40s) with intelligence as measured by the Wonderlic test. (When added together, the overall score for the three kinds of intelligence correlated about .55 with the Wonderlic test.) As for performance in the psychology course, all three aspects of intelligence—again, not just analytical—correlated in the .20s and .30s with course examination grades; when added together, the overall score on the three "triarchic" tests correlated about .40 with those grades, a value that was actually slightly higher than that yielded by the Wonderlic test. Thus, these results suggest that the three aspects of intelligence are not independent, but instead are all related to a general mental ability (or g) and are all related to criteria (such as academic performance) that depend, in part, on that general mental ability.

To summarize, there is not much evidence so far to support Sternberg's suggestion of three separate aspects of intelligence. The study by Koke and Vernon (2003) described earlier found that the analytical, creative, and practical aspects of intelligence were all substantially correlated with each other, and hence strongly related to an overall, general intelligence. Moreover, although there may be some validity for "practical intelligence" tests designed as predictors of performance in specific jobs, these tests are likely to measure a kind of "situational judgment" that depends on specific job experience in addition to general intelligence.

10.9.3 Emotional Intelligence

Since the 1990s, there has been a great deal of interest in the idea of "emotional intelligence." Promoted in best-selling books, this concept has received much attention in newspapers, radio, TV, and the internet, apparently because of the suggestion that emotional intelligence can be more important than the traditional concept of intelligence, which is generally measured using IQ tests of mental ability.

There have been two rather different approaches to the study and measurement of emotional intelligence. The original approach was developed by John Mayer and Peter Salovey, who studied emotional intelligence as an ability to perceive and understand one's emotions and those of others (e.g., Mayer & Salovey, 1993). A later approach was popularized by journalist Daniel Goleman, whose best-selling book on the topic (Goleman, 1995) described emotional intelligence in terms of an ability to regulate one's emotions. Let us consider these two ways of conceptualizing emotional intelligence, beginning with the more recent and widely popularized approach.

The concept of emotional intelligence as described by Goleman (e.g., 1995) involves an ability to regulate one's emotions and includes such characteristics as self-control, self-confidence, trustworthiness, empathy, optimism, achievement orientation, conflict management, teamwork, and awareness of one's emotions. Some instruments have been developed to measure the various aspects of emotional intelligence as described here, and these generally rely on self-reports or on observer reports (e.g., Bar-On, 1997).

In reading the preceding description of emotional intelligence and its measurement, you might wonder how this concept differs from that of personality. Many psychologists have raised this same question, because most of the various characteristics related to emotional intelligence are generally viewed as socially desirable personality traits. When self-report measures of these emotional intelligence characteristics have been examined along with personality inventories, the results have shown strong correlations between emotional intelligence and familiar personality traits. For example, consider two investigations (Brackett & Mayer, 2003; Newsome, Day, & Catano, 2000) of the relations between emotional intelligence (measured using the inventory by Bar-On, 1997) and personality traits as assessed by traditional personality inventories. In both studies, emotional intelligence was negatively related to Neuroticism (or anxiety), and positively related to Extraversion and Conscientiousness (or self-control); the correlations were rather strong, with the highest well above .50.

Interestingly, both of the preceding studies were based on samples of college students, and both studies obtained information on the grade point average and the mental ability (i.e., IQ or SAT scores) of the students. In both investigations, grade point average was correlated with IQ or SAT and with Conscientiousness (or self-control), but not with emotional intelligence; also, self-reported emotional intelligence was unrelated to IQ or SAT scores (Brackett & Mayer, 2003; Newsome et al., 2000).

Thus, it appears that when emotional intelligence is measured using self-reports (or observer reports), it largely represents a blend of several desirable personality traits. Those traits—such as low anxiety, high extraversion, and high self-control—are important predictors of many important outcome variables, including one's subjective sense of life satisfaction (see Chapter 9). Therefore, emotional intelligence is also likely to be associated with self-reports of well-being and of psychological health, and some researchers have found emotional intelligence measures to be just as good as traditional personality scales in predicting those outcomes, if not somewhat better (Day, Therrien, & Carroll, 2005). But the validity of self-report emotional intelligence scales appears to be due to the fact that they assess several important personality traits, with a particular emphasis on traits that are associated with psychological health. What this means is that it is not really necessary to invent a new concept—"emotional intelligence"—to describe variables that are already familiar to personality psychologists.

The status of emotional intelligence is rather different when we consider it not as a collection of desirable personality traits, but rather as the ability to think accurately about emotions. As you will recall, this was the way in which emotional intelligence was originally defined by Salovey and Mayer (1990; Mayer & Salovey, 1993), the researchers who began much of the recent work on this topic. As described by Salovey and Mayer, emotional intelligence includes the abilities to monitor one's own emotions and those of others, to discriminate among various emotions, and to use information about emotions as a guide to one's own thinking and action. Accordingly, these researchers have developed a test whose items assess these abilities (Mayer, Salovey, & Caruso, 2002). For example, some items ask the respondent to indicate which emotions are expressed in pictures of people's faces (or even of landscapes or designs). Some other items ask the respondent to choose effective ways to manage their own emotions and the emotions of others within hypothetical situations. (On this test, women score higher on average than do men, with a difference between one-half and one full standard deviation.)

In several studies, performance-based tests of emotional intelligence have been examined in relation to overall intelligence and to personality characteristics (e.g., Brackett & Mayer, 2003; Brackett, Mayer, & Warner, 2004). The results of these studies have indicated that emotional intelligence shows modest positive correlations with self-report measures of Big Five Agreeableness and Openness to Experience and also with verbal-based tests of mental ability. These correlations were rather modest, reaching only the .20s for the personality characteristics, and the .30s for verbal ability. However, the size of these correlations is limited by the modest reliability of the measures of emotional intelligence and of personality and mental ability; when this unreliability is accounted for, the relations become considerably stronger (Fiori & Antonakis, 2011; see also MacCann, Joseph, Newman, & Roberts, 2014). Taken together, these results suggest that emotional intelligence—when measured as an ability—is substantially related to personality and general mental ability but also has some limited unique aspects.

The preceding investigations were based on college student participants, and these studies also examined relations of emotional intelligence with some important outcome variables, such as drug and alcohol use, smoking, grade point average, and deviant behaviors (e.g., fighting, vandalism). Overall, the relations with emotional intelligence were rather weak, although low emotional intelligence was modestly associated with higher levels of deviance, even when personality and mental ability were held constant (Brackett & Mayer, 2003; Brackett et al., 2004). However, other research has found that emotional intelligence is only a very weak predictor of life satisfaction, when personality and mental ability are held constant (Bastian, Burns, & Nettelbeck, 2005). Future research might examine the validity of emotional intelligence for predicting outcomes that are more directly connected to emotional skills, such as success in interacting with other people in a variety of individual and group settings.

10.10 SUMMARY AND CONCLUSIONS

As described in this chapter, there are positive correlations between diverse tasks measuring many different kinds of mental ability; that is, on average, people who are relatively good at one mental ability task tend to be relatively good at any other mental ability task also. This indicates that the domain of mental abilities can be summarized in terms of a large factor of general mental ability, known as *g*. However, tasks measuring similar aspects of mental ability tend to correlate quite strongly with each other, and this indicates that, in addition to *g*, there are several smaller "group factors" of mental ability. Each of these corresponds to a different aspect of mental ability, such as spatial, numerical, or verbal abilities. Thus, whereas the *g* factor describes the individual's overall level of mental ability, the group factors provide some additional information about areas of relative strength or weakness.

Differences between age groups in levels of mental ability vary according to the particular ability being measured. Verbal abilities and arithmetic reasoning average somewhat higher in middle-aged adults than in young adults, and older adults average close to young adults. Spatial ability, perceptual speed, and to some extent short-term memory are much higher in young adults than in older adults, with middle-aged adults in between. Researchers have disagreed about the extent to which these latter differences reflect real age-related changes, as opposed to differences due to the cohort in which people were born. In any case, individual differences in mental ability are very stable, even between childhood and old age: That is, children who are "smart" relative to their age peers will usually be "smart" relative to their age peers in old age.

Much research has been conducted in search of possible biological bases of mental ability. One consistent finding is that individuals with larger brains tend to have higher IQs, with correlations typically in the .20s. IQ scores are typically correlated in the −.30s with faster reaction times and show similar relations with speed of inspection time (i.e., with the ability to discriminate between stimuli that are presented for only a vanishingly brief interval).

Research on the genetic and environmental origins of mental ability has been based on methods essentially the same as those described for personality, in Chapter 6. The results of many investigations—as conducted in broad middle-class samples from economically developed countries—suggest that the heritability of IQ is typically about .40 when assessed in children, but in the .60s when assessed in adults. The genetic contribution to variation in mental ability is partly additive and partly nonadditive. The effects of the common environment on IQ show a pattern opposite to that of genetic effects: The common environment shows a moderately strong influence during childhood, with values in the .30s, but this declines to less than .20 by adulthood. However, some research suggests that variation in the womb environment—both between mothers and also between pregnancies of the same mother—is an important contributor to variation in mental ability. The lack of attention to these womb effects may have led researchers to overestimate somewhat the heritability of mental ability, which even in adulthood might be only about .50. With regard to environmental influences on IQ, one possible influence is breastfeeding, but some research suggests that the link between breastfeeding and mental ability is due to the tendency for mothers who are more intelligent to be both more likely to breastfeed and also more likely to have smarter children. On average, the earlier-born children of a family have slightly higher IQs in adulthood than do the later-born children; this difference appears to be due to the more stimulating cognitive environment that the earlier-born children experience, not due to changes in the mother's womb environment.

Scores on IQ tests—and hence on the g factor that is the main element of those tests—are related to a variety of "life outcome" variables of practical significance. Academic achievement and performance are substantially correlated with IQ, with correlations sometimes in the .60s or .70s for standardized tests of academic achievement. These correlations become somewhat lower if the IQ tests are based only on nonverbal tasks.

In the workplace, job performance is also related to mental ability, with correlations typically in the .50s for performance in complex jobs and about .20 for performance in simpler jobs. Individuals' levels of occupational status are also correlated with IQ, even when the individuals' parents' levels are controlled. Longevity is also modestly related to IQ, as individuals who score higher on mental ability tests tend to have longer-than-average life expectancies; this relation is likely due in some part to health-related behaviors, as higher-IQ persons tend to have healthier patterns of behavior. Higher levels of IQ are also associated with lower levels of criminal or delinquent behavior, as measured both by arrest records and also by anonymous self-reports. There is also a moderately strong tendency for spouses to be similar in their levels of verbal aspects of mental ability, but there is little of this "assortative mating" for mathematical aspects of mental ability.

Tasks that are good indicators of g often relate in similar ways to other variables, but there are exceptions. For example, during the past century people's scores have increased greatly on nonverbal reasoning tasks (such as Raven's matrices), but hardly at all on tasks that resemble school tests (such as vocabulary or arithmetic problem solving). Also, the personality trait of intellectual curiosity is correlated substantially with tasks assessing verbal knowledge, but hardly at all with tasks assessing mathematical problem solving.

Several popular theories of mental ability have been offered as alternatives or as supplements to traditional concepts of mental ability. Gardner's theory of multiple intelligences describes several areas of mental ability. Sternberg's triarchic theory includes analytical intelligence (similar to academic ability), creative intelligence, and practical intelligence (i.e., "street smarts" or common sense). Recent ideas about emotional intelligence emphasize either (1) a variety of socially desirable personality characteristics, or (2) the *ability* to understand the emotions and behavior of oneself and others. Thus far, Gardner's and Sternberg's theories have not shown important improvements on the traditional theories of mental ability, which are based on a *g* factor and on several group factors. Researchers currently disagree about the question of whether tests of emotional intelligence—tests based on the *ability* to think accurately in the context of emotions—can provide some predictive validity beyond that given by traditional measures of personality and mental abilities.

CHAPTER 11

Vocational Interests

Contents

The measurement of work-related interests—also known as *occupational interests* or *vocational interests*—has been an active area of psychological research for several decades, beginning with the work of Edward Strong in the 1920s and of Frederick Kuder in the 1930s. It is no surprise that vocational interests have attracted much attention: Satisfaction with one's job is an important part of satisfaction with life, and job satisfaction depends in part on having work that fits with one's interests. Accordingly, researchers have tried to develop instruments that can predict which occupations and which kinds of work are best suited to an individual's pattern of interests. The information provided by such instruments (often called *surveys*) may potentially be useful in counseling young persons who have not yet entered the work force and also in counseling older persons who may be considering a change in their career path.

In this chapter, we will begin by discussing several issues in the measurement of vocational interests. We will then examine the factor structure of vocational interests, their relations with personality characteristics, and their validity in predicting important job-related criteria. Finally, we will also address such issues as the stability, heritability, biological bases, and evolutionary function of vocational interests.[1]

---

[1] For an engaging review of vocational interests research, see also the relevant chapter of Silvia (2006).

Individual Differences and Personality
ISBN 978-0-12-809845-5, http://dx.doi.org/10.1016/B978-0-12-809845-5.00011-1

11.1 HOW VOCATIONAL INTERESTS ARE MEASURED

Vocational interest surveys typically ask the respondent to indicate his or her probable liking for various kinds of occupations and work activities. Some surveys also ask about the liking for various kinds of leisure activities and school subjects. Responses to these items are then used to determine which occupations and work activities would be best suited to the respondent.

Different vocational interest surveys use different formats for administering items. Consider the examples in the upper panel of Table 11.1. In some surveys, the item states a single activity, and the person who takes the survey estimates how much he or she would like that activity, using a multipoint response scale. After the person has responded to the entire survey, his or her responses to the items are aggregated to produce scores on the various scales measuring interests in various areas of work or occupations.

This "single stimulus" format has the advantages of clarity and simplicity. However, one potential disadvantage of this format is that some people may indicate rather high

Table 11.1 Examples of single-stimulus and forced-choice vocational interest items

---

Single-stimulus items

For each of the activities below, please indicate how much you think you would like to do that activity. Circle one of the options according to the following scale:

SD = strongly dislike
D = dislike
I = indifferent (neither like nor dislike)
L = like
SL = strongly like

SD	D	I	L	SL	Taking care of elderly people.
SD	D	I	L	SL	Raising vegetable crops.
SD	D	I	L	SL	Writing a newspaper article.
SD	D	I	L	SL	Fixing a motor.
SD	D	I	L	SL	Designing new clothing.
SD	D	I	L	SL	Arresting criminal suspects.

Forced-choice items

For each pair of activities below, please indicate which you would like better, by circling A or B.

A   Calculating interest payments on a loan.
B   Making pottery.

A   Designing an advertisement.
B   Leading a rescue mission.

A   Conducting a chemistry experiment.
B   Giving advice to troubled youths.

---

levels of interest across almost all activities, whereas other people may indicate rather low levels of interest. This probably reflects real differences among people in the variety of activities that are of interest to them, but it probably also reflects differences among people merely in their style of responding to such items: Some people have a habit of indicating high levels of liking and other people low levels, even when their "true" levels are about the same. As a result, some people will obtain very high scores across most scales, and other people very low scores across most scales. This can make interpretation of results somewhat difficult, because the aim is to identify a respondent's areas of higher and lower interest, so that the most suitable areas of work and occupations can be identified.

The lower panel of Table 11.1 also shows an alternative format for administering items. In this format, respondents are asked to choose which of two activities they would like more (alternatively, in some surveys, respondents are asked to choose which of three activities they would like most and least). This "forced-choice" item response format produces scale scores that indicate the respondent's level of interest in one area relative to other areas, and thus eliminates the problem that some respondents tend to indicate high (or low) levels of interest across all areas. One minor drawback of the forced-choice format is that respondents take considerably longer time to complete an inventory consisting of these items, due to the additional thinking involved in comparing activities.

In a survey consisting of forced-choice items, each item should involve different combinations of various kinds of activities, so that the same kinds of activities are not repeatedly matched with each other. For example, if "business" items and "engineering" items were always pitted against each other in forced-choice items, then it would be impossible for a respondent to obtain high scores on both, even if these were in fact his or her two areas of greatest interest.

Thus, both the single-stimulus item format and the forced-choice item format have some strengths and some weaknesses. Both item formats have been successfully used in constructing some valid measures of vocational interests.

11.2 SCORE REPORTS FROM VOCATIONAL INTEREST SURVEYS

When a respondent takes a vocational interest survey in the context of obtaining counseling about career choices, his or her responses are used to generate a report that contains several different kinds of information. The precise features of the report will differ from one inventory to another, but here we will describe the most common features. Table 11.2 shows an (artificial) example report similar to those of several widely used interest surveys.

Typically, a report includes the respondent's standard scores on various scales that assess his or her interest in various *areas of work* (see Part A of Table 11.2). In other words, these scales are meant to indicate how much the respondent would enjoy various kinds of work activity. Many inventories will include scores for several (perhaps only six or seven)

Table 11.2 Sample score report for a hypothetical respondent on a hypothetical vocational interest survey

Part A: Areas of work

Area of work	Standard score	Score category
Realistic/practical		
Mechanical	52	Average
Carpentry	50	Average
Farming/forestry	58	High
Plants/gardens	56	High
Animals	56	High
Outdoor adventure	58	High
Investigative/scientific		
Mathematics & physical science	54	Average
Life & medical science	62	High
Social sciences	67	Very high
Artistic/expressive		
Performing arts & entertainment	39	Low
Visual arts	49	Average
Writing	66	Very high
Fashion	48	Average
Culinary	44	Average
Social/helping		
Teaching	64	High
Social service	54	Average
Child care	54	Average
Religious activity	50	Average
Medical activity	54	Average
Enterprising/assertive		
Sales	37	Low
Advertising & marketing	46	Average
Management & supervision	43	Low
Public speaking	51	Average
Law & politics	56	High
Law enforcement & military	46	Average
Conventional/organizing		
Data management	38	Low
Financial services	33	Very low
Office practices	33	Very low

Table 11.2 Sample score report for a hypothetical respondent on a hypothetical vocational interest survey—cont'd

Part B: Occupations		
Occupation	**Standard score**	**Score category**
Realistic/practical		
Architect	50	Average
Auto mechanic	52	Average
Bus driver	53	Average
Carpenter	49	Average
Conservation officer	57	High
Draftsperson	49	Average
Electrician	53	Average
Emergency medical technician	50	Average
Engineer	54	Average
Farmer	59	High
Firefighter	50	Average
Forester	57	High
Gardener	54	Average
Machinist	48	Average
Mail carrier	48	Average
Painter	46	Average
Park ranger	56	High
Plumber	50	Average
Tool/die maker	53	Average
Surveyor	55	Average
Veterinarian	56	High
Investigative/scientific		
Biologist	54	Average
Chemist	51	Average
Computer programmer	47	Average
Dentist	55	Average
Economist	60	High
Electronic technician	49	Average
Engineer	53	Average
Geologist	55	Average
Mathematician/statistician	52	Average
Medical lab technician	56	High
Optometrist	57	High
Pharmacist	52	Average
Physician	55	Average
Physicist	50	Average
Psychologist, academic	66	Very high

Continued

Table 11.2 Sample score report for a hypothetical respondent on a hypothetical vocational interest survey—cont'd

Part B: Occupations

Occupation	Standard score	Score category
Artistic/expressive		
Advertising artist/writer	48	Average
Architect	49	Average
Artist	48	Average
Author/writer	66	Very high
Broadcaster	56	High
Chef	44	Low
Florist	45	Average
Fashion designer	49	Average
Interior designer	46	Average
Journalist	62	High
Liberal arts professor	60	High
Librarian	56	High
Musician	42	Low
Photographer	47	Average
Restaurant manager	44	Low
Translator	59	High
Social/helping		
Athletic trainer	57	High
Child care provider	53	Average
Counselor	55	Average
Dental hygienist	52	Average
Dietitian	54	Average
Elementary school teacher	61	High
Fitness instructor	57	High
Flight attendant	53	Average
Nurse	58	High
Occupational therapist	58	High
Psychologist, clinical	67	Very high
Recreation director	53	Average
Religious leader	52	Average
Social worker	57	High
Special education teacher	59	High
Enterprising/assertive		
Buyer/merchandiser	38	Low
Corporate executive	44	Low
Hotel/motel manager	41	Low
Insurance agent	34	Very low
Lawyer	56	High
Manufacturing representative	44	Low
Military officer	45	Average

Table 11.2 Sample score report for a hypothetical respondent on a hypothetical vocational interest survey—cont'd

Part B: Occupations

Occupation	Standard score	Score category
Police officer	46	Average
Public relations director	52	Average
Purchasing agent	46	Average
Real estate agent	48	Average
School principal	52	Average
Conventional/organizing		
Accountant	35	Low
Actuary	40	Low
Administrative assistant	32	Very low
Bank manager	39	Low
Bank teller	32	Very low
Bookkeeper	35	Low
Executive secretary	38	Low
Hospital administrator	38	Low
Investment manager	40	Low
Store manager	34	Very low

Standard scores are based here on a mean of 50 and standard deviation of 10 across all respondents.

very broad areas of work; full-length surveys will include scores for many more specific areas of work (perhaps about 30), which can be classified within the broader areas. (Note that any given area of work will represent many different occupations.) By examining his or her standard scores on these scales, the respondent can identify the areas of work for which his or her interests tend to be particularly strong in comparison with those of people in general. (As described in Section 1.1.2, standard scores give information about people's relative standing on a variable. These scores can be computed with reference to people in general or to men and women separately.)[2]

As just mentioned, vocational interest scores provide information about areas of work that match a respondent's interests. In addition, score reports from vocational interest surveys generally also include scores on scales that indicate how closely the respondent's pattern of interests resembles that of workers in various *occupations* (see Part B of Table 11.2). By examining his or her scores on these scales, the respondent can identify

---

[2] Note that a score report based on standard scores (or percentiles) indicates how much a person would like an area of work *in comparison with how much other people would like it*. This means that if an area of work were very unpopular—such that almost no one really likes to do it—then even if a person had a rather high standard score or percentile for activity, he or she might not actually like that area of work. Therefore, a person's standard scores can also be considered in combination with his or her raw responses to particular items.

the occupations for which he or she is similar to the typical worker (or at least, more similar than the average person is). Note that the interests of the typical worker in a given occupation might include many activities other than those that are directly related to their work.[3]

Thus, as described in this section, vocational interest surveys typically report at least two sets of scores: one set of scores indicates how much a respondent appears to like a given area of work, and another set of scores indicates how similar a respondent is to people who work in a particular occupation. These two kinds of information tend to overlap heavily—for example, if you like artistic areas of work, then you are probably similar to people who work in artistic occupations—but they are not necessarily identical. Potentially, a person who does not really know how much he or she would like a given area of work might gain some insight into his or her interests by considering which kinds of workers have interests most similar to his or her own.

Using the information provided by the score reports, the respondent can then begin (usually with the assistance of a professional counselor) to learn more about the areas of work or the occupations for which he or she appears to have a suitable pattern of interests. In addition, the respondent can also consider the training or education that is required for various occupations in the relevant areas of work.[4]

11.3 CONSTRUCTING VOCATIONAL INTEREST SCALES: EMPIRICAL AND RATIONAL STRATEGIES

Psychologists who construct vocational interest surveys typically use a combination of the rational and empirical strategies of test construction. (Recall the description of these strategies in Chapter 2.)

The rational approach is usually applied in developing scales to measure interests in *areas of work*: The psychologist starts by writing many items that are conceptually related to interest in each of the various areas of work; that is, the items written for a given scale will seem clearly relevant to the intended area of work. (As noted earlier, the items would describe interests in work activities or occupations, and perhaps also in leisure activities or school subjects.) After the entire pool of items is administered to a large sample of respondents, some items may be discarded if they are not correlated with the other items measuring the same area of work.

---

[3] Some inventories also report similar kinds of information for various college major programs, in addition to occupations. That is, a respondent can learn how much he or she resembles the typical student of various college major programs.

[4] Most vocational interest surveys also report scores on a scale that detects invalid responding, as might occur when a respondent chooses responses randomly or makes an error in transcribing responses onto an answer sheet. These scales alert the respondent or the counselor that the scores on the other scales are unlikely to provide meaningful information.

The empirical approach is usually applied in developing *occupational* scales, which show how closely a person's pattern of interests matches that of the typical worker in a given occupation: Typically, the psychologist administers a large, diverse pool of items to a sample of employed workers—ideally, this sample consists of several thousand men and women of diverse ages and educational levels, representing dozens of common and widely varied occupations. The psychologist then selects items according to how well they distinguish the workers of one occupation from workers of all other occupations combined.

Note that even though the empirical strategy does not consider the content of the items, many of the items selected by that strategy will be conceptually relevant to their respective occupations. For example, an occupational scale for "Restaurant Manager" in one major survey (the CISS; Campbell, Hyne, & Nilsen, 1992) contains items related to preparing food and to running a business. However, the items belonging to any given occupational scale tend to be somewhat diverse, and some items do not have any immediately obvious relevance to the occupation in question. To consider the CISS Restaurant Manager scale again, some items related to teaching and to religious activities are included as *negatively keyed* items (see Chapter 2), such that lower levels of liking for these activities contribute to higher scores on the Restaurant Manager scale. Apparently, restaurant managers tend on average to be less interested in teaching or in religious activities than are workers in most other occupations.

11.4 MAJOR DIMENSIONS OF VOCATIONAL INTERESTS

One of the goals of researchers who study vocational interests is to find a few basic dimensions that can explain the wide variety of people's interests in occupations and work activities. Ideally, researchers could find a few major dimensions of vocational interests, much as have been done for personality characteristics (recall Chapter 3). These dimensions could then be used to give a simple and efficient summary of people's interests.

One difficulty in finding the major dimensions of vocational interests is the question of which interests to include in a factor analysis. Personality researchers can use the lexical hypothesis to guide their selection of personality characteristics, but vocational interest researchers cannot use this approach, because languages contain few words that describe people in terms of their vocational interests. Therefore, when trying to find the structure of vocational interests, researchers have to use their own subjective judgment in deciding how to make a list of interests to include in their analyses. As a result, any given factor analysis of vocational interests might give somewhat biased results, to the extent that some areas of interest are under- or overrepresented in the variable set.

The most widely used set of vocational interest dimensions is based on the research of John Holland (1966). This set of six interest dimensions is known by the acronym,

RIASEC, taken from the first letters of the names of the six dimensions: Realistic, Investigative, Artistic, Social, Enterprising, and Conventional. The "profile" shown in Table 11.2 summarizes the areas of interest that are generally included within each of these dimensions.

Note that some researchers favor somewhat different sets of basic dimensions. For example, Campbell et al. (1992) include an "Adventuring" dimension, which involves interests in dangerous or combative occupations. Goldberg (see Pozzebon, Visser, Ashton, Lee, & Goldberg, 2010) also includes this dimension, as well as an "Erudition" dimension, which involves interests in literary and intellectual occupations.

One somewhat unusual feature of Holland's model is that although it contains six dimensions, those dimensions are supposed to be somewhat correlated with each other. Holland portrayed the relations among these six themes in terms of a two-dimensional space, that is, a plane (see Fig. 11.1). In this figure, the interests that tend to be somewhat positively correlated with each other are placed beside each other, whereas interests that tend to be uncorrelated (or even slightly negatively correlated) with each other are placed opposite from each other. This gives the six broad interests a roughly hexagon-like arrangement within the plane, and Holland has referred to his framework as a hexagonal model. (Do not confuse this with the HEXACO model of *personality* structure, described in Section 3.5, which involves six personality dimensions. Those dimensions do not possess this kind of two-dimensional, hexagonal arrangement.)

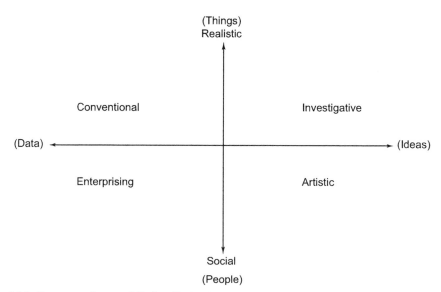

Figure 11.1 Correspondence of Holland's RIASEC interests with the Things/People and Ideas/Data dimensions.

The idea that these six major categories of interests can be summarized by two dimensions has led some researchers to suggest that Holland's framework can be simplified. The most widely known proposal is that of Dale Prediger, who described the plane of Holland's hexagon as a set of two contrasts between different kinds of vocational interests (e.g., Prediger, 1982); see Fig. 11.1. One of Prediger's dimensions is called *People versus Things*, where the People pole corresponds to Holland's Social theme, and the Things pole corresponds to Holland's Realistic theme. The other of Prediger's dimensions is called *Ideas versus Data*, where the Ideas pole corresponds to Holland's Artistic and Investigative themes, and the Data pole corresponds to Holland's Conventional and Enterprising themes.[5]

The two-dimensional structure of vocational interests as reported by Prediger is based on analyses of each person's *relative* levels of interest in the six broad interest areas proposed by Holland. For example, interest in People and interest in Things are strongly negatively correlated, but only if one compares each respondent's levels of interest in these areas *relative to their overall level of interest across all areas*. (By taking into account a person's overall level of interest, one controls for differences between people in the tendency to express interest across all activities.) If instead one simply assesses each respondent's levels of interest in these areas *without* taking into account his or her overall level of interest across all areas, then there is no strong negative correlation; instead, interest in People and interest in Things are almost unrelated. The same situation applies for Data and Ideas; these areas of interest are negatively related only if one compares each respondent's level of interest in these areas relative to their overall interest across all areas; otherwise, interest in Data and interest in Ideas are roughly uncorrelated.[6]

The two dimensions described by Prediger make good conceptual sense, and analyses of some vocational interest surveys do support this structure (e.g., Day & Rounds, 1998). But any attempt to summarize vocational interests in terms of only two dimensions tends to oversimplify that structure. There are many interests that are not adequately accounted for by only two dimensions, but that are well summarized within structures of six or more dimensions.

---

[5] Some researchers have suggested a third dimension of interests, which involves a contrast between occupations having higher and lower "prestige", which generally corresponds to the level of education required for the occupation. Here we do not consider the prestige dimension in detail, because it does not contrast different areas of work; instead, there are occupations of high and low prestige within each area.

[6] This situation again raises the issue of whether it is better to consider a respondent's interest in each area taken on its own, or instead to consider a respondent's interest in each area compared to his or her overall level of interest. On one hand, it is true that some people may really have a higher level of interest in a wide variety of activities than do other people. But on the other hand, it may be more useful to know which activities a person finds most and least interesting.

11.5 VOCATIONAL INTERESTS AND PERSONALITY

Vocational interests are likely to be a reflection, at least in part, of personality characteristics, and a great deal of research has examined the links between interests and personality. A review by Larson, Rottinghaus, and Borgen (2002; see also Barrick, Mount, & Gupta, 2003) summarized the results of over 20 previous studies that had examined the correlations between respondents' scores on scales measuring the Big Five personality factors and on scales measuring the six RIASEC dimensions of occupational interests proposed by Holland. The findings showed several moderately strong relations between personality characteristics and occupational interests:

Extraversion was correlated about .40 and .30 with Enterprising and Social interests, respectively;

Openness to Experience was correlated nearly .50 and .30 with Artistic and Investigative interests, respectively;

Conscientiousness was correlated about .25 with Conventional interests; and,

Agreeableness was correlated about .20 with Social interests.

The Big Five Emotional Stability factor did not correlate substantially with any of the interest dimensions, and the Realistic interest dimension did not correlate substantially with any of the personality dimensions.

A few recent studies have examined the links between vocational interests and self-reports on the HEXACO personality dimensions (McKay & Tokar, 2012; Pozzebon et al., 2010; Sverko & Babarovic, 2016). Across these studies, Artistic and Investigative interests have been found to correlate fairly strongly with Openness to Experience. In addition, Enterprising interests have shown modest negative correlation with Honesty-Humility, and Realistic interests have shown small negative correlations with Emotionality. (In the Pozzebon et al. study, interests in "adventure-related" areas of work—such as the military, law enforcement, and competitive sports—were examined as a separate category rather than as part of the Realistic or Enterprising categories. The Adventuring interests showed substantial negative correlations with Emotionality.)

Thus, there are several important links between personality and vocational interests. But these relations are only moderate in strength; even though vocational interests may emerge partly as a function of personality, an individual's personality can give only a rough indication as to his or her likely pattern of vocational interests.

11.6 VOCATIONAL INTERESTS AND MENTAL ABILITIES

Vocational interest surveys assess interest in various areas of work, not abilities in those areas of work. Nevertheless, there is usually some association between interest in a given area of work and ability in that same area of work. In fact, if we consider people's *perceptions* of their own abilities or skills, the relations with interests are very strong.

Campbell et al. (1992) reported that the correlations between interests and self-perceived skills in the same area of work averaged nearly .70. If you are very much interested in a given area of work, you likely see yourself as having a high level of ability in that area of work.

When abilities are measured by tests rather than estimated by self-report, the correlations with interests are much weaker, but still tend to be positive (see review by Ackerman & Heggestad, 1997). For example, tests of spatial or mechanical abilities tend to be related to Realistic or Investigative interests in Holland's framework. Verbal ability tests tend to be related to some aspects of Artistic or Investigative interests, particularly those that have some element of writing. Perceptual speed (typically assessed as quickness in identifying similarities or differences between strings of numbers or letters or shapes) tends to be related to Conventional interests. With regard to abilities of the kinds not measured by mental ability tests—for example, social skills or manual dexterity—there is not much research. However, it is plausible that these would also be modestly associated with interests in Social or Realistic occupations, respectively.

11.7 VALIDITY OF VOCATIONAL INTEREST SURVEYS

The issues discussed above—specifically, the structure of vocational interests and their relations with personality and ability—are of considerable scientific interest. But there is also the important practical question of whether the scales of vocational interest inventories actually "work": Do they predict important occupation-related variables, such as job satisfaction, job turnover, and job performance? In other words, what is the evidence of the criterion validity of vocational interest surveys? This validity can be evaluated in several ways.

11.7.1 Relations With Job Satisfaction and (Lack of) Turnover

One strategy for assessing vocational interest scales' validity is to obtain workers' ratings of their level of job satisfaction, and to find out whether these job satisfaction ratings are correlated positively with the workers' scores on the vocational interest scales that are relevant to their occupations. The same strategy can also be applied using job *turnover* (i.e., quitting one's job) as the criterion, except that the interest scale scores would be expected to correlate negatively with turnover.

The correlations between vocational interest survey scores and self-reports of job satisfaction have varied somewhat from one investigation to the next. But a review of 18 such investigations by Hough, Barge, and Kamp (2001) found that, in most studies, scores on a given occupational interest scale correlated between .25 and .35 with job satisfaction in the relevant occupation. In addition, negative correlations of similar size were observed in three other studies in which turnover was used instead of self-reported job satisfaction.

A more recent review by Van Iddekinge, Roth, Putka, and Lanivich (2011) examined vocational interest scales in relation to turnover intentions and also to actual turnover. They found that, on average, scores on occupational scales (i.e., for the occupations of the workers being studied) correlated about $-.20$ with actual turnover and slightly less with turnover intentions. The correlations involving scales measuring interest in areas of work were slightly weaker than those involving occupational scales.

11.7.2 Relations With Job Performance

Another way to evaluate the validity of vocational interest scales is to obtain supervisor ratings or objective records of workers' performance on the job (or in training), and to find out whether these job performance ratings are correlated positively with the workers' scores on vocational interest scales that are relevant to that occupation. The reasoning behind this method is that a worker who is more interested in a given area of work is likely to be a more effective worker, other things being equal.

Research findings suggest that vocational interest surveys have some validity for predicting job performance and training performance. Hough et al. (2001) reviewed 14 studies in which scores on vocational interest scales were compared with supervisor ratings or other indicators of job performance and found that the correlations were typically in the .20 to .30 range. Similar results were observed across 13 other studies that measured performance in a job training program as the criterion variable rather than actual on-the-job performance.

Van Iddekinge et al. (2011) reviewed a larger set of previous studies and found that the validity of vocational interest scales differed according to the kind of scale: Scores on occupational scales correlated about .20, on average, with measures of job performance in relevant occupations, whereas scores on scales measuring interest in areas of work correlated below .10, on average, with those job performance criteria. The correlations were somewhat higher when job performance was measured by objective records than when it was measured by supervisor ratings.

11.7.3 "Congruence" (or "Fit") of Interests: Relations With Performance and Satisfaction

The preceding summaries of research on vocational interests and job outcomes—both satisfaction (or turnover) and performance—were based on workers' scores on various scales. Another approach to examining the validity of vocational interest surveys involves computing, for each worker, an overall score indicating how closely his or her combination of interests in broad areas of work matches the combination of broad areas of work represented by his or her occupation. For example, consider a job such as high-school "shop" teacher: this work presumably combines Realistic interests (e.g., mechanical work) and Social interests (e.g., teaching). Therefore, a high-school shop teacher who has high levels of interest in the Realistic and Social areas would be said to have a good "fit" or "congruence" with his or her occupation. The validity of a vocational interest survey could be examined by finding out whether workers with higher fit or congruence scores tend to have higher levels of job satisfaction or job performance.

Some recent research studies have used the approach of computing "fit" or "congruence" between a person and his or her chosen occupation (Marcus & Wagner, 2015) or academic major area (Pozzebon, Ashton, & Visser, 2014). The resulting scores for fit or congruence were then examined in relation to job (or academic) performance and satisfaction. Both studies, however, found weak or near-zero associations between the fit or congruence scores and the outcomes of satisfaction and performance. Thus, these investigations do not support the validity of fit or congruence scores based on the overall patterns of vocational interests.

11.7.4 Limits to Validity

The relations between vocational interest scales and variables such as job satisfaction and job performance are rather modest. But to some extent these results are to be expected when we consider the difficulties in measuring job satisfaction and job performance. With regard to job satisfaction, most workers who have stayed in an occupation for a considerable period of time tend to report a fairly high level of job satisfaction. (Those who have a very low level of satisfaction with their current job are likely to move, sooner or later, to a different job.) As a result, the amount of variation in job satisfaction may be somewhat narrow, and predictor variables are therefore unlikely to correlate strongly with that criterion. Job satisfaction also depends on many variables other than liking of one's area of work as such. For example, various features of one's specific job (e.g., supervisor, coworkers, pay, benefits, etc.) also influence job satisfaction. The same limitations also apply when assessing job performance: The range of job performance levels tends to be somewhat limited (because very incompetent workers are less likely to remain in a job), and job performance itself depends on variables such as ability and work ethic in addition to interest in the work as such.

Overall, the evidence suggests that the mainstream vocational interest inventories show at least modest levels of criterion validity, as evaluated using the various approaches summarized above. Certainly, scores on vocational interest scales cannot indicate precisely which occupations or areas of work would be most liked or most disliked by a respondent. But those scales do appear to give at least some rough indications as to which occupations or areas of work would likely be of high or low interest to the respondent.

11.8 ORIGINS OF VOCATIONAL INTERESTS: DEVELOPMENTAL CHANGE AND STABILITY, GENETIC AND ENVIRONMENTAL INFLUENCES, BIOLOGICAL BASES, AND EVOLUTION

Vocational interests are usually studied in the very practical context of career counseling. But we can ask some scientific questions about the nature and origins of vocational interests, just as we have done for personality traits and other individual differences:

Are the differences among people in their vocational interests relatively stable over the life span? What are the genetic and environmental contributions to variation in these interests, and what is the biological basis of that variation? What, if any, would have been the adaptive trade-offs between high and low levels of these interests during the evolutionary past?

11.8.1 Stability of Vocational Interests

Let us first consider the stability of vocational interests across long periods of time. One recent review (Low, Yoon, Roberts, & Rounds, 2005) summarized over 60 studies that had examined respondents' interests at time intervals many years apart. On the basis of those results, Low et al. estimated the extent to which vocational interests remained stable across different periods of the life course between adolescence (about 12 years of age) and early middle age (about 40 years of age). The results showed that these interests were fairly stable across this interval. Even during the teenage years, when interests might be expected to change substantially, the stability was rather high; correlations between levels of a given interest at age 12 and at age 17 were generally above .50. This result is important, because it had previously been believed that vocational interests were very unstable before roughly the age of 16. The findings of Low et al. suggest otherwise; instead, there is a moderately high degree of stability to vocational interests even during adolescence.

Low et al. (2005) also found that vocational interests became even more stable during young adulthood, with correlations of about .65 between levels of an interest measured at ages 18 and 22. This rather high (but not extremely high) level of stability was then maintained throughout the 20s and 30s. Presumably, the increase in the stability of vocational interests that occurs at the beginning of young adulthood might result from increased exposure to different kinds of jobs, recreational activities, and academic subjects during the later high-school years. In general, differences among various kinds of interests in their degree of stability were small; however, there was slightly higher stability for interests in "hands-on" physical activities and in artistic expression than for interests in other areas, such as the scientific, clerical, social, or business-related areas.

11.8.2 Genetic and Environmental Influences on Vocational Interests

Next, let us consider the question of whether the variation among people in those interests has any important genetic component. A large-scale study of this question was reported by Lykken, Bouchard, McGue, and Tellegen (1993), who obtained self-reports of a wide variety of interests from over 1800 adults, including about 500 pairs of identical twins raised together, about 50 pairs of identical twins raised apart, and about 400 pairs of fraternal twins raised together. When averaged across the various kinds of interests, the correlations between members of a twin pair for a given interest were almost .25 for fraternal twins, but were about .45 for identical twins (with little difference between identical twins raised together or apart). These results suggested that the heritabilities of these interests were substantial, not much less than .50, and that there was no common environment influence on these interests.

The finding of substantial heritability of vocational interests also raises the question of the biological mechanisms by which genes might influence those interests. There has been a lack of research on the biological bases of vocational interests, but it is likely that those bases will be shared in considerable part with those that underlie personality characteristics. As described earlier in this chapter, vocational interests are correlated with personality dimensions and probably arise in part as a result of those traits. In addition, vocational interests may also develop as a function of the levels of ability that people have, and these abilities are also likely to be heritable (see Section 10.5 for the heritability of general mental ability). In other words, the genes that contribute to differences among people in personality and in ability—presumably by influencing the functioning of their brain mechanisms, in their hormone levels, and in their neurotransmitters—will likely also contribute to differences in vocational interests.

11.8.3 Evolutionary Function of Vocational Interests

Finally, we can also consider the question of the evolutionary adaptive function of vocational interests. In some sense, this question might not need to be asked at all, given that most kinds of occupations have only arisen during the modern era. Because many kinds of work have emerged so recently, there might not yet have been enough time for interests in those kinds of work to have been favored or disfavored by natural selection.

However, the sex differences associated with certain kinds of interests suggest the possibility that natural selection in the human evolutionary past would have favored different levels of these interests within the sexes. For example, the sex differences in average levels of interest for child development occupations (women averaging about one standard deviation unit higher than men) or in mechanical occupations (men averaging about one standard deviation unit higher than women) might reflect a division of labor that existed throughout human prehistory. According to this view, reproductive success in the human evolutionary past was likely higher for women who had at least some interest in child-raising activities and for men who had at least some interest in tool-making activities. As another example, the sex differences in the average levels of interest for fashion- or aesthetic-related occupations (women averaging about one standard deviation unit higher than men) and for competitive, military-like occupations (men averaging about one standard deviation unit higher than women) might reflect different forms of within-sex competition during human prehistory. According to this view, reproductive success was likely somewhat higher for women who had at least some interest in adornment and for men who had at least some interest in combat-like competition. However, these accounts are speculative; moreover, it should be kept in mind that for all of these areas of work, there is considerable overlap between the distributions of men and women, so that in each area of work there are both men and women who show high levels of interest.

11.9 SUMMARY AND CONCLUSIONS

Vocational interest surveys typically ask the respondent to indicate his or her probable liking for various kinds of occupations and work activities, and sometimes leisure activities and school subjects. Responses to these items are then used to predict which occupations and work activities would be best suited to the respondent.

Measures of vocational interests are sometimes based on "single-stimulus" items (in which the respondent indicates his or her degree of interest separately for each activity), and sometimes on "forced-choice" items (in which the respondent chooses which of two or more activities are more and less interesting).

Most vocational interest surveys contain scales of two kinds. Some scales assess perceived liking of various work activities and occupations (and perhaps also school subjects and leisure activities) that are conceptually relevant to particular *areas of work*. Other scales assess similarity to workers in various *occupations*, by comparing the respondent's answers with those of workers in each occupation.

Several studies suggest that vocational interests can be classified into a few broad dimensions as identified through factor analysis. In Holland's widely used framework, there are six dimensions, named Realistic, Investigative, Artistic, Social, Enterprising, and Conventional; each of these broad dimensions subsumes several related areas of work. (Other researchers use somewhat different frameworks, some with additional dimensions that might be separate from Holland's six.) Some researchers have suggested that Holland's six areas can be reduced to two very broad dimensions of interests, one called People versus Things and the other called Ideas versus Data. However, these two dimensions discard much of the information that is given by six or more areas.

Vocational interests tend to show moderate correlations with conceptually similar personality characteristics. For example, people who are interested in areas of work that involve artistic creativity tend to be high in Openness to Experience; likewise, people who are interested in areas of work that involve social interaction and leadership tend to be high in Extraversion. Because the correlations of interests with personality characteristics are not very strong, an individual's personality gives only a rough guide as to his or her pattern of vocational interests.

Vocational interests in a given area of work are strongly associated with self-perceived ability in that area of work. Relations of vocational interests with measured abilities tend to be much more modest, but are still positive.

Many investigations have examined the validity of vocational interest surveys, by comparing individuals' scores with their future levels of such variables as job choice, job turnover, job satisfaction, and job performance. These studies generally show some modest level of validity for those surveys in predicting these variables, with correlations typically about .20 for occupational scales relevant to the jobs being studied.

Vocational interest surveys tend to be rather stable across long periods of time, even when first measured during adolescence. Heredity plays a strong role in vocational interests, but the biological mechanisms underlying these interests are not understood. Sex differences in certain areas of vocational interest are moderately large and might have resulted from evolutionary selection pressures that differed between men and women.

CHAPTER 12

Religion and Politics

Contents

In this chapter we will consider religion and politics—two topics that you are not supposed to discuss in polite company. These topics are the source of much passion and conflict in people's lives, and they are of great interest to psychologists. For the personality psychologist, several major questions come to mind. What are the main ways in which people differ in their religious beliefs and political attitudes? How are those beliefs and attitudes related to personality characteristics? Why do people differ so sharply in their religious and political orientations?

12.1 RELIGION

Religion is of profound importance in the lives of millions of people, yet millions of others profess no religious beliefs at all. Although religiosity often differs greatly between

Individual Differences and Personality
ISBN 978-0-12-809845-5, http://dx.doi.org/10.1016/B978-0-12-809845-5.00012-3

generations and between nations,[1] there are also very large individual differences *within* societies in the extent of religious belief and practice. This raises the obvious question of whether *individual differences* in religiosity—that is, among persons who have grown up in the same society and at the same time—are associated with personality differences. Are some personality characteristics consistently and strongly related to religiosity? For example, are religious people gentler or harsher? More open-minded or more closed-minded?

12.1.1 Is Religiosity a Personality Characteristic?

Before answering the questions just asked, it is worth reflecting for a moment on a different question: Is religiosity itself a personality trait? There are certainly many ways in which religiosity is a kind of trait: It is manifested in a wide variety of correlated behaviors that are expressed in various situations (praying before going to bed, reading scriptures, watching religious television, observing dietary restrictions, attending weekly services, seeking advice from religious authorities, etc.). And, on an intuitive level, a person's religiosity (or lack thereof) seems to be a very important part of his or her personality, in the broad sense of the term, given that religiosity involves such a wide range of behaviors, thoughts, and feelings.

However, religiosity also involves several features that do not characterize personality characteristics. Saroglou (2011) has summarized four basic components of religion, which he calls believing, bonding, behaving, and belonging.

Believing refers to the fact that a religious person accepts some beliefs about the spiritual or supernatural world, such as the existence of God or of a soul.

Bonding refers to the importance in religions of uniting oneself with something greater than oneself, for example by praying, by meditating, or by participating in group rituals.

Behaving refers to the "way of living" that religions encourage as a way of achieving harmony with God or with the universe. For example, a religion may provide its followers with various rules about their diet, their dress, their sexuality, their family life, their leisure time, and their drug use.

Belonging refers to the sense of identity that religious persons gain from being part of a community of believers.

---

[1] In this chapter, we will focus mostly on religiosity as expressed in Western societies, in which the religion of the majority is Christianity. This emphasis reflects the fact that most research on the topic of religiosity has been based on samples of Christians in Western countries. An important task for future research will be to find out whether or not the correlations of religiosity with other variables will be similar in non-Western or non-Christian countries (for recent examples of cross-cultural research, see Aghababaei et al., 2014; Gebauer, Paulhus, & Neberich, 2013; Clobert & Saroglou, 2015).

BOX 12.1 Cross-Generational and Cross-National Differences in Religiosity

As you might expect, there is evidence of some very large differences in religiosity between generations and between countries or cultures. With regard to generational differences, some societies have shown rapid changes in their levels of religious belief and practice, as was strikingly apparent in many Western countries during the late 20th century. A classic example is the Canadian province of Quebec: In the late 1950s, about 99% of French-speaking Quebec residents belonged to a Roman Catholic congregation; by 1990, the proportion had dropped to 18% (Bibby, 1993). With regard to national or cultural differences, the contrasts are equally striking. For example, a survey conducted in 2002 found that, in many African and Asian countries, more than 80% of the people considered religion to be an important part of their lives (Pew Global Attitudes Project, 2002). However, the proportion was less than 20% in some other Asian countries and in some European countries.

These differences between countries and generations are massive and probably much greater than any such differences involving personality characteristics. As shown in the case of Quebec, a change in people's ideas about religious belief and practice can spread rapidly throughout a society, but a similarly rapid change in the general dispositions that make up personality has not been observed (see Section 7.4).

A person's level of a personality trait—unlike his or her level of religiosity—does not depend on beliefs, on feelings of unity with a higher power, on adopting a way of living, or on membership in a community. Thus, although religiosity seems to share some features of personality traits, it also involves some unique features that personality traits do not possess.[2]

12.1.2 Religiosity and the Major Dimensions of Personality

In considering how religiosity relates to the major dimensions of personality, we should first be clear about what we will mean by religiosity. As you have probably noticed, people who follow various religious practices may have very different motivations for doing so: Some people's religious behavior is a reflection of their deepest beliefs, whereas for other people, expressions of religiosity are intended mainly for the purpose of "keeping up appearances" within their community. In other words, some people are genuinely religious in the sense that they would follow their religious practices even if no one were watching, whereas other people observe religious rituals simply to gain and maintain social approval. In the following sections, we will focus mainly on aspects of

[2] One other difference between religiosity and personality traits is the distribution of people's levels. On self- or observer report personality trait scales, the distribution of scale scores is roughly "normal", with most people close to the middle and with fewer and fewer people toward the extremes at either end. But for self-report or observer report scales measuring religiosity, the scale scores show a nonnormal distribution in which there are many people who show extremely low or extremely high levels of religiosity (e.g., Ashton, Lee, & Goldberg, 2004; Paunonen, 2002).

religiosity of the former kind; some researchers refer to this as *intrinsic* religiosity, because the person's religious activity is based on a view that religion is important in its own right, or intrinsically. Only when specifically noted we will consider the latter kind of religiosity; this other variety is often called *extrinsic* religiosity, because religion is treated as a way of obtaining some other, extrinsic goals rather than as something important for its own sake. Now—keeping in mind that we will consider religiosity in the "intrinsic" sense just described—let us consider how religiosity relates to the major dimensions of personality.

Several studies have examined the links between religiosity and the Big Five dimensions of personality, and a recent review of those studies (Saroglou, 2010) has summarized their results. Probably the most striking finding is that the relations tend to be weak: Religiosity is not strongly associated with any of the Big Five factors. There is, however, some tendency for people who are more religious to have higher levels of Agreeableness and of Conscientiousness, with correlations of about .20 (slightly less for Conscientiousness). Other research suggests similar associations of religiosity with HEXACO Honesty—Humility and (to a lesser extent) Emotionality (e.g., Aghababaei, Wasserman, & Nannini, 2014; Lee, Ogunfowora, & Ashton, 2005). Taken together, these results suggest that more religious people are somewhat more altruistic and "better behaved" than are nonreligious people, but again, the tendency is fairly weak.[3]

These results raise the interesting question of why religious people tend to be a bit higher in personality dimensions such as Agreeableness and Conscientiousness. Are better-behaved people more likely to be attracted to religion? Or, does religion tend to make people better behaved? Or both? The relative importance of these influences is not yet known. However, the results of several longitudinal studies suggest that personality tends to influence religiosity rather than the other way around (Heaven & Ciarrocchi, 2007; McCullough, Enders, Brion, & Jain, 2005; McCullough, Tsang, & Brion, 2003; Wink, Ciciolla, Dillon, & Tracy, 2007).

In addition to the results just described, there are also some interesting relations between religiosity and the personality factor of Openness to Experience. Overall, religiosity is roughly uncorrelated with Openness to Experience, but this fact conceals some intriguing contrasts between two very different ways in which religiosity is expressed. First, consider what might be called *religious fundamentalism*, which involves a strict obedience and unquestioning devotion toward the rules and teachings of one's religion. Next, consider what might be called *spirituality*, which involves a sense of unity or togetherness with God and the universe and an intense feeling of religious fervor or inspiration.

---

[3] Note that these results are based primarily on personality self-reports but that similar patterns are also obtained when personality is assessed by observer reports (Saroglou, 2010).

Can you guess how these two aspects of religiosity are related to Openness to Experience? As reported in Saroglou's (2010) review, religious fundamentalism is correlated *negatively* with Openness to Experience, whereas spirituality is correlated *positively* with Openness to Experience. These results would seem to make sense if one considers the traits that make up the Openness to Experience factor in relation to these two expressions of religiosity. Persons high in Openness to Experience are inquisitive and unconventional, and these tendencies would likely lead them to question traditional religious teachings. But, in addition, persons high in Openness are imaginative and feel a sense of awe toward nature, and these tendencies would likely lead them to seek a kind of spiritual unity with God or with the universe. (Note that the average correlations as observed by Saroglou were rather weak—about .20 in absolute value—but that the relations can be considerably stronger depending on the scales that are used to measure fundamentalism or spirituality.)

Saucier and Skrzypinska (2006) reported a particularly detailed study of these two forms of religiosity. Their findings were consistent with the pattern just described: Religious fundamentalism (or traditional religiosity) was associated with low Openness to Experience, whereas spirituality was associated with high Openness to Experience. Saucier and Skrzypinska also explored a wide range of other variables that were related to the traditional and spiritual forms of religious expression. For example, traditionally religious people tended to avoid using alcohol or drugs; they expressed more belief in miracles and reported attitudes favoring authorities but opposed to evolution scientists. In contrast, spiritual people reported being fantasy-prone and eccentric; also, they expressed more belief in magic, witchcraft, and astrology.

Overall, the results summarized here suggest that the major dimensions of personality are not strongly related to religiosity. But this is perhaps not surprising if we realize that our level of religious belief and commitment is partly determined by the religiosity of the household in which we grow up. (We will discuss this influence of the shared or common environment in more detail later in the chapter.) If the religiosity of one's upbringing has a strong effect on one's level of religiosity, then there might not be so much variation left over for one's personality to explain. But what about those people whose level of religiosity differs sharply from that of the household in which they were raised? Is there anything special about the personalities of people who entirely abandon the religion with which they grew up, or of people who become deeply religious despite having had a thoroughly nonreligious upbringing?

So far, only a few investigations have addressed this question. McCullough et al. (2003) studied a sample of nearly 500 persons who had been identified as "gifted" children and who had later provided a variety of information about themselves during adulthood. (This sample was drawn from the group of gifted children identified by Terman and later studied by Friedman et al. in their study of personality and longevity; see Section 9.4.2.)

The results showed that the children who had been raised in religious households tended to be more religious in adulthood (the correlation was in the .40s). But this tendency was somewhat stronger among people lower in emotional stability than among people higher in emotional stability McCullough et al. suggested that this finding might be explained by a tendency for emotionally unstable persons to be more strongly motivated to avoid the tension and conflict that would arise as a result of departing from the religious traditions (or the very nonreligious traditions) of their families.

Another study of the personalities of people who are much more or much less religious than their parents is that of Altemeyer and Hunsberger (1997). These researchers did not collect any standardized measures of personality, but they conducted detailed interviews with several dozen persons who were either (1) very nonreligious despite having been raised in a very religious household or (2) very religious despite having been raised in a very nonreligious household. Altemeyer and Hunsberger referred to the people who had abandoned their religion as "Amazing Apostates," and they referred to the people who had spontaneously become very religious as "Amazing Believers." (Note that both of these kinds of individuals are quite rare, each representing less than 2% of the large sample of young adults in which Altemeyer and Hunsberger found them.)

The interviews revealed that the Amazing Apostates had generally experienced increasing doubts about their religion. These doubts were due to what they perceived as moral hypocrisy in religious people and as logical inconsistency and factual inaccuracy in religious teachings. Most of the Amazing Apostates were very good students in school, and upon having thought a great deal about their religion, they had eventually concluded that they no longer believed in that religion. With regard to the Amazing Believers, the conversion to religion had generally followed a period of intense personal crisis due, for example, to the death of a loved one or to problems with drug or alcohol use. The conversion of the Amazing Believers had been sudden and was characterized by emotion and passion rather than reason and reflection—thus opposite to the typical case of the Amazing Apostates—and suggests that the Amazing Believers had felt a strong need for a sense of community and structure in their lives.

12.1.3 Religiosity and Mental Ability

Beyond the major personality dimensions, another psychological characteristic that might be correlated with religiosity is that of general mental ability, as assessed with IQ tests. A recent review of over 60 studies of the links between religiosity and mental ability was reported by Zuckerman, Silberman, and Hall (2013). They found that, on average, persons with higher mental ability were slightly less religious than were people with lower mental ability: the correlation between IQ and religious belief was about $-.20$ to $-.25$, and if one divides people into "believers" and "nonbelievers", this corresponds to a difference of about six to eight IQ points or roughly one-half of a standard deviation unit. Zuckerman et al. (2013) discussed several possible reasons for this association. For example, persons with higher mental ability may be less likely to conform to religious dogma or more likely to have an analytical style of thinking that could undermine religious belief.[4] Note, however, that the association between mental ability and (lack of) religiosity is fairly modest, which means that there will still be many religious persons of very high mental ability.

12.1.4 Developmental Change and Stability in Religiosity

We now consider a couple of important questions about change and stability in religiosity levels. First, how do people's levels of religiosity typically change across the life span? In other words, do people in general tend to become more religious or less religious during certain phases of their lives? Second, how much stability is there to individual differences in religiosity? Put another way, to what extent do the differences in religiosity levels among a group of people remain similar across the life span?

Some answers to these questions are provided from the same data set as that used in the McCullough et al. (2003) study described earlier in this chapter. In a follow-up investigation, McCullough et al. (2005) examined the self-rated levels of religiosity of participants in an early study of gifted children. As part of this study, the participants were contacted at various times throughout their adulthood (specifically, about every 10 years between 1940, when the participants were 24–40 years old, and 1991). This allowed McCullough et al. (2005) to examine overall trends in the average level of religiosity across the life span, and it also allowed them to examine whether or not the participants' relative levels of religiosity were stable across the life span.

With regard to developmental change, the results showed a modest tendency for religiosity levels to increase between young adulthood and middle age, and then a slightly weaker tendency for those levels to decrease between middle age and old age. Overall, the average participant was very slightly more religious in old age than in young adulthood. But even these changes were not the same for all participants. Instead, McCullough et al. (2005) found that the participants showed three different patterns of change in religiosity: Some participants showed the pattern described previously; however, some other participants showed initially high levels of religiosity that gradually increased across the years, and some remaining other participants showed initially low levels of religiosity that remained low, or even decreased slightly, across the years.

Thus, the patterns of developmental change in religiosity do not show any dramatic changes for the average person, but there is some weak tendency for religiosity to be higher in middle age than in young adulthood or in old age. Future research will be

---

[4] In relation to the latter possibility, it is interesting to note that at least in the United States, scientists tend to be much less religious than are people in general (Pew Research Center for People and the Press, 2009).

needed to find out why these developmental changes occur or even to find out whether these findings are true of people in general. Note that the McCullough et al. (2005) findings were obtained in a sample of very intelligent persons, and it is not known whether the changes would have been similar for people in general. Moreover, the people studied in that sample all lived in the United States during the twentieth century, and it is possible that the age trends would differ in other countries and other eras.

The results of McCullough et al. (2005) also provide some information about stability in levels of religiosity—that is, the extent to which the differences among people in religiosity remain constant across the years. In general, there was a fairly high level of stability: Even across the half-century span between 1940 and 1991, the correlation between levels of religiosity at these two times was above .50. Given the very long span of time involved, this does seem to be a rather high level of stability. (Over shorter time periods, the stability was higher, with correlations approaching .90 for religiosity self-ratings at times 10 years apart.)

12.1.5 Religiosity and Life Outcomes

Another interesting question is that of how religiosity is related to important life outcomes in contemporary, modern societies. Here we will consider four variables: Health outcomes, life satisfaction, law-abidingness, and number of children.

First, many investigations have examined the links between religiosity and health, and the results of these studies were summarized in a review by McCullough, Hoyt, Larson, Koenig, and Thoresen (2000). By averaging the results obtained across 42 studies, involving over 125,000 participants, McCullough et al. were able to estimate the extent to which religious involvement was associated with health outcomes, and particularly with the odds of survival during the period of the investigation. The results showed that persons who were more religious were about 25% less likely to die during the period of study than were persons who were less religious. This finding indicates a fairly important link between religiosity and longevity; however, it leaves open the question of why that link exists. For example, it might be the case that religious people tend to have healthier lifestyles, either because of adherence to the teachings of their religion or because of some tendency for people who live healthy lifestyles to be more oriented toward religion. It is also possible that social support from one's religious community has important benefits, whether psychological, financial, or otherwise, that help people to maintain health and to recover from illness. Another possibility is that religious people have a more optimistic or a more courageous outlook that helps them to withstand stress and to recover from illness; in particular, perhaps the practice of prayer or meditation may itself provide these benefits. One of the challenges for future research will be to explore the reasons for the link between religiosity and health outcomes.

Regarding the relations between religiosity and life satisfaction, some investigations report modest positive correlations of around .20 or .30 (Salsman, Brown, Brechting, & Carlson, 2005). In the study by Salsman et al., this link between religiosity and life satisfaction was partly attributable to a tendency for more religious persons to be somewhat more optimistic and to have somewhat more social support than less religious persons.

Many studies have examined the links between religiosity and law-abidingness, and the results have been fairly consistent, usually showing a weak tendency for more religious persons to commit fewer criminal or delinquent acts (Baier & Wright, 2001). The relation between religiosity and law-abidingness is quite small (about .10) and appears to operate through the development of conventional attitudes and the avoidance of delinquent peers (Simons, Simons, & Conger, 2004).

Finally, various lines of evidence suggest that higher levels of religiosity are associated with having more children. At the level of the society as a whole, this link can be observed in many Roman Catholic countries that became much less religious during the second half of the twentieth century: When Italy, Spain, and Quebec experienced a decline in religious belief and activity, a sharp decline in the birthrate occurred also. (This likely reflects in part, but only in part, an abandonment of traditional Roman Catholic prohibition of contraception.) Within societies, there is also a tendency for the more religious persons to have more children (e.g., Balakrishnan & Chen, 1990).

12.2 POLITICS

Intuitively, it seems likely that personality should have some influence on one's political attitudes. Most of us would probably think that if we know an individual's personality in some depth, then we could have at least some rough idea as to his or her outlook on political issues. But before we can investigate the links between personality and politics, it would be helpful to examine the structure of political attitudes themselves—that is, to identify the main ways in which people differ in their orientations toward various kinds of political issues.

12.2.1 Right-Wing Authoritarianism

Much of our current knowledge on this topic of individual differences in political attitudes has been derived from the research of Bob Altemeyer. Altemeyer's work (e.g., 1981, 1988, 1996) focused on a variable known as *Right-Wing Authoritarianism*, which he defined in terms of three related tendencies called *conventionalism*, *authoritarian submission*, and *authoritarian aggression*. As studied by Altemeyer, conventionalism refers to a strong adherence to the norms endorsed by society and the authorities. Authoritarian submission refers to obedience toward the authorities perceived as legitimate in one's society. Authoritarian aggression refers to hostility toward people or groups that are considered "deviant" or deserving of punishment.

Altemeyer's construct of Right-Wing Authoritarianism was partly based on some earlier efforts by several other psychologists who, in the years following World War II, had tried to develop scales to measure "fascist" tendencies (Adorno, Frenkel-Brunswik,

Levinson, & Sanford, 1950). Those researchers—who had fled Nazi Germany shortly before World War II—believed that some personality characteristics or attitudes were associated with a tendency to support anti-Semitic policies and the fascist, authoritarian governments that implemented those policies. Adorno et al. developed a set of self-report items called the "F-scale" (short for "Fascist scale") to measure these tendencies, but unfortunately there were several major problems with the F-scale.

One problem was that many of the items in this scale had nothing to do with authoritarianism at all, and instead assessed a variety of characteristics such as cynicism, superstition, sexual repression, glorification of toughness, dislike of artistic sensitivity, and a tendency to "project" one's impulses onto others.[5] Adorno et al. had believed that authoritarian individuals would tend to show all of these tendencies; this belief was partly based on their own observations, and partly based on ideas derived from Sigmund Freud's writings about psychoanalysis. However, these characteristics were not much related to each other or to the core elements of authoritarianism that Altemeyer later identified.

Another problem with the F-scale was that it did not contain any reverse-keyed items (recall our earlier discussion in Section 2.4 about the use of reverse-keyed items). As a result, it was not clear whether persons who had high scores on the F-scale were really "fascists" having strongly authoritarian views, or whether they simply tended to "acquiesce" or agree when asked to respond to statements expressing various attitudes.

One interesting result of this problem of acquiescence was that F-scale scores tended to show strong negative correlations with educational level: Because the item statements seemed to be rather extreme generalizations, few educated people indicated strong agreement with those statements, whereas some less educated people (who may have had some difficulty in comprehending the items) did indicate agreement.[6]

Altemeyer (1981) developed an improved measure of authoritarianism—the Right-Wing Authoritarianism scale—by including some reverse-keyed items and by focusing on items that measured conventionalism, authoritarian submission, and authoritarian aggression, leaving aside the other kinds of items in the earlier F-scale. (See some example Right-Wing Authoritarianism items in Table 12.1.) This scale had better reliability than did the old F-scale, and it was also less strongly associated with educational level. In a series of studies, Altemeyer (1981, 1988, 1996) investigated the validity of the new Right-Wing Authoritarianism scale. Some of those studies examined the relations of Right-Wing

---

[5] The idea of projection is that one might unconsciously have some socially undesirable impulse—for example, to behave aggressively, or to engage in some forbidden kind of sexual activity—and that to reduce the anxiety caused by having this forbidden urge, one might come to imagine that those impulses are held by other people, not by oneself.

[6] The problem of acquiescence tends to be more severe for political attitudes than for personality characteristics in general: Many people do not have any opinion at all on many issues, but few people have no idea about their own behavior.

Table 12.1 Example items from the Right-Wing Authoritarianism and Social Dominance Orientation scales

Right-Wing Authoritarianism
Obedience and respect for authority are the most important virtues children should learn.
Once our government leaders and the authorities condemn the dangerous elements in our society, it will be the duty of every patriotic citizen to help stomp out the rot that is destroying our country from within.
Young people sometimes get rebellious ideas, but as they grow up they ought to get over them and settle down.

Social Dominance Orientation
To get ahead in life, it is sometimes necessary to step on other groups.
If certain groups stayed in their place, we would have fewer problems.
It's probably a good thing that certain groups are at the top and other groups are at the bottom.

Altemeyer, B. (1998). The other "authoritarian personality". In M.P. Zanna (Ed.). *Advances in experimental social psychology* (Vol. 30, pp. 47–92). San Diego: Academic Press. Sidanius, J., & Pratto, F. (1999). Social dominance: An intergroup theory of social hierarchy and oppression. New York: Cambridge University Press.

Authoritarianism with willingness to punish others. For example, higher scores on the scale were associated with willingness to give harsh prison sentences to hypothetical criminals and to give stronger electric shocks to a participant who made mistakes in a learning experiment. In other studies, Altemeyer found that higher scores were also associated with approval of restrictions on civil liberties, such as police raids and wiretaps conducted without warrants from a judge. In addition, another finding in Altemeyer's research was that higher scores on Right-Wing Authoritarianism were substantially correlated with "ethnocentrism"—a tendency to favor one's own ethnic group over other groups—and also with negative attitudes toward gay and lesbian persons.

From the point of view of our question about political attitudes, some of the interesting findings about the Right-Wing Authoritarianism scale involved its relations with political party preferences, with voting, and with attitudes on specific issues. Altemeyer (e.g., 1996) found (not surprisingly) that Right-Wing Authoritarianism was strongly correlated with preference for more "right-wing" political parties: In the United States, higher Right-Wing Authoritarianism scores were associated with preference for the Republicans over the Democrats, and in Canada higher scores were associated with preference for the Conservatives over the Liberals and (especially) the New Democratic Party. These differences were also observed among elected politicians in federal and in state or provincial legislatures.

12.2.2 Social Dominance Orientation

Based on the results of Altemeyer's work, many other researchers began to use the Right-Wing Authoritarianism scale as a basic measure of political attitudes. But, in the 1990s, a second variable began to be studied in depth also, beginning with the work of Felicia Pratto and Jim Sidanius. They developed a scale to measure *Social Dominance Orientation* (Pratto, Sidanius, Stallworth, & Malle, 1994), which captured some aspects of political attitudes that were not assessed by Right-Wing Authoritarianism. Overall, the two variables were similarly strong predictors of many important criteria, and together they were very effective in explaining a wide array of political attitudes.

The idea of Social Dominance Orientation is that people differ in their preference for hierarchy, as opposed to equality, in relations among social groups. In other words, some people like the idea that certain groups of people (e.g., ethnic or racial groups, religious groups, social classes, or sexes) should have higher status than others, whereas other people like the idea that all groups should be treated equally. In fact, most people in modern Western countries tend to favor equality over hierarchy, but there are large individual differences in the degree of this preference, and there are certainly some people who show a clear preference for hierarchy.

In developing the Social Dominance Orientation construct, Pratto and Sidanius began with the observation that virtually all human societies have social hierarchies of some kind. In addition, Pratto and Sidanius perceived that people differ in their endorsement of attitudes (or ideologies) that justify those hierarchies. For example, some people might believe that the members of a lower social class or a disadvantaged ethnic group tend to be lazy or impulsive or unintelligent, and that their lower position is therefore natural or appropriate; in contrast, other people might reject these beliefs. The researchers reasoned that such attitudes could be important in explaining a wide array of more specific social and political attitudes. The Social Dominance Orientation scale was constructed to assess this general preference for social hierarchy versus social equality. (See some example Social Dominance Orientation items in Table 12.1.)

In their original study, Pratto et al. (1994) found that the Social Dominance Orientation scale was correlated substantially (typically about .40) with attitudes on a variety of specific issues. Higher Social Dominance Orientation scores were associated with lower levels of support for several policies, including government social programs, assistance for racial minorities, environmental protection, and reduced defense spending. In other studies, Social Dominance Orientation has been studied in relation to attitudes about immigrants—in particular, whether immigrants should preserve their culture (multiculturalism) or change to fit in with the majority culture (assimilation). People with higher levels of Social Dominance Orientation tend to oppose multiculturalism and favor assimilation (Guimond et al., 2013).[7] Other research even indicates that higher Social Dominance Orientation is associated with greater favorability toward the exploitation of animals (e.g., Dhont, Hodson, Costello, & MacInnis, 2014).

---

[7] These results are found when most participants belong to the nonimmigrant, majority group of a society. Within the various immigrant or minority groups of a society, it is likely that favorability toward multiculturalism will be higher when members of a group are more concerned about the loss of their culture.

12.2.3 Relations Between Right-Wing Authoritarianism and Social Dominance Orientation

In most research studies, Social Dominance Orientation and Right-Wing Authoritarianism are moderately positively correlated with each other, often around .30 but higher in some countries and lower in others (e.g., Roccato & Ricolfi, 2005). The fact that Right-Wing Authoritarianism and Social Dominance Orientation tend to be only modestly correlated with each other has interesting implications for the prediction of other variables, such as attitudes toward minority ethnic groups. When these two predictors are considered, each of them often shows fairly high correlations with the criterion variable, and in combination, the "multiple correlation" yielded by the two predictors is very high. This is because each scale is accounting for some aspect of the criterion variable that the other scale does not. For example, consider attitudes toward a particular ethnic minority group: Some people may have unfavorable attitudes toward that group because of a perception that this group's members tend not to follow a society's norms of behavior; in contrast, other people may have unfavorable attitudes because of a tendency to perceive all other ethnic groups as inferior to their own. Because Right-Wing Authoritarianism assesses adherence to social norms, whereas Social Dominance Orientation assesses a general preference for hierarchy, the two variables together can account for a great deal of the variation among people in attitudes toward an ethnic minority group (e.g., Altemeyer, 1998; Duckitt, 2000). Similar results are found when these two variables are used in predicting attitudes toward gay or lesbian persons (e.g., Altemeyer, 1998).

The relations of Right-Wing Authoritarianism and Social Dominance Orientation with prejudice toward other groups might be explained in part by the ways in which those two scales are related to one's perception of the world. Some studies have found an interesting difference between the two scales (e.g., Altemeyer, 1998; Duckitt, 2000; Duckitt, Wagner, du Plessis, & Birum, 2002). First, persons high in Right-Wing Authoritarianism tend to see the world as a dangerous place in which one's most important values and traditions are being threatened, whereas persons low in Right-Wing Authoritarianism tend to see the world as a safe place in which one's values are secure. In contrast, persons high in Social Dominance Orientation tend to see the world as a competitive place (a "jungle") in which people struggle for resources and power, whereas persons low in Social Dominance Orientation tend to see the world as a cooperative place in which people help and share with each other. Thus, the people with the most negative attitudes toward other groups would tend to be high in both Right-Wing Authoritarianism and Social Dominance Orientation: Those people would tend to see other groups as dangerous and as threatening, and also to see those groups as rivals in a competitive struggle. These two perceptions of the world are roughly independent of each other—you can see the world as dangerous but not competitive, or vice versa—but if someone has both of these perceptions, then he or she is unlikely to have favorable views of other groups.

BOX 12.2 Personality and Rescue of Others During the Holocaust

As noted in this chapter, the psychological study of authoritarianism began as an attempt to understand the personality characteristics and attitudes of persons who supported fascist governments. Other research has examined people who showed the opposite tendencies, focusing in particular on the persons who risked their lives to rescue Jewish persons from the Nazis during the Holocaust—the mass murder of about 6 million Jewish men, women, and children by the Nazi regime during World War II.

A small proportion of the non-Jewish population of Nazi-occupied Europe was active in hiding or rescuing Jews from the Nazis. By helping Jewish people to escape the Nazis, these rescuers put themselves at great risk, and many were themselves killed by the Nazis. Any given person's decision as to whether or not to help their Jewish neighbors would likely have depended on various circumstances. But it is also likely that on average, rescuers would have differed from nonrescuers in some personality characteristics.

Some researchers have studied the persons who did try—for humanitarian reasons—to rescue Jews from the Nazis. For example, in some studies, researchers conducted detailed interviews with rescuers and nonrescuers several decades after the Holocaust (e.g., Oliner & Oliner, 1988). The results of those studies showed that rescuers—who were identified as such by Jewish survivors—tended to have a strong sense of social responsibility and of empathy for persons who were suffering.

Other research has used a similar strategy but has also included self-report personality assessments. For example, Midlarsky, Fagin Jones, and Corley (2005) compared personality self-reports of rescuers and of "bystanders" (i.e., people who lived in the same communities as the rescuers but were not involved in the rescue of Jews). They found that the rescuers tended to be considerably higher than bystanders in several characteristics, such as altruistic moral reasoning, social responsibility, empathy, risk taking, and autonomy (i.e., independent-mindedness). By using a combination of these and other characteristics, the researchers were able to differentiate nearly all of the rescuers from nearly all of the bystanders. Thus, the results of Midlarsky et al. (2005) supported but also extended previous findings based on other samples of rescuers.

Midlarsky et al. also noted that some of the characteristics that differentiated rescuers from bystanders—such as responsibility and empathy—are similar to characteristics that predict much smaller and less costly forms of altruism in other psychological research. But what was striking about the rescuers was their very high levels of those characteristics and also their willingness to accept great personal risks and costs, at a time when very few others did so.

12.2.4 Social Values

The finding of two major dimensions of political attitudes has an interesting parallel in a related area of research. Some investigators have examined individual differences in people's *social values*—that is, in the goals that people view as important guiding principles in their lives (e.g., Schwartz & Bilsky, 1987). Much of the research in this area has been conducted by the Israeli psychologist Shalom Schwartz, who in the 1980s began to expand on some earlier work by Milton Rokeach (e.g., Rokeach, 1973). Schwartz began by generating thorough lists of values that people might consider to be important, for example "wisdom," "self-indulgence," "freedom," "environmental protection," "social power," and so on. He asked research participants in various countries to rate the personal importance of more than 50 such values. The results of these responses suggested that the various values could be grouped into about 10 categories. In turn, further analyses (based on techniques similar to factor analysis) suggested that those 10 types of values could be summarized by two broad dimensions (see Fig. 12.1).

One of the two broad dimensions of values in Schwartz's framework is called *Conservation* versus *Openness to Change*. In terms of the value types, Conservation values include *Conformity* (e.g., obedience, respect for parents/elders), *Security* (e.g., family safety, national security), and *Tradition* (e.g., devotion, respect for tradition). At the opposite pole, Openness to Change values include *Self-Direction* (e.g., freedom, independence) and *Stimulation* (e.g., excitement, variety). According to Schwartz's research, people who view Conservation values as particularly important guiding principles in their lives tend to view Openness to Change values as less important, and vice versa. People with high levels of Conservation values also tend to be religious (Saroglou, Delpierre, & Dernelle, 2004), and tend in particular to have traditional religious beliefs.

The other broad dimension of values observed by Schwartz was one that he called *Self-Enhancement* versus *Self-Transcendence*. From the perspective of the value types described by Schwartz, Self-Enhancement values include *Power* (e.g., wealth, authority) and *Achievement* (e.g., success, ambition). At the opposite pole of this dimension, Self-Transcendence values include *Benevolence* (e.g., helpfulness, loyalty) and *Universalism*

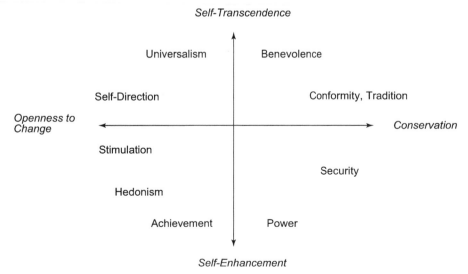

Figure 12.1 The two-dimensional arrangement of the 10 values identified by Schwartz (1992).

(e.g., peace, equality). (Note that one of Schwartz's value types, *Hedonism* (e.g., self-indulgence, enjoyment), is associated both with the Self-Enhancement pole of the second dimension and with the Openness to Change pole of the first dimension; see Fig. 12.1.) Again, Schwartz's findings suggest that people who view Self-Enhancement values as particularly important guiding principles in their lives tend to view Self-Transcendence values as less important, and vice versa.

Given the descriptions of the two dimensions of values identified by Schwartz, you can probably predict how those dimensions will relate to Right-Wing Authoritarianism and Social Dominance Orientation. As you would likely expect, Conservation (vs. Openness to Change) values are correlated positively with Right-Wing Authoritarianism, and Self-Enhancement (vs. Self-Transcendence) values are correlated positively with Social Dominance Orientation (e.g., Lee, Ashton, Ogunfowora, Bourdage, & Shin, 2010).

12.2.5 Attitudes, Values, and Personality

Next comes the question of how the differences among people in their attitudes and values are related to the differences in their personalities. In other words, can we view people's attitudes and values as expressions of their personality characteristics?

A study by Lee et al. (2010) examined the relations of personality dimensions with values and attitudes. Lee et al. measured people's personality characteristics, social values, and political attitudes in three countries: South Korea, the United States, and Canada. The researchers found two main results.

First, the Openness to Experience personality factor was negatively related to Right-Wing Authoritarian attitudes and to Conservation (vs. Openness to Change) values. These results suggest that people who have high levels of Openness to Experience tend to value independence and innovation more than obedience and tradition and tend to prefer a society in which people question authority rather than conform to conventions.

Also, the Honesty—Humility personality factor was negatively related to Social Dominance Orientation and to Self-Enhancement (vs. Self-Transcendence) values. These results suggest that people who have high levels of Honesty—Humility tend to value helping and sharing more than status and wealth, and tend to prefer egalitarian rather than hierarchical relationships between groups of people.[8]

We can summarize the relations among attitudes, values, and personality in a two-dimensional space, as shown in Fig. 12.2. One dimension is shared by Right-Wing Authoritarian attitudes, by Conservation (vs. Openness to Change) values, and by low levels of the Openness to Experience personality factor. (This dimension is also strongly

---

[8] The Openness to Experience personality factor was also negatively related to Social Dominance Orientation and to Self-Enhancement (vs. Self-Transcendence) values, but the correlations were considerably weaker than those shown by Honesty—Humility.

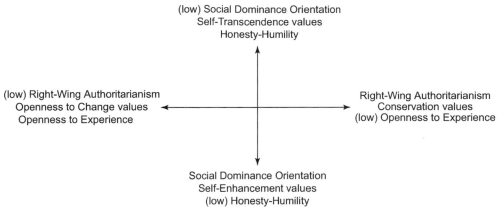

Figure 12.2 Approximation of two-dimensional arrangement of political attitude scales (Right-Wing Authoritarianism and Social Dominance Orientation), Schwartz's values dimensions (Conservation versus Openness to Change and Self-Transcendence versus Self-Enhancement), and HEXACO personality dimensions (Ashton et al., 2005; Choma, Ashton, & Hafer, 2010; Lee et al., 2010).

associated with traditional religious beliefs.) The other dimension is shared by Social Dominance Orientation attitudes, by Self-Enhancement (vs. Self-Transcendence) values, and by low levels of the Honesty—Humility personality factor. (This dimension is not related to religious or spiritual beliefs in either direction.)

12.2.6 Developmental Change and Stability in Political Attitudes

Relatively few studies have examined the patterns of developmental change and stability in political attitudes. However, some data on this topic have been reported by Altemeyer (1988, 1996) for the Right-Wing Authoritarianism scale. In one study, Altemeyer administered this scale to a sample of nearly 80 students at the beginning of their first year of college and again at the end of their fourth year. Altemeyer found that authoritarianism levels tended to decrease on average, by an amount about equal to half of a standard deviation unit. This result could suggest that attending college tends to reduce one's level of authoritarianism. On the other hand, it is also possible that young adults in general tend to experience a decline in authoritarian attitudes during this period of life, regardless of college attendance. Interestingly, though, Altemeyer found that the largest decreases in authoritarianism were observed for students in "liberal arts" programs. This finding suggests that the decline might be due to exposure to new and unconventional ideas about people and society, as these ideas would likely be discussed by liberal arts students and professors.

Altemeyer (1988, 1996) also examined the changing levels of authoritarianism across the entire span of young adulthood, from the college years to the 30s. In two samples totaling nearly 180 persons, Altemeyer obtained Right-Wing Authoritarianism scale scores from first-year college students, and then obtained scores on the same scale from those same persons either 12 or 18 years later, by which time they were in their 30s. The results showed that these persons' authoritarianism scores decreased somewhat across this period, but that the decrease was a bit less than that observed between the first and last years of college (as found in the study described in the previous paragraph). Taken together, the results of the two studies suggest that authoritarianism levels tend to decline during the late teens or early 20s but then increase slightly during the mid-to-late 20s or early 30s. One especially interesting finding of Altemeyer's research was that persons who had become parents tended to have authoritarianism scores that were about as high as they had been at the start of college, whereas persons who had not become parents showed authoritarianism scores that were somewhat lower than they had been at the start of college. This raises the possibility that the experience of being a parent tends to increase one's level of authoritarianism, offsetting what would otherwise be a decrease. Presumably, parents would be more likely to prefer a society that is oriented toward security and obedience than would people who do not have children.

In conducting the studies just described, Altemeyer (1988, 1996) was also able to examine the stability of individual differences in Right-Wing Authoritarianism scores across long periods of time. In his study of students' authoritarianism scores at the beginning and end of their college careers, Altemeyer found that the correlation between scores across this 4-year period was .75. In his study of people's authoritarianism scores at the beginning of college and in their 30s (i.e., 12 or 18 years later), the correlation between scores was nearly .60. These results suggest that the differences among people in their authoritarianism scores are rather stable, even across a fairly long period of time during early adulthood. Put another way, most people who are more authoritarian than their peers before the age of 20 will also be more authoritarian than their peers after the age of 30. However, the levels of stability are not extremely high, and this indicates that some shifts do occur in people's relative levels of political attitudes during the period of young adulthood.

12.3 ORIGINS OF RELIGIOUS BELIEFS AND POLITICAL ATTITUDES: BIOLOGICAL BASES, GENETIC AND ENVIRONMENTAL INFLUENCES, AND EVOLUTIONARY FUNCTION

In Chapters 5—7, we examined some basic questions about why personality variation exists, as we explored the biological bases, the genetic and environmental origins, and the evolutionary adaptive functions of personality characteristics. But these same issues can also be considered with regard to individual differences in religious beliefs and political attitudes. Why is it that people differ so widely in these important variables?

12.3.1 Biological Bases

Thus far, there has not been very much research examining the biological bases of individual differences in religious and political variables. Some few studies that have been conducted so far have suggested links of religious or spiritual beliefs with levels of certain hormones or neurotransmitters, but sample sizes have been small and in some cases the findings have failed to be replicated in other research. For the time being, our understanding of the biological bases of religious and political variation is very limited.

12.3.2 Genetic and Environmental Influences (and Spousal Similarity)

In comparison, much more research has examined the genetic and environmental origins of variation in religiosity and in political attitudes. The results of these studies have been interesting, insofar as the findings differ in important ways from those observed for personality characteristics (see Section 6.4). The most striking of these differences involves the influence of the common or shared environment: This influence has been weak for personality traits but much stronger for religious and political variables.

Recall that for most personality traits, the common or shared environment has had a very small impact: For example, adopted persons do not resemble the parents or siblings of their adoptive family in terms of personality trait levels. However, for religiosity, there is a fairly strong similarity between adopted persons and the parents and siblings of their adopted family. In a study of 650 adopted and nonadopted adolescents (Abrahamson, Baker, & Caspi, 2002), correlations above .40 were observed between the religiosity levels of relatives, with the values being almost as high for adoptive relatives as for biological relatives. A similar pattern of results, but with slightly weaker correlations, was also observed for conservatism of political attitudes.[9] This indicates that—at least during adolescence—the shared environment does influence religiosity and political attitudes substantially, even though it has little impact on the personality characteristics that we considered in the previous chapters.

There is some additional evidence, however, that the influence of the common or shared environment on religiosity and political attitudes tends to diminish as people reach adulthood. Koenig, McGue, Krueger, and Bouchard (2005) found that *fraternal* twins of the same pair tended to be very similar in religiosity when they were growing up together in the same household, but only moderately similar when they were in their 30s, after they had grown up and moved away. The correlation between fraternal twins' religiosity levels during adolescence was about .60, but this correlation had dropped to only slightly over .40 by the time the twins were in their 30s. In contrast, *identical* twins of the same pair did not show as much of a decrease in similarity of religiosity, with a decline from a correlation of nearly .70 when growing up to slightly over .60 when in their 30s. For twins of both kinds, the common environment in which they were raised was presumably having a much weaker effect in adulthood than during childhood or adolescence.

---

[9] The conservatism scale used in this study was related to both aspects of political attitudes as discussed in this chapter; that is, it contained items relevant both to authoritarianism and also to social dominance orientation.

However, Koenig et al. suggested that the genetic tendencies of the identical twins (who share 100% of their genes) were helping to maintain similar levels of religiosity, whereas this effect was not so strong for the fraternal twins (who share about 50% of their genes). On the basis of their results, Koenig et al. estimated that the heritability of religiosity is higher during adulthood (at least .40) than when growing up (under .15), and that, conversely, the effect of the common environment is lower during adulthood (under .20) than when growing up (at least .50).

A similar decline in the influence of the common environment (and a similar rise in the influence of heredity) was observed in another study that examined political attitudes (Eaves et al., 1997). This study involved nearly 7000 twin pairs—roughly half identical and half fraternal—including adolescents as well as young, middle-aged, and elderly adults. Eaves et al. administered the same conservatism scale that Abrahamson et al. (2002) later used in the study described earlier in this section. Interestingly, the similarity in conservatism levels showed a very different pattern of differences across age groups, depending on whether identical twins or fraternal twins were considered. Fraternal twins of the same pair tended to be rather similar in conservatism during their teenage years (correlations averaging in the .50s) but somewhat less so after the age of 20 (correlations averaging about .40). Identical twins of the same pair also tended to be rather similar in conservatism during their teenage years (correlations again averaging in the .50s); however, identical twins were actually somewhat *more* similar in conservatism after the age of 20 (correlations averaging above .60). These results suggest that common environment influences have strong effects on political attitudes prior to the age of 20, making fraternal twins of the same pair nearly as similar as identical twins of the same pair. After the age of 20, however, those common environment influences weaken while genetic influences strengthen, with the result that fraternal twins become less similar in political attitudes whereas identical twins do not.

In some recent studies, researchers have studied the heritability of political attitudes but have examined Right-Wing Authoritarianism and Social Dominance Orientation rather than an overall political conservatism variable. Kandler, Bell, and Riemann (2016) obtained self-reports of Right-Wing Authoritarianism and Social Dominance Orientation from several hundred pairs of German twins (with average ages in the 30s), along with observer reports from persons who knew them well (typically a different person for each twin of a given pair). By analyzing the self-reports and observer reports jointly, they were able to estimate the genetic and environmental influences more accurately than could be done using either source of information alone (recall Section 6.4.1 for a similar approach applied to personality characteristics). Kandler et al. found that Right-Wing Authoritarianism was highly heritable (above 55%) but also had a considerable common environment contribution (about 30%) and a small unique environment contribution (above 10%). But in contrast, Kandler et al. found that Social Dominance Orientation had very low heritability (about 10%) and a very strong common environment influence (almost 60%), as well as a considerable unique environment influence (above 30%). The relatively high heritability of Right-Wing Authoritarianism is broadly consistent with previous findings of high heritability—in adulthood—for traditional religiosity, which tends to be highly correlated with Right-Wing Authoritarianism. The low heritability of Social Dominance Orientation suggests that people's attitudes about group hierarchy or equality depend heavily on their own experiences, both those shared with their siblings (such as growing up in the same household and neighborhood) and those not shared with their siblings. However, the findings for Social Dominance Orientation might differ across countries, as some research from the United States suggests that egalitarian attitudes are substantially heritable, to about the same extent as Right-Wing Authoritarianism (e.g., Funk et al., 2013).

To summarize, Right-Wing Authoritarianism and traditional religiosity appear to be substantially heritable at least in adulthood, but findings are less clear about the heritability of Social Dominance Orientation (and hierarchical versus egalitarian attitudes more generally).

In investigating the effects of heredity and environment on religiosity and political attitudes, researchers also examine the extent to which spouses are similar in these variables. As explained in Section 6.5.2, if spouses tend to be alike in a trait that is influenced by genetic differences, then it is as if their children have more than 50% of their genes in common with each other (and with each of their parents). As a result of the extra genetic similarity between siblings whose parents are similar to each other on a trait, researchers' estimates of the heritability of the trait may be inaccurate. (That is, the researchers might overestimate or underestimate the heritability, depending on the type of design used in their investigation; see Section 6.5.2.) In such a case, the researchers would need to make statistical adjustments to their heritability estimates, to account for the effects of assortative mating. However, in the case of personality characteristics, this is not really a problem, because there is very little assortative mating: As we discussed in Section 9.2.1, there are only some modest tendencies for spouses to be similar (or dissimilar) in personality traits.

For religiosity and political attitudes, the situation is much different: People do tend to marry people whose level of religiosity and political views are similar to their own. Therefore, researchers must take this fact into account when they study biological relatives to examine the heritability of these variables. One example of the finding that spouses tend to be similar for religiosity and political attitudes comes from a study of spouses' characteristics by Watson et al. (2004). Watson et al. found near-zero correlations between spouses for personality characteristics (a typical result for such research; recall Section 9.2.1), and found moderately high correlations (about .45) between spouses for verbal intelligence (but not for nonverbal intelligence; recall Section 10.7.5). However, Watson et al. also found very strong correlations between spouses for religiosity and for political conservatism. Religiosity, as assessed by items regarding religious beliefs, practices, and the importance of religion, showed correlations of about .75 between husbands and wives. Political conservatism, as assessed by items regarding attitudes toward issues related to authority, moral regulation, and traditional values, showed correlations approaching .65. This result is also similar to previous findings (e.g., Lykken & Tellegen, 1993), and it indicates that husbands and wives tend to be very similar in their religious beliefs and political attitudes. Apparently, these variables play an important role in determining who will marry whom, as spouses are usually not very different from each other in these characteristics. This finding makes some sense: A person is more likely to enter into a close relationship with someone whose beliefs and attitudes about the world, society, life, and the supernatural are similar to one's own.[10]

12.3.3 Evolutionary Function

Next, let us turn to the question of why individual differences in religiosity and in political attitudes have been maintained across the generations. In other words, why has the process of evolution by natural selection not eliminated variation in these characteristics, by favoring some single optimal level? For the time being, we can only speculate on this issue, but future research will allow some tests of hypotheses such as those outlined below. Here we will focus on adaptive trade-offs associated with the two broad dimensions that span the domains of religious beliefs, social values, and political attitudes.

Let us first consider the dimension that involves high versus low levels of religious traditionalism, conservation values, and authoritarian attitudes. One potential advantage for persons having higher levels of these characteristics is that, within any given group, those persons would likely receive more rewards and fewer punishments than would persons who are more nonconforming or rebellious.[11] In contrast, however, there would also be some disadvantages associated with being an obedient person: By strictly following the leaders of their group, they might make sacrifices that would be avoided by less obedient persons. (For example, in time of war, the persons who are more obedient toward authority might be more likely to be killed or otherwise affected by the conflict.) Presumably, when the customs and the leaders of a group are successful in promoting the society's interests, the persons who are most socially conservative will usually gain the most; when the group is unsuccessful, however, those same persons will often lose the most.

Now let us consider the dimension that involves high versus low levels of self-enhancement values and of socially dominant attitudes. The likely benefit for individuals

---

[10] An alternative explanation for spousal similarity in beliefs and attitudes is "convergence", whereby spouses become more similar as their marriage progresses. However, further analyses by Watson et al. indicated that the similarity between spouses was not due to convergence; instead, there would have been substantial similarity even at the beginning of the relationship.

[11] One evolutionary biologist (Wilson, 2002) has proposed that the primary function of organized religion is to encourage (and to enforce) cooperation within a group, which also has the consequence of making that group more effective in competition with other groups.

having high levels of these characteristics is that those persons' groups would sometimes succeed in exploiting persons in other groups; for example, by conquering a neighboring group, or by enslaving some segment of their own society. However, these power-oriented individuals would also risk some heavy costs due to retaliation by those other groups, which would likely resist violently any attempts at being conquered or being enslaved. Thus, there is a trade-off associated with self-enhancement values and socially dominant attitudes, as persons having lower levels of these characteristics would tend to avoid both the benefits and the costs associated with higher levels. Depending on the relative strength of one's group—which might sometimes be badly overestimated—persons who encourage their group to dominate other groups might experience great gains or great losses.

12.4 SUMMARY AND CONCLUSIONS

In this chapter, we have examined religious beliefs and political attitudes, studying these variables in relation to personality characteristics and other individual differences. Although religiosity is an important individual difference characteristic, its features of "believing, bonding, behaving (way of living), and belonging" set religiosity apart from personality traits. Religious belief generally shows weak positive correlations with some of the major personality dimensions, such as Honesty—Humility, Agreeableness, Conscientiousness, and Emotionality. In addition, there are interesting links between Openness to Experience and religiosity: Persons high in Openness tend to have a greater sense of spirituality, and persons low in Openness tend to adhere more strictly to traditional religious teachings. Religiosity shows a small negative association with IQ.

Some research suggests that, on average, people are slightly more religious during middle adulthood than during adolescence or during old age. Also, even though some people show sharp changes in their level of religiosity, the overall stability of individual differences in religiosity is rather high, even across a span of several decades. Religiosity shows positive but weak associations with several life outcomes involving health, law-abidingness, and life satisfaction, and is also associated with having more children.

With regard to political attitudes, two of the most widely studied variables are Right-Wing Authoritarianism and Social Dominance Orientation. Right-Wing Authoritarianism involves a combination of conventional attitudes, submission to authorities, and aggression against targets designated by the authorities. Social Dominance Orientation involves favorability to inequalities among groups, such that some groups would be dominant and others subordinate. Right-Wing Authoritarianism and Social Dominance Orientation are only modestly related to each other. These two variables are related to the two main dimensions of individual differences in social values—the abstract goals that serve as guiding principles in people's lives. Specifically, Right-Wing

Authoritarianism is related to the values dimension of "Conservation versus Openness to Change" (and also to religious traditionalism and low Openness to Experience), and Social Dominance Orientation is related to the values dimension of "Self-Enhancement versus Self-Transcendence" (and also to low Honesty—Humility); see Fig. 12.2.

Although the developmental trends in political attitudes have not been studied in depth, the existing evidence suggests that one's level of Right-Wing Authoritarianism scores tends to decline during the college-age years but tends to increase on becoming a parent. Individual differences in Right-Wing Authoritarianism show fairly high levels of stability between the college-age years and the 30s.

Thus far, there has not been much systematic, large-scale research on the biological bases of religious beliefs and political attitudes. Studies of the heritability of religious beliefs suggest that the genetic influence on religiosity increases between adolescence and middle age, whereas the influence of the common environment decreases during that interval. Other research suggests that Right-Wing Authoritarianism is heritable in adulthood, but the heritability of Social Dominance Orientation may be lower. Religious beliefs and political attitudes show a high level of "assortative mating," with correlations between spouses in the .60s and .70s; that is, most people marry someone whose beliefs and attitudes are similar to their own.

Finally, some speculations have been offered on the evolutionary function of individual differences in the two major dimensions that underlie religious beliefs, social values, and political attitudes.

CHAPTER 13

Sexuality

Contents

Sex, in case you did not notice, is an important part of the human condition. And just as people differ in their personality characteristics, so too do they differ in their sexual behaviors, attitudes, and preferences. In this chapter, we will begin by identifying some important aspects of sexuality and examining their relations with personality. We will then examine several important issues concerning the nature of these sexuality dimensions, including their biological bases, their genetic and environmental origins, and their evolutionary function.

13.1 MAJOR DIMENSIONS OF SEXUALITY

To study individual differences in sexuality, it is useful to start by finding the basic ways in which people differ in their sexual behaviors, preferences, and attitudes—that is, by summarizing the many ways in which people differ in their sexuality. One approach to this

Individual Differences and Personality
ISBN 978-0-12-809845-5, http://dx.doi.org/10.1016/B978-0-12-809845-5.00013-5

problem is to adopt a lexically based strategy, one that is similar to that used in identifying the major dimensions of personality (see Chapter 3).

Using this lexical method, David Schmitt and David Buss (2000) identified a set of 67 familiar adjectives that describe various aspects of a person's sexuality. Schmitt and Buss then obtained self- and observer ratings on these adjectives from several hundred American participants (mostly college students), including roughly similar numbers of men and women. When factor analyzed, the ratings on these adjectives produced a set of seven factors; however, several of those factors were correlated with each other and could in turn be summarized in terms of only two very broad factors (Schmitt & Buss, 2000; D. P. Schmitt, personal communication, 2006). Because this two-factor solution provides a simple yet reasonably complete summary of human sexuality variation, we will focus on those two dimensions in the rest of this chapter. However, we will also consider one other important aspect of sexuality that, as Schmitt and Buss noted, was not well summarized by the two broad factors.

One of the two large dimensions obtained by Schmitt and Buss (2000) was labeled as *Sexual Arousal*. This factor was defined by adjectives such as *seductive, sensual, sexual, arousing, sexy*, and *erotic* versus (at the opposite pole) *celibate, abstinent*, and *prudish*, and thus represents individual differences in the tendency to feel sexually aroused, sexually attractive, and generally interested in sex.

The other of the two large dimensions found by Schmitt and Buss (2000) was called *Sexual Commitment*. This factor was defined by adjectives such as *devoted, loving, faithful*, and *monogamous* versus (at the opposite pole) *polygamous, promiscuous, loose*, and *unfaithful*, and thus represents individual differences in the inclination to be strongly committed or attached to one sex partner, as opposed to the inclination to prefer multiple partners or to be weakly devoted to any one partner.

Interestingly, some adjectives showed moderate loadings on both factors, and thus represented combinations or blends of these dimensions (see Fig. 13.1). For example, adjectives such as *passionate, romantic*, and *affectionate* loaded about equally on the positive poles of both Sexual Arousal and Sexual Commitment; thus, these terms describe someone who has a high level of both factors. Some other adjectives, such as *obscene, vulgar*, and *indecent* loaded about equally on the positive pole of Sexual Arousal and on the negative pole of Sexual Commitment; thus, these terms describe someone who is high in sexual arousal but low in sexual commitment.

The two large factors just described showed quite different patterns of sex differences. For Sexual Arousal, there was virtually no difference between the average ratings for men and for women[1]; however, for Sexual Commitment, there was a moderately large

---

[1] Other research, however, does suggest somewhat higher sex drive for the average man than for the average woman. For example, Lippa (2009) reported that sex drive in men averaged about 0.6 standard deviation units higher than in women.

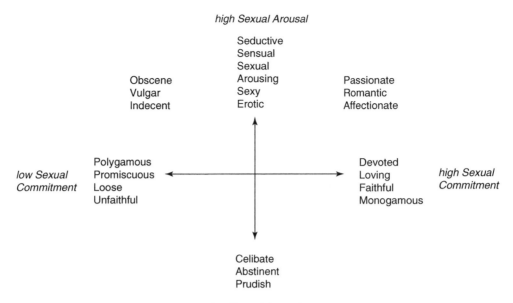

Figure 13.1 Graph showing loadings of sexuality adjectives on two factors of Sexual Arousal and Sexual Commitment. *(Based on Schmitt, D. P., & Buss, D. M. (2000). Sexual dimensions of person description: beyond or subsumed by the Big Five?* Journal of Research in Personality, 34, 141—177; *Schmitt, D. P. (Personal Communication, 2006).)*

difference between the sexes, with women having higher ratings on average than did men. For example, terms such as *faithful* versus *unfaithful* showed sex differences of about two-thirds of a standard deviation unit overall.[2] This suggests that more than 60% of women, but less than 40% of men, have above average levels of Sexual Commitment. Note that even though this represents a fairly substantial difference between the sexes, there is also a great deal of variation within each sex, with a considerable fraction of men who are high in Sexual Commitment and a considerable fraction of women who are low.

As mentioned earlier in this section, there were some sexuality-related terms that did not show substantial loadings on either of these two large factors. These relatively few terms included *heterosexual* versus *homosexual* and *bisexual*, and thus describe a person's *sexual orientation*. Because this is obviously an important way in which people differ from

[2] When data from both men and women are analyzed together, the second factor is also defined by adjectives such as *feminine* versus *masculine*. This reflects the fact that women tended to be somewhat higher in Sexual Commitment than did men, and also that women generally rated themselves as feminine, whereas men generally rated themselves as masculine. If data are analyzed separately for each sex, then there is much less variation in ratings on *feminine* and *masculine*, and these terms do not load strongly on either of the two factors.

each other, we will consider Sexual Orientation as an additional dimension of sexuality when we discuss relations with personality and other variables.

Now that we have identified some basic dimensions of sexuality, we can examine the question of how personality is related to sexuality. We will consider Sexual Arousal, Sexual Commitment, and Sexual Orientation, relying in part on results obtained by Schmitt and Buss (2000) and in part on results from other research studies.

13.2 SEXUALITY AND PERSONALITY

13.2.1 Sexual Arousal and Personality

Along with the sexuality adjectives that Schmitt and Buss (2000) administered to their research participants were some self-report scales measuring the Big Five personality factors. Of these characteristics, the one that showed the clearest links with Sexual Arousal was Extraversion, which correlated about .45 with this dimension of sexuality (Schmitt & Buss, 2000; D. P. Schmitt, personal communication, 2006). That is, people who were more extraverted tended to report a stronger sex drive and a stronger sense of being sexually attractive—to put it simply, the more extraverted people tended to feel sexier. Thus, there is a moderately strong tendency for people who are outgoing and lively to feel a strong sex drive and a strong sense of being sexually attractive, although there are certainly some people with more shy or passive personalities who also feel very sexy.

Other evidence supporting the link between Sexual Arousal and Extraversion comes from the personality trait levels of persons who describe themselves as "asexual" or "nonsexual"—that is, as having essentially no feelings of sexual attraction toward others. Asexual persons—who represent somewhat more than 1% of women and nearly 1% of men—can thus be considered to be very low in Sexual Arousal. Research based on a very large online sample of persons who gave personality self-reports has shown that asexual persons average about three-quarters of a standard deviation lower in Extraversion than do persons who are not asexual (Bogaert, Ashton, & Lee, 2017). This finding that persons very low in Sexual Arousal tend to be low in Extraversion is consistent with the earlier findings that persons who are more extraverted tend to have stronger sex drives.

13.2.2 Sexual Commitment and Personality

Next, with regard to Sexual Commitment, the findings of Schmitt and Buss (2000; D. P. Schmitt, personal communication, 2006) showed that self-reports on the Big Five Agreeableness and Conscientiousness factors were correlated with this dimension of sexuality. In particular, higher levels of Agreeableness and higher levels of Conscientiousness were both associated with a stronger inclination to be faithful and devoted to a single partner, rather than to be promiscuous.[3] Both correlations were about .50, thus indicating a rather strong link between these personality characteristics and Sexual Commitment.

Some additional research that is relevant to Sexual Commitment has been based on a variable called *sociosexual orientation* (Simpson & Gangestad, 1991). (Be careful not to confuse this with sexual orientation!) Simpson and Gangestad described sociosexual orientation as a dimension that has two opposing poles, "restricted" and "unrestricted." A person who has a *sociosexually restricted* orientation can be comfortable in a sexual relationship only if he or she feels a strong emotional bond with his or her partner. In contrast, a person who has a *sociosexually unrestricted* orientation can be perfectly willing to engage in sexual relations even in the absence of any emotional commitment to his or her partner. In short, people with an "unrestricted" orientation are potentially very much willing to have sex without love, whereas people with a "restricted" orientation only want sex within a relationship that is based on love.

As can be seen from this description, the variable of sociosexual orientation closely resembles the Sexual Commitment factor, with a restricted orientation representing high commitment and an unrestricted orientation representing low commitment. Some research suggests that sociosexual orientation does show roughly the same relations with personality as does Sexual Commitment: Bourdage, Lee, Ashton, and Perry (2007) found that a restricted orientation was associated with higher levels of HEX-ACO Honesty—Humility and, to a lesser extent, higher levels of the HEXACO Emotionality, Conscientiousness, and Agreeableness factors. In addition, Reise and Wright (1996) found that more sociosexually unrestricted persons had somewhat higher levels of traits such as narcissism and psychopathy (which are related to low Honesty—Humility).

13.2.3 Sexual Orientation and Personality

As noted before, Sexual Orientation represents another aspect of sexuality, additional to the two broad dimensions of Sexual Arousal and Sexual Commitment. But one interesting difference between Sexual Orientation and the other two aspects of sexuality involves the distributions of people's levels of these variables. To see this, first consider Sexual Arousal: Some people have a very strong sex drive, whereas others have a very weak sex drive, and most people are somewhere in between. Or, consider Sexual Commitment: Most people

---

[3] The *opposite* pole of the Sexual Commitment dimension includes both unfaithfulness and promiscuity, even though these are not exactly the same thing. Although unfaithful people are likely to be promiscuous and vice versa, there could be exceptions: For example, consider someone who has an ongoing extramarital affair with only one person, or conversely someone who has had many "one-night stands" but who has never actually cheated on a partner. The personality variables associated with these two tendencies are slightly different; for example, promiscuity has a weak association with Extraversion, whereas unfaithfulness does not (Schmitt, 2004).

Table 13.1 Proportions of men and women reporting sexual fantasies and attractions that are heterosexual and/or homosexual

	Gender	
Sexual fantasies and attractions	**Men (%)**	**Women (%)**
Entirely heterosexual	92	92
Partly homosexual but equally or mainly heterosexual	4	7
Mainly or entirely homosexual	4	1

Based on Bailey, J. M., Dunne, M. P., & Martin, N. G. (2000a). Genetic and environmental influences on sexual orientation and its correlates in an Australian twin sample. *Journal of Personality and Social Psychology, 78*, 524–536.

are inclined to be devoted and monogamous, but many others tend to be unfaithful and promiscuous, and still others are somewhere in between. Thus, for both of those variables—as for personality characteristics and most other individual differences considered in this book—there is a continuous distribution of people along the entire length of a dimension that extends from one extreme to another.

Sexual Orientation is different from the preceding two dimensions, because the very large majority of people (both women and men) describe themselves as being entirely heterosexual in their preferences (see Bailey, Dunne, & Martin, 2000). Among both men and women, about 92% of people report having sexual fantasies and attractions that are entirely heterosexual (see Table 13.1). In contrast, only about 4% of men and 1% of women report having sexual fantasies or attractions that are mainly or completely homosexual; and in between, about 4% of men and 7% of women report having fantasies and attractions that are partly homosexual but equally or mainly heterosexual. Thus, for Sexual Orientation, most people are at one pole of the "dimension," with a few people at the other pole, and a few others in between.[4]

But regardless of the distribution of the Sexual Orientation dimension, the question of how personality relates to sexual orientation is an interesting one. What differences are there, if any, between the average gay man and the average heterosexual man, or between the average lesbian and the average heterosexual woman? What about the personalities of persons (of either sex) who describe themselves as bisexual?

Relatively few studies have compared the personalities of heterosexual and nonheterosexual people. However, Lippa (2005) reviewed the results of several such studies that he had conducted using measures of the Big Five personality factors. The most noteworthy difference in personality between heterosexual and nonheterosexual people was in Openness to Experience. On average, gay men were nearly half of a standard

---

[4] Asexuality, as described in the previous section, is sometimes considered as a fourth sexual orientation, additional to heterosexual, gay/lesbian (homosexual), and bisexual, but for the purposes of this chapter we will consider it in relation to the Sexual Arousal dimension rather than to the Sexual Orientation dimension.

deviation higher than heterosexual men in Openness to Experience; similarly, lesbian women were nearly half of a standard deviation higher than heterosexual women.

Some recent research based on the HEXACO personality factors has also found that nonheterosexual persons on average have higher self-reported levels of Openness to Experience than do heterosexual persons. In data from a large online sample, Bogaert et al. (2017) found that, on average, bisexual persons had the highest levels of Openness to Experience, with bisexual men averaging about one-third of a standard deviation above heterosexual men, and with bisexual women averaging about one-half of a standard deviation above heterosexual women. Gay men and lesbians also averaged higher in Openness to Experience than did heterosexual persons of the same sex, but the differences were smaller, about one-fifth of a standard deviation unit in each case.

It is interesting to consider why it is that on average, nonheterosexual persons have higher levels of Openness to Experience than do heterosexual persons. Researchers do not yet know why this is so, but there are a few possible reasons (e.g., Bogaert et al., 2017). One possibility is that some of the same genetic or environmental influences that increase Openness to Experience also directly promote attractions to persons of the same sex. A second possibility is that having a nonheterosexual orientation—which involves departing from the social norm of heterosexuality—tends to lead one to develop a more unconventional, nonconforming personality. A third possibility is that having a higher level of Openness to Experience somehow makes a person some-what more likely to develop attractions to persons of the same sex. Yet another possibility, related to the previous one, is that persons higher in Openness to Experience are more likely to *identify* themselves as nonheterosexual, even if they have no greater tendency to have nonheterosexual attractions. To appreciate this possibility, consider two persons—one high in Openness and one low in Openness—who each feel a mild tendency to be attracted to people of the same sex. The person who is lower in Openness might be more likely to identify himself or herself as heterosexual (the statistically "conventional" orientation), whereas the person who is higher in Openness might be more likely to identify himself or herself as bisexual (a statistically "unconventional" orientation).

Some other noteworthy differences in average personality trait levels between heterosexual and nonheterosexual persons have also been found. Lippa (2008), using self-report data from a very large online sample, found that gay men averaged about one-third of a standard deviation unit higher than heterosexual men in Big Five Agreeableness and also in Big Five Neuroticism. Lippa also found that lesbian women averaged slightly lower than heterosexual women in these same two Big Five factors, but the difference was very small.

Recall from Chapter 3 that the Big Five Agreeableness and Neuroticism factors are both related to HEXACO Emotionality, such that persons higher in Big Five

Agreeableness and Neuroticism tend to be higher in HEXACO Emotionality. Given these relations, you might expect that the sexual orientation differences that have been found for Big Five Agreeableness and Neuroticism would also be found for HEXACO Emotionality. And this is in fact the case: Bogaert et al. (2017) found that gay men averaged about one-half of a standard deviation unit higher in Emotionality than did heterosexual men; also, lesbian women averaged about one-quarter of a standard deviation unit lower in Emotionality than did heterosexual women.

Recall also from Box 7.4 that men have lower levels of Emotionality, on average, than do women. In the data of Bogaert et al. (2017), the difference was about one full standard deviation unit. Taking this result together with the sexual orientation differences in Emotionality, the average gay man has an Emotionality level that is about halfway between those of the average heterosexual man and the average heterosexual woman; also, the average lesbian woman is in between the average gay man and the average heterosexual woman.[5,6]

Another area in which gay men and lesbians show average levels in between those of heterosexual men and heterosexual women is that of vocational interests (Lippa, 2002). On average, gay men tend to be more interested in traditionally "feminine" occupations (e.g., flight attendant) and less interested in traditionally "masculine" occupations (e.g., auto mechanic) than are heterosexual men. Conversely, lesbian women tend to be more interested in traditionally "masculine" occupations and less interested in traditionally "feminine" occupations than are heterosexual women.

13.3 ORIGINS OF VARIATION IN SEXUALITY: DEVELOPMENTAL STABILITY AND CHANGE, GENETIC AND ENVIRONMENTAL INFLUENCES, BIOLOGICAL BASES, AND EVOLUTION

For sexuality, as for personality characteristics, there is the important issue of "nature versus nurture": Are individual differences in sexuality due mainly to genetic differences or to environmental differences? Some researchers have tried to answer these questions

---

[5] Sexual orientation differences in Emotionality might also reflect, at least in part, differences between sexual orientation groups in the tendency to describe oneself in ways that conform to norms or stereotypes for persons of one's sex. For example, if heterosexual men feel motivated to describe themselves as low in Emotionality (as is consistent with the way men in general are perceived), but if gay men feel less motivated to describe themselves in this way, then this difference in motivations could produce differences between heterosexual and gay men in scores on self-report Emotionality scales, beyond any "real" differences in Emotionality (e.g., Bogaert et al., 2017). But there is not yet any evidence to support this possibility.

[6] In considering sexual orientation differences in personality trait levels, keep in mind that the large majority of persons are heterosexual. Therefore, even though nonheterosexual persons average higher in Openness to Experience than do heterosexual persons, most persons who are very high in Openness are heterosexual. Similarly, even though gay men average higher in Emotionality than do heterosexual men, most men who are very high in Emotionality are heterosexual.

using methods very similar to those used in investigating the heritability of personality characteristics. In addition, researchers have examined the question of *how* those genetic or environmental influences might affect sexuality: What are the biological variables that contribute to differences among people in sexual behavior, and how do they operate? And finally, the existence of these individual differences leads to the question of why the variation in sexuality would persist across evolutionary time: In other words, what have been the "trade-offs" associated with higher and lower levels of each dimension of sexuality, as judged in terms of reproductive success?[7,8]

13.4 SEXUAL AROUSAL

13.4.1 Genetic and Environmental Influences

Few, if any, studies have examined the heritability of sex drive or related characteristics. But a study by Dawood, Kirk, Bailey, Andrews, and Martin (2005) did investigate the heritability of orgasm frequency in women, using a large sample of Australian twin pairs. The heritability of orgasm frequency, as occurring during sexual intercourse or during sexual contact other than intercourse, was between .30 and .40, and the heritability of orgasm during masturbation was about .50. (Presumably, the latter figure is higher because it does not depend on interaction with a sex partner.) These results indicate that differences among women in orgasm frequency have an important genetic basis, and suggest that the broad dimension of Sexual Arousal is also likely to be influenced substantially by genetic differences.

13.4.2 Biological Bases

Next, let us take a quick look at possible biological bases of individual differences in Sexual Arousal. One way to understand the causes of variation in any aspect of sexuality is to find the causes of the personality characteristics that are strongly related to it. In the case of

---

[7] Perhaps surprisingly, there has been little research on the topics of developmental change and stability in sexuality-related variables. One exception, however, is a study by Schmitt et al. (2002), who obtained self-reports of Sexual Arousal—related variables from large samples of men and women of widely varying ages. Schmitt et al. found that women's sexual arousal reached a peak in the early 30s, whereas men's sexual arousal reached a peak in the late 20s (not in the late teens, as many might expect). Another exception, as noted later in this chapter, is the finding that some characteristics observable during childhood can predict sexual orientation in adulthood. It will be interesting to see the results of future studies that use a longitudinal design, assessing the major dimensions of sexuality at several intervals across a span of many years in the same sample of persons.

[8] Keep in mind that we are discussing about individual differences *within* a given society: If we instead consider differences *between* societies, such as those considered in Box 13.1, we might find rather different results. For example, cultural attitudes that influence sexuality can vary widely, and can change relatively quickly. These attitudes, and the environmental forces that produce them, are likely to be far more important than any genetic changes in explaining the trends in a society's sexuality. The same is true of changes in a society's levels of religiosity, as discussed in Box 12.1. For relations between sexuality and religiosity, see Box 13.2.

Box 13.1 Cross-Generational and Cross-National Differences in Sexuality

Sexuality can show wide variation across generations and across countries, much like the religious and political variables of the previous chapter (see Box 12.1). Some behaviors that are considered perfectly acceptable in one culture may be considered criminal in another; some attitudes that were almost universally shared in one generation may become very rare in the next. A few researchers have tried to study these differences systematically, to find out how (and how much) sexuality differs across times and places.

With regard to differences across generations or age cohorts, Wells and Twenge (2005) conducted a review of previous studies that had assessed the sexuality of young people in North America between the 1940s and late 1990s. They found that young people—especially young women—reported increasing favorability toward sexual activity throughout this period. For example, in the 1940s, only 12% of young women and 40% of young men indicated attitudes approving of premarital sex, but by the late 1990s, 73% of young women and 79% of young men indicated approval.

Regarding cross-national differences, Schmitt (2005) examined this topic in a study of 14,000 participants in 48 countries. Schmitt obtained self-reports on a scale designed to measure sociosexual orientation (i.e., "restricted" versus "unrestricted," as described before). The average levels of self-reported sociosexuality differed substantially across countries, and there were some fairly clear differences between regions of the world. Among the most "restricted" nations were those of East Asia, south Asia, and Africa; among the most "unrestricted" nations, in contrast, were several European countries. In between were nations in North America, Latin America, and the Middle East, as well as a few other European, Asian, and African countries. The differences between the most and least unrestricted countries were fairly large, amounting to more than one standard deviation unit. Interestingly, countries with higher fertility rates and higher childhood malnutrition tended to be more restricted overall. Schmitt interpreted this result as indicating that people tend to be more monogamous (and less promiscuous) when the demands of raising families are greater and more stressful.

One interesting aspect of the cross-national comparisons of sexuality involves the degree of sex differences observed in various countries. Within every one of the 48 countries studied by Schmitt (2005), men tended to be more "unrestricted" in self-reported attitudes than did women, with the difference averaging about three-quarters of a standard deviation unit. (This means that, in a typical country, men make up almost two-thirds of people who are more *unrestricted* than the "average" person, whereas women make up almost two-thirds of people who are more *restricted* than average.) Nations did differ, however, in the sizes of these sex differences, with somewhat smaller sex differences within countries that had greater equality of political status for men and women.

Sexual Arousal, the moderately strong relations with Extraversion suggest that the biological bases of that personality dimension would also be involved in Sexual Arousal. But as we discussed in Chapter 5, there is a great deal to be learned about the biological bases of personality, and therefore we still have much to learn about the causes of individual differences in Sexual Arousal.

Box 13.2 Religiosity and Sexuality

Most religions tend to disapprove of extramarital and premarital sex, and hence we might expect that religious persons would tend to be higher in Sexual Commitment or, in other words, more restricted in sociosexual orientation. Some investigations of the relations between religiosity and sexuality do indeed show a positive correlation between religiosity and Sexual Commitment. However, there is an interesting difference in results depending on whether *intrinsic* religiosity or *extrinsic* religiosity (recall Section 12.1.2) is examined (Leak, 1993; Rowatt & Schmitt, 2003; Wulf, Prentice, Hansum, Ferrar, & Spilka, 1984). People who report being "intrinsically" religious—in other words, people who value religious contemplation, prayer, and scriptures for their own sake—tend on average to be more sexually committed, that is, less promiscuous or less unfaithful. In contrast, people who report being "extrinsically" religious—in other words, people who value participation in religion as a way of gaining social status, social contacts, or even rewards from God—actually tend on average to be less sexually committed, that is, more promiscuous and more unfaithful. Thus, people who are genuinely religious are somewhat higher on average in Sexual Commitment, whereas people who are religious only for the purpose of "keeping up appearances" are somewhat lower on average in Sexual Commitment.

A study by Ben Zion et al. (2006) examined the relations between Sexual Arousal and levels of the neurotransmitter called dopamine (recall Section 5.2.1.1). This investigation compared the self-reported levels of Sexual Arousal of about 150 persons who had various alleles (i.e., different versions) of a gene that influences dopamine levels. The researchers found that individuals who had the alleles associated with higher dopamine tended to be higher in Sexual Arousal than did individuals who had the alleles associated with lower dopamine levels. These results suggest that dopamine may have an influence not only on personality characteristics—such as the novelty seeking—related traits suggested by Cloninger (see Section 5.2.1.1)—but also on this aspect of sexuality in particular. However, further research will be needed to verify these results.[9]

13.4.3 Evolutionary Function

These findings regarding the heritability and biological basis of Sexual Arousal also raise the challenging question of why genetic variation in this dimension would have been maintained throughout the human evolutionary past. Of course, persons having virtually no interest in sex might have been less likely to have had children, and so it is not difficult

---

[9] Another potential cause of individual differences in Sexual Arousal is testosterone, the hormone that is associated with many aspects of sexual behavior. In a later section of this chapter (Section 13.5.2), we will consider studies examining possible links between testosterone and number of sex partners. The findings reported there are discussed in terms of the biological bases of (low) Sexual Commitment, but those findings might also be relevant to Sexual Arousal.

to imagine that genes causing a very low level of sexual arousability would tend to disappear from the population. But why are some people genetically inclined to be highly sexually arousable, and others so much less so? There is no clear evidence on this question so far, but the correlations between Sexual Arousal and Extraversion, as described before, suggest that the evolutionary forces that maintain Sexual Arousal might be analogous to those for Extraversion (see Chapter 7). That is, persons with high levels of Sexual Arousal (or of Extraversion) were likely to have been more attractive to potential mates, and might therefore have had more opportunities to choose among potential mates. However, persons with high levels of Sexual Arousal (or of Extraversion) might also have had less time and energy for investment in work-related or other endeavors and might also have been the focus of hostility from competitors.

13.5 SEXUAL COMMITMENT (OR RESTRICTED VERSUS UNRESTRICTED SOCIOSEXUALITY)

13.5.1 Genetic and Environmental Influences

Some of the largest investigations of the heritability of sexuality-related variables have been conducted in a sample of 4900 Australian twins. Using data from this sample, Bailey, Kirk, Zhu, Dunne, and Martin (2000) examined the genetic and environmental influences on sociosexuality. (As discussed before, "restricted" sociosexuality corresponds to high Sexual Commitment, and "unrestricted" sociosexuality corresponds to low Sexual Commitment.) Their results showed that the members of an identical twin pair were usually similar to each other in their level of sociosexuality: Correlations were above .50, both for male twin pairs and for female twin pairs. For the members of fraternal twin pairs, there was still some similarity, but the correlations were weaker, with values in the .30s both for male twin pairs and for female twin pairs, and less than .20 for opposite-sex twin pairs.

Overall, the results of Bailey, Kirk, et al. (2000) suggested that individual differences in sociosexuality were almost 50% heritable, and that the environmental influences were due not to the common environment, but almost entirely to the unique environment. In other words, sociosexuality variation is not caused by aspects of the environment that differ *between* one family and the next; instead, it is caused by genetic variation and by aspects of the environment that differ across siblings *within* each family. (As you will recall from Chapter 6, a similar pattern of results is observed for personality characteristics. Recall also that estimates of unique environment influence might be overestimated due to the imperfect measurement of characteristics (see Section 6.3.6).)

13.5.2 Biological Bases

Now let us consider the possible biological bases of individual differences in Sexual Commitment. To some extent, we will understand the causes of variation in Sexual

Commitment by understanding the causes of variation in the major dimensions of personality. As described earlier in this chapter, Sexual Commitment is related to several aspects of personality; therefore, if we can find the biological bases of those personality dimensions, then we will have at least a partial knowledge of the biological bases of Sexual Commitment. But as noted in Chapter 5, the causes of personality variation are not yet well understood, and therefore the causes of variation in Sexual Commitment also remain obscure.

One biological variable that might be considered as a possible contributor to lower levels of Sexual Commitment is the "male" hormone testosterone. Some studies of young men have suggested at least modest links between higher levels of testosterone and higher numbers of sexual partners (e.g., Bogaert & Fisher, 1995; Halpern, Udry, Campbell, Suchindran, & Mason, 1994), and similar patterns might also exist among young women (Halpern, Udry, & Suchindran, 1997). Other research based on a larger sample of older adults found that testosterone levels showed a small positive link with lifetime number of opposite-sex sexual partners among men, although this association was nearly zero among women (Pollet, van der Meij, Cobey, & Buunk, 2011). These links with testosterone are somewhat weak, and might not be any stronger for sexuality in particular than for personality in general (recall Section 5.4.1).

Another biological variable that might be associated with lower levels of Sexual Commitment is the neurotransmitter called dopamine (see Chapter 5). One study (Garcia et al., 2010) of nearly 200 persons examined self-reports of promiscuity (specifically, "one-night stands") and of sexual infidelity in relation to those persons' different alleles of a gene that influences dopamine levels. [This study involved the same gene as that examined by Ben Zion et al. (2006) in their study of sexual arousal (described earlier in this chapter), but involved comparisons of different alleles.] The researchers found that individuals who had the alleles associated with higher dopamine levels reported somewhat more promiscuity and infidelity than did individuals who had alleles associated with lower dopamine levels. However, these findings will need to be tested in future research using larger participant samples.

13.5.3 Evolutionary Function

Findings regarding the heritability and the biological bases of Sexual Commitment (or of sociosexuality) lead to the question of why the variation in sociosexuality has been maintained during the course of human evolution. This question has been considered in some detail by researchers, who have considered both the differences between the sexes and the differences among members of each sex.

Most researchers have agreed that some sex difference in sociosexuality would be expected, because of evolutionary forces that would have favored a more restricted orientation in women during prehistoric times. The reason for this is simple: Women can become pregnant. Consider the consequences for a prehistoric woman who has sex with a man who is *not* emotionally committed to her: If she becomes pregnant, then she will undergo a nine-month pregnancy, followed by childbirth and then a prolonged period of breastfeeding and intensive child care. During this period, she may find it very difficult to obtain enough food and to defend herself and her child, and she is unlikely to get any help from the man who impregnated her. As a result, the woman will have paid the heavy biological cost of reproduction, but her child may be unlikely to survive, and her own life may also be at considerable risk.

In contrast, suppose that our prehistoric woman has sex with a man who *is* emotionally committed to her: She will then likely obtain much help from him in the form of food and protection, and the chances that she and her child will survive may be much higher. Thus, the likelihood of having surviving offspring would have been greater for women who were sociosexually restricted, and therefore a restricted orientation would have predominated in later generations.

Now let us consider the consequences for a prehistoric man who has sex with a woman despite not being in a committed relationship with her. If she becomes pregnant, he will likely feel little inclination to help her or the child. If the child does not survive, then there is no biological cost to the man, who can still impregnate another woman; if the child instead does survive, then the man achieves some reproductive success at no cost. Therefore, men who were sociosexually unrestricted would not have been at the same disadvantage as unrestricted women would have been, and the unrestricted orientation would not have become as rare among men as among women.

The reasoning just described may be largely accurate, but it leaves unexplained an important fact about sociosexuality: Despite the difference between the sexes, there is still wide variation within each sex, with many men being restricted and many women being unrestricted. Why should this be the case? One strong possibility is that frequency-dependent selection may be at work (recall Section 7.2.3 and Box 7.1), preserving variation in sociosexuality both among women and among men.

First, let us consider women. As explained before, natural selection would have tended to favor a more restricted sociosexuality among women than among men, because the biological cost of reproduction is so much greater for women than for men. But nevertheless, an unrestricted orientation might still have been advantageous for some women (see Gangestad & Simpson, 1990). Consider again a prehistoric woman who has sex with a man who is not emotionally committed to her. This unrestricted woman will not randomly choose any man to be her sex partner; instead, she will choose a man whom she (and probably most other women) would find to be attractive, physically and socially. If the woman becomes pregnant, she is unlikely to receive any help from the man, and there is some chance that the child will not survive. But there is also some chance that the child will survive, and, if so, that child will inherit the father's genes, and will thereby inherit, to some extent, his attractiveness. If the child happens to be a boy, then he may well grow up to be a man who is considered attractive by many women. As a result, the mother could end up having many grandchildren, because her son may end up impregnating many different women. In this way, being sociosexually unrestricted could have been a successful "strategy" for some women. However, this "sexy son" strategy (as it is fittingly named) would not work if too many women were to use it: If many women were unrestricted, then having a "sexy son" would no longer be so rare, and the unrestricted strategy would no longer possess any advantage. As a result, most women would still tend to be restricted in their sociosexuality.[10]

Now, let us consider men. As explained before, natural selection would not have tended to favor restricted sexuality so strongly among men as among women, because the biological cost of reproduction is so much less for men than for women. However, a restricted orientation could still have had some important advantages for at least some men. Consider a prehistoric man who develops an emotional commitment to a woman with whom he then has sex: If this woman becomes pregnant, he will help to feed and protect her and her child, and thus the man's child is more likely to survive. If this man had instead felt no such emotional attachment, he could have tried to have sex with various other women. But this is not guaranteed to be a successful "strategy": There may be much competition from other men for sexual access to women, and even if this man has some success in mating, he might not have any surviving children. Thus, for many men, a sociosexually restricted tendency would have been more successful. In this way frequency-dependent selection would maintain variation among men in sociosexual orientation: Some men would follow a restricted strategy, and others would follow an unrestricted strategy.

Finally, it is also possible that sociosexuality would be governed by the "fluctuating optimum" level of this trait, as influenced by features of the environment. For example, in environments in which it is very difficult for a woman to have surviving children without the help of a man, a more restricted sociosexuality would be favored. In contrast, in environments in which it is somewhat easier for a woman to have surviving children without the help of a man, a more unrestricted sociosexuality would be favored.

13.6 SEXUAL ORIENTATION

13.6.1 Genetic and Environmental Influences and Biological Bases

13.6.1.1 Estimating the Heritability of Sexual Orientation

Now let us consider the origins of sexual orientation: Are the differences between heterosexual and homosexual persons due mainly to genetic or to environmental differences

---

[10] The word strategy is given in quotation marks because it is not meant to suggest any conscious planning. That is, women (or men) would not have chosen their level of sociosexuality by deliberately calculating their likely reproductive success. On this point, note that the "sexy son" hypothesis was developed originally to explain the behavior of female *birds*, not of women (Weatherhead & Robertson, 1979).

between them? In other words, are some people "born straight" and others "born gay" and "born lesbian," or are people's sexual orientations determined by experiences during development? One difficulty in addressing this question is that, as discussed before, sexual orientation has a distribution much different from that of most other individual differences. As noted earlier in this chapter, slightly more than 90% of people describe themselves as completely heterosexual; as a result, even when researchers obtain a fairly large sample of research participants taken from the general population, they usually have only a small subsample of participants who have nonheterosexual orientations. With these small samples, it is difficult to have confidence in estimates of the heritability of sexual orientation.

Researchers have tried to obtain larger samples of participants for sexual orientation research by advertising their investigations toward gay and lesbian persons who have twin siblings of the same sex. This approach has been successful in increasing the sample sizes, but it does create a potential problem: A gay or lesbian twin is somewhat more likely to participate in such a research project if his or her twin has the same sexual orientation. Because twins with *different* sexual orientations will therefore tend to be underrepresented, the researchers may get a misleadingly high estimate of the extent to which twins are similar in sexual orientation.

Some early studies that used the above approach for obtaining participants had found that the heritability of sexual orientation was rather high, but these findings were probably overestimates. More recently, researchers have avoided this problem by studying large random samples of twins. These studies, as conducted in Australia (Bailey, Dunne, et al., 2000), the United States (Kendler, Thornton, Gilman, & Kessler, 2000), and Sweden (Langström, Rahman, Carlström, & Lichtenstein, 2010), have found somewhat varying results. However, they have all found that identical twins are somewhat more likely to have the same sexual orientation than are fraternal twins, and this difference seems to be stronger among men than among women. (Note that even in the case of identical twins, most twins who are gay or lesbian have a twin who is *not* gay or lesbian; however, the proportion of gay or lesbian twins whose twin *is* gay or lesbian is considerably higher than the proportion of gay or lesbian persons in the general population.)

These findings suggest some genetic basis to sexual orientation, particularly men's sexual orientation; for women, the common environment might also be involved. For both men and women, however, much of the variance in sexual orientation appears to be due to the unique environment, rather than to genetic or to common environmental influences. It is not yet known, however, exactly which features of the unique environment are responsible.

13.6.1.2 Development of Sexual Orientation? "Exotic Becomes Erotic"
In one of the twin-based studies described in the previous section, the researchers also examined the heritability of a characteristic that is closely linked to sexual orientation.

Bailey, Dunne, et al. (2000) asked the twins to recall some aspects of their behavior during childhood, to examine each individual's level of *childhood gender nonconformity*. Specifically, the researchers asked the participants to indicate their preferences, as children, for activities that are typically preferred by boys and by girls. For example, boy-typical activities include playing with toy trucks or blocks or playing rough-and-tumble sports, whereas girl-typical activities include playing with dolls and with toy clothes. If a child tends to prefer the activities that are more typical of children of the opposite sex, then this is a case of childhood gender nonconformity.

Previous investigations have found that childhood gender nonconformity is strongly correlated with sexual orientation in later life, as boys who prefer girl-typical activities are likely to become gay men, and girls who prefer boy-typical activities are somewhat likely to become lesbian women. (The link is not quite as strong among women as among men.) In the Australian twin study of Bailey, Dunne, et al. (2000), the same pattern of results was found: Among men who reported a homosexual orientation, levels of childhood gender nonconformity were about two standard deviation units higher than among men who reported a heterosexual orientation. (Men who were "bisexual," having a partly heterosexual and partly homosexual orientation, were about halfway in between in their levels of childhood gender nonconformity.) For women, the same pattern of differences was observed, but the effect sizes were somewhat smaller.

In studying heritability, childhood gender nonconformity is an easier variable to examine than is sexual orientation. This is because, even though most people behave largely in a gender-typical way during childhood, there exist a substantial fraction of people who have at least moderate levels of childhood gender nonconformity. In the study by Bailey, Dunne, et al. (2000), the correlations between twins' levels of childhood gender nonconformity were fairly high for identical twins, but rather low for fraternal twins. Overall, those results suggest that the heritability of childhood gender nonconformity would be fairly high, probably close to 50%. Thus, it appears that childhood gender nonconformity—one of the best predictors of a person's eventual sexual orientation—is substantially heritable, even though the evidence regarding the heritability of sexual orientation itself is less clear.

The finding that childhood gender nonconformity has a substantial genetic component is of some importance for an interesting theory of how sexual orientation develops. Childhood gender nonconformity plays a major role in what is called the "exotic becomes erotic" theory of sexual orientation (Bem, 1996). According to this theory, most children engage mainly in activities that are typical of their own sex, and thus tend to play and associate with children of the same sex as themselves. Bem suggested that, when children reach puberty, they then develop a sexual attraction toward the strange and unfamiliar "other" children: Boys become attracted to girls, and girls become attracted to boys. In this sense, members of the opposite sex appear to be mysterious and "exotic," and when puberty arrives, this becomes sexually attractive, or "erotic."

But what happens if a child is involved mainly in activities that are typical of the opposite sex? According to Bem (1996), people differ in the hormonal and other physiological characteristics that influence their level of male- or female-typical behavior during childhood. Depending on these hormonal and other causes, some boys will tend to prefer "girlish" activities, and some girls will tend to prefer "boyish" activities. As a result, the boys with girlish interests will tend to play with girls, and the girls with boyish interests will tend to play with boys. When puberty arrives, these gender-nonconforming persons will tend to see members of the same sex as the "exotic" ones, and will thus develop an "erotic" attraction toward them. That is, the boys who had girlish interests will now be attracted to other boys, and the girls who had boyish interests will now be attracted to other girls.

An alternative hypothesis is also plausible: Perhaps childhood gender nonconformity is inherited genetically and is influenced by the same genes that, after puberty, will cause a homosexual attraction. But the results reported by Bailey, Dunne, et al. (2000) are at least consistent with Bem's suggestion that childhood gender nonconformity is genetically influenced, and that it then leads to a homosexual orientation in adulthood.

13.6.1.3 Development of Sexual Orientation? Number of Older Brothers

In addition to the possibility of genetic influences on sexual orientation, there is some evidence that some features of the environment are also involved, at least as far as men's sexual orientation is concerned. But the aspect of the environment that has shown the clearest relation with male sexual orientation is not one that you might expect. According to a series of studies (e.g., Blanchard & Bogaert, 1996; Bogaert, 2003), the more older brothers a man has, the more likely he is to be gay. This does not mean that most men with several older brothers will be gay; in fact, most such men are heterosexual. But in several large studies, results have shown that the chances of a man having a homosexual orientation are about 38% higher for every older brother that he has. If, for example, the chances of being gay are 3% for a man with no older brothers, then the chances of being gay would be about 15% for a man with five older brothers.[11] According to other calculations (Cantor, Blanchard, Paterson, & Bogaert, 2002), about one in seven gay men have acquired their sexual orientation through the influence of the number of older brothers.

The existence of this effect raises an obvious question: *Why* is the number of older brothers associated with sexual orientation in men? One important clue is that the effect of older brothers on men's sexual orientation applies only in the case of *biological* older brothers, and not in the case of nonbiological older brothers, such as adopted brothers or stepbrothers (Bogaert, 2006). The most likely explanation of the relation between

---

[11] This value is calculated as $.03 \times (1.38)^5 = .03 \times 5.00 = .15$.

number of older brothers and male sexual orientation involves the womb environment. According to this hypothesis (e.g., Blanchard & Bogaert, 1996; Bogaert, 2003), some substances that are involved in the development of a male fetus may be recognized by the mother's body as "foreign" substances. If another male fetus is conceived at the start of a subsequent pregnancy, then the presence of this foreign substance will cause the mother's body to release antibodies that tend to counteract the effects of these substances. As a result of the antibodies, these substances involved in male fetal development might not operate at full strength, and the development of a "male-typical" brain—including the features that would later produce a heterosexual orientation—may not fully occur. This effect would become stronger with each additional pregnancy involving a son, and the likelihood that a male fetus would develop a homosexual orientation would increase each time.

One important aspect of the preceding hypothesis is that the mother's body would have no such reaction to a female fetus, because the substances involved in the development of a female fetus would not be recognized as foreign. As a result, the number of older sisters would not be expected to relate to the development of a homosexual orientation among women. This is consistent with the evidence: A woman's likelihood of being lesbian is unrelated to the number of older sisters that she has (e.g., Bogaert, 2003). Apparently, the effect of having older siblings of the same sex on one's sexual orientation is observed for men only.

The influence of number of older brothers on male sexual orientation can account for the sexual orientation of about one in seven gay men. However, this leaves unexplained the sexual orientation of most gay men, as well as that of all lesbians. Also, as noted earlier, the fact that even identical twins are often different from each other in sexual orientation indicates that genetic influences are unlikely to account for all of the variation in sexual orientation. This raises the question of what additional variables could explain sexual orientation, and one controversial explanation is that sexual orientation might be in some way transmitted, perhaps by a virus or a bacterium that does not cause any recognized physical or mental illness. Some researchers (see Hooper, 1999) have suggested that this is the most likely explanation of male exclusive homosexuality (i.e., attraction to men only, as opposed to bisexuality, in which there is attraction to both sexes).

13.6.2 Evolutionary Function

The finding of some genetic influence on sexual orientation is in some sense surprising, because one would expect that any genes that tend to produce an exclusively homosexual orientation—especially in men—would soon be eliminated by natural selection. For example, the results of one study suggest that gay men have only about one-fifth the number of biological children that heterosexual men do (Bell & Weinberg, 1978).

Perhaps this number would have been considerably higher during earlier eras, when social pressures might have caused more gay men to have gotten married to women and to have had children, but it still seems likely that gay men would have had substantially lower "reproductive success" than heterosexual men would have had.[12] Therefore, the genes causing male homosexuality would have become less and less frequent with each generation, and would have soon disappeared altogether.

Alternatively, it has been proposed that even though gay men tend to have fewer children than do straight men, it might also be the case that the *relatives* of gay men have more children than do the relatives of straight men. In other words, genes causing homosexuality (and, hence, low reproductive success for gay men) might also cause gay men's relatives to have high reproductive success, therefore balancing out the effects of the genes on biological fitness. How might this work?

One possibility is that gay men might contribute heavily to the well-being of their siblings and to their siblings' children. However, any such tendency for gay men to be helpful brothers or uncles would have to be very strong, to compensate for the decreased number of children fathered by gay men. Moreover, some evidence suggests that gay men do not contribute any more assistance to their siblings than straight men do, whether in terms of money, child care, or emotional support (Bobrow & Bailey, 2001). But some research from the Pacific island of Samoa has suggested that, at least in some traditional societies, gay men might in fact be particularly helpful as uncles (Vasey & VanderLaan, 2010). In Samoa, there are men known as *fa'afafine* who are considered as a "third gender," and who would be considered gay in Western countries. Those men apparently do give considerable help to their siblings' children; for example, by giving money and doing frequent babysitting. Further research will likely examine whether other traditional societies also have a similar category of men whose sexual orientation is gay and who invest heavily in their nieces and nephews. To the extent that these "avuncular" (uncle-like) tendencies in gay men would lead to their siblings having more surviving children, this would compensate for some part of the fitness cost of exclusive male homosexuality.

Another possibility is that the same genes that sometimes cause male homosexuality may also cause relatives of gay men to have more children than do the relatives of straight men. Some research studies have found that the mothers and aunts of gay men have about 33% more children than do the mothers and aunts of straight men (e.g., Camperio Ciani, Corna, & Capiluppi, 2004). It is not yet clear exactly why the female relatives of gay men tend to have more children, and this effect is not always found (Blanchard, 2012), but this tendency would help to make up at least in part for the tendency of

---

[12] For women, the link between an exclusively homosexual orientation and reduced reproductive success might not have been so strong, because until relatively recently women would likely not have had as much choice about getting married and having children. For this reason, the persistence in women of some heritable tendency toward homosexuality is less surprising.

gay men themselves to have very few children. Given the uncertainties with the above hypotheses, however, it seems that researchers have not yet answered the question of how the heritable variation in men's sexual orientation has been maintained. In addition, the smaller amount of heritable variation in women's sexual orientation also remains to be explained.

13.7 SUMMARY AND CONCLUSIONS

Let us summarize the major points of this chapter. First, research on the structure of individual differences in sexuality suggests at least three major aspects of sexuality, which can be called Sexual Arousal, Sexual Commitment, and Sexual Orientation. These aspects have distinctive patterns of correlations with dimensions of personality: Sexual Arousal is associated with Extraversion; Sexual Commitment is associated with several personality dimensions (in the HEXACO framework, Conscientiousness, Agreeableness, Emotionality, and Honesty—Humility); Sexual Orientation is associated with Openness to Experience (such that nonheterosexual persons tend to be higher in Openness) and also with Emotionality (such that gay men and lesbians both tend to be intermediate between heterosexual men and heterosexual women). In addition, Sexual Orientation is also related to vocational interests that show differences between men and women in general (again with gay men and lesbians having intermediate levels).

With regard to the origins of individual differences in sexuality, the biological bases of these dimensions are not yet well understood. Investigations of the heritability of these variables do suggest some genetic influences for all aspects of sexuality. It is possible that genetic influences on Sexual Orientation operate through childhood gender nonconformity, and it appears that Sexual Orientation in men is influenced by an environmental variable, specifically, the number of biological older brothers that a man has. Finally, speculations on the evolutionary origins of variation in sexuality dimensions are similar in nature to those for personality dimensions more generally, but there is greater uncertainty with regard to the possible evolutionary basis for the heritable variation in Sexual Orientation.

CONCLUSIONS

We now come to the end of our exploration of personality traits and related individual differences. In surveying this field of study, we have examined a wide variety of questions, and we can now summarize some of the important answers that have been gained from personality research, as well as some of the unanswered questions to be resolved in future study.

WHAT WE HAVE LEARNED SO FAR

We Can Describe People Meaningfully by Their Levels of Various Personality Traits

This point would seem obvious to most people, but there was a time when many psychologists believed that the whole idea of a personality trait was mistaken. As discussed in Chapter 2, some researchers suggested that the differences among people in their behavior showed very little consistency across situations. But it was soon demonstrated that there is a great deal of consistency when we consider people's behavior "in the big picture," as aggregated or averaged across many situations. For example, the people who are the most organized in one situation might not be the most organized in another, but if you observe people's overall pattern of behavior across a wide variety of situations, you can easily tell that some people are more organized than others are.

The fact that people can be described in terms of personality trait levels allows us to do two very important things. One is to summarize a given individual's personality in some detail by assessing his or her levels of various different traits or characteristics. Another is to study the causes and the consequences of personality variation. For example, the relations between levels of a personality trait and some important life outcome variable could show us something about the practical significance of that aspect of personality. In the same way, the relations between levels of a personality trait and some biological variable (whether a neurotransmitter, hormone, or brain structure) could give us some hints about the origins of that dimension of personality.

We Can Measure People's Personality Trait Levels Fairly Accurately Using Self- and Observer Report Personality Inventories

Under at least some conditions, self-report personality inventories can provide reasonably valid assessment of people's relative levels of various personality traits. When self-report scales are administered in anonymous research settings, the scale scores show substantial convergent correlations with scores on observer report scales and with some objectively measured criteria. Moreover, when observer reports of the same person are given by two different observers who know that person well, the correlations between those observer reports are moderately large, even when those observers do not know each other. Ideally, personality would be assessed most accurately using a combination of self-reports and several observer reports, but even self-reports alone can be fairly good indicators of people's personalities.

Interestingly, self-report measures of personality retain at least some of their validity even when people provide those self-reports under conditions that tend to encourage unrealistically desirable responses, such as a job application. The problem of how to measure personality accurately in these "high-stakes" situations does pose a challenge for researchers. But for the purposes of psychological research, and even for some purposes involving practical decision making, the use of self-reports and observer reports works rather well.

Personality Traits (and People's Personalities) Can Be Summarized in Terms of Six Broad Dimensions

Although the domain of personality characteristics contains many hundreds of traits, a rough summary of personality can be given in terms of six broad dimensions, or factors. (Until recently, the most widely accepted view has been that there are five major factors of personality, but much recent research has indicated that there are in fact six such factors.) One implication of this finding is that we can understand each personality trait, in considerable part, as an aspect of one of these broad dimensions of personality, or as a blend of two or more such dimensions. Another implication is that the personality of any given individual can be understood, in broad outline, as a combination of his or her levels of each of these dimensions. Because the number of combinations is very large, a great deal of information about an individual can be expressed using only half a dozen broad factors.

The identification of these major personality dimensions is useful, because it makes it feasible to assess people's personalities in research and in applied settings. But we should be careful not to oversimplify personality. Personality traits are not perfectly summarized in terms of the major factors, and as a result, some important outcome variables are predicted better by specific traits than by the more general dimensions to which those traits belong. Also, even though we can obtain a good overview of an individual's personality by assessing his or her levels of the broad factors, this obviously cannot capture every detail of his or her personality.

Some Important Individual Differences—Including Some Aspects of Mental Ability, of Religiosity, and of Sexuality—Are Only Modestly Related to Personality Characteristics

The major dimensions of personality are related to individual differences in a variety of other areas of human individual differences, such as mental abilities, religious or political views, and sexuality. For example, higher levels of the Openness to Experience factor are associated to some extent with higher verbal ability, with higher spiritual religiosity (and lower religious fundamentalism), and with higher likelihood of having a nonheterosexual orientation. But relations such as these are not particularly strong, and so we cannot simply describe these characteristics as being expressions of the major personality factors. Instead, it appears that these other individual differences are important variables in their own right. Therefore, a complete portrait of an individual's psychological characteristics would need to include—in addition to the personality factors—measurements of mental abilities, religious or political views, and sexuality.

Personality Characteristics are Moderately Heritable, and Are Not Much Influenced by the Common Environment

Perhaps the most surprising results observed in personality research have come from studies of the heritability of personality characteristics. One major finding of those investigations is that genetic differences account for as much as two-thirds of the personality variation among people.

A related finding of these studies involves the nature of environmental influences on personality: Persons raised in the same household tend to have only slightly more similar personalities than do persons raised in different households. This indicates that personality is influenced more strongly by the unique environment (i.e., aspects of the environment that differ among siblings within the same family) than by the common environment (i.e., aspects of the environment that differ between families). Apparently, an individual's levels of the various personality traits are not much influenced by, for example, the socioeconomic status or the child-rearing style of his or her parents. This result was a surprise to many researchers who had assumed that personality would be heavily influenced by the household in which one was raised.

Somewhat different results have been observed for mental ability and religiosity, which do show a substantial influence of the common environment, especially during earlier periods of development. However, the heritability of mental ability increases, and the influence of the common environment on mental ability decreases, as individuals progress from childhood to adulthood. A similar pattern of change occurs slightly later in the life span for religiosity, whereby genetic effects increase and common environment effects decrease between adolescence and later adulthood.

Personality and Other Psychological Individual Differences Are Moderately Predictive of Some Important Life Outcomes

Another conclusion that we can draw from research on personality and other individual differences is that these characteristics do matter, in the sense of being at least modestly related to some important life outcomes. For example, persons who are generally achievement oriented do tend to get high marks in school and good performance ratings on the job. Similarly, persons who are generally dishonest and impulsive do tend to commit more delinquent and criminal acts. Also, persons who are impulsive and unstable are more likely to abuse drugs or alcohol, and persons who are hostile and dominant are more likely to suffer from heart disease. In addition, persons who are generally cheerful and calm tend to report higher levels of life satisfaction.

Several other important examples involve the g factor of general mental ability, which (as approximated by IQ test scores) is a strong predictor not only of school performance but also of job performance; in addition, mental ability is also related to health and longevity and to law-abidingness. Of course, individual differences such as personality factors and mental ability cannot predict these outcomes with extremely high accuracy, because there are so many other variables that are involved. But it is clear that a person's levels of various psychological characteristics have a considerable influence on the likelihood of many life outcomes.

Personality Does Not Predict Which People Will Marry Each Other, But Some Other Psychological Individual Differences Do

Despite the importance of personality as a predictor of life outcomes, it does not appear to be a good predictor of how married couples are formed. Some personality traits show a modest degree of similarity between spouses, but for most personality traits, the personalities of wives and husbands are neither similar nor opposite. However, marital satisfaction is related both to one's own personality and also to that of one's spouse: In general, people who are agreeable, emotionally stable, and conscientious tend to be happier with their marriages and also to have spouses who feel the same way.

Other psychological variables, unlike personality characteristics, do show considerable "assortative mating"—that is, substantial similarity between the spouses of a given couple. In general, spouses tend to have fairly similar levels of verbal (but not mathematical) ability, and also to have very similar levels of religiosity and of political conservatism.

WHAT WE HAVE YET TO LEARN

The Biological Bases of Personality Are Not Yet Well Understood (and Neither Is the Development or Evolution of Personality)

During the second half of the 20th century, many researchers investigated the biological bases of personality, examining the links of brain structures, neurotransmitters, and hormones with levels of various personality traits. These studies have revealed some interesting findings, but have also indicated that the biological bases of personality are very complicated; moreover, the levels of various neurotransmitters and hormones appear to be only weakly related to personality trait levels. Thus far, we do not have a good understanding of which biological variables influence which personality characteristics, or of how that influence works.

Identifying the biological bases of personality will be an important task for future personality researchers. In some related domains of human individual differences, there has already been some encouraging progress. With regard to mental ability, researchers have identified some biological variables (such as brain size) that are modestly correlated with IQ. We might hope to see similar progress during the next few decades in identifying the bases of the major personality dimensions. But it will likely be some time (if ever) before we can predict an individual's personality trait levels with any accuracy by measuring the levels of some biological variables—that is, of some substances or some kinds of activity—within his or her brain or body.

There also remains a great deal to learn about the development of personality during childhood. We noted in Chapter 4 the challenges involved in measuring personality during early childhood. This makes it difficult to identify the extent to which the major dimensions of personality—as observed in adulthood, adolescence, or even later childhood—emerge in the very early stages of life. For example, is it meaningful to describe, say, 3-year-olds in terms of dimensions such as Openness to Experience or Honesty—Humility? If so, in what ways are those dimensions expressed at that early age? To what extent are individual differences in personality trait levels stable between early childhood and later life?

Some similar questions exist with regard to the evolutionary origins of personality. There has recently been an increase in research on the personalities of animals, and future work may help us to identify how the various personality dimensions emerged during the distant evolutionary past. Other research that will help us to understand why people differ in personality involves examining people's behavior in games designed to simulate the costs and benefits of various personality trait levels.

The Specific Features of the Unique Environment That Influence Personality Trait Levels Are Not Yet Known

As noted earlier in this chapter, the research evidence suggests that environmental influences on personality are more of the "unique" (i.e., nonshared or within family) variety than of the "common" (i.e., shared or between family) variety. But this leaves open the question as to which particular aspects of the unique environment actually influence personality. Some researchers have suggested that an individual's birth order—that is, his or her age rank among the siblings raised in the same household—might influence personality even in adulthood; however, the existing evidence suggests that this has only a weak effect on personality trait levels. (Birth order is, however, somewhat related to mental ability.) Another hypothesis is that peer influences have a lasting influence on personality, but it is difficult to measure peer influences, and the little existing research suggests a modest effect (if any) of the peer environment on personality. More research will be needed to establish how strong these influences are, and to identify any other aspects of the unique environment that might influence personality. And some of the unique environment influence on personality might not come from any specific cause at all, being instead the result of random variation in early development.

FINAL REMARKS

The science of personality is a special field of study, because personality—unlike the vast majority of the sciences—is a subject that is so much a part of our own lives as human beings. We all have a personality, we all observe each other's personality, we all communicate about personality, and we all make decisions based on personality. Because personality seems so specially and uniquely human, this tends to make us think of it as something beyond scientific study. But the story of this book has been that it is possible to investigate personality in a systematic way—and thus to answer some fundamental questions that, until recently, were considered suitable only for philosophical speculation.

REFERENCES

Abrahamson, A. C., Baker, L. A., & Caspi, A. (2002). Rebellious teens? Genetic and environmental influences on the social attitudes of adolescents. *Journal of Personality and Social Psychology, 83*, 1392–1408.

Ackerman, P. L., Bowen, K. R., Beier, M. E., & Kanfer, R. (2001). Determinants of individual differences and gender differences in knowledge. *Journal of Educational Psychology, 93*, 797–825.

Ackerman, P. L., & Heggestad, E. D. (1997). Intelligence, personality, and interests: Evidence for overlapping traits. *Psychological Bulletin, 121*, 219–245.

Adorno, T. W., Frenkel-Brunswik, E., Levinson, D. J., & Sanford, R. N. (1950). *The authoritarian personality*. New York: Harper and Row.

Aghababaei, N., Wasserman, J. A., & Nannini, D. (2014). The religious person revisited: Cross-cultural evidence from the HEXACO model of personality structure. *Mental Health, Religion, and Culture, 17*, 24–29.

Allgaier, K., Zettler, I., Göllner, R., Hilbig, B. E., & Trautwein, U. (2013). Development and first validation of the HEXACO elementary school inventory (HEXACO-ESI). In *Stellenbosch, South Africa: Paper presented at the 1st world conference on personality*.

Allport, G. W. (1937). *Personality: A psychological interpretation*. New York: Holt, Rinehart, & Winston.

Allport, G. W., & Odbert, H. S. (1936). Trait-names: A psycho-lexical study. *Psychological Monographs, 47* (1, Whole No. 211).

Altemeyer, B. (1981). *Right-wing authoritarianism*. Winnipeg: University of Manitoba Press.

Altemeyer, B. (1988). *Enemies of freedom: Understanding right-wing authoritarianism*. San Francisco: Jossey-Bass.

Altemeyer, B. (1996). *The authoritarian specter*. Cambridge, MA: Harvard University Press.

Altemeyer, B. (1998). The other "authoritarian personality.". In M. P. Zanna (Ed.), *Advances in experimental social psychology* (Vol. 30, pp. 47–92). San Diego: Academic Press.

Altemeyer, B., & Hunsberger, B. (1997). *Amazing conversions: Why some turn to faith and others abandon religion*. New York: Prometheus.

Aluja, A., Kuhlman, M., & Zuckerman, M. (2010). Development of the Zuckerman–Kuhlman–Aluja Personality Questionnaire (ZKA–PQ): A factor/facet version of the Zuckerman–Kuhlman Personality Questionnaire (ZKPQ). *Journal of Personality Assessment, 92*, 416–431.

American Psychiatric Association. (2013). *Diagnostic and statistical manual of mental disorders: DSM-5*. Washington, DC: American Psychiatric Association.

Anderson, C., John, O. P., Keltner, D., & Kring, A. M. (2001). Who attains social status? Effects of personality and physical attractiveness in social groups. *Journal of Personality and Social Psychology, 81*, 116–132.

Anusic, I., Schimmack, U., Pinkus, R., & Lockwood, P. (2009). The nature and structure of correlations among Big Five ratings: The halo-alpha-beta model. *Journal of Personality and Social Psychology, 97*, 1142–1156.

Asendorpf, J. B. (2003). Head-to-head comparison of the predictive validity of personality types and dimensions. *European Journal of Personality, 17*, 327–346.

Ashton, M. C., Danso, H. A., Maio, G. R., Esses, V. M., Bond, M. H., & Keung, D. K.-Y. (2005). Two dimensions of political attitudes and their individual difference correlates: A cross-cultural perspective. In R. M. Sorrentino, D. Cohen, J. Olson, & M. Zanna (Eds.), *Culture and social behavior: The Ontario symposium* (pp. 1–29). Hillsdale, NJ: Erlbaum.

Ashton, M. C., de Vries, R. E., & Lee, K. (2016). Trait variance and response style variance in the scales of the Personality Inventory for *DSM-5* (PID-5). *Journal of Personality Assessment, 99*, 192–203.

Ashton, M. C., Jackson, D. N., Helmes, E., & Paunonen, S. V. (1998). Joint factor analysis of the Personality Research Form and the Jackson Personality Inventory: Comparisons with the Big Five. *Journal of Research in Personality, 32*, 243–250.

Ashton, M. C., & Lee, K. (2001). A theoretical basis for the major dimensions of personality. *European Journal of Personality, 15*, 327–353.

Ashton, M. C., & Lee, K. (2005a). A defence of the lexical approach to the study of personality structure. *European Journal of Personality, 19*, 5—24.

Ashton, M. C., & Lee, K. (2005b). Honesty—humility, the Big Five, and the Five-Factor Model. *Journal of Personality, 73*, 1321—1353.

Ashton, M. C., & Lee, K. (2007). Empirical, theoretical, and practical advantages of the HEXACO model of personality structure. *Personality and Social Psychology Bulletin, 11*, 150—166.

Ashton, M. C., & Lee, K. (2009a). The HEXACO-60: A short measure of the major dimensions of personality. *Journal of Personality Assessment, 91*, 340—345.

Ashton, M. C., & Lee, K. (2009b). An investigation of personality types within the HEXACO personality framework. *Journal of Individual Differences, 30*, 181—187.

Ashton, M. C., & Lee, K. (2010). Trait and source factors in HEXACO-PI-R self- and observer reports. *European Journal of Personality, 24*, 278—289.

Ashton, M. C., & Lee, K. (2016). Age trends in HEXACO-PI-R self-reports. *Journal of Research in Personality, 64*, 102—111.

Ashton, M. C., Lee, K., de Vries, R. E., Hendrickse, J., & Born, M. P. (2012). The maladaptive personality traits of the Personality Inventory for DSM-5 (PID-5) in relation to the HEXACO personality factors and schizotypy/dissociation. *Journal of Personality Disorders, 26*, 641—659.

Ashton, M. C., Lee, K., & Goldberg, L. R. (2004a). A hierarchical analysis of 1,710 English personality-descriptive adjectives. *Journal of Personality and Social Psychology, 87*, 707—721.

Ashton, M. C., Lee, K., Goldberg, L. R., & de Vries, R. E. (2009). Higher-order factors of personality: Do they exist? *Personality and Social Psychology Review, 13*, 79—91.

Ashton, M. C., Lee, K., & Paunonen, S. V. (2002). What is the central feature of extraversion? Social attention versus reward sensitivity. *Journal of Personality and Social Psychology, 83*, 245—252.

Ashton, M. C., Lee, K., Perugini, M., Szarota, P., de Vries, R. E., Di Blas, L., et al. (2004b). A six-factor structure of personality-descriptive adjectives: Solutions from psycholexical studies in seven languages. *Journal of Personality and Social Psychology, 86*, 356—366.

Ashton, M. C., Lee, K., Vernon, P. A., & Jang, K. L. (2000). Fluid intelligence, crystallized intelligence, and the openness/intellect factor. *Journal of Research in Personality, 34*, 198—207.

Ashton, S. G., & Goldberg, L. R. (1973). In response to Jackson's challenge: The comparative validity of personality scales constructed by the external (empirical) strategy and scales developed intuitively by experts, novices, and laymen. *Journal of Research in Personality, 7*, 1—20.

Aylward, G. P., Pfeiffer, S. I., Wright, A., & Verhulst, S. J. (1988). Outcome studies of low birth weight infants published in the last decade: A meta-analysis. *Journal of Pediatrics, 115*, 515—520.

Baier, C. J., & Wright, B. R. E. (2001). "If you love me, keep my commandments": A meta-analysis of the effect of religion on crime. *Journal of Research in Crime and Delinquency, 38*, 3—21.

Bailey, J. M., Dunne, M. P., & Martin, N. G. (2000a). Genetic and environmental influences on sexual orientation and its correlates in an Australian twin sample. *Journal of Personality and Social Psychology, 78*, 524—536.

Bailey, J. M., Kirk, K. M., Zhu, G., Dunne, M. P., & Martin, N. G. (2000b). Do individual differences in sociosexuality represent genetic or environmentally contingent strategies? Evidence from the Australian twin registry. *Journal of Personality and Social Psychology, 78*, 537—545.

Balakrishnan, T. R., & Chen, J. (1990). Religiosity, nuptiality and reproduction in Canada. *Canadian Review of Sociology and Anthropology, 27*, 316—340.

Bar-On, R. (1997). *The Bar-On Emotional Quotient Inventory: A test of emotional intelligence*. Toronto: Multi-Health Systems.

Barrick, M. R., & Mount, M. K. (1991). The Big Five personality dimensions and job performance: A meta-analysis. *Personnel Psychology, 44*, 1—26.

Barrick, M. R., Mount, M. K., & Gupta, R. (2003). Meta-analysis of the relationship between the five-factor model of personality and Holland's occupational types. *Personnel Psychology, 56*, 45—74.

Bastian, V., Burns, N. R., & Nettelbeck, T. (2005). Emotional intelligence predicts life skills, but not as well as personality or cognitive abilities. *Personality and Individual Differences, 39*, 1135—1145.

Baumgarten, F. (1933). *Die Charaktereigenschaften* [The character traits.] (Whole No. 1). Bern: A. Francke. *Beiträge zur Charakter- und Persönlichkeitsforschung*, (Whole No. 1). Bern: A. Francke.

Beck, A. T., Freeman, A., & Davis, D. D. (2004). *Cognitive therapy of personality disorders*. New York: Guilford.

Bell, A. P., & Weinberg, M. (1978). *Homosexualities: A study of diversity among men and women*. New York: Simon and Schuster.

Bem, D. J. (1996). Exotic becomes erotic: A developmental theory of sexual orientation. *Psychological Review, 103*, 320–335.

Ben Zion, I. Z., Tessler, R., Cohen, L., Lerer, E., Raz, Y., Bachner-Melman, R., et al. (2006). Polymorphisms in the dopamine D4 receptor gene (DRD4) contribute to individual differences in human sexual behavior: Desire, arousal and sexual function. *Molecular Psychiatry, 11*, 782–786.

Benjamin, J., Li, L., Patterson, C., Greenberg, B. D., Murphy, D. L., & Hamer, D. H. (1996). Population and familial association between the D4 dopamine receptor gene and measures of novelty seeking. *Nature Genetics, 12*, 81–84.

Bibby, R. W. (1993). *Unknown gods: The ongoing story of religion in Canada*. Toronto: Stoddart.

Blanchard, R. (2012). Fertility in the mothers of firstborn homosexual and heterosexual men. *Archives of Sexual Behavior, 41*, 551–556.

Blanchard, R., & Bogaert, A. F. (1996). Homosexuality in men and number of older brothers. *American Journal of Psychiatry, 153*, 27–31.

Bobrow, D., & Bailey, J. M. (2001). Is male homosexuality maintained via kin selection? *Evolution and Human Behavior, 22*, 361–368.

Bogaert, A. F. (2003). Number of older brothers and sexual orientation: New tests and the attraction/behavior distinction in two national probability samples. *Journal of Personality and Social Psychology, 84*, 644–652.

Bogaert, A. F. (2006). Biological versus nonbiological older brother and men's sexual orientation. *Proceedings of the National Academy of Sciences, 103*, 10771–10774.

Bogaert, A. F., Ashton, M. C., & Lee, K. (2017). Personality and sexual orientation: extension to asexuality and the HEXACO model. *Journal of Sex Research* (in press).

Bogaert, A. F., & Fisher, W. A. (1995). Predictors of university men's numbers of sexual partners. *Journal of Sex Research, 32*, 119–130.

Bogg, T., & Roberts, B. W. (2004). Conscientiousness and health-related behaviors: A meta-analysis of the leading behavioral contributors to mortality. *Psychological Bulletin, 130*, 887–919.

Boomsma, D. I., Willemsen, G., Martin, N. G., Distel, M. A., Trull, T. J., Rebollo-Mesa, I., et al. (2009). Familial resemblance of borderline personality disorder features. Genetic or cultural transmission? *PLoS One, 4*(4), e5334.

Borkenau, P., Riemann, R., Angleitner, A., & Spinath, F. M. (2001). Genetic and environmental influences on observed personality: Evidence from the German Observational Study of Adult Twins. *Journal of Personality and Social Psychology, 80*, 655–668.

Bottlender, M., & Soyka, M. (2005). Impact of different personality dimensions (NEO Five-Factor Inventory) on the outcome of alcohol-dependent patients 6 and 12 months after treatment. *Psychiatry Research, 136*, 61–67.

Botwin, M. D., Buss, D. M., & Shackelford, T. K. (1997). Personality and mate preferences: Five factors in mate selection and marital satisfaction. *Journal of Personality, 65*, 107–136.

Bouchard, T. J., Jr., & Loehlin, J. C. (2001). Genes, evolution, and personality. *Behavior Genetics, 31*, 243–273.

Bouchard, T. J., Jr., Lykken, D. T., McGue, M., Segal, N. L., & Tellegen, A. (1990). Sources of human psychological differences: The Minnesota study of twins reared apart. *Science, 250*, 223–228.

Bourdage, J. S., Lee, K., Ashton, M. C., & Perry, A. (2007). Big Five and HEXACO model correlates of sexuality. *Personality and Individual Differences, 43*, 1506–1516.

Brackett, M. A., & Mayer, J. D. (2003). Convergent, discriminant, and incremental validity of competing measures of emotional intelligence. *Personality and Social Psychology Bulletin, 29*, 1147–1158.

Brackett, M. A., Mayer, J. D., & Warner, R. M. (2004). Emotional intelligence and its relation to everyday behavior. *Personality and Individual Differences, 36*, 1387–1402.

Burisch, M. (1984). Approaches to personality inventory construction: A comparison of merits. *American Psychologist, 39*, 214–227.

Burt, S. A., McGue, M., & Iacono, W. G. (2009). Nonshared environmental mediation of the association between deviant peer affiliation and adolescent externalizing behaviors over time: Results from a cross-lagged monozygotic twin differences design. *Developmental Psychology, 45*, 1752—1760.

Buss, A. R. (1979). The trait-situation controversy and the concept of interaction. *Personality and Social Psychology Bulletin, 5*, 191—195.

Buss, D. M. (1996). Social adaptation and five major factors of personality. In J. S. Wiggins (Ed.), *The Five-Factor Model of Personality* (pp. 180—207). New York: Guilford.

Buss, D. M., & Greiling, H. (1999). Adaptive individual differences. *Journal of Personality, 67*, 209—243.

Cabot, P. S. de Q. (1938). The relationship between personality and physique. *Psychological Bulletin, 35*, 710.

Calvin, C., Fernandes, C., Smith, P., Visscher, P. M., & Deary, I. J. (2009). Is there still a cognitive cost of being a twin in the UK? *Intelligence, 37*, 243—248.

Campbell, A. (1999). Staying alive: Evolution, culture, and women's intrasexual aggression. *Behavioral and Brain Sciences, 22*, 223—252.

Campbell, D. P., Hyne, S. A., & Nilsen, D. L. (1992). *Manual for the Campbell Interest and Skill Survey*. Minneapolis, MN: National Computer Systems.

Campbell, D. T., & Fiske, D. W. (1959). Convergent and discriminant validation by the multitrait multi-method matrix. *Psychological Bulletin, 56*, 81—104.

Camperio Ciani, A., Corna, F., & Capiluppi, C. (2004). Evidence for maternally inherited factors favouring male homosexuality and promoting female fecundity. *Proceedings of the Royal Society of London, Series B: Biological Sciences, 271*, 2217—2221.

Cantor, J. M., Blanchard, R., Paterson, A. D., & Bogaert, A. F. (2002). How many gay men owe their sexual orientation to fraternal birth order? *Archives of Sexual Behavior, 31*, 63—71.

Carver, C. S., & White, T. L. (1994). Behavioral inhibition, behavioral activation, and affective responses to impending reward and punishment: The BIS/BAS scales. *Journal of Personality and Social Psychology, 67*, 319—333.

Caspi, A., Roberts, B. W., & Shiner, R. L. (2005). Personality development: Stability and change. *Annual Review of Psychology, 56*, 453—484.

Castellanos, F. X., Giedd, J. N., Marsh, W. L., Hamburger, S. D., Vaituzis, A. C., Dickstein, D. P., et al. (1996). Quantitative brain magnetic resonance imaging in attention-deficit hyperactivity disorder. *Archives of General Psychiatry, 53*, 607—616.

Cattell, R. B. (1947). Confirmation and clarification of primary personality factors. *Psychometrika, 12*, 197—220.

Cattell, R. B. (1971). *Abilities: Their structure, growth, and action*. Oxford, England: Houghton Mifflin.

Child, I. L. (1950). The relation of somatotype to self-ratings on Sheldon's temperamental traits. *Journal of Personality, 18*, 440—453.

Choma, B. L., Ashton, M. C., & Hafer, C. L. (2010). Conceptualizing political attitudes in Canadian political candidates: a tale of two (correlated) dimensions. *Canadian Journal of Behavioural Science, 42*, 24—33.

Christensen, J. C., Shiyanov, P. A., Estepp, J. R., & Schlager, J. J. (2014). Lack of association between human plasma oxytocin and interpersonal trust in a prisoner's dilemma paradigm. *PLoS One, 9*(12), e116172.

Christie, R., & Geis, F. L. (1970). *Studies in Machiavellianism*. New York: Academic Press.

Clobert, M., & Saroglou, V. (2015). Religion, paranormal beliefs, and distrust in science: Comparing east versus west. *Archive for the Psychology of Religion, 37*, 185—199.

Cloninger, C. R. (1987). A systematic method for clinical description and classification of personality disorders: A proposal. *Archives of General Psychiatry, 44*, 573—588.

Cloninger, C. R., Przybeck, T. R., Svrakic, D. M., & Wetzel, R. D. (1994). *The Temperament and Character Inventory (TCI): A guide to its development and use*. St. Louis, MO: Center for Psychobiology of Personality, Washington University.

Cloninger, C. R., Svrakic, D. M., & Przybeck, T. R. (1993). A psychobiological model of temperament and character. *Archives of General Psychiatry, 50*, 975—990.

Cohen, T. R., Panter, A. T., Turan, N., Morse, L., & Kim, Y. (2015). Moral character in the workplace. *Journal of Personality and Social Psychology, 107*, 943—963.

Cohen, T. R., Wolf, S. T., Panter, A. T., & Insko, C. A. (2011). Introducing the GASP scale: A new measure of guilt and shame proneness. *Journal of Personality and Social Psychology, 100*, 947–966.

Cokely, E. T., Feltz, A., Ghazal, S., Allan, J. N., Petrova, D., & Garcia-Retamero, R. (2017). Decision making skill: from intelligence to numeracy and expertise. In K. A. Ericsson, R. R. Hoffman, A. Kozbelt, & A. M. Williams (Eds.), *Cambridge handbook of expertise and expert performance* (2nd ed.). New York, NY: Cambridge University Press (in press).

Cokely, E. T., Galesic, M., Schulz, E., Ghazal, S., & Garcia-Retamero, R. (2012). Measuring risk literacy: The Berlin Numeracy Test. *Judgment and Decision Making, 7*, 25–47.

Comings, D. E., Gade-Andavolu, R., Gonzalez, N., Wu, S., Muhleman, D., Blake, H., et al. (2000). A multivariate analysis of 59 candidate genes in personality traits: The Temperament and Character Inventory. *Clinical Genetics, 58*, 375–385.

Conn, S. R., & Rieke, M. L. (1994). *The 16PF fifth edition technical manual*. Champaign, IL: Institute for Personality and Ability Testing.

Cooper, T., Detre, T., & Weiss, S. M. (1981). Coronary-prone behavior and coronary heart disease: A critical review. *Circulation, 63*, 1199–1215.

Costa, P. T., Jr., Herbst, J. H., McCrae, R. R., Samuels, J., & Ozer, D. J. (2002). The replicability and utility of three personality types. *European Journal of Personality, 16*, S73–S87.

Costa, P. T., Jr., & McCrae, R. R. (1985). *The NEO Personality Inventory manual*. Odessa, FL: Psychological Assessment Resources.

Costa, P. T., Jr., & McCrae, R. R. (1988a). From catalog to classification: Murray's needs and the Five-Factor Model. *Journal of Personality and Social Psychology, 55*, 258–265.

Costa, P. T., Jr., & McCrae, R. R. (1988b). Personality in adulthood: A six-year longitudinal study of self-reports and spouse ratings on the NEO Personality Inventory. *Journal of Personality and Social Psychology, 54*, 853–863.

Costa, P. T., Jr., & McCrae, R. R. (1992a). Four ways five factors are basic. *Personality and Individual Differences, 13*, 653–665.

Costa, P. T., Jr., & McCrae, R. R. (1992b). *NEO Personality Inventory–Revised (NEO-PI-R) and NEO Five-Factor Inventory (NEO-FFI) Professional manual*. Odessa, FL: Psychological Assessment Resources.

Costa, P. T., Jr., & McCrae, R. R. (1992c). Trait psychology comes of age. In T. B. Sonderegger (Ed.), *Nebraska symposium on motivation 1991 psychology and aging. Current theory and research in motivation* (Vol. 39, pp. 169–204). Lincoln, NE: University of Nebraska Press.

Cramer, K. M., & Imaike, E. (2002). Personality, blood type, and the Five-Factor Model. *Personality and Individual Differences, 32*, 621–626.

Cronbach, L. J., & Meehl, P. E. (1955). Construct validity in psychological tests. *Psychological Bulletin, 51*, 281–302.

Cunningham, M. R., Wong, D. T., & Barbee, A. P. (1994). Self-presentation dynamics on overt integrity tests: Experimental studies of the Reid Report. *Journal of Applied Psychology, 79*, 643–658.

Dabbs, J. M., Hargrove, M. F., & Heusel, C. (1996). Testosterone differences among college fraternities: well-behaved vs rambunctious. *Personality and Individual Differences, 20*, 157–161.

Dahlstrom, W. G., Hopkins, D., Dahlstrom, L., Jackson, E., & Cumella, E. (1996). MMPI findings on astrological and other folklore concepts of personality. *Psychological Reports, 78*, 1059–1070.

Danner, D. D., Snowdon, D. A., & Friesen, W. V. (2001). Positive emotions in early life and longevity: Findings from the nun study. *Journal of Personality and Social Psychology, 80*, 804–813.

Darwin, C. (1859). *On the origin of species by means of natural selection, or the preservation of favoured races in the struggle for life*. London: John Murray.

Dawood, K., Kirk, K. M., Bailey, J. M., Andrews, P. W., & Martin, N. G. (2005). Genetic and environmental influences on frequency of orgasm in women. *Twin Research and Human Genetics, 8*, 27–33.

Day, A. L., Therrien, D. L., & Carroll, S. A. (2005). Predicting psychological health: Assessing the predictive validity of emotional intelligence beyond personality, type A behaviour, and daily hassles. *European Journal of Personality, 19*, 519–536.

Day, S. X., & Rounds, J. (1998). Universality of vocational interest structure among racial and ethnic minorities. *American Psychologist, 53*, 728–736.

De Raad, B., Barelds, D. P. H., Levert, E., Ostendorf, F., Mlacic, B., Di Blas, L., et al. (2010). Only three factors of personality description are fully replicable across languages: A comparison of fourteen trait taxonomies. *Journal of Personality and Social Psychology, 98*, 160—173.

De Raad, B., Barelds, D. P. H., Timmerman, M. E., De Roover, K., Mlacic, B., & Church, A. T. (2014). Towards a pan-cultural personality structure: Input from 11 psycholexical studies. *European Journal of Personality, 28*, 497—510.

Deary, I. J., Der, G., & Ford, G. (2001). Reaction times and intelligence differences: A population-based cohort study. *Intelligence, 29*, 389—399.

Deary, I. J., Strand, S., Smith, P., & Fernandes, C. (2007). Intelligence and educational achievement. *Intelligence, 35*, 13—21.

Deary, I. J., Taylor, M. D., Hart, C. L., Wilson, V., Smith, G. D., Blane, D., et al. (2005). Intergenerational social mobility and mid-life status attainment: Influences of childhood intelligence, childhood social factors, and education. *Intelligence, 33*, 455—472.

Deary, I. J., Thorpe, G., Wilson, V., Starr, J. M., & Whalley, L. J. (2003). Population sex differences in IQ at age 11: The Scottish mental survey 1932. *Intelligence, 31*, 533—542.

Deary, I. J., Whiteman, M. C., Starr, J. M., Whalley, L. J., & Fox, H. C. (2004). The impact of childhood intelligence on later life: Following up the Scottish mental surveys of 1932 and 1947. *Journal of Personality and Social Psychology, 86*, 130—147.

Der, G., Batty, G. D., & Deary, I. J. (October 4, 2006). Effect of breast feeding on intelligence in children: Prospective study, sibling pairs analysis, and meta-analysis. *British Medical Journal.*

Detterman, D. K. (1987). What does reaction time tell us about intelligence? In P. A. Vernon (Ed.), *Speed of information-processing and intelligence* (pp. 177—200). Westport, CT: Ablex.

de Vries, R. E., Lee, K., & Ashton, M. C. (2008). The Dutch HEXACO Personality Inventory: Psychometric properties, self-other agreement, and relations with psychopathy among low and high acquaintanceship dyads. *Journal of Personality Assessment, 90*, 142—151.

de Vries, R. E., Zettler, I., & Hilbig, B. E. (2014). Rethinking trait conceptions of social desirability scales: Impression management as an expression of honesty-humility. *Assessment, 21*, 286—299.

Devlin, B., Daniels, M., & Roeder, K. (1997). The heritability of IQ. *Nature, 388*, 468—471.

DeYoung, C. G. (2006). Higher-order factors of the Big Five in a multi-informant sample. *Journal of Personality and Social Psychology, 91*, 1138—1151.

Dhont, K., Hodson, G., Costello, K., & MacInnis, C. C. (2014). Social dominance orientation connects prejudicial human-human and human-animal relations. *Personality and Individual Differences, 61—62*, 105—108.

Dickens, W. T., & Flynn, J. R. (2001). Heritability estimates versus large environmental effects: The IQ paradox resolved. *Psychological Review, 108*, 346—359.

Dickens, W. T., & Flynn, J. R. (2006). Black American reduce the IQ gap: Evidence from standardization samples. *Psychological Science, 17*, 913—920.

Diener, E. (2000). Subjective well-being: The science of happiness and a proposal for a national index. *American Psychologist, 55*, 34—43.

Digman, J. M. (1997). Higher-order factors of the Big Five. *Journal of Personality and Social Psychology, 73*, 1246—1256.

Digman, J. M., & Takemoto-Chock, N. K. (1981). Factors in the natural language of personality: Re-analysis, comparison, and interpretation of six major studies. *Multivariate Behavioral Research, 16*, 149—170.

Donnellan, M. B., Trzesniewski, K. H., Robins, R. W., Moffitt, T. E., & Caspi, A. (2005). Low self-esteem is related to aggression, antisocial behavior, and delinquency. *Psychological Science, 16*, 328—335.

Duckitt, J. (2000). Culture, personality, and prejudice. In S. Renshon, & J. Duckitt (Eds.), *Political psychology: Cultural and cross-cultural foundations* (pp. 89—107). New York: New York University Press.

Duckitt, J., Wagner, C., du Plessis, I., & Birum, I. (2002). The psychological basis of ideology and prejudice: Testing a dual process model. *Journal of Personality and Social Psychology, 83*, 75—93.

Dyrenforth, P. S., Kashy, D. A., Donnellan, M. B., & Lucas, R. E. (2010). Predicting relationship and life satisfaction from personality in nationally representative samples from three countries: The relative importance of actor, partner, and similarity effects. *Journal of Personality and Social Psychology, 99*, 690—702.

Eaves, L., Martin, N., Heath, A., Schieken, R., Meyer, J., Silberg, J., et al. (1997). Age changes in the causes of individual differences in conservatism. *Behavioral Genetics, 27*, 121—124.

Edwards, A. G. P., & Armitage, P. (1992). An experiment to test the discriminating ability of graphologists. *Personality and Individual Differences, 13*, 69—74.

Elkins, I. J., King, S. M., McGue, M., & Iacono, W. G. (2006). Personality traits and the development of nicotine, alcohol, and illicit drug disorders: Prospective links from adolescence to young adulthood. *Journal of Abnormal Psychology, 115*, 26—39.

Epstein, S. (1979). The stability of behavior: I. On predicting most of the people much of the time. *Journal of Personality and Social Psychology, 37*, 1097—1126.

Exner, J. E. (1974). *The Rorschach: A comprehensive system* (Vol. 1). New York: Wiley.

Eysenck, H. J. (1947). *Dimensions of personality*. London: Routledge and Kegan Paul.

Eysenck, H. J. (1970). *The structure of human personality* (3rd ed.). London: Methuen.

Eysenck, H. J., & Eysenck, S. B. G. (1975). *Manual of the Eysenck Personality Questionnaire*. San Diego: EdITS.

Eysenck, H. J., & Wilson, G. D. (1991). *The Eysenck Personality Profiler*. London: Corporate Assessment Network.

Eysenck, S. B. G., & Eysenck, H. J. (1967). Salivary response to lemon juice as a measure of introversion. *Perceptual and Motor Skills, 24*, 1047—1053.

Eysenck, S. B. G., & Eysenck, H. J. (1968). The measurement of psychoticism: A study of factor stability and reliability. *British Journal of Social and Clinical Psychology, 7*, 286—294.

Farrell, A. H., Brook, C., Dane, A. V., Marini, Z. A., & Volk, A. A. (2014). Relations between adolescent ratings of Rothbart's temperament questionnaire and the HEXACO Personality Inventory. *Journal of Personality Assessment, 97*, 163—171.

Finn, S. E. (1986). Stability of personality self-ratings over 30 years: Evidence for an age/cohort interaction. *Journal of Personality and Social Psychology, 50*, 813—818.

Fiori, M., & Antonakis, J. (2011). The ability model of emotional intelligence: Searching for valid measures. *Personality and Individual Differences, 50*, 329—334.

Fleeson, W. (2004). Moving personality beyond the person-situation debate: The challenge and the opportunity of within-person variability. *Current Directions in Psychological Science, 13*, 83—87.

Fleeson, W., & Noftle, E. E. (2009). In favor of the synthetic resolution to the person-situation debate. *Journal of Research in Personality, 43*, 150—154.

Flynn, J. R. (1984). The mean IQ of Americans: Massive gains 1932 to 1978. *Psychological Bulletin, 95*, 29—51.

Flynn, J. R. (1987). Massive IQ gains in 14 nations: What IQ tests really measure. *Psychological Bulletin, 101*, 171—191.

Flynn, J. R. (2006). [Introduction to the psychology of individual differences] [Efeito Flynn: Repensando a inteligência e seus efeitos.] [The Flynn Effect: Rethinking intelligence and what affects it.]. In C. Flores-Mendoza, & R. Colom (Eds.), *Introduçao à psicologia das diferenças individuais* (pp. 387—411). Porto Alegre, Brazil: ArtMed.

Fossati, A., Madeddu, F., & Maffei, C. (1999). Borderline personality disorder and childhood sexual abuse: A meta-analytic study. *Journal of Personality Disorders, 13*, 268—280.

Friedman, H. S., Tucker, J. S., Schwartz, J. E., Martin, L. R., Tomlinson-Keasey, C., Wingard, D. L., et al. (1995). Childhood conscientiousness and longevity: Health behaviors and cause of death. *Journal of Personality and Social Psychology, 68*, 696—703.

Friedman, H. S., Tucker, J. S., Tomlinson-Keasey, C., Schwartz, J. E., Wingard, D. L., & Criqui, M. H. (1993). Does childhood personality predict longevity? *Journal of Personality and Social Psychology, 65*, 176—185.

Friedman, M., & Rosenman, R. H. (1959). Association of a specific overt behavior pattern with increases in blood cholesterol, blood clotting time, incidence of arcus senilis, and clinical coronary artery disease. *Journal of the American Medical Association, 169*, 1286—1296.

Funder, D. C. (2008). Persons, situations, and person—situation interactions. In O. P. John, R. W. Robins, & L. A. Pervin (Eds.), *Handbook of personality: Theory and research* (pp. 568—580). New York: Guilford.

Funder, D. C., Kolar, D. W., & Blackman, M. C. (1995). On the basis of agreement among judges of personality: Interpersonal relations, similarity, and acquaintanceship. *Journal of Personality and Social Psychology, 69*, 656—672.

Funk, C. L., Smith, K. B., Alford, J. R., Hibbing, M. V., Eaton, N. R., Krueger, R. F., et al. (2013). Genetic and environmental transmission of political orientations. *Political Psychology, 34*, 805—819.

Furnham, A., Chamorro-Premuzic, T., & Callahan, I. (2003). Does graphology predict personality and intelligence? *Individual Differences Research, 1*, 78—94.

Furr, R. M., & Funder, D. C. (1998). A multimodal analysis of personal negativity. *Journal of Personality and Social Psychology, 74*, 1580—1591.

Furukawa, T. (1930). A study of temperament and blood groups. *Journal of Social Psychology, 1*, 494—509.

Galton, F. (1884). Measurement of character. *Fortnightly Review, 36*, 179—183.

Gangestad, S. W., & Simpson, J. A. (1990). Toward an evolutionary history of female sociosexual variation. *Journal of Personality, 58*, 69—96.

Garcia, J. R., MacKillop, J., Aller, E. L., Merriwether, A. M., Wilson, D. S., & Lum, K. (2010). Associations between dopamine D4 receptor gene variation with both infidelity and sexual promiscuity. *PLoS One, 5*(11), e14162.

Gardner, H. (1983). *Frames of mind*. New York: BasicBooks.

Gardner, H. (1999). *Intelligence reframed*. New York: BasicBooks.

Gaughan, E. T., Miller, J. D., & Lynam, D. R. (2012). Examining the utility of general models of personality in the study of psychopathy: Comparing the HEXACO-PI-R and NEO PI-R. *Journal of Personality Disorders, 26*, 513—523.

Gebauer, J. E., Paulhus, D. L., & Neberich, W. (2013). Big two personality and religiosity across cultures: Communals as religious conformists and agentics as religious contrarians. *Social Psychological and Personality Science, 4*, 21—30.

Geen, R. G. (1984). Preferred stimulation levels in introverts: Effects on arousal and performance. *Journal of Personality and Social Psychology, 46*, 1303—1312.

Gleitman, H. (1986). *Psychology* (2nd ed.). New York: Norton.

Goffin, R. D., & Christiansen, N. D. (2003). Correcting personality tests for faking: A review of popular personality tests and an initial survey of researchers. *International Journal of Selection and Assessment, 11*, 340—344.

Goldberg, L. R. (1990). An alternative "description of personality": The Big-Five factor structure. *Journal of Personality and Social Psychology, 59*, 1216—1229.

Goldberg, L. R. (1999). A broad-bandwidth, public-domain, personality inventory measuring the lowerlevel facets of several five-factor models. In I. Mervielde, I. Deary, F. De Fruyt, & F. Ostendorf (Eds.), *Personality psychology in Europe* (Vol. 7, pp. 7—28). The Netherlands: Tilburg University Press.

Goleman, D. (1995). *Emotional intelligence*. New York: Bantam.

Gosling, S. D., Kwan, V. S. Y., & John, O. P. (2003). A dog's got personality: A cross-species comparative approach to personality judgments in dogs and humans. *Journal of Personality and Social Psychology, 85*, 1161—1169.

Gottfredson, L. S. (2003). Dissecting practical intelligence theory: Its claims and evidence. *Intelligence, 31*, 343—397.

Gottfredson, L. S. (2004). Intelligence: Is it the epidemiologists' elusive "fundamental cause" of social class inequalities in health? *Journal of Personality and Social Psychology, 86*, 174—199.

Gottfredson, L. S., & Deary, I. J. (2004). Intelligence predicts health and longevity, but why? *Current Directions in Psychological Science, 13*, 1—4.

Gottfredson, M. R., & Hirschi, T. (1990). *A general theory of crime*. Stanford, CA: Stanford University Press.

Gough, H. G. (1996). *California Psychological Inventory* (3rd ed.). Palo Alto: CA: Consulting Psychologists Press.

Gray, J. A. (1981). A critique of Eysenck's theory of personality. In H. J. Eysenck (Ed.), *A model for personality* (pp. 246—276). New York: Springer-Verlag.

Gray, J. A. (1987). Perspectives on anxiety and impulsivity: A commentary. *Journal of Research in Personality, 21*, 493—509.

Gross, M. R. (1991). Evolution of alternative reproductive strategies: Frequency-dependent sexual selection in male bluegill sunfish. *Philosophical Transactions of the Royal Society of London, Series B: Biological Sciences, 332*, 59—66.

Grudnik, J. L., & Kranzler, J. H. (2001). Meta-analysis of the relationship between intelligence and inspection time. *Intelligence, 29*, 523—535.

Guimond, S., Crisp, R. J., De Oliveira, P., Kamiejski, R., Kteily, N., Kuepper, B., et al. (2013). Diversity policy, social dominance, and intergroup relations: Predicting prejudice in changing social and political contexts. *Journal of Personality and Social Psychology, 104*, 951—958.

Gustafsson, J.-E. (2002). Measurement from a hierarchical point of view. In H. I. Braun, D. N. Jackson, & D. E. Wiley (Eds.), *The role of constructs in psychological and educational measurement* (pp. 73—95). Mahwah, NJ: Erlbaum.

Halpern, C. T., Udry, J. R., Campbell, B., Suchindran, C., & Mason, G. A. (1994). Testosterone and religiosity as predictors of sexual attitudes and activity among adolescent males: A biosocial model. *Journal of Biosocial Science, 26*, 217—234.

Halpern, C. T., Udry, J. R., & Suchindran, C. (1997). Testosterone predicts initiation of coitus in adolescent females. *Psychosomatic Medicine, 59*, 161—171.

Halpern, D. F. (1997). Sex differences in intelligence: Implications for education. *American Psychologist, 52*, 1091—1102.

Halverson, C. F., Havill, V. L., Deal, J., Baker, S. R., Victor, J. B., Pavlopoulos, V., et al. (2003). Personality structure as derived from parental ratings of free descriptions of children: The inventory of child individual differences. *Journal of Personality, 71*, 995—1026.

Hamilton, W. D. (1964). The genetical evolution of social behavior. I, II. *Journal of Theoretical Biology, 7*, 1—52.

Hampson, S. E., & Goldberg, L. R. (2006). A first large cohort study of personality trait stability over the 40 years between elementary school and midlife. *Journal of Personality and Social Psychology, 91*, 763—779.

Hampson, S. E., Goldberg, L. R., Vogt, T. M., & Dubanoski, J. P. (2006). Forty years on: Teachers' assessments of children's personality traits predict self-reported health behaviors and outcomes at midlife. *Health Psychology, 25*, 57—64.

Harpur, T. J., Hare, R. D., & Hakstian, A. R. (1989). Two-factor conceptualization of psychopathy: Construct validity and assessment implications. *Psychological Assessment, 1*, 6—17.

Harris, G. T., & Rice, M. E. (2006). Treatment of psychopathy: A review of empirical findings. In C. J. Patrick (Ed.), *Handbook of psychopathy* (pp. 555—572). New York: Guilford.

Harris, J. R. (1995). Where is the child's environment? A group socialization theory of development. *Psychological Review, 102*, 458—489.

Harris, J. R. (1998). *The nurture assumption: Why children turn out the way they do.* New York: Free Press.

Hartshorne, H., & May, M. A. (1928). Studies in the nature of character. In *Studies in deceit* (Vol. 1). New York: Macmillan.

Haworth, C. M. A., Wright, M. J., Luciano, M., Martin, N. G., de Geus, E. J. C., van Beijsterveldt, C. E. M., et al. (2010). The heritability of general cognitive ability increases linearly from childhood to young adulthood. *Molecular Psychiatry, 15*, 1112—1120.

Heaven, P. C. L., & Ciarrocchi, J. (2007). Personality and religious values among adolescents: A three-wave longitudinal analysis. *British Journal of Psychology, 98*, 681—694.

Highfill, L. E., & Kuczaj, S. A. (2007). Do bottlenose dolphins (*Tursiops truncatus*) have distinct and stable personalities? *Aquatic Mammals, 33*, 380—389.

Hilbig, B. E., Zettler, I., Leist, F., & Heydasch, T. (2013). It takes two: Honesty-humility and agreeableness differentially predict active versus reactive cooperation. *Personality and Individual Differences, 54*, 598—603.

Hirschi, T., & Hindelang, M. J. (1977). Intelligence and delinquency: A revisionist review. *American Sociological Review, 42*, 571—587.

Hodson, G. (2009). The puzzling person—situation schism in prejudice research. *Journal of Research in Personality, 43*, 247—248.

Hofstee, W. K. B., De Raad, B., & Goldberg, L. R. (1992). Integration of the Big Five and circumplex approaches to trait structure. *Journal of Personality and Social Psychology, 63*, 146—163.

Hogan, R. (1996). A socioanalytic perspective on the Five-Factor Model. In J. S. Wiggins (Ed.), *The Five-Factor Model of Personality* (pp. 163—179). New York: Guilford.

Hogan, R. (2009). Much ado about nothing: The person-situation debate. *Journal of Research in Personality, 43*, 249.

Hogan, J., & Holland, B. (2003). Using theory to evaluate personality and job-performance relations: A socioanalytic perspective. *Journal of Applied Psychology, 88*, 100−112.

Hogan, R., & Hogan, J. (1995). *Hogan Personality Inventory* (2nd ed.). Tulsa, OK: Hogan Assessment Systems.

Holden, R. R., Wood, L. L., & Tomashewski, L. (2001). Do response time limitations counteract the effect of faking on personality inventory validity? *Journal of Personality and Social Psychology, 81*, 160−169.

Holland, J. L. (1966). *The psychology of vocational choice*. Waltham, MA: Blaisdell.

Holzinger, K. J., & Swineford, F. (1939). A study in factor analysis: The stability of a bi-factor solution. In *Supplementary educational monographs, No. 48*. Chicago: University of Chicago, Department of Education.

Hooper, J. (February 1999). A new germ theory. *Atlantic Monthly, 283*, 41−53.

Horn, J. L., & Cattell, R. B. (1966). Refinement and test of the theory of fluid and crystallized general intelligences. *Journal of Educational Psychology, 57*, 253−270.

Hough, L. A., Barge, B. N., & Kamp, J. D. (2001). Assessment of personality, temperament, vocational interests, and work outcome preferences. In J. P. Campbell, & D. J. Knapp (Eds.), *Exploring the limits in personnel selection and classification* (pp. 111−154). Mahwah, NJ: Erlbaum.

Houston, B. K., Babyak, M. A., Chesney, M. A., Black, G., & Ragland, D. R. (1997). Social dominance and 22-year all-cause mortality in men. *Psychosomatic Medicine, 59*, 5−12.

Hudson, N. W., Roberts, B. W., & Lodi-Smith, J. (2012). Personality trait development and social investment in work. *Journal of Research in Personality, 46*, 334−344.

Huesmann, L. R., Dubow, E. F., & Boxer, P. (2009). Continuity of aggression from childhood to early adulthood as a predictor of life outcomes: Implications for the adolescent-limited and life-course persistent models. *Aggressive Behavior, 35*, 136−149.

Humbad, M. N., Donnellan, M. B., Iacono, W. G., McGue, M., & Burt, S. A. (2010). Is spousal similarity for personality a matter of convergence or selection? *Personality and Individual Differences, 49*, 827−830.

Hunter, J. E., & Hunter, R. F. (1984). Validity and utility of alternative predictors of job performance. *Psychological Bulletin, 96*, 72−98.

Hurtz, G. M., & Donovan, J. J. (2000). Personality and job performance: The Big Five revisited. *Journal of Applied Psychology, 85*, 869−879.

Jackson, D. N. (1970). A sequential system for personality scale development. *Current Topics in Clinical and Community Psychology, 2*, 61−96.

Jackson, D. N. (1971). The dynamics of structured personality tests: 1971. *Psychological Review, 78*, 229−248.

Jackson, D. N. (1975). The relative validity of scales prepared by naïve item writers and those based on empirical methods of personality scale construction. *Educational and Psychological Measurement, 35*, 361−370.

Jackson, D. N. (1984a). *Multidimensional Aptitude Battery manual*. Port Huron, MI: Research Psychologists Press.

Jackson, D. N. (1984b). *Personality Research Form manual* (3rd ed.). Port Huron, MI: Research Psychologists Press.

Jackson, D. N. (1994). *Jackson Personality Inventory—Revised manual*. Port Huron, MI: Sigma Assessment Systems.

Jackson, D. N., & Messick, S. (1961). Acquiescence and desirability as response determinants on the MMPI. *Educational and Psychological Measurement, 21*, 771−790.

Jackson, D. N., & Paunonen, S. V. (1985). Construct validity and the predictability of behavior. *Journal of Personality and Social Psychology, 49*, 554−570.

Jackson, D. N., Wroblewski, V. R., & Ashton, M. C. (2000). The impact of faking on integrity tests: Does forced-choice offer a solution? *Human Performance, 13*, 371−388.

Jackson, J. J., Bogg, T., Walton, K. E., Wood, D., Harms, P. D., Lodi-Smith, J., et al. (2009). Not all Conscientiousness scales change alike: a multimethod, multisample study of age differences in the facets of Conscientiousness. *Journal of Personality and Social Psychology, 96*, 446−459.

Jacobs, N., Van Gestel, S., Derom, S., Thiery, E., Vernon, P., Derom, R., et al. (2001). Heritability estimates of intelligence in twins: Effect of chorion type. *Behavior Genetics, 31*, 209−217.

Jefferson, T., Jr., Herbst, J. H., & McCrae, R. R. (1998). Associations between birth order and personality traits: Evidence from self-reports and observer ratings. *Journal of Research in Personality, 32*, 498−509.

Jencks, C. (1979). *Who gets ahead? The determinants of economic success in America.* New York: Basic Books.

John, O. P., Donahue, E. M., & Kentle, R. L. (1991). *The "Big Five" Inventory—Versions 4a and 54. Berkeley, Institute of Personality and Social Research.* Berkeley: University of California, Berkeley, Institute of Personality and Social Research.

Johnson, W., & Deary, I. J. (2011). Placing inspection time, reaction time, and perceptual speed in the broader context of cognitive ability: The VPR model in the Lothian Birth Cohort 1936. *Intelligence, 39,* 405—417.

Kandler, C., Bell, E., & Riemann, R. (2016). The structure and sources of right-wing authoritarianism and social dominance orientation. *European Journal of Personality, 30,* 406—420.

Kandler, C., Riemann, R., Spinath, F. M., & Angleitner, A. (2010). Sources of variance in personality facets: A multiple-rater twin study of self-peer, peer-peer, and self-self (dis)agreement. *Journal of Personality, 78,* 1565—1594.

Karpman, B. (1948). The myth of the psychopathic personality. *American Journal of Psychiatry, 103,* 523—534.

Kaufman, A. S. (1979). *Intelligent testing with the WISC-R.* New York: Wiley.

Kaufman, A. S. (2010). "In what way are apples and oranges alike?" A critique of Flynn's interpretation of the Flynn effect. *Journal of Psychoeducational Assessment, 28,* 382—398.

Kendler, K. S., Thornton, L. M., Gilman, S. E., & Kessler, R. C. (2000). Sexual orientation in a US national sample of twin and non-twin sibling pairs. *American Journal of Psychiatry, 157,* 1843—1846.

King, J. E., & Figueredo, A. J. (1997). The Five-Factor Model plus dominance in chimpanzee personality. *Journal of Research in Personality, 31,* 257—271.

Knudson, R. M., & Golding, S. L. (1974). Comparative validity of traditional versus S—R format inventories of interpersonal behavior. *Journal of Research in Personality, 8,* 111—127.

Koenig, L. B., McGue, M., Krueger, R. F., & Bouchard, T. J., Jr. (2005). Genetic and environmental influences on religiousness: Findings for retrospective and current religiousness ratings. *Journal of Personality, 73,* 471—488.

Koke, L. C., & Vernon, P. A. (2003). The Sternberg Triarchic Abilities Test (STAT) as a measure of academic achievement and general intelligence. *Personality and Individual Differences, 35,* 1803—1807.

Kolar, D. W., Funder, D. C., & Colvin, C. R. (1996). Comparing the accuracy of personality judgments by the self and knowledgeable others. *Journal of Personality, 64,* 311—337.

Kramer, M. S., Aboud, F., Mironova, E., Vanilovich, I., Platt, R. W., Matush, L., et al. (2008). Breastfeeding and child cognitive development: New evidence from a large randomized trial. *Archives of General Psychiatry, 65,* 578—584.

Kretschmer, E. (1925). *Physique and character.* Oxford: Kegan Paul.

Kristensen, P., & Bjerkedal, T. (2007). Explaining the relation between birth order and intelligence. *Science, 316,* 1717.

Krueger, R. F., Derringer, J., Markon, K. E., Watson, D., & Skodol, A. E. (2012). Initial construction of a maladaptive personality trait model and inventory for DSM-5. *Psychological Medicine, 42,* 1879—1890.

Krueger, R. F., Eaton, N. R., Derringer, J., Markon, K. E., Watson, D., & Skodol, A. E. (2011). Personality in DSM-5: Helping to delineate personality disorder content and framing the meta-structure. *Journal of Personality Assessment, 93,* 325—331.

Lamb, M. E., Chuang, S. S., Wessels, H., Broberg, A. G., & Hwang, C. P. (2002). Emergence and construct validation of the Big Five factors in early childhood: A longitudinal analysis of their ontogeny in Sweden. *Child Development, 73,* 1517—1524.

Langström, N., Rahman, Q., Carlström, E., & Lichtenstein, P. (2010). Genetic and environmental effects on same-sex sexual behavior: A population study of twins in Sweden. *Archives of Sexual Behavior, 39,* 75—80.

Larsen, R. J., & Diener, E. (1987). Affect intensity as an individual difference characteristic: A review. *Journal of Research in Personality, 21,* 1—39.

Larson, L. M., Rottinghaus, P. J., & Borgen, F. H. (2002). Meta-analysis of Big Six interests and Big Five personality factors. *Journal of Vocational Behavior, 61,* 217—239.

Leak, G. K. (1993). Relationship between religious orientation and love styles, sexual attitudes, and sexual behaviors. *Journal of Psychology and Theology, 21,* 315—318.

Lee, K., & Ashton, M. C. (2004). Psychometric properties of the HEXACO Personality Inventory. *Multivariate Behavioral Research, 39*, 329–358.

Lee, K., & Ashton, M. C. (2006). Further assessment of the HEXACO Personality Inventory: Two new facet scales and an observer report form. *Psychological Assessment, 18*, 182–191.

Lee, K., & Ashton, M. C. (2008). The HEXACO personality factors in the indigenous personality lexicons of English and 11 other languages. *Journal of Personality, 76*, 1001–1053.

Lee, K., & Ashton, M. C. (2012). *The H factor of personality: Why some people are manipulative, self-entitled, materialistic, and exploitive—and why it matters for everyone.* Waterloo, ON: Wilfrid Laurier University Press.

Lee, K., & Ashton, M. C. (2013). Prediction of self- and observer report scores on HEXACO-60 and NEO-FFI scales. *Journal of Research in Personality, 47*, 668–675.

Lee, K., & Ashton, M. C. (2017). Psychometric properties of the HEXACO-100. *Assessment* (in press).

Lee, K., Ashton, M. C., Ogunfowora, B., Bourdage, J., & Shin, K.-H. (2010). The personality bases of sociopolitical attitudes: The role of honesty-humility and openness to experience. *Journal of Research in Personality, 44*, 115–119.

Lee, K., Ashton, M. C., Pozzebon, J. A., Visser, B. A., Bourdage, J. S., & Ogunfowora, B. (2009). Similarity and assumed similarity in personality reports of well-acquainted persons. *Journal of Personality and Social Psychology, 96*, 460–472.

Lee, K., Ashton, M. C., Wiltshire, J., Bourdage, J. S., Visser, B. A., & Gallucci, A. (2013). Sex, power, and money: Prediction from the dark triad and honesty-humility. *European Journal of Personality, 27*, 167–184.

Lee, K., Gizzarone, M., & Ashton, M. C. (2003). Personality and the likelihood to sexually harass. *Sex Roles, 49*, 59–69.

Lee, K., Ogunfowora, B., & Ashton, M. C. (2005). Personality traits beyond the Big Five: Are they within the HEXACO space? *Journal of Personality, 73*, 1437–1463.

Lenzenweger, M. F. (2010). *Schizotypy and schizophrenia: The view from experimental psychopathology.* New York: Guilford.

Lesch, K.-P., Bengel, D., Heils, A., Sabol, S. Z., Greenberg, B. D., Petri, S., et al. (1996). Association of anxiety-related traits with a polymorphism in the serotonin transporter gene regulatory region. *Science, 274*, 1527–1531.

Levenson, M. R., Kiehl, K. A., & Fitzpatrick, C. M. (1995). Assessing psychopathic attributes in a noninstitutionalized population. *Journal of Personality and Social Psychology, 68*, 151–158.

Linehan, M. M., & Dexter-Mazza, E. T. (2008). Dialectical behavior therapy for borderline personality disorder. In D. H. Barlow (Ed.), *Clinical handbook of psychological disorders: A step-by-step treatment manual* (4th ed., pp. 365–420). New York: Guilford.

Lippa, R. (2009). Sex differences in sex drive, sociosexuality, and height across 53 nations: Testing evolutionary and social structural theories. *Archives of Sexual Behavior, 38*, 631–651.

Lippa, R. A. (2002). Gender-related traits of heterosexual and homosexual men and women. *Archives of Sexual Behavior, 31*, 83–98.

Lippa, R. A. (2005). Sexual orientation and personality. *Annual Review of Sex Research, 16*, 119–153.

Lippa, R. A. (2008). Sex differences and sexual orientation differences in personality: Findings from the BBC Internet survey. *Archives of Sexual Behavior, 37*, 173–187.

Loehlin, J. C. (1997). A test of J. R. Harris's theory of peer influences on personality. *Journal of Personality and Social Psychology, 72*, 1197–1201.

Loehlin, J. C. (2005). Resemblance in personality and attitudes between parents and their children: Genetic and environmental contributions. In S. Bowles, H. Gintis, & M. Osborne Groves (Eds.), *Unequal chances: Family background and economic success* (pp. 192–207). Princeton, NJ: Princeton University Press.

Loehlin, J. C., & Nichols, R. C. (1976). *Heredity, environment, and personality: A study of 850 sets of twins.* Austin, TX: University of Texas Press.

Loney, B. R., Butler, M. A., Lima, E. N., Counts, C. A., & Eckel, L. A. (2006). The relation between salivary cortisol, callous-unemotional traits, and conduct problems in an adolescent non-referred sample. *Journal of Child Psychology and Psychiatry, 47*, 30–36.

Low, K. S. D., Yoon, M., Roberts, B. W., & Rounds, J. (2005). The stability of vocational interests from early adolescence to middle adulthood: A quantitative review of longitudinal studies. *Psychological Bulletin, 131,* 713–737.

Lucas, R. E., & Donnellan, M. B. (2009). If the person-situation debate is really over, why does it still generate so much negative affect? *Journal of Research in Personality, 43,* 146–149.

Luciano, M., Wright, M. J., Geffen, G. M., Geffen, L. B., Smith, G. A., & Martin, N. G. (2004). A genetic investigation of the covariation among inspection time, choice reaction time, and IQ subtest scores. *Behavior Genetics, 34,* 41–50.

Lykken, D. T., Bouchard, T. J., McGue, M., & Tellegen, A. (1993). Heritability of interests: A twin study. *Journal of Applied Psychology, 78,* 649–661.

Lykken, D. T., & Tellegen, A. (1993). Is human mating adventitious or the result of lawful choice? A twin study of mate selection. *Journal of Personality and Social Psychology, 65,* 56–68.

Lynn, R., Wilson, R. G., & Gault, A. (1989). Simple musical tests as measures of Spearman's. g. *Personality and Individual Differences, 10,* 25–28.

Määttänen, I., Jokela, M., Hintsa, T., Firtser, S., Kähönen, M., Jula, A., et al. (2013). Testosterone and temperament traits in men: Longitudinal analysis. *Psychoneuroendocrinology, 38,* 2243–2248.

MacCann, C., Joseph, D. L., Newman, D. A., & Roberts, R. D. (2014). Emotional intelligence is a second-stratum factor of intelligence: Evidence from hierarchical and bifactor models. *Emotion, 14,* 358–374.

MacDonald, K. (1995). Evolution, the Five-Factor Model, and levels of personality. *Journal of Personality, 63,* 525–567.

MacKinnon, D. W. (1967). Stress interview. In D. N. Jackson, & S. Messick (Eds.), *Problems in human assessment* (pp. 669–676). New York: McGraw-Hill.

Malouff, J. M., Thorsteinsson, E. B., Schutte, N. S., Bhullar, N., & Rooke, S. E. (2010). The Five-Factor Model of personality and relationship satisfaction of intimate partners: A meta-analysis. *Journal of Research in Personality, 44,* 124–127.

Marcus, B. (2004). Self-control in the general theory of crime: Theoretical implications of a measurement problem. *Theoretical Criminology, 8,* 33–55.

Marcus, B., Lee, K., & Ashton, M. C. (2007). Personality dimensions explaining relationships between personality dimensions and counterproductive behavior: Big Five, or one in addition? *Personnel Psychology, 60,* 1–34.

Marcus, B., & Wagner, U. (2015). What do you want to be? Criterion-related validity of attained vocational aspirations versus inventoried person-vocation fit. *Journal of Business and Psychology, 30,* 51–62.

Markon, K. E., Quilty, L. C., Bagby, R. M., & Krueger, R. F. (2013). The development and psychometric properties of an informant-report form of the Personality Inventory for *DSM-5* (PID-5). *Assessment, 20,* 370–383.

Martin, L. R., Friedman, H. S., Tucker, J. S., Tomlinson-Keasey, C., Criqui, M. H., & Schwartz, J. E. (2002). A life-course perspective on childhood cheerfulness and its relation to mortality risk. *Personality and Social Psychology Bulletin, 28,* 1155–1165.

Mattia, J. I., & Zimmerman, M. (2001). Epidemiology. In W. J. Livesley (Ed.), *Handbook of personality disorders: Theory, research, and treatment.* New York: Guilford.

Mayer, J. D., & Salovey, P. (1993). The intelligence of emotional intelligence. *Intelligence, 17,* 433–442.

Mayer, J. D., Salovey, P., & Caruso, D. (2002). *Mayer–Salovey–Caruso Emotional Intelligence Test (MSCEIT), Version 2.0.* Toronto: Multi-Health Systems.

Maynard Smith, J., & Price, G. R. (1973). The logic of animal conflict. *Nature, 246,* 15–18.

McCrae, R. R. (2002). NEO-PI-R data from 36 cultures: Further intercultural comparisons. In R. R. McCrae, & J. Allik (Eds.), *The Five-Factor Model of personality across cultures.* New York: Kluwer.

McCrae, R. R., & Costa, P. T., Jr. (1989). Re-interpreting the Myers–Briggs Type Indicator from the perspective of the five-factor model of personality. *Journal of Personality, 57,* 17–40.

McCrae, R. R., & Costa, P. T., Jr. (1997). Personality trait structure as a human universal. *American Psychologist, 52,* 509–516.

McCrae, R. R., & Costa, P. T., Jr. (1999). A five-factor theory of personality. In L. A. Pervin, & O. P. John (Eds.), *Handbook of personality: Theory and research* (2nd ed.). New York: Guilford.

McCrae, R. R., Costa, P. T., Jr., Terracciano, A., Parker, W. D., Mills, C. J., De Fruyt, F., et al. (2002). Personality trait development from age 12 to age 18: Longitudinal, cross-sectional, and cross-cultural analyses. *Journal of Personality and Social Psychology, 83*, 1456–1468.

McCrae, R. R., Kurtz, J. E., Yamagata, S., & Terracciano, A. (2011). Internal consistency, retest reliability, and their implications for personality scale validity. *Personality and Social Psychological Review, 15*, 28–50.

McCrae, R. R., Martin, T. A., Hrebickova, M., Urbanek, T., Boomsma, D. I., Willemsen, G., et al. (2008). Personality trait similarity between spouses in four cultures. *Journal of Personality, 76*, 1137–1163.

McCrae, R. R., Scally, M., Terracciano, A., Abecasis, G. R., & Costa, P. T., Jr. (2010). An alternative to the search for single polymorphisms: Toward molecular personality scales for the Five-Factor Model. *Journal of Personality and Social Psychology, 99*, 1014–1024.

McCrae, R. R., & Terracciano, A. (2006). National character and personality. *Current Directions in Psychological Science, 15*, 156–161.

McCrae, R. R., Yik, M. S. M., Trapnell, P. D., Bond, M. H., & Paulhus, D. P. (1998). Interpreting personality profiles across cultures: Bilingual, acculturation, and peer rating studies of Chinese undergraduates. *Journal of Personality and Social Psychology, 74*, 1041–1055.

McCrae, R. R., Zonderman, A. B., Costa, P. T., Jr., Bond, M. H., & Paunonen, S. V. (1996). Evaluating replicability of factors in the Revised NEO Personality Inventory: Confirmatory factor analysis versus procrustes rotation. *Journal of Personality and Social Psychology, 70*, 552–566.

McCullough, M. E., Enders, C. K., Brion, S., & Jain, A. R. (2005). The varieties of religious development in adulthood: A longitudinal investigation of religion and rational choice. *Journal of Personality and Social Psychology, 89*, 78–89.

McCullough, M. E., Hoyt, W. T., Larson, D. B., Koenig, H. G., & Thoresen, C. (2000). Religious involvement and mortality: A meta-analytic review. *Health Psychology, 19*, 211–222.

McCullough, M. E., Tsang, J.-E., & Brion, S. (2003). Personality traits in adolescence as predictors of religiousness in early adulthood: Findings from the Terman longitudinal study. *Personality and Social Psychology Bulletin, 29*, 980–991.

McDaniel, M., & Whetzel, D. L. (2005). Situational judgment test research: Informing the debate on practical intelligence theory. *Intelligence, 33*, 515–525.

McGue, M., Keyes, M., Sharma, A., Elkins, I., Legrand, L., Johnson, W., et al. (2007). The environments of adopted and non-adopted youth: Evidence on range restriction from the sibling interaction and behavior study (SIBS). *Behavior Genetics, 37*, 449–462.

McHoskey, J. W., Worzel, W., & Szyarto, C. (1998). Machiavellianism and psychopathy. *Journal of Personality and Social Psychology, 74*, 192–210.

McKay, D. A., & Tokar, D. M. (2012). The HEXACO and five-factor models of personality in relation to RIASEC vocational interests. *Journal of Vocational Behavior, 81*, 138–149.

Meehl, P. E. (1990). Toward an integrated theory of schizotaxia, schizotypy, and schizophrenia. *Journal of Personality Disorders, 4*, 1–99.

Midlarsky, E., Fagin Jones, S., & Corley, R. P. (2005). Personality correlates of heroic rescue during the Holocaust. *Journal of Personality, 43*, 907–934.

Miller, T. Q., Smith, T. W., Turner, C. W., Guijarro, M. L., & Hallet, A. J. (1996). Meta-analytic review of research on hostility and physical health. *Psychological Bulletin, 119*, 322–348.

Milojev, P., & Sibley, C. G. (2017). Normative personality trait development in adulthood: a 6-Year cohort-sequential growth model. *Journal of Personality and Social Psychology, 112*, 510–526.

Mischel, W. (1968). *Personality and assessment*. New York: Wiley.

Mischel, W., & Peake, P. K. (1982). Beyond déjà vu in the search for cross-situational consistency. *Psychological Review, 89*, 730–755.

Mischel, W., Shoda, Y., & Peake, P. K. (1988). The nature of adolescent competencies predicted by preschool delay of gratification. *Journal of Personality and Social Psychology, 54*, 687–696.

Moffitt, T. E., Gabrielli, W. F., Mednick, S. A., & Schulsinger, F. (1981). Socioeconomic status, IQ, and delinquency. *Journal of Abnormal Psychology, 90*, 152–156.

Moffitt, T. E., & Silva, P. A. (1988). IQ and delinquency: A direct test of the differential detection hypothesis. *Journal of Abnormal Psychology, 97*, 330–333.

Mortensen, E. L., Michaelsen, K. F., Sanders, S. A., & Reinisch, J. M. (2002). The association between duration of breastfeeding and adult intelligence. *Journal of the American Medical Association, 287,* 2365−2371.

Mount, M. K., Barrick, M. R., & Strauss, J. P. (1994). Validity of observer ratings of the Big Five personality factors. *Journal of Applied Psychology, 79,* 272−280.

Munafo, M. R., Freimer, N. B., Ng, W., Ophoff, R., Veijola, J., Miettunen, J., et al. (2009). 5-HTTLPR genotype and anxiety-related personality traits: A meta-analysis and new data. *American Journal of Medical Genetics: Part B. Neuropsychiatric Genetics, 150,* 271−281.

Munafo, M. R., Yalcin, B., Willis-Owen, S. A., & Flint, J. (2008). Association of the dopamine D4 receptor (DRD4) gene and approach-related personality traits: Meta-analysis and new data. *Biological Psychiatry, 63,* 197−206.

Murray, H. A. (1943). *Thematic Apperception Test manual.* Cambridge, MA: Harvard University Press.

Musek, J. (2007). A general factor of personality: Evidence for the Big One in the Five-Factor model. *Journal of Research in Personality, 41,* 1213−1233.

Myers, I. B., & McCaulley, M. H. (1985). *Manual: A guide to the development and use of the Myers−Briggs type indicator.* Palo Alto, CA: Consulting Psychologists Press.

Nathan, B. R., & Alexander, R. A. (1988). A comparison of criteria for test validation: A meta-analytic investigation. *Personnel Psychology, 41,* 517−535.

Neisser, U., Boodoo, G., Bouchard, T. J., Jr., Boykin, A. W., Brody, N., Ceci, S. J., et al. (1996). Intelligence: Knowns and unknowns. *American Psychologist, 51,* 77−101.

Neppl, T. K., Donnellan, M. B., Scaramella, L. V., Widaman, K. F., Spilman, S. K., Ontai, L. L., et al. (2010). Differential stability of temperament and personality from toddlerhood to middle childhood. *Journal of Research in Personality, 44,* 386−396.

Nettelbeck, T. (1987). Inspection time and intelligence. In P. A. Vernon (Ed.), *Speed of information-processing and intelligence* (pp. 295−346). Westport, CT: Ablex.

Nettle, D. (2006). The evolution of personality variation in humans and other animals. *American Psychologist, 61,* 622−631.

Newcomb, A. F., Bukowski, W. M., & Pattee, L. (1993). Children's peer relations: A meta-analytic review of popular, rejected, neglected, controversial, and average sociometric status. *Psychological Bulletin, 113,* 99−128.

Newsome, S., Day, A. L., & Catano, V. M. (2000). Assessing the predictive validity of emotional intelligence. *Personality and Individual Differences, 29,* 1005−1016.

New, A. S., Triebwasser, J., & Charney, D. S. (2008). The case for shifting borderline personality disorder to Axis I. *Biological Psychiatry, 64,* 653−659.

Neyer, F. J., & Lehnart, J. (2007). Relationships matter in personality development: Evidence from an 8-year longitudinal study across young adulthood. *Journal of Personality, 75,* 535−568.

Nilsson, L.-G., Sternäng, O., Rönnlund, M., & Nyberg, L. (2009). Challenging the notion of an early-onset of cognitive decline. *Neurobiology of Aging, 30,* 521−524.

Nisbett, R. E., Aronson, J., Blair, C., Dickens, W., Flynn, J., Halpern, D. F., et al. (2012). Intelligence: New findings and theoretical developments. *American Psychologist, 67,* 130−159.

Noftle, E. E., & Robins, R. W. (2007). Personality predictors of academic outcomes: Big Five correlates of GPA and SAT scores. *Journal of Personality and Social Psychology, 93,* 116−130.

Norman, W. (1967). *2800 personality trait descriptors: Normative operating characteristics for a university population.* Ann Arbor, MI: University of Michigan.

Oliner, S. P., & Oliner, P. M. (1988). *The altruistic personality: Rescuers of Jews in Nazi Europe.* New York: Free Press.

Osler, W. (1910). The Lumelin Lectures on angina pectoris. *Lancet, 1,* 839−844.

O'Steen, S., Cullum, A. J., & Bennett, A. F. (2002). Rapid evolution of escape ability in Trinidadian guppies (*Poecilia reticulata*). *Evolution, 56,* 776−784.

O'Toole, B. I., & Stankov, L. (1992). Ultimate validity of psychological tests. *Personality and Individual Differences, 13,* 699−716.

Park, G., Lubinski, D., & Benbow, C. P. (2007). Contrasting intellectual patterns predict creativity in the arts and sciences: Tracking intellectually precocious youth over 25 years. *Psychological Science, 18,* 948−952.

Paulhus, D. L., & John, O. P. (1998). Egoistic and moralistic biases in self-perception: The interplay of self-deceptive styles with basic traits and motives. *Journal of Personality, 66,* 1025—1060.

Paulhus, D. L., Robins, R. W., Trzesniewski, K. H., & Tracy, J. L. (2004). Two replicable suppressor situations in personality research. *Multivariate Behavioral Research, 39,* 303—328.

Paulhus, D. L., & Trapnell, P. D. (2008). Self-presentation of personality: An agency-communion framework. In O. P. John, R. W. Robins, & L. A. Pervin (Eds.), *Handbook of personality* (3rd ed., pp. 492—517). New York: Guilford.

Paulhus, D. L., Trapnell, P. D., & Chen, D. (1999). Birth order effects on personality and achievement within families. *Psychological Science, 10,* 482—488.

Paulhus, D. L., & Williams, K. M. (2002). The Dark Triad of personality: Narcissism, Machiavellianism, and psychopathy. *Journal of Research in Personality, 36,* 556—563.

Paunonen, S. V. (2002). *Design and construction of the Supernumerary Personality Inventory* (Research Bulletin #763). London, ON: University of Western Ontario.

Paunonen, S. V., & Ashton, M. C. (2001a). Big Five factors and facets and the prediction of behavior. *Journal of Personality and Social Psychology, 81,* 524—539.

Paunonen, S. V., & Ashton, M. C. (2001b). Big Five predictors of academic achievement. *Journal of Research in Personality, 35,* 78—90.

Paunonen, S. V., Jackson, D. N., & Keinonen, M. (1990). The structured nonverbal assessment of personality. *Journal of Personality, 58,* 481—502.

Pederson, A. K., King, J. E., & Landau, V. I. (2005). Chimpanzee (*Pan troglodytes*) personality predicts behavior. *Journal of Research in Personality, 39,* 534—549.

Perugini, M., Gallucci, M., Presaghi, F., & Ercolani, A. P. (2003). The personal norm of reciprocity. *European Journal of Personality, 17,* 251—283.

Perugini, M., & Richetin, J. (2007). In the land of the blind, the one-eyed man is king. *European Journal of Personality, 21,* 977—981.

Pew Global Attitudes Project. (2002). *Among wealthy nations U.S. stands alone in its embrace of religion.* Washington, DC: Pew Research Center for the People and the Press.

Pew Research Center for People and the Press. (2009). *Public praises science: Scientists fault public, media.* Retrieved from: http://people-press.org/reports/pdf/528.pdf.

Pietschnig, J., Penke, L., Wicherts, J. M., Zeiler, M., & Voracek, M. (2015). Meta-analysis of associations between human brain volume and intelligence differences: How strong are they and what do they mean? *Neuroscience and Biobehavioral Reviews, 57,* 411—432.

Plomin, R., & DeFries, J. C. (1985). *Origins of individual differences in infancy: The Colorado Adoption Project.* New York: Academic Press.

Plomin, R., DeFries, J. C., & Fulker, D. W. (1988). *Nature and nurture during infancy and early childhood.* New York: Cambridge University Press.

Plomin, R., Haworth, C. M. A., Meaburn, E. L., Price, T. S., Wellcome Trust Case Control Consortium, & Davis, O. S. P. (2013). Common DNA markers can account for more than half of the genetic influence on cognitive abilities. *Psychological Science, 24,* 562—568.

Plomin, R. C., & Caspi, A. (1999). Behavioral genetics and personality. In L. A. Pervin, & O. P. John (Eds.), *Handbook of personality: Theory and research* (2nd ed., pp. 251—276). New York: Guilford.

Pollet, T. V., van der Meij, L., Cobey, K. D., & Buunk, A. P. (2011). Testosterone levels and their associations with lifetime number of opposite sex partners and remarriage in a large sample of American elderly men and women. *Hormones and Behavior, 60,* 72—77.

Poropat, A. E. (2011). A meta-analysis of the Five-Factor Model of personality and academic performance. *Psychological Bulletin, 135,* 322—338.

Pozzebon, J. A., Ashton, M. C., & Visser, B. A. (2014). Major changes: personality, ability, and congruence in the prediction of academic outcomes. *Journal of Career Assessment, 22,* 75—88.

Pozzebon, J. A., Visser, B. A., Ashton, M. C., Lee, K., & Goldberg, L. R. (2010). Psychometric characteristics of the Oregon vocational interest scales. *Journal of Personality Assessment, 92,* 168—174.

Pratto, F., Sidanius, J., Stallworth, L. M., & Malle, B. F. (1994). Social dominance orientation: A personality variable predicting social and political attitudes. *Journal of Personality and Social Psychology, 67,* 741—763.

Prediger, D. J. (1982). Dimensions underlying Holland's hexagon: Missing link between interests and occupations? *Journal of Vocational Behavior, 21,* 259–287.

Raven, J. C. (1941). Standardisation of progressive matrices. *British Journal of Medical Psychology, 19,* 137–150.

Reise, S. P., & Wright, T. M. (1996). Personality traits, cluster B personality disorders, and sociosexuality. *Journal of Research in Personality, 30,* 128–136.

Riemann, R., Angleitner, A., & Strelau, J. (1997). Genetic and environmental influences on personality: A study of twins reared together using the self- and peer-report NEO-FFI scales. *Journal of Personality, 65,* 449–475.

Riemann, R., & Kandler, C. (2010). Construct validation using multitrait multimethod twin data: The case of a general factor of personality. *European Journal of Personality, 24,* 258–277.

Ritchie, S. J., Booth, T., Hernandez, M. D. C. V., Corley, J., Maniega, S. M., Gow, A. J., et al. (2015). Beyond a bigger brain: Multivariable structural brain imaging and intelligence. *Intelligence, 51,* 47–56.

Roberts, B. W., Caspi, A., & Moffitt, T. (2001). The kids are alright: Growth and stability in personality development from adolescence to adulthood. *Journal of Personality, 81,* 670–683.

Roberts, B. W., & DelVecchio, W. F. (2000). The rank-order consistency of personality traits from childhood to old age: A quantitative review of longitudinal studies. *Psychological Bulletin, 126,* 3–25.

Roberts, B. W., Wood, D., & Smith, J. L. (2005). Evaluating five-factor theory and social investment perspectives on personality trait development. *Journal of Research in Personality, 39,* 166–184.

Robins, R. W., Fraley, R. C., Roberts, B. W., & Trzesniewski, K. (2001). A longitudinal study of personality change in young adulthood. *Journal of Personality, 73,* 489–521.

Roccato, M., & Ricolfi, L. (2005). On the correlation between right-wing authoritarianism and social dominance orientation. *Basic and Applied Social Psychology, 27,* 187–200.

Rogers, M., & Glendon, A. I. (2003). Blood type and personality. *Personality and Individual Differences, 34,* 1099–1112.

Rokeach, M. (1973). *The nature of human values.* New York: Free Press.

Romero, E., Gómez-Fraguela, J. A., Luengo, M. A., & Sobral, J. (2003). The self-control construct in the general theory of crime: An investigation in terms of personality psychology. *Psychology, Crime, and Law, 9,* 61–86.

Ronalds, G. A., De Stavola, B. L., & Leon, D. A. (2005). The cognitive cost of being a twin: Evidence from comparisons within families in the Aberdeen children of the 1950s cohort study. *British Medical Journal, 331,* 1306.

Rorschach, H. (1921). *Psychodiagnostics: A diagnostic test based on perception.* New York: Grune & Stratton.

Rosse, J. G., Stecher, M. D., Miller, J. L., & Levin, R. A. (1998). The impact of response distortion on pre-employment personality testing and hiring decisions. *Journal of Applied Psychology, 83,* 634–644.

Rothbart, M. K., & Bates, J. E. (1998). Temperament. In W. Damon, & N. Eisenberg (Eds.), *Handbook of child psychology: Social, emotional, and personality development* (5th ed., Vol. 3, pp. 105–176). New York: Wiley.

Rowatt, W. C., & Schmitt, D. P. (2003). Associations between religious orientation and varieties of sexual experience. *Journal for the Scientific Study of Religion, 42,* 455–465.

Ruch, W. (1992). Pavlov's types of nervous system, Eysenck's typology and the Hippocrates–Galen temperaments: An empirical examination of the asserted correspondence between three temperament typologies. *Personality and Individual Differences, 13,* 1259–1271.

Rushton, J. P., Brainerd, C. J., & Pressley, M. (1983). Behavioral development and construct validity: The principle of aggregation. *Psychological Bulletin, 94,* 18–38.

Rusting, C. L., & Larsen, R. J. (1999). Clarifying Gray's theory of personality: A response to Pickering, Corr, and Gray. *Personality and Individual Differences, 24,* 200–213.

Sackett, P. R., & Harris, M. M. (1984). Honesty testing for personnel selection: A review and critique. *Personnel Psychology, 37,* 221–245.

Salovey, P., & Mayer, J. D. (1990). Emotional intelligence. *Imagination, Cognition, and Personality, 9,* 185–211.

Salsman, J. M., Brown, T. L., Brechting, E. H., & Carlson, C. R. (2005). The link between religion and spirituality and emotional adjustment: The mediating role of optimism and social support. *Personality and Social Psychology Bulletin, 31,* 522–535.

Salthouse, T. A. (2009). When does age-related cognitive decline begin? *Neurobiology of Aging, 30,* 507–514.

Saroglou, V. (2010). Religiousness as a cultural adaptation of basic traits: A five-factor model perspective. *Personality and Social Psychology Review, 14,* 108–125.

Saroglou, V. (2011). Believing, bonding, behaving, and belonging: The big four religious dimensions and cultural variation. *Journal of Cross-Cultural Psychology, 42,* 1320–1340.

Saroglou, V., Delpierre, V., & Dernelle, R. (2004). Values and religiosity: A meta-analysis of studies using Schwartz's model. *Personality and Individual Differences, 37,* 721–734.

Sattler, J. M. (1988). *Assessment of children* (3rd ed.). San Diego: Sattler.

Saucier, G. (1992). Benchmarks: Integrating affective and interpersonal circles with the Big-Five personality factors. *Journal of Personality and Social Psychology, 62,* 1025–1035.

Saucier, G. (2009). Recurrent personality dimensions in inclusive lexical studies: Indications for a Big Six structure. *Journal of Personality, 77,* 1577–1614.

Saucier, G., & Goldberg, L. R. (1996). Evidence for the Big Five in analyses of familiar English personality adjectives. *European Journal of Personality, 10,* 61–77.

Saucier, G., & Skrzypinska, K. (2006). Spiritual but not religious? Evidence for two independent dispositions. *Journal of Personality, 74,* 1257–1292.

Saucier, G., Thalmayer, A. G., Payne, D. L., Carlson, R., Sanogo, L., Ole-Kotikash, L., et al. (2014). A basic bivariate structure of personality attributes evident across nine languages. *Journal of Personality, 82,* 1–14.

Scarr, S., & Carter-Saltzman, L. (1979). Twin method: Defense of a critical assumption. *Behavior Genetics, 9,* 527–542.

Schaie, K. W. (2009). When does age-related cognitive decline begin?" Salthouse again reifies the "cross-sectional fallacy. *Neurobiology of Aging, 30,* 528–529.

Schimmack, U., Radhakrishnan, P., Oishi, S., Dzokoto, V., & Ahadi, S. (2002). Culture, personality, and subjective well-being: Integrating process models of life-satisfaction. *Journal of Personality and Social Psychology, 82,* 582–593.

Schmidt, F. L., & Hunter, J. (2004). General mental ability in the world of work: Occupational attainment and job performance. *Journal of Personality and Social Psychology, 86,* 162–173.

Schmitt, D. P. (2004). The Big Five related to risky sexual behaviour across 10 world regions: Differential personality associations of sexual promiscuity and relationship infidelity. *European Journal of Personality, 18,* 301–319.

Schmitt, D. P. (2005). Sociosexuality from Argentina to Zimbabwe: A 48-nation study of sex, culture, and strategies of human mating. *Behavioral and Brain Sciences, 28,* 247–311.

Schmitt, D. P., & Buss, D. M. (2000). Sexual dimensions of person description: Beyond or subsumed by the Big Five? *Journal of Research in Personality, 34,* 141–177.

Schmitt, D. P., Shackelford, T. K., Duntley, J., Tooke, W., Buss, D. M., Fisher, M. L., et al. (2002). Is there an early-30s peak in female sexual desire? Cross-sectional evidence from the United States and Canada. *Canadian Journal of Human Sexuality, 11,* 1–18.

Schönbrodt, F. D., & Perugini, M. (2013). At what sample size do correlations stabilize? *Journal of Research in Personality, 47,* 609–612.

Schwartz, S. H. (1992). Universals in the content and structure of values: Theoretical advances and empirical tests in 20 countries. In M. Zanna (Ed.), *Advances in experimental social psychology* (Vol. 25, pp. 1–65). San Diego: Academic Press.

Schwartz, S. H., & Bilsky, W. (1987). Toward a universal psychological structure of human values. *Journal of Personality and Social Psychology, 53,* 550–562.

Shedler, J. (2010). The efficacy of psychodynamic psychotherapy. *American Psychologist, 65,* 98–109.

Sheldon, W. H. (1940). *The varieties of human physique.* Oxford: Harper.

Sheldon, W. H. (1942). *The varieties of temperament.* Oxford: Harper.

Shiner, R. L., & Caspi, A. (2003). Personality differences in childhood and adolescence: Measurement, development, and consequences. *Journal of Child Psychology and Psychiatry, 44,* 2–32.

Sibley, C. G., & Pirie, D. J. (2013). Personality in New Zealand: Scale norms and demographic differences in the mini-IPIP6. *New Zealand Journal of Psychology, 42,* 13–30.

Sidanius, J., & Pratto, F. (1999). *Social dominance: An intergroup theory of social hierarchy and oppression.* New York: Cambridge University Press.

Siever, L. J., & Davis, K. L. (1991). A psychobiological perspective on the personality disorders. *American Journal of Psychiatry, 148,* 1647–1658.

Silvia, P. J. (2006). *Exploring the psychology of interest.* New York: Oxford University Press.

Simons, L. G., Simons, R. L., & Conger, R. D. (2004). Identifying the mechanisms whereby family religiosity influences the probability of adolescent antisocial behavior. *Journal of Comparative Family Studies, 35,* 547–563.

Simpson, J. A., & Gangestad, S. W. (1991). Individual differences in sociosexuality: Evidence for convergent and discriminant validity. *Journal of Personality and Social Psychology, 60,* 870–883.

Smith, T. W., & Ruiz, J. M. (2002). Coronary heart disease. In A. J. Christensen, & M. H. Antoni (Eds.), *Chronic medical disorders: Behavioral medicine's perspective* (pp. 83–111). Malden, MA: Blackwell.

Smith, T. W., & Spiro, A., III (2002). Personality, health, and aging: Prolegomenon for the next generation. *Journal of Research in Personality, 36,* 363–394.

Soto, C. J., & John, O. P. (2012). Development of Big Five domains and facets in adulthood: mean-level age trends and broadly versus narrowly acting mechanisms. *Journal of Personality, 80,* 881–914.

Soto, C. J., & John, O. P. (2016). The next Big Five Inventory (BFI-2): Developing and assessing a hierarchical model with 15 facets to enhance bandwidth, fidelity, and predictive power. *Journal of Personality and Social Psychology* (in press).

Spangler, W. D. (1992). Validity of questionnaire and TAT measures of need for achievement: Two meta-analyses. *Psychological Bulletin, 112,* 140–154.

Spearman, C. (1904). "General intelligence, " objectively determined and measured. *American Journal of Psychology, 15,* 201–292.

Spearman, C. (1927). *The abilities of man.* Oxford, England: Macmillan.

Spearman, C., & Jones, L. W. (1950). *Human ability.* Oxford, England: Macmillan.

Starr, J. M., Pattie, A., Whiteman, M. C., Whalley, L. J., & Deary, I. J. (2005). Vitamin B12, serum folate, and cognitive change from age 11 to age 79. *Journal of Neurology, Neurosurgery, and Psychiatry, 76,* 219–292.

Sternberg, R. J. (1985). *Beyond IQ: A triarchic theory of human intelligence.* New York: Cambridge University Press.

Sternberg, R. J. (1993). *The Sternberg Triarchic Abilities Test (level H)* (Unpublished test).

Sternberg, R. J., Forsythe, G. B., Hedlund, J., Horvath, J. A., Wagner, R. K., Williams, W. M., et al. (2000). *Practical intelligence in everyday life.* New York: Cambridge University Press.

Strelau, J., Angleitner, A., Bantelmann, J., & Ruch, W. (1990). The Strelau Temperament Inventory—Revised (STI-R): Theoretical considerations and scale development. *European Journal of Personality, 4,* 209–235.

Stubbe, J. H., Posthuma, D., Boomsma, D. I., & De Geus, E. J. C. (2005). Heritability of life satisfaction in adults: A twin-family study. *Psychological Medicine, 35,* 1581–1588.

Sulloway, F. J. (1995). Birth order and evolutionary psychology: A meta-analytic overview. *Psychological Inquiry, 6,* 75–80.

Sulloway, F. J. (1996). *Born to rebel: Birth order, family dynamics, and creative lives.* New York: Pantheon.

Sutin, A. R., Costa, P. T., Miech, R., & Eaton, W. W. (2009). Personality and career success: Concurrent and longitudinal relations. *European Journal of Personality, 23,* 71–84.

Sverko, I., & Babarovic, T. (2016). Integrating personality and career adaptability into vocational interest space. *Journal of Vocational Behavior, 94,* 89–103.

Taylor, S. E., Klein, L. C., Lewis, B. P., Gruenewald, T. L., Gurung, R. A. R., & Updegraff, J. A. (2000). Biobehavioral responses to stress in females: Tend-and-befriend, not fight-or-flight. *Psychological Review, 107,* 411–429.

Tellegen, A. (2016). *MPQ (Multidimensional Personality Questionnaire): Manual for administration, scoring, and interpretation.* Minneapolis, MN: University of Minnesota Press (in press).

Tellegen, A., Watson, D., & Clark, L. A. (1999). On the dimensional and hierarchical structure of affect. *Psychological Science, 10,* 297–303.

Terman, L. M. (1925). *Genetic studies of genius. Medical and physical traits of a thousand gifted children.* Oxford, England: Stanford University Press.

Terracciano, A., & Costa, P. T., Jr. (2004). Smoking and the Five-Factor Model of personality. *Addiction, 99,* 472–481.

Terracciano, A., Costa, P. T., Jr., & McCrae, R. R. (2006). Personality plasticity after age 30. *Personality and Social Psychology Bulletin, 32*, 999–1009.

Terracciano, A., Löckenhoff, C. E., Zonderman, A. B., Ferrucci, L., & Costa, P. T., Jr. (2008). Personality predictors of longevity: Activity, emotional stability, and conscientiousness. *Psychosomatic Medicine, 70*, 621–627.

Terracciano, A., McCrae, R. R., Brant, L. J., & Costa, P. T., Jr. (2005). Hierarchical linear modeling analyses of NEO-PI-R scales in the Baltimore Longitudinal Study of Aging. *Psychology and Aging, 20*, 493–506.

Tett, R. P., Jackson, D. N., & Rothstein, M. G. (1991). Personality measures as predictors of job performance: A meta-analytic review. *Personnel Psychology, 44*, 703–742.

Tett, R. P., & Palmer, C. A. (1997). The validity of handwriting elements in relation to self-report personality trait measures. *Personality and Individual Differences, 22*, 11–18.

Thielmann, I., Hilbig, B. E., & Niedtfeld, I. (2014). Willing to give but not to forgive: Borderline personality features and cooperative behavior. *Journal of Personality Disorders, 28*, 778–795.

Thurstone, L. L. (1938). Primary mental abilities. In *Psychometric monographs, No. 1*. Chicago: University of Chicago Press.

Townsend, F. (2000). Birth order and rebelliousness: Reconstructing the research in Born to Rebel. *Politics and the Life Sciences, 19*, 135–156.

Trivers, R. L. (1971). The evolution of reciprocal altruism. *Quarterly Review of Biology, 46*, 35–57.

Tucker-Drob, E. M., & Bates, T. C. (2016). Large cross-national differences in gene × socioeconomic status interaction on intelligence. *Psychological Science, 27*, 138–149.

Tucker-Drob, E. M., & Salthouse, T. A. (2011). Individual differences in cognitive aging. In T. Chamorro-Premuzic, S. von Stumm, & A. Furnham (Eds.), *The Wiley-Blackwell handbook of individual differences* (1st ed., pp. 242–267). London: Wiley-Blackwell.

Tupes, E. C., & Christal, R. E. (1961). *Recurrent personality factors based on trait ratings* (USAF Tech. Rep. No. 61–97). TX: U.S. Air Force: Lackland Air Force Base.

Tupes, E. C., & Christal, R. E. (1992). Recurrent personality factors based on trait ratings. *Journal of Personality, 60*, 225–251.

Twenge, J. M. (2000). The age of anxiety? Birth cohort change in anxiety and Neuroticism, 1952–1993. *Journal of Personality and Social Psychology, 79*, 1007–1021.

Twenge, J. M. (2001). Birth cohort changes in extraversion: A cross-temporal meta-analysis, 1966–1993. *Personality and Individual Differences, 30*, 745–748.

Tyrer, P., & Bateman, A. W. (2004a). Psychological treatment for personality disorders. *Advances in Psychiatric Treatment, 10*, 378–388.

Tyrer, P., & Bateman, A. W. (2004b). Drug treatment for personality disorders. *Advances in Psychiatric Treatment, 10*, 389–398.

van Beijsterveldt, C. E. M., Overbeek, L. I. H., Rozendaal, L., McMaster, M. T. B., Glasner, T. J., Bartels, M., et al. (2016). Chorionicity and heritability estimates from twin studies: the prenatal environment of twins and their resemblance across a large number of traits. *Behavior Genetics, 46*, 304–314.

Van Iddekinge, C. H., Roth, P. L., Putka, D. J., & Lanivich, S. E. (2011). Are you interested? A meta-analysis of relations between vocational interests and employee performance and turnover. *Journal of Applied Psychology, 96*, 1167–1194.

Van Iddekinge, C. H., Roth, P. L., Raymark, P. H., & Odle-Dusseau, H. N. (2012). The criterion-related validity of integrity tests: An updated meta-analysis. *Journal of Applied Psychology, 97*, 499–530.

van Scheppingen, M. A., Jackson, J. J., Specht, J., Hutteman, R., Denissen, J. J., & Bleidorn, W. (2016). Personality trait development during the transition to parenthood: A test of Social Investment Theory. *Social Psychological and Personality Science, 7*, 452–462.

Vasey, P. L., & VanderLaan, D. P. (2010). Avuncular tendencies and the evolution of male androphilia in Samoan fa'afafine. *Archives of Sexual Behavior, 39*, 821–830.

Vazire, S. (2010). Who knows what about a person? The self-other knowledge asymmetry (SOKA) model. *Journal of Personality and Social Psychology, 98*, 281–300.

Vernon, P. A. (1991). Studying intelligence the hard way. *Intelligence, 15*, 389–395.

Vernon, P. A., Wickett, J. C., Bazana, P. G., & Stelmack, R. M. (2000). The neuropsychology and psychophysiology of human intelligence. In R. J. Sternberg (Ed.), *Handbook of intelligence* (pp. 245–264). New York: Cambridge University Press.

Visser, B. A., Ashton, M. C., & Vernon, P. A. (2006). Beyond *g*: Putting multiple intelligences theory to the test. *Intelligence, 34,* 487−502.

Watson, D., Klohnen, E. C., Casillas, A., Nus Simms, E., Haig, J., & Berry, D. S. (2004). Match makers and deal breakers: Analyses of assortative mating in newlywed couples. *Journal of Personality, 72,* 1029−1068.

Weatherhead, P. J., & Robertson, R. J. (1979). Offspring quality and polygyny threshold: The "sexy son" hypothesis. *American Naturalist, 113,* 201−208.

Wechsler, D. (2008). *WAIS-IV Administration and Scoring manual.* San Antonio, TX: The Psychological Corporation.

Weiss, A., Adams, M. J., Widdig, A., & Gerald, M. S. (2011). Rhesus macaques (*Macaca mulatta*) as living fossils of hominoid personality and subjective well-being. *Journal of Comparative Psychology, 125,* 72−83.

Wells, B. E., & Twenge, J. M. (2005). Changes in young people's sexual behavior and attitudes, 1943−1999: A cross-temporal meta-analysis. *Review of General Psychology, 9,* 249−261.

Whalley, L. J., & Deary, I. J. (2001). Longitudinal cohort study of childhood IQ and survival up to age 76. *British Medical Journal, 322,* 819.

Whiteman, M. C., Deary, I. J., & Fowkes, F. G. R. (2000). Personality and health: Cardiovascular disease. In S. E. Hampson (Ed.), *Advances in personality psychology* (Vol. 1, pp. 157−198). New York: Psychology Press.

Williams, J. E. (2010). Anger/hostility and cardiovascular disease. In M. Potegal, G. Stemmler, & C. Spielberger (Eds.), *International handbook of anger* (pp. 435−447). New York: Springer.

Williams, K. M., Paulhus, D. L., & Hare, R. D. (2007). Capturing the four-factor structure of psychopathy in college students via self-report. *Journal of Personality Assessment, 88,* 205−219.

Wilson, D. S. (1994). Adaptive genetic variation and human evolutionary psychology. *Ethology and Sociobiology, 15,* 219−235.

Wilson, D. S. (2002). *Darwin's cathedral: Evolution, religion, and the nature of society.* Chicago: University of Chicago Press.

Wilson, J. Q., & Herrnstein, R. J. (1985). *Crime and human nature.* New York: Simon and Schuster.

Wink, P., Ciciolla, L., Dillon, M., & Tracy, A. (2007). Religiousness, spiritual seeking, and personality: Findings from a longitudinal study. *Journal of Personality, 75,* 1051−1070.

Wisdom, N. M., Mignogna, J., & Collins, R. L. (2012). Variability in Wechsler adult intelligence scale—IV subtest performance across age. *Archives of Clinical Neuropsychology, 4,* 389−397.

Wood, J. M., Lilienfeld, S. O., Garb, H. N., & Nezworski, M. T. (2000). The Rorschach test in clinical diagnosis: A critical review, with a backward look at Garfield (1947). *Journal of Clinical Psychology, 56,* 395−430.

Wu, K., Lindsted, K. D., & Lee, J. W. (2005). Blood type and the five factors of personality in Asia. *Personality and Individual Differences, 38,* 797−808.

Wulf, J., Prentice, D., Hansum, D., Ferrar, A., & Spilka, B. (1984). Religiosity and sexual attitudes and behaviors among evangelical Christian singles. *Review of Religious Research, 26,* 119−131.

Zak, P. J., Kurzban, R., & Matzner, W. T. (2005). Oxytocin is associated with human trustworthiness. *Hormones and Behavior, 48,* 522−527.

Zametkin, A. J., Nordahl, T. E., Gross, M., King, A. C., Semple, W. E., Rumsey, J., et al. (1990). Cerebral glucose metabolism in adults with hyperactivity of childhood onset. *New England Journal of Medicine, 323,* 1361−1366.

Zelenski, J. M., & Larsen, R. J. (1999). Susceptibility to affect: A comparison of three personality taxonomies. *Journal of Personality, 67,* 761−791.

Zettler, I., & Hilbig, B. E. (2010). Honesty−humility and a person−situation interaction at work. *European Journal of Personality, 24,* 569−582.

Zettler, I., Hilbig, B. E., Moshagen, M., & de Vries, R. E. (2015). Dishonest responding or true virtue: A behavioral test of impression management. *Personality and Individual Differences, 81,* 107−111.

Zuckerman, M. (2002). Zuckerman-Kuhlman Personality Questionnaire (ZKPQ): An alternative five-factorial model. In B. de Raad, & M. Perugini (Eds.), *Big five assessment* (pp. 377−396). Göttingen, Germany: Hogrefe & Huber.

Zuckerman, M. (2005). *Psychobiology of personality* (2nd ed.). New York: Cambridge University Press.

Zuckerman, M., Kuhlman, D. M., & Camac, C. (1988). What lies beyond E and N? Factor analyses of scales believed to measure basic dimensions of personality. *Journal of Personality and Social Psychology, 54,* 96−107.

Zuckerman, M., Kuhlman, D. M., Joireman, J., Teta, P., & Kraft, M. (1993). A comparison of three structural models of personality: The Big Three, the Big Five, and the Alternative Five. *Journal of Personality and Social Psychology, 65*, 757–768.

Zuckerman, M., Kuhlman, D. M., Thornquist, M., & Kiers, H. (1991). Five (or three) robust questionnaire scale factors of personality without culture. *Personality and Individual Differences, 12*, 929–941.

Zuckerman, M., Silberman, J., & Hall, J. A. (2013). The relation between intelligence and religiosity: a meta-analysis and some proposed explanations. *Personality and Social Psychology Review, 17*, 325–354.

INDEX

'*Note*: Page numbers followed by "f" indicate figures, "t" indicate tables, and "b" indicate boxes.'